Manipulating the World Economy

The Rise of Modern Monetary Theory & the Inevitable Fall of Classical Economics

Is there an alternative?

By Martin A. Armstrong

Fifth Edition

DISCLAIMER

The information contained in this report is NOT intended for speculation on any financial market referred to within this report. AE Global Solutions, Inc. makes no such warrantee regarding its opinions or forecasts in reference to the markets or economies discussed in this report. Anyone seeking consultation on economic future trends in a personal nature must do so under written contract.

This is neither a solicitation nor an offer to Buy or Sell any cash or derivative (such as futures, options, swaps, etc.) financial instrument on any of the described underlying markets. No representation is being made that any financial result will or is likely to achieve profits or losses similar to those discussed. The past performance of any trading system or methodology discussed here is not necessarily indicative of future results.

Futures, Options, and Currencies trading all have large potential rewards, but also large potential risk. You must be aware of the risks and be willing to accept them in order to invest in these complex markets. Don't trade with money you can't afford to lose and NEVER trade anything blindly. You must strive to understand the markets and to act upon your conviction when well researched.

Indeed, events can materialize rapidly and thus past performance of any trading system or methodology is not necessarily indicative of future results particularly when you understand we are going through an economic evolution process and that includes the rise and fall of various governments globally on an economic basis.

CFTC Rule 4.41 – Any simulated or hypothetical performance results have certain inherent limitations. While prices may appear within a given trading range, there is no guarantee that there will be enough liquidity (volume) to ensure that such trades could be actually executed. Hypothetical results thus can differ greatly from actual performance records, and do not represent actual trading since such trades have not actually been executed, these results may have under- or over-compensated for the impact, if any, of certain market factors, such as lack of liquidity. Simulated or hypothetical trading programs in general are also subject to the fact that they are designed with the benefit of hindsight and back testing. Such representations in theory could be altered by Acts of God or Sovereign Debt Defaults.

It should not be assumed that the methods, techniques, or indicators presented in this publication will be profitable or that they will not result in losses since this cannot be a full representation of all considerations and the evolution of economic and market development. Past results of any individual or trading strategy published are not indicative of future returns since all things cannot be considered for discussion purposes. In addition, the indicators, strategies, columns, articles and discussions (collectively, the "Information") are provided for informational and educational purposes only and should not be construed as investment advice or a solicitation for money to manage since money management is not conducted. Therefore, by no means is this publication to be construed as a solicitation of any order to buy or sell. Accordingly, you should not rely solely on the Information in making any investment. Rather, you should use the Information only as a starting point for doing additional independent research in order to allow you to form your own opinion regarding investments. You should always check with your licensed financial advisor and tax advisor to determine the suitability of any such investment.

Manipulating the World Economy: The Rise of Modern Monetary Theory & the Inevitable Fall of Classical Economics — Is there an Alternative?

Published by Gatekeeper Press

2167 Stringtown Rd, Suite 109

Columbus, OH 43123-2989

www.GatekeeperPress.com

Library of Congress Control Number: 2021939250

ISBN (hardcover): 9781662914461

eISBN: 9781662914478

Manipulating Interest Rates

Contents

Preface

I have assembled this book to illustrate the proposition that government can manipulate any nation's economy, no less the world, is threatening our future as a free society and that of our posterity. Those in government will always act out of their own self-interest as all humans do, regardless of their position. In my personal dealings with various governments around the globe, I have come to realize that they will never act to prevent a crisis. Governments enjoy a crisis, for then and only then can they act authoritatively, which usually ends with creating more power.

A politician cannot run for office and ask you to vote for them because they saved your job and prevented a recession. Nobody would believe them. Politicians run for office by promising action and change. Just look at the slogans politicians use to run for office, such as 1976 Jimmy Carter's "A Leader, For a Change," 2008 Barack Obama's "Change We Can Believe In," or 2016 Donald Trump's "Make America Great Again." If you lose your job first, then they can run for office, vowing to prosecute the culprit responsible. That is how politics truly work. They never actually prevent an event, and they cannot prove that an event would have taken place.

What I hope to demonstrate in this book is that economics has deviated from any true science. Economics is no longer about discovering how the economy functions, but rather altering it in ways that are unsustainable for personal gain.

Preface

Governments have assumed the role of manipulating their respective economies, and in the process, have disrupted the very nature of how the world economy functions. This threatens our future; our present form of society will once again be buried in a common grave with the failures of all the empires, nations, and city-states that have gone before us.

Not even religion has resulted in as many deaths as economics in this futile attempt to change and manipulate society in search of Utopia. What has been done under the banner of economics has been far worse than religion. The class warfare unleashed by Karl Marx has transformed economics into the bloodiest theory in recorded history.

Economics, unfortunately, has been usurped as a political philosophy instead of a science. These political philosophies rest upon the exploitation of one group for the benefit of another. The very purpose of civilization is that everyone comes together, and the synergy which emerges is greater than the sum of the individuals. Someone becomes a baker, which relieves you of the daily burden of baking bread, freeing you to explore your own talents. Civilization is all about harmony and cooperation, which is why it rises and falls throughout history once it loses that benefit for all.

Whenever a society turns in upon itself, polarizing one group against another, the very purpose of civilization ceases to exist. Politics has degenerated into a self-defeating force. Even when Obama was elected, those who opposed him simply moved on with their lives. Today, society no longer accepts the loss of their candidate. Instead, we have deteriorated into a state of obstruction where dying democracy is becoming a faint memory of its original intent.

Others claim capitalism is collapsing and point to the lobbying of multinational corporations and bankers. Simply because it involves money, they call that capitalism when it is plain corruption. Capitalism is the freedom to decide your own future, whereas in the Marxist philosophy of communism/socialism, the state comes first. This has led governments to wrongly assume that they are the embodiment of the nation rather than "We the People."

Welcome to the 21st century that has marked the decline and fall of our most basic principle of civilization — the equal protection of the law.

Introduction

Karl Marx
(1818-1883)

Economics is by no means a science where we seek to discover how the economy works. Instead, economics has become a social experiment where people devise theories in an attempt to change human nature without success. No matter how many times people have attempted to apply Karl Marx's theories (1818–1883) known as Marxism, they have failed, and it often resulted in the worst bloodshed in human history. They tried to avoid the labels of "communism" or "socialism" by recharacterizing it as "income inequality" to achieve the same goals with arguments of fairness or equality.

No matter how many have tried to recharacterize Marxism, their goals have led to outright class warfare that has resulted in more deaths than religious wars. Just glance at the Communist Revolutions in Russia and China. The twentieth-century Socialist movement was the bloodiest of all wars. It is generally estimated to have resulted in the deaths of about 61 million in the Soviet Union, 78 million in China, and roughly 200 million worldwide.

Soldiers raising the Soviet flag over the German Reichstag, 1945

The most curious aspect of this recharacterization of Marxism is that perhaps ancient wisdom concluded long ago that socialistic economics is both dangerous and destructive to civilization. For we find in the Ten Commandments, it expressly forbids Socialist philosophy that still dominates our present politics.

> "You shall not covet your neighbor's house. You shall not covet your neighbor's wife, or his male or female servant, his ox or donkey, or anything that belongs to your neighbor"
> — The Tenth Commandment, Exodus 20:17

It appears that this prohibition even predates the Bible. We find the essence of this prohibition in *The Egyptian Book of the Dead* known as the "42 Negative Confessions." This features a list of 42 sins that the soul of the deceased had to state affirmatively that they never committed when they stood in the final judgment in the afterlife. The most famous list comes from *The Papyrus of Ani*, a text prepared for the priest Ani of Thebes (1250 BC). Therefore, the Tenth Commandment is also found in this list as the combination of 13, 20, 21, 29, and 33.

Egyptian - 42 Negative Confessions

1. I have not done iniquity.
2. I have not robbed with violence.
3. I have not stolen.
4. I have done no murder; I have done no harm.
5. I have not defrauded offerings.
6. I have not diminished obligations.
7. I have not plundered the Netcher.
8. I have not spoken lies.
9. I have not snatched away food.
10. I have not caused pain.
11. I have not committed fornication.
12. I have not caused shedding of tears.
13. I have not dealt deceitfully.
14. I have not transgressed.
15. I have not acted guilefully.
16. I have not laid wasted the ploughed land.
17. I have not been an eavesdropper.
18. I have not set my lips in motion (against any man).
19. I have not been angry and wrathful except for a just cause.
20. I have not defiled the wife of any man.
21. I have not defiled the wife of any man. (repeated twice)
22. I have not polluted myself.
23. I have not caused terror.
24. I have not transgressed. (repeated twice)
25. I have not burned with rage.
26. I have not stopped my ears against the words of Right and Truth (Ma'at)
27. I have not worked grief.
28. I have not acted with insolence.
29. I have not stirred up strife.
30. I have not judged hastily.
31. I have not been an eavesdropper. (repeated twice)
32. I have not multiplied words exceedingly.
33. I have not done neither harm nor ill.
34. I have never cursed the King.
35. I have never fouled the water.
36. I have not spoken scornfully.
37. I have never cursed the Netcher.
38. I have not stolen.
39. I have not defrauded the offerings of the Netcher.
40. I have not plundered the offerings of the blessed dead.
41. I have not filched the food of the infant, neither have I sinned against the Netcher of my native town.
42. I have not slaughtered with evil intent the cattle of the Netcher.

"Covet" means to crave or desire. The Tenth Commandment does not tell us that all of our desires are immoral. It tells us that some desires are most certainly wrong. Coveting is an immoral longing for something that is not rightfully ours, which is the very essence of Marxism. The Tenth Commandment expressly directs us that our desire for something that already belongs to someone else is morally wrong. Therefore, it forbids us from wanting far more than we would legitimately deserve or that would be our rightful share. The Tenth Commandment's focus is that we are not to illicitly desire anything that already belongs to anyone else, which is, of course, the foundation of Marxist socialism.

Aristotle
(384–322BC)

The most interesting economic developments throughout millennia have been the misconception of the exploitation of labor viewed by Marx and the structural change into a capitalistic system. This was observed by Aristotle (384–322 BC), who influenced Marx. Much of this entire idea of socialism and communism was driven by the evolutionary process of all economies.

For example, economies generally begin as agriculturally based. I call this the "Villa Economy," meaning these economies tend to be predominantly self-sufficient. Peripheral trades emerged like the role of a blacksmith who would shoe the horses to plow. There emerged the manufacturing of harnesses and various products, and the market was the farmers. The Physiocrats of France believed that all wealth was derived from land and agriculture, which inspired the age of empire building. They viewed these peripheral trades, which became Mercantilism, as parasites that sucked the wealth from the farmer. Adam Smith (1720–1790) wrote his *Wealth of Nations* (1776) as the counter-argument to the Physiocrats, illustrating that all activities contributed to the wealth of a nation, and not just agriculture.

Indeed, Mercantilism existed both in China and Europe, which led to the evolution from the Villa Economy to a Market Economy. Gradually, tradesmanship offered an alternative to farming. This evolution of a Market Economy developed in Athens, where people encouraged farmers to grow excess supplies that they, in turn, would sell to others. Aristotle indirectly termed this practice basically as people who made money from money or brokers.

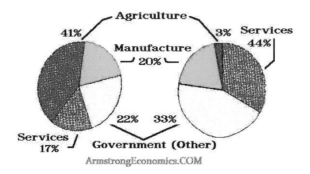

US Civil Work Force
1900   1980

As society evolves from a Villa Economy to a Market Economy, there is naturally a displacement of labor as it shifts into other fields and away from agriculture. During the 19th century, this emerged as the Industrial Revolution that created factories and fueled the urbanization of society at first using the steam engine from about 1776 onward. By 1810, London finally reached a population of one million equal to that of ancient Rome, which had reached that in 133 BC. As urbanization emerges, this displaced the traditional agriculture of the Villa Economy, which is what Aristotle observed in ancient Athens.

As technology advances, it creates new opportunities, but it also makes the prior technology redundant. Joseph Schumpeter (1883-1950) termed this phenomenon waves of "creative destruction." For example, the invention of the automobile put the horse and buggy makers out of business. England lost the edge on the Industrial Revolution because it enacted laws to protect the buggy makers when the politicians were bribed by the oligarchy.

The Locomotive Act (1865) required self-propelled vehicles on public roads in England to be preceded by a man on foot waving a red flag and blowing a horn. The legislation orchestrated by the status quo of the English oligarchy prevented England from fully participating in the Industrial Revolution during this early stage. They were fighting against this wave of creative destruction. The English Parliament finally removed the need for the red flag in 1878 and then went on to abolish the law entirely in 1896.

The Black Death killed about 50% of the population. The shortage in labor led to the birth of wages and the end of serfdom. As there was a shortage in labor, wages rose. In 1362, a petition was filed in the English House of Commons in Parliament that blamed the inflation on workers "who refuse to bear the burden

of poverty patiently." This was intended to justify freezing wages. Again, government sought to prevent the wave of creative destruction.

Today, we see the internet expanding, once again, and unleashing a totally new wave of creative destruction. Local stores find it hard to compete with online services. Even newspapers and printed magazines are declining. VHS tapes were replaced by CD-ROMs, which were then replaced by DVDs, and now we have movies streaming over the internet. The wave of creative destruction is never-ending.

Cyrus II the Great of Persia
(601 - 530BC)

Unfortunately, analysis typically fails to see the commonality throughout the centuries. To make matters worse, analysis is often far too biased and becomes more propaganda than objective. People start with a conclusion or presumption and then only look for evidence to support that objective. In this manner, they doom society, for they never reach the true understanding of the trend or the causes behind the trend.

Only Adam Smith sought to understand how the economy functioned. Almost everyone since Marx began with the presumption that the economy is truly random, and thus it can be altered and manipulated to perform as they desire. They never accept how the economy functions, nor do they understand that by trying to alter the economy as Marx did, they are actually trying to change human nature itself. This has resulted in economics becoming a social experiment rather than a science.

Smith discovered that we all act in our own self-interest, and in doing so, we create an economy where a synergy emerges that is greater than the sum of individuals themselves. Someone else grows the turnups, which allows you to spend your time on your talents. This is the very fundamental foundation of how civilization itself is created.

Civilization emerges because the collective interaction of individuals coming together is beneficial for everyone. This is what has been called the invisible hand discovered by Smith. The goal of all economic theories since Karl Marx has been based on how to manipulate the invisible hand.

Communism failed because it sought to replace the individual with centralized planning. Governments cannot respond to the opportunities that only individuals can see in their daily actions. It is the individual that can see that there is a need for a baker, candlestick marker, or social media like Facebook. Governments are also incapable of creating new innovations. The entrepreneurship of individuals creates economic progress. Regulation and centralized control do not.

Even the creation of empires has often been the vision of a single person. The Achaemenid Persian Empire under Cyrus the Great (601–530 BC) grew substantially in less than 30 years and reached its greatest extent within 75 years. The Roman Republic was founded by a revolution against their king in 509 BC, but the Roman Empire didn't reach its greatest extent until 180 AD because it lacked a single individual continuously.

In 336 BC, when Alexander the Great embarked on his major campaign for the Persian Empire's conquest, his military leadership abilities made him a legend in his own time. By 327 BC, the Persian Empire was firmly under his control. However, his conquest of Persia was largely enabled because that civilization had peaked and was on the decline.

The Roman Republic was a militaristic society, yet it did not generally set out to conquer territory. Instead, it often defended itself as in the Punic Wars. Moreover, following its victory over its enemies, the Roman Republic offered them some level of citizenship in exchange for loyalty. A few individuals greatly expanded the empire, such as Sulla (138–78 BC) and Julius Caesar (100–44 BC) during the Republican days. Its greatest expansion was still due to the vision of one person rather than a collective decision-making event from central government.

Alexander III the Great of Macedon
(356 - 323BC)

Many empires rise from a collective foundation of individuals, such as the United States, rather than a single individual. However, these types of advances will often give rise to a single individual who then aids its advancement in short bursts of economic expansion. There are often periods at the beginning that create the spark of life in an empire, such as with Cyrus the Great, or there is one individual who emerges that creates a burst of economic growth and innovation. We see these advancements under one individual's vision throughout history, such as Lenin in Russia, Hitler in Germany, or Napoleon in France.

Edward Gibbon said it best in his *Decline and Fall of the Roman Empire*:

> "[Rome in h]er primeval state, … was then a savage and solitary thicket; in the time of the poet, it was crowned with the golden roofs of a temple, the temple is overthrown, the gold has been pillaged, the wheel of Fortune has accomplished her revolution, and the sacred ground is again disfigured with thorns and brambles. The hill of the Capitol, on which we sit, was formerly the head of the Roman Empire, the citadel of the earth, the terror of kings; illustrated by the footsteps of so many triumphs, enriched with the spoils and tributes of so many nations. This spectacle of the world, how is it fallen!"

What is fascinating is that the rise and fall of empires, nations, and city-states seem to follow the same path as corporations as they adopt centralized authoritarian

control as advocated by Karl Marx. Great advancements and creations are due to an individual's vision. Once that creative individual is gone, the entity is dominated by a bureaucracy that inevitably becomes arrogant and assumes the entire foundation is based upon their power. Apple discarded Steve Jobs and became bureaucratic. The company was then compelled to bring him back, for he was the creative spark of innovation and not the board of directors.

"[T]he different forms of government make law democratical, aristocratical, tyrannical, with a view to their several interests; and these laws, which are made by them for their own interests, are the justice which they deliver to subjects, and him who transgresses them they punish as a breaker of the law, and unjust. And that is what I mean when I say that in all states there is the same principle of justice, which is the interest of the government; and as the government must be supposed to have power, the only reasonable conclusion as, that everywhere there is one principle of justice, which is the interest of the stronger."

Thrasymachus (Θρασύμαχος)
(ca. 459-400 BC)

In the case of governments, they presume they are sovereign, and the people are subjects to be exploited. The might of the Athenian Empire encouraged an arrogance in the policy makers of the day who grew intolerable to their neighbors and led to the Peloponnesian War.

All empires rise and fall because they grow intolerable, arrogant, and the rule of law is corrupted in favor of the state. When the rule of law fails, everything else crumbles. As Thrasymachus warned Socrates, justice is always the same no matter what form of government is in power. It is simply their self-interest.

Population of Rome (3000BC - 1900AD)

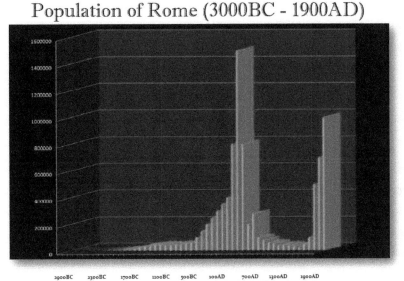

SOURCE: Livy, Cassius Dio, Tacitus, Suetonius, Josephus, Virgil, Quintus Fabius Pictor, Polybius, Zozimus
Aldrete, Gregory S. (2004), Daily life in the Roman city; Rome, Pompeii and Ostia, Westport, CT: Greenwood Press, p. 22 (ISBN 0-323-33174-X)

ArmstrongEconomics.COM

All empires rise and then fall because they have attempted to manipulate the invisible hand. They forget that they are not the creators of great societies in civilization. Empires always peak and begin to decline as the bureaucracy rises, for they inevitably exploit the very bonds that made civilization work from the outset. They historically turn one segment of society against another — a house divided cannot stand.

Society will always divide into opposing groups and no longer accept a common bond. The synergy that built the civilization is then lost, and the rule of law no longer provides equal protection for all. Civilization loses its purpose, and it is no longer beneficial to stay together and create the synergy that made it great. Hence, all great empires begin to decline, divide, and return to their separate origins from which they came.

Rome reached the 1 million mark in population in 133 BC and peaked by 180 AD. It would take London until 1810 to reach a population of 1 million, and New York finally reached that number in 1875. There is a cycle to everything, and that includes civilizations. The theories of Karl Marx have exploited societies and divided them into opposition forces. Once you divide a civilization, the decline and fall begins. One group cannot exploit another, for the freedom which once existed transforms into economic slavery and ends equal justice for all.

While we classify economics as a science, it is really just a social experiment driven by the greed, jealousy, and ignorance of many who seek to punish others for their own failures. The proposition that government can actually manage the economy to create the perfect world has never materialized in 6,000 years of recorded history. If economics were a true science, we would merely try to live in harmony with how it develops rather than attempt to change how it functions. I remember my physics professor saying that nothing is random, and then the economics professor said everything is random. Obviously, by arguing that the economy is simply random, that means it can be manipulated.

Politics has evolved by adapting itself to Marxism. Politicians promise change and impose laws in an effort to manipulate the economy. Yet, politicians in a republic inevitably become corrupt, for they are easily bought. Republics typically die by their own hand, committing suicide mired in corruption, and legislation is sold to the highest bidder.

Marx believed if you confiscated all assets from people and handed them to government, this would end the boom and bust of the business cycle. His philosophy resulted in the deaths of hundreds of millions of people. Ironically, all the economic theories that have emerged post-Marx have dominated the field during the 20th and into the 21st century. They have all been a derivative of Marx advocating that government can manipulate the economy for the better of human society. They have never been able to prevent a single recession and always launch investigations to blame someone in the private sector. Economics has empowered governments and inspired promises that can never be realized. Politicians have created New Deals with promises of pensions but never funded these promises.

Introduction

Attempts to manipulate the world economy have prejudiced society and unleashed the battle cry of class warfare. This has been dividing the people, creating the very seed that has been the destroyer of civilizations throughout history. This presumption that government is capable of manipulating the world economy, and thus the business cycle, has been the core of every other economic theory to emerge ever since Marx. Even this new Modern Monetary Theory (MMT) is shrouded in the presumption that the government is all-powerful and good-intentioned, no different than the beliefs that inspired the Communist Revolutions. But all governments die in a pool of corruption.

Former U.S. Secretary of the Treasury and past President of Harvard University Lawrence Summers, who was also an economic adviser to President Obama during the economic crisis from 2009 through 2010, wrote an article that appeared on December 6, 2015, in the *Washington Post.*

Washington Post

By Lawrence Summers December 6, 2015

"While the risk of recession may seem remote given recent growth, it bears emphasizing that since World War II, no postwar recession has been predicted a year in advance by the Fed, the White House or the consensus forecast."

Subsequently, *Bloomberg News* interviewed Summers on this very issue. They asked:

"Why it's so hard for smart guys like you to predict some form of economic slowdown? In part it's hard because the economy is an enormously complex system meteorologists turns out are not very good at predicting the weather that's a complex system too.

In part there is something in the logic of economics if it were predictable that the economy was going to decline people would stop investing; people would reduce their spending and the economy would have already declined. So, there is a sense in which in the logic of the system that once expectation of recession takes hold, you're in recession and therefore it's very difficult to predict in advance when that is going to take place. The argument is not unlike that at least there's a good approximation that speculative prices should follow random walks."

15

Introduction

In the *Bloomberg* interview, Larry Summers again conceded it is impossible to forecast the direction of the business cycle because it is like that of the weather system — too complex. It was Summers who had supported negative interest rates. He had championed the role of what he has called "secular stagnation" in current economic conditions. Summers argued that the "neutral interest rate" had declined substantially and was likely to be lower in the future. He argued that the idea that real interest rates, defined as interest rates adjusted for inflation, will be lower going forward.

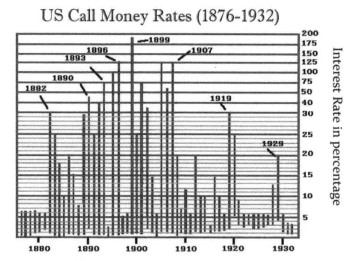

US Call Money Rates (1876-1932)

(Source: Contemporary newspaper reporting of rates at NYSE)

When we look at the call money interest rates from the New York Stock Exchange, something dramatic emerges from the observation. This very idea of a neutral interest rate assumes, as always, that all things remaining equal. What academics fail to understand is that markets move in anticipation. It does not matter if what they think is happening is true or not. Markets do not move in such a plain, logical, or orderly manner.

The United States was virtually bankrupt in 1896 when J.P. Morgan had to organize a gold loan to save the government. We can see that interest rates reached 125% during the crisis of 1896. In 1899, the Bank of England doubled its discount interest rate to 6% in November, up from 3% in February 1899, to curb what it thought was excessive speculative inflation in Britain. A full-scale panic unfolded as a global contagion when British investors began selling American assets to cover losses back home. Call money rates reached nearly 125% during the Panic of 1907. Yet when capital concentrated in the United States post-1914 World War I, we can see that the peak in interest rates during the Panic of 1929 only reached 20% during the worst speculative bubble in history up to that point in time.

The chart of call money rates from 1876 to 1932 illustrates that the peak in interest rates is far more complex than a simple calculation with respect to inflation. There has always been an international component that cannot be judged by simply looking at the domestic economic numbers. This is why economists cannot forecast the economy, for they fail to understand this is a global economy where we are all connected.

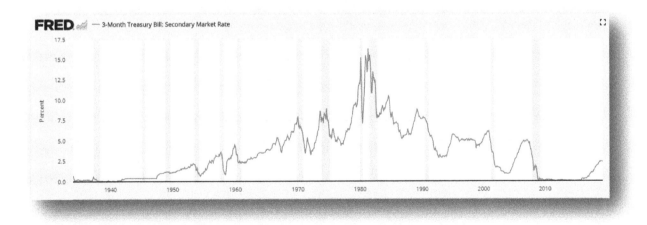

We can see from the Federal Reserve chart of 90-day T-Bill rates that completely opposite events took place during the early 1980s compared to the 2007-2009 Subprime Mortgage Crisis. During the 1980s, it was perceived that inflation was the problem (devaluation of the currency), so people fled to the private sector assets including gold. Then the 2007-2009 Subprime Mortgage Crisis hit, and confidence in the banking system collapsed as people fled the private sector to rush into government Treasuries. For a brief shining moment, even U.S. T-Bills moved to a negative interest rate, reflecting that people were just parking their money for security without regard for profit because they did not trust the banks.

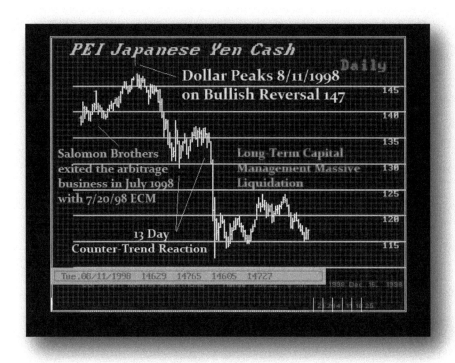

Any attempt to claim there is a neutral interest rate fails to understand that the system will swing between two extremes based entirely upon where people perceive the risk to lie. It is a fictional dream to propose there is some neutral interest rate and 100% full employment will ever exist. Moreover, it is impossible for any government to manage its own domestic economy because an external crisis can impact a domestic economy, as was the case in 1899. There was the liquidity crisis of 1998 when the collapse in Russian bonds took place and investors, including Long-Term Capital Management, were then forced to sell assets everywhere else to raise money to cover losses elsewhere. The dollar crashed against the Japanese yen simply because they needed money. It had nothing to do with the Japanese economy.

This global interconnection has existed for centuries. Investors in Rome were impacted by natural disasters in Asia, which sent panic down the Via Sacra, which was the ancient Wall Street. There were the South Sea and Mississippi Bubbles of 1720 in America. International investment has always impacted domestic economies.

Introduction

With all the economic theories presented post-Marx, each has been based upon a basic assumption that this complexity does not even exist, and the economic driver can be reduced to a single cause and effect. That basic assumption has colored all economic theories that have emerged post-Marx and his publication of the *Communist Manifesto* published in 1848. Ever since, most economic theories have adopted the proposition that government is capable of manipulating the economy. Yet, these theories fail inevitably as they cannot control external factors from global contagions.

There has been no theory to date that has been employed by governments to prevent an economic recession. As Larry Summers admitted, "No postwar recession has been predicted a year in advance by the Fed, the White House or the consensus forecast."

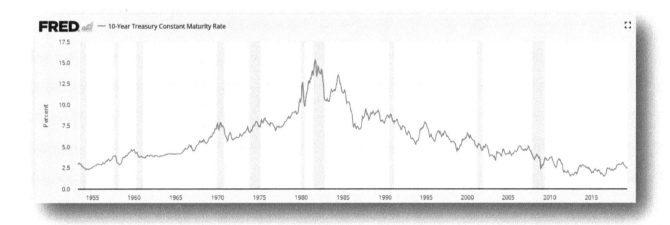

The crisis we now face is truly monumental. Central banks have employed Quantitative Easing to "stimulate" the economy in the quest to manipulate the economy and thus the business cycle. They have become like some medieval doctor who tries cutting off your ear in the hope of stopping a chronic earache. They just keep removing body parts until the pain subsides.

The European Central Bank (ECB) lowered interest rates to negative in hopes of forcing people to spend rather than save. They have lowered the economic living standards of those retired, undermining the entire pension system. They also regulate pensions and require them to invest some portion in government bonds, which are now negative yielding. There is now virtually $17 trillion of negative yielding bonds that will collapse in price to reflect a positive yield once again of about 8%.

The ECB has simply kept the governments in the EU on life support with unrealistic negative yields. The ECB owns nearly 40% of government debt. The central banks are now trapped. Their efforts to employ Quantitative Easing have been only one side of the coin. The other remains the political fiscal spending on various programs and agencies. Central banks cannot control fiscal spending. If the central banks allow interest rates to return to normal, the fiscal budgets will explode.

In Europe, governments will be compelled to raise taxes dramatically to maintain the pretend Maastricht Treaty, which imposed limits on government public spending dictated through limits on government debt and deficit as a proportion of gross domestic product (GDP). A rise in interest rates will threaten the existence of the Eurozone. This will also lead to civil unrest.

Due to the failure of Quantitative Easing, many now assume that government can freely create money without inflation. After trillions of dollars have been created to buy government debt with no appreciable inflation, many conclude that everything has changed. They are calling this the Modern Monetary Theory (MMT), where all the Marxist dreams of creating endless social programs can be funded without consequence. If they are correct, then why bother with taxes? They are simply borrowing money continually with no intention of ever paying off national debts. Governments can just create an endless supply of money to fund a new modern version of Utopia.

Does this proposed theory ignore global connections? Can it really be that simple to create money without regard for economic history? Do they comprehend the implications this experiment will have on the global economy and the very foundation of civilization itself? These questions are not asked because they fail to look at the global interconnections that have existed throughout time and circumstance for centuries.

So How Did We Get Here?

The internet and bookstores are filled with doom and gloom. It has been curious why people ascribe to such theories and always look for the end of the world behind every new headline. Some people are just obsessed with the numerous conspiracy theories from the Bilderberg Group, Davos, to the bankers owning and controlling the central banks. While that makes for great scary headlines and conspiracy theories, the underlying premise has been that the world is merely a puppet of the evil super-rich who control the future. What if all these people like to posture their own importance, yet lack the power to control anything? We cannot see Congress or Parliaments ever reach a complete agreement. Why should these diverse groups ever speak with a single mind?

The horrifying reality behind all these conspiracy theories is that no one has been in control. Even Goldman Sachs had to be rescued in 2007–2009. The real frightening factor is what if nobody is in charge? What if they all trot around like peacocks showing off their power, but behind the façade, they remain economically impotent?

The economist Kenneth Rogoff said that the conventional wisdom of Davos participants is always wrong. Indeed, they have never been able to forecast the future any more than weathermen, as Larry Summer put it. As mentioned, Summers wrote in the *Washington Post* back on December 6, 2015, "… since World War II, no postwar recession has been predicted a year in advance by the Fed, the White House or the consensus forecast." Obviously, Davos and the Bilderberg Group's meetings may be great sources for conspiracy theories that these people control the world, but the evidence fails to support those conclusions.

Take 2016 for example. Nobody at either the Bilderberg meetings or Davos believed that Donald Trump would win the presidency, and in the UK, they never saw Brexit winning. No participant ever foresaw either political event. All these elite groups were completely blind to the political storm on the horizon. Even with Europe, they just assumed they could force the people to accept the waves of immigrants without a single day of resistance. In France, Macron tried to use global warming as an excuse to raise taxes on fuel and ignited civil unrest. Today, that civil unrest is reported to be supported by 80% of the French population.

The proposition that some elite groups can crash the economies at will so they can buy things cheap is truly absurd. The super-rich are deeply in debt, and many lose a lot during every crash. Make no mistake about it; there are truly evil groups who try to manipulate the outcome of events by infiltrating governments and bribing political powers. They too have collapsed and needed bailouts for events that took them by surprise.

Throughout history there have been powerful confrontations between those who seek to control society, as in ancient Athens, the Roman Republic under the Optimates, and every society and empire that has followed right up to the present. There are always people who look above and assume such people are all-powerful. But throughout history, the pages are littered with stories of how the powerful have always fallen.

What we face is far worse. Those who think they can control events pose a serious risk, for they assume they can dictate the outcome by paying bribes. The 1998 Long-Term Capital Management collapse was betting on the IMF supporting the Russian bond market. When that proved to be a false assumption, everything came crashing down in the blink of an eye. Even during the 2007–2009 Subprime Mortgage Crisis, Lehman Brothers and Bear Stearns investment banks failed overnight. Warren Buffett had to lend $5 billion to Goldman Sachs to prevent their fall. As they say, "Oh, how hard the mighty fall."

There is no historical evidence whatsoever that the elite has been able to survive such events. During the Great Depression of the early '30s, farmers had less and less money to spend and could not meet their loans. This resulted in banks failing at an alarming rate and did not help the Sovereign Debt Crisis of 1931. Before the Great Depression during the '20s, about 70 banks would fail on average annually in the United States. After the 1929 crash, during the first 10 months of 1930, 744 banks failed. By the end of the Great Depression, some 9,000 banks failed.

It is an old saying among professional traders to buy/sell the rumor and sell/buy the news. Indeed, people act in anticipation of events so often that the markets will move on anticipation of events that are false or may never take place.

In December 1930, New York's Bank of the United States collapsed. The bank had more than $200 million in deposits at the time, making it the largest single bank failure in American history. It was indeed one of the larger banks in New York City with over 30 branches at that time. Unfortunately, its name was misinterpreted to be the U.S. government or central bank, so its failure became symbolic.

DAILY NEWS, THURSDAY, DECEMBER 11, 1930

$3,000,000 Cash Stops Bank 'Run'

Three million dollars in cash was rushed to the branch of the Bank of United States at Freeman st. and Southern blvd., Bronx, last night to stem a run started by idle gossip of one of the neighborhood merchants.

A score of clerks were rushed from the fifty-eight other branches of the bank throughout the city to help pay out the money as officials reassured depositors there were plenty more millions to meet any demand that might be made.

Plenty of Cash Ready.

Governors of the Federal Reserve bank, of which system the Bank of United States is a member, gave reassuring statements that the bank would be furnished with an unlimited supply of cash and that there was no reason for the run. They were preparing an amplified statement last night.

A small neighborhood merchant reported to have become alarmed when plans to merge the Manu-

(Continued on page 4, col. 3)

USE $3,000,000 CASH TO STOP 'RUN' ON BANK

(Continued from page 2)

facturers Trust company, the Public National Bank and Trust company, the International Trust company and the Bank of the United States with total resources of $1,000,000,000, were abandoned Tuesday after an all night conference in an attempt to reach an agreement as to terms.

Advised to Keep Stock.

In the fear that failure of the merger to materialize would send the bank's stock crashing, the merchant went into the branch early today to sell. Bank officials advised him to keep it and the merchant returned to his store to tell friends and patrons that the bank had refused to buy the stock.

As the story passed from person to person it grew until a few timid depositors decided to hurry to the branch and withdraw their accounts.

Fear of Loss Spreads.

Their action created more fear and by 3 p. m. several hundreds were lined up in front of the bank. Frantic wives telephoned husbands at work to hurry home and get their money out of the bank. Then they rushed over to join the harassed throng that was slowly filling up the street.

As the fear of the depositors increased with every arrival, police reserves were called out to maintain order.

There were fully 5,000 depositors storming the bank at 6 p. m., after subways had disgorged frightened men and women hurrying home from downtown offices.

Finally a mounted officer rode his horse up the steps of the bank to prevent them crashing down the doors. Meanwhile, as a semblance of calm was restored by 7 p. m., the bank continued to pay out steadily.

A run on the Bank of the United States began when a merger failed, and a local merchant went into the bank to sell his shares. Banks would typically sell their own shares directly to customers. The clerk told him he should keep the stock, and after leaving, he told people the bank refused to accept its own shares. Thousands of people then set out to withdraw their funds, and the bank was forced to close in days.

There were allegations that the bank had sold its shares to customers with a guarantee of no losses for one year. The price of their shares had peaked in 1928 at $231.25. By 1930, it had fallen to $11.50 before the bank run. When the dust settled, the share price collapsed to just $2.00.

When we step back from these conspiracy theories and look at this objectively, the actual story is far worse than the wildest grand conspiracy controlling the world. The shocking truth is that nobody is in control, so no one can come to rescue society to save the day. Those in power realize that this is a confidence game. In the midst of every panic, the head of state will always come out and pronounce that everything is fundamentally sound. On October 25, 1929, President Herbert Hoover came out and made a public announcement:

Herbert Hoover
(1874 - 1964)
(President 1929 - 1933)

"The fundamental business of the country, that is the production and distribution of commodities, is on a sound and prosperous basis. The best evidence is that although production and consumption are at high levels, the average prices of commodities as a whole have not increased and there have been no appreciable increases in the stocks of manufactured goods. Moreover, there has been a tendency of wages to increase, the output per worker in many industries again shows an increase, all of which indicates a healthy condition..."

President Hoover was still looking at the economy as one that was predominantly commodity-based. After all, the Dust Bowl did not yet take place. In 1900, 40% of the civil workforce was employed in agriculture. You can see from his words that he was looking at the economy from a traditional viewpoint, unaware that the events unfolding were external.

A major fraud took place in London that created a liquidity crisis which resulted in foreign selling of U.S. securities. This contributed to the October Crash in New York. The Hatry Group's fraud and collapse was particularly bad for it involved fraudulent, duplicate stock certificates created by Clarence Hatry (1888–1965) that were posted as collateral at several banks. The Hatry Group collapsed in September 1929 and was a contributing factor to the Wall Street Crash of 1929.

Hatry asserted that in late August 1929, he had made a secret visit to the Bank of England (BoE) to appeal to the central banker, Montagu Norman, for financing to allow him to complete a merger with United Steel Companies, a UK firm. The BoE refused Hatry's bid for a bridge loan in September 1929. By the 17th of September, Hatry Group shares began to fall on the London Royal Exchange. It turned out that Hatry's total liabilities stood at

£19 million while his assets were a mere £4 million. On September 19, after Hatry had approached Lloyds Bank and was turned down, he asked Sir Gilbert Garnsey of Price Waterhouse, a chartered accountant firm, to intervene on his behalf. They submitted accounts, and then after the fraud, they said that Hatry did not tell them he had been issuing duplicate fraudulent shares.

THE OBSERVER, SUNDAY, OCTOBER 13, 1929.

MONEY AND MARKETS.

"GROUP" FINANCE ON ITS TRIAL.

REVISED METHODS NEEDED—RUBBER & RESTRICTION — INVERESK MYSTERY — GRAMOPHONE PROFITS—CHEMICAL INDUSTRIES PROGRESS.

(By Our Financial Editor.)

The indefinite postponement of the "Hatry" Settlement was far from welcome to members of the Stock Exchange. No doubt it was inevitable in view of the extremely complicated tangle that has to be straightened out. Registrars of the companies concerned can neither certify transfers nor guarantee the genuineness of the securities involved. It is quite impossible, therefore, that the many bargains yet to be settled can be closed satisfactorily. The effect of the postponement on business, however, is almost disastrous. It is hoped and believed that the losses sustained by members of the Stock Exchange will be moderate. Until the Settlement is completed, however, no one can know who is involved or to what extent, and an atmosphere of uneasiness and suspicion exists which is a severe handicap to active business.

Such an atmosphere is the breeding ground of adverse rumours, and the output during the past week has been prolific. Men whisper to each other of the difficulties of this man or that group, and no one can tell what to believe and what to disregard. Share values slump as the whispers circulate. Confidence, the basis of all Stock Exchange activity, is undermined, and everyone is looking for the next "crash." Times are indeed difficult. They will pass, of course, but the immediate outlook is full of uncertainty and doubt.

Revised Methods Needed.

The loss of confidence which has resulted from recent events has been directed particularly at "group" concerns. Such combinations, sometimes confined to one industry, in other cases including several, are generally dominated by some outstanding personality. The information available regarding their financial operations is too often entirely inadequate. The shareholders have to take a great deal on trust. The dangers inherent in investments of this class have been brought home to investors generally, with the result that there has been considerable liquidation of holdings and a consequent marked reaction in market values.

At the moment it is impossible to say whether this "flight from the groups" is justified or not. Official information has so far either been too general or too scanty to enable a reasoned judgment to be formed. It is becoming quite clear, however, that if "group" finance is to continue to receive the support of the investing public some revision of its methods will be needed. Directors, other than the central figure, will be called on to take an intelligent interest in the affairs of the "group." Interlocking shareholdings will come under grave suspicion unless the full facts in regard to them are made public. Holding companies will have to give far more justification than heretofore for the values placed on investments in subsidiaries.

More Information Essential.

Some progress will be brought about in the direction needed by the new Company Act when its provisions become operative. Information now withheld will then be compulsory. Even then, however, the "group" which limits the information it divulges to the strict letter of the law will leave much to be desired. Investors in the past have been inclined to place their faith rather in the man than in the figures. This attitude is slowly but surely changing. The demand on all hands is for fuller and franker information, and those who meet this demand to the fullest possible extent will receive a bountiful return in the confidence inspired in those who supply the capital.

The only sound reason for withholding information is that its publication may injure the business of the company concerned. That reason is really operative in very few cases. It is used, however, time and again to hide facts which, if published, would be injurious not to the company but to those who have secured power and position in it.

Gilt-edged Stocks Firm.

The lack of confidence in the general markets has brought a larger amount of business to the gilt-edged and high-class investment sections. Under normal conditions the rise in the Bank Rate to 6½ per cent. would have meant a serious reaction in the quotations for all "money" stocks. On the present occasion the whole class has been remarkably firm, showing, in some cases, an actual appreciation in value. War Loan 5 per cents. have been as high as 102¼, finally closing at just under the figure.

Home railways have attracted more attention under the stimulation of the exceptionally good traffic returns, North-Eastern stock in particular being marked up. Actual business has, however, been limited in character. Still further improvement should result from the settlement of the 2½ per cent. wages reduction question. As we anticipated some weeks ago the discussions between the companies and their workmen have been amicable and have resulted satisfactorily. Foreign bonds have been steady, while Oil shares have been inclined to move upwards on better advices from New York, but dealings have been mainly professional, the public showing little interest.

THE OBSERVER, SUNDAY, SEPTEMBER 22, 1929.

MONEY AND MARKETS.

"HATRY GROUP" COLLAPSE EFFECTS.

WAKEFIELD MYSTERY — GILT-EDGE FIRMNESS — CELANESE UNCERTAINTY— TRUST AND SEVEN PER CENT.—BRAZILIAN BONDS.

(By Our Financial Editor.)

Acute nervousness characterised the situation on the Stock Exchange when business ceased on Friday. This is Account week, and grave fears were entertained that serious trouble may arise owing to the extraordinary situation that has arisen in connection with what is known as "the Hatry group" of companies. Within two days the market valuation of the shares of these companies collapsed in the most sensational manner, over £5,000,000 being wiped out. The companies immediately concerned were as follows:—

On Friday morning some efforts were made to deal in the shares, but in view of representations made to the Committee for General Purposes, a notice was posted in the Stock Exchange suspending all dealings in these shares, and adding to them the Wakefield Corporation 4½ per cent. stock, 1949-59 and the shares of the Drapery Trust, Ltd. Later it was officially announced that Sir Gilbert Garnsey, of Price, Waterhouse and Co., the well-known firm of chartered accountants, had undertaken an investigation into the affairs of the group of companies

	Highest this Year	Wed.	Thurs.
	s. d.	s. d.	s. d.
Corp. and Gen. Securities £1	22 1½	16 3	5 0
Oak Investment £1	20 6	16 3	4 0
Retail Trade Securities 10s.	16 0	6 3	1 6
Photomaton P. Corp. 5s.	12 7½	5 9	1 6
Associated Automatic 5s.	15 3	5 9	4 0

The scheme was to issue the same share certificates he had printed twice. He had tendered these as collateral to different lending banks. A clerk at the City of Wakefield spotted the discrepancy. Montagu Norman of the BoE informed the chairman of the London Stock Exchange that the Hatry Group was bankrupt. Trading in all shares was suspended on September 20, 1929.

When the Hatry Group shares were suspended, they had a market value of about £24 million. Hatry and his leading associates confessed to fraud and forgery and were arrested after lunching at the Charing Cross Hotel. The worst part of this fraud was that no one knew how many institutions had fraudulent shares. This resulted in a wholesale panic that created a contagion that impacted the U.S. share market as well.

Conspiracy theories have a tendency to attribute supreme power to groups or individuals who do not exist. Of course, when their failed manipulations bring down the world economy, as Hatry Group in 1929 or the case during the 2007–2009 collapse of the mortgage-backed securities, the mighty also fall. These conspiracy theories also assume that some group or cabal has control when in fact we are on a runaway train with no engineer.

Throughout history, every society has assumed that they are sophisticated. Therefore the fate of all those empires, nations, and city-states who have gone before us will never be our fate. This time is always different, we tell ourselves. We have the internet and have traveled to the moon. How can we simply decline and fall? Surely, we are beyond such primitive ancestors. Yet, the truth behind such self-indulgent narcissism lies a very interesting fact. The common thread that runs through history is not that we advance technologically. Countless wars have been fought to end all wars since ancient times. What never changes aside from the evolution of weapons is human nature. A mother still cries for her son's death in war today as they did in ancient times.

Buffet to invest in Goldman Sachs

BY BEN WHITE
New York Times News Service

Warren E. Buffett, America's most famous investor and one of the world's richest men, announced on Tuesday that he would invest $5 billion in Goldman Sachs, the embattled Wall Street titan, in a move that could bolster confidence in the financial markets.

Until now, Buffett, who has navigated the stock market with legendary prowess, has largely refrained from investing in the stricken financial industry, saying repeatedly that things could get worse.

Thousands of people on and off Wall Street follow Buffett's moves, so his decision to invest in Goldman immediately heartened investors. After falling nearly 1.6 percent during the day, the Standard & Poor's 500 index erased its loss in after-hours trading Tuesday evening on news of the investment.

Buffett's conglomerate, Berkshire Hathaway, unveiled the move only days after Goldman, long the premier investment house on Wall Street, embarked on a radical plan to transform itself into a traditional bank in order to ensure its survival. Goldman, which examined various options over the past week as its shares tumbled and some clients abandoned the firm, also said Tuesday it would sell at least $2.5 billion of common stock to the public.

Since the credit crisis flared more than a year ago, Buffett had stayed his hand even as other investors poured money into ailing American financial companies like Citigroup and Merrill Lynch, only to see their investments wither.

Such wariness is a hallmark of Buffett's investing style, and many on Wall Street have wondered when he might jump in.

Buffett, in the statement, called Goldman Sachs an exceptional institution.

"It has an unrivaled global franchise," Buffett said, "a proven and deep management team and the intellectual and financial capital to continue its track record of outperformance."

Berkshire Hathaway will receive perpetual preferred shares in Goldman, which will pay a 10 annual percent dividend, or $500 million a year. Those dividends take precedence over other payments to common shareholders. Goldman has the right to buy back the shares at any time for premium of 10 per cent.

Berkshire Hathaway will receive warrants to buy $5 billion in common stock at a strike price of $115 a share, which are exercisable at any time in a five-year period. Those warrants are already in the money: Goldman shares closed Tuesday at $125.05, up $4.27, and rose to $133 in after-hours trading on Tuesday evening.

Thomas Paine
(1737-1809)

Common Sense

Some writers have so confounded society with government, as to leave little or no distinction between them; whereas they are not only different, but have different origins. Society is produced by our wants, and government by our wickedness; the former promotes our POSITIVELY by uniting our affections, the latter NEGATIVELY by restraining our vices. The one encourages intercourse, the other creates distinctions. The first a patron, the last a punisher.

"These are the times that try men's souls."

History repeats for a single reason — the passions and behaviors of humans never change. No matter what form of government we have devised throughout the centuries, whether they are monarchies, dictatorships, tyrannies, aristocracies, republics, democracies, or socialistic-communistic states, the commonality remains the same. Justice is always defined by the self-interest of those in power. They call Edward Snowden a traitor because he exposed that the government was acting illegally. Yet, the sovereignty of the United States is not the government — it is the people. Edward Snowden cannot be a traitor for exposing government corruption.

Nobody explained that confusion better than Thomas Pain in his *Common Sense*. Those in power confuse society (people) with government. They become drunk with power and can no longer see things through the eyes of the people who became the great unwashed.

We must understand that the frailties of human nature decide the fate of all nations. When the United States Constitution was completed, Ben Franklin was leaving the convention. He was stopped and asked, "What kind of government do we have?" He responded, "A republic if you can keep it."

It has often been said that the best form of government is a benevolent dictatorship. Perhaps the reason some have reached that conclusion is that a benevolent dictator is beyond reproach. At the time of the founding of the United States, many were deeply influenced by the knowledge emerging from history about the Roman Republic thanks to Edward Gibbons' *Decline and Fall of the Roman Empire* published in 1776. The American and French Revolutions were against monarchies, for the idea sprung from the Roman Republic's history who overthrew their kings.

Nevertheless, the idealism which many believed existed within the Roman Republic overlooked its fatal flaw. No form of a republic has ever survived throughout history, for those pretending to represent the people are easily bribed. The propaganda hurled at Julius Caesar (100–44 BC) came from very corrupt political groups that forced Caesar to cross the Rubicon. The senators of the oligarchy had to flee as the people cheered Caesar who they saw as their liberator from a massive debt crisis.

Our calendar was revised by Julius Caesar to end the political corruption. The Romans used the moon calendar, but knew that was incorrect. The high priest, Pontiff Maximus, was given the discretion to add days to the calendar to compensate for the error in time. Politicians would bribe the priest to add days to avoid elections. It was Caesar who standardized the calendar and eliminated the discretion that allowed for bribery.

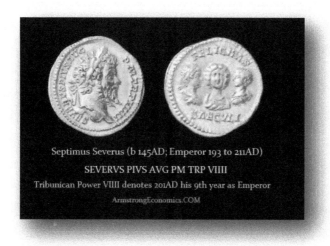

Septimus Severus (b 145AD; Emperor 193 to 211AD)

SEVERVS PIVS AVG PM TRP VIIII

Tribunican Power VIIII denotes 201AD his 9th year as Emperor

ArmstrongEconomics.COM

Even during the Imperial Era of the Roman Empire that followed Julius Caesar's assassination, the pretense of the Republic was maintained. We call them emperors, but their title was "Augustus" — the father of his country. The Republic's image maintained that they were elected consul for one year as if they stood for election. Here is a coin of Septimius Severus (193–211 AD) from his 9th year as the pretend elected head of state, also known as the Tribunician Power.

The elite presumes that if they can crash an economy at will, they can also manipulate it at will. The harsh reality is no one can manage the economy, no less manipulate it. We have experienced 10+ years of Quantitative Easing without creating inflation. The quantity of money theory that central banks and governments relied upon has proven to be completely false.

We also have a crisis in qualifications. People can run for politics and have zero experience in understanding how the economy even works. Nevertheless, they promise to manipulate the economy to achieve some social goal. This is no different than allowing someone to be a brain surgeon simply because they smile nicely and have a good sales pitch. We allow people to run for office with promises of altering the economy with no understanding of how it even works.

Politics also remains infected with the theories of Karl Marx. While people do not want to call themselves Marxists, anyone who advocates that government has the power to manipulate the economy follows Karl Marx, who rejected laissez-faire. They do not respect that the economy unfolds according to the invisible hand, as discovered by Adam Smith (1723–1790). Smith observed that the complexity of the business cycle was driven by each one of us pursuing our own self-interest.

The dominant economic theory employed by central banks is that of John Maynard Keynes. It took Keynes a lifetime to realize everything he had fought against by advocating that government could manipulate society was wrong. People sometimes forget that Karl Marx and John Keynes have a lot in common. They both advocated government intervention to temper, control, and eliminate the business cycle.

The failure of Socialist/Communist forms of government is the attempt to impose central planning. The individual and people coming together to work freely create the synergy we call our economy. It is the sum of the individuals that creates a greater whole. Communism failed because centralized planning by government is incapable of managing the economy, for they cannot respond to anything other than in their own self-interest.

But when representative government becomes angered, it will burn down the barn to get a rat out of it.

memoirs p-130-131

Herbert Hoover
(1874 - 1964)
(President 1929 - 1933)

With every crash in the share market and economy, government immediately launches investigations. Of course, the culprit is always assumed to be someone in the private sector. There are no mirrors in government. Never in history has any government accepted blame for creating an economic crash. The only apology I have come across was from Herbert Hoover for launching the investigation into market manipulation to cause the stock market to crash for political reasons. Nobody was ever found to have been short from Rockefeller on down. They all lost. Hoover simply apologized in his memoirs, writing, "When representative government becomes angered, it will burn down the barn to get a rat out of it."

Government cannot see the opportunities to create a local bakery shop. It would be like a man attempting to write a book to explain how it "feels" to birth a child. Experience is the root of all wisdom. There are but three methods by which we may obtain wisdom: (1) by reading and contemplation, which is noblest; (2) by imitation and learning by example from others, which is the easiest; and (3) the most common by experience, which is the bitterest but most practical. What child does not stick their finger in the flame of a candle despite their parent saying it will hurt? We all made decisions that we probably regret to various degrees in life, yet wisdom emerges most profoundly from our failures, not our successes in life. Government is a collective body. It is incapable of learning from experience when those in charge keep changing.

Behavioral Economics

The science of explaining why market participants make systematic irrational decisions. People possess free will yet display animalistic instincts such as having a herd mentality.

There is something emerging in the field of economics. People are opening their eyes to what those who have risen from the trading pits have known all along — markets move in anticipation even if that view is completely unjustified. Hence, the trader's maxim — buy the rumor and sell the news. Those who wait for the confirmation typically buy the high.

What is fascinating is that we elect people to run nations who have ideas of how to manipulate the economy, yet they have no experience in dealing with the economy. We also have academics who have read books on economics but have no practical experience whatsoever. As mentioned, it is akin to a man writing a book on what it feels like to give birth to a child. If you have not experienced childbirth, how could you ever describe how it feels?

This newly emerging field of economics has been dubbed behavioral economics, which studies the effects of psychological, cognitive, emotional, cultural, and social factors on the economic decisions of individuals and institutions. But trying to isolate a decision to a single cause and effect leads to attempting to create a simple cause and effect. Trying to reduce everything to a single decision is absurd. We are very much still creatures that respond in herd instincts.

A zebra herd is a classic example. A lion approaches, one zebra spots him and begins to run. The others begin running because another zebra is running. They did not see the lion. Markets function in the same manner. People begin selling because the market is going down, and they may have no idea what is going on, as was the case during the 1987 Crash. I refer to this as our "herd instinct," because we respond because others are buying or selling.

I was giving an institutional conference in Tokyo at the Imperial Hotel in the early 1990s following the December 1989 high in the Japanese share market. A retail investor bribed his way in through with someone he knew at the hotel. He approached me when I finished, saying he had to speak to me and apologized for his intrusion.

He was in his late 60s and explained he had bought the Nikkei 225 the very day of the high at the end of December 1989. He had invested $50 million. What fascinated me was that he said it was the first time in his life that he had invested in stocks.

Imperial Hotel Tokyo

Now I was intrigued. Here was the man who actually bought the high of the whole bull market in 1989 in Tokyo. I asked him what made him buy that fateful day when he had never bought stocks before. He told me brokers had called him every year and said the Nikkei rallied 5% on average every January. He did nothing but watched for seven years. Finally, at the very top, he invested $50 million, waiting to earn a quick buck in January. The market crashed and he held, waiting to break even, but that never occurred. This was the herd instinct. He bought because everyone else was buying. He was cautious and waited for consistent proof. But all things come to an end because everything in the universe operates on cyclical frequencies.

Critics of behavioral economics typically stress the rationality of economic agents, contending that experimentally observed behavior has limited application to market situations. They still generally insist that there must be a single cause and effect that is rational and logical. They claim that competition ensures at least a close approximation of rational behavior. They ignore the fact that in the middle of a bear market recession, a company can report good earnings, and its share price will still decline because the overall sentiment is bearish. The TV commentators will simply report the good earnings and quickly add that they were not good enough.

The traditional economists also remain skeptical as the idea they cannot create a single solution robs them of their influence with government, such as raising taxes to improve some idealized program or rebalance the concentration of wealth. However, such criticisms offer no alternative solution, for they may have inspired interventionists like Karl Marx and John Maynard Keynes, but they have produced no picture of how to manage the economy, no less why markets trade the way they do.

The Capital Asset Pricing Model of the 1960s became a joke and the Efficient Market Theory or hypothesis that the market was "informationally efficient" at all times. Eugene Fama was considered the father of this Efficient Market Hypothesis. Fama began with his Ph.D. thesis back in May 1970, which appeared in the issue of the *Journal of Finance*, entitled, *Efficient Capital Markets: A Review of Theory and Empirical Work.* Nonetheless, all these various theories have eventually proven to be inefficient in themselves and led to the Black–Scholes model of attempting to price these under and over valuations within a given market. Of course, that blew up in the collapse of Long–Term Capital Management in 1998.

Markets and the economy are by no means efficient or logical. There are simply times when markets do not trade rationally because perhaps some people are acting on events externally. The 1987 Crash took place, but it was not for any fundamental change within the United States. Externally, foreigners sold U.S. assets because they viewed that the dollar would crash. The Brady Commission Report on the 1987 Crash concluded:

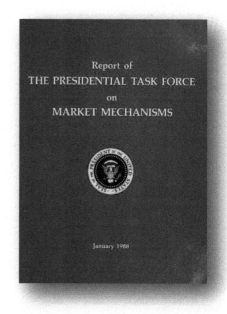

"Expertise in individual market segments is, therefore, not sufficient for effective response to intermarket crises. The October experience demonstrates that the intermarket agency must consider the interactions among a wide variety of markets encompassing stocks, stock index futures, stock options, bonds, foreign exchange and the credit and banking system, in both domestic and foreign markets."

Clearly, even the official government investigation into the 1987 Crash uncovered that everything is connected. The Long-Term Capital Management Crisis of 1998 was a liquidity crisis where investments in Russia became illiquid, so to raise cash, they began selling everything else around the world. Even the Japanese yen

crashed from 147 to 108 in a major meltdown over a 109-day trading period. They sold everything everywhere to raise money to cover losses in Russia.

The very idea that we can reduce everything to a single decision of some generic person to forecast the economy is truly absurd. Such a proposal merely illustrates the lack of knowledge to craft or formulate such a theory.

The theories implied by classical economics support the idea that government possesses the intellect and power to manipulate the economy are without a historical foundation. Even when we attempt to embark on a study into the new field of behavioral economics, we must respect that if we again attempt to reduce society's thinking process down to a single cause and effect, we will quickly get lost in the corridors of our mind.

This is true even when we turn to microeconomics, which many refer to as the law of supply and demand. This economic model maintains that price determination in a market correlates to supply and demand. The qualification in economic theories is always the same — assuming all things remain equal. The belief is that the unit price for a particular good will be determined by the supply relative to the demand. They then go forward and claim that under the law of supply and demand, an economic equilibrium for price and quantity will take place in any transaction.

Supply & Demand

The first to articulate the concept of supply and demand was John Law (1671 – 1729). There is perhaps no other major contributor to our understanding of the modern political economy than the notorious financier John Law. He was also the first to envision the concept of a Gross National or Domestic Product. Indeed, being a trader who observed the markets in Amsterdam at the turn of the 18th century fed his inquisitive mind to comprehend the nature of the economy.

John Law (1671-1729)

John Law explained his Water/Diamond Paradox. There are two distinct interpretations of the word "value." On the one hand, something has a value based upon its use, like water, but has no value with respect to a medium of exchange. Conversely, something which has a value as a medium of exchange, like gold, silver, or paper money, has no value for use like water.

The Water/Diamond Paradox was a central observation made by John Law that led to his understanding behind the concept of replacing precious metals with paper money, which is interestingly relevant to the Modern Monetary Theory (MMT).

What John Law had witnessed was a supply/demand balance between money and assets. He was able to see that when the demand for money rose, the prices (value) of useful things it could buy declined. When the supply of money increased in excess of its demand, the prices of useful things rose. John Law expressed this dynamic relationship quite well.

> "Though Parliament could give money to the nation in as great a quantity as there was occasion for the Parliament could not justly know what sum would serve the nation for the demand changes. If the quantity is less than the demand for it the landed man who owes money and has his rent paid in the product of the ground is wronged, for money being more valuable it will cost him a greater quantity of his goods to pay the debt he owes. If the quantity of money is greater than the demand for it the money'd [sic] man is wronged for money being less valuable £100 will not buy him the same quantity of goods £100 bought before." (John Law, *Essay on a Land Bank*, 77)

John Law came to understand that money was actually a commodity itself where its value rose and fell, no different than anything else. In his later work, *Money and Trade*, he saw the value of money could also impact international capital flows as did Gresham. He warned that if the supply of money in one nation rose beyond its proportion to the product of the nation, "It would undervalue money there, or, according to the way of speaking, it would raise goods: But as money would be undervalued everywhere the same, or near to what it were there; it would be of great advantage to that country, though thereby money were less valuable."

Law's observations came after the great imports of gold and silver into Europe from America by Spain. He wrote in *Money and Trade*, "When the Spaniards bring money or bullion into Europe, they lessen its value, but gain by bringing it; because they have the whole benefit of the greater quantity and only bear a share of the lesser value." (*Money and Trade*, 104).

John Law made critical observations we attribute to the Quantity Theory of Money and the Monetarist Theory of the Chicago School. However, John Law is stating that as modern states continue borrowing, accumulating their national debts, the value of those debts depreciate as the quantity of new money is created. The crisis comes when the people realize this is the trend in motion and stop buying the new debt. Then the free markets anticipate a decline in the value of a currency and capital flees to other countries.

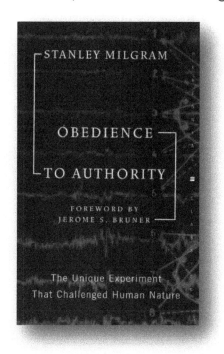

Capital can flee to safety in foreign lands, but an individual's labor cannot flee to a safe haven unless the person physically leaves. John Law was visualizing that there was a link between money and trade, or in other words the Gross Domestic Product of the people. Clearly, any assumption that markets are somehow driven by logic according to old theories such as supply and demand cannot hold up when dealing with an international economy where capital can move in and out, distorting the domestic perspective.

However, while supply can be quantified, demand is an emotional affair dependent upon people having confidence at that instant in time. The clash between the old world of fundamental analysis where people always try to explain what happens, reducing it to a simple cause and effect, involves personal judgment. Therein lies the conflict that is centered upon opinion. Shedding this link to old theories is essential to move forward in the analytical field.

Human Behavior is Not So Simple

Stanley Milgram
(1933-1984)

Behavioral economics and the consequences for market and economic trends cannot be isolated to a single cause and effect of some logical decision process. There is also the madness of crowds and herd instincts that humans clearly possess.

The studies of Stanley Milgram (1933–1984) cracked the door on this field of observing human behavior. The assumption that Germans were somehow different and could kill Jews without remorse during World War II prompted investigations into how that happened. Milgram conducted his experiment in the USA by attaching wires to an actor and soliciting people off the street. He instructed them to ask their subject a series of questions, and every time they answered incorrectly, they were to give the participant an electric shock. The results themselves were shocking, and he called it *Obedience to Authority*. People would torture another

person if instructed to do so. They felt obligated to obey the higher authority.

Stanley Milgram also conducted fascinating studies that revealed the herd mentality instinctive within human culture that is also displayed by traffic jams. There can be an accident on the left side of a divided highway, and the right side will slow down to look. We call these "rubber-neck" delays.

Milgram also experimented by placing a single person on the street, staring into the sky at nothing. People walked by and probably just thought the individual was nuts. When he placed five people out there staring into the sky at nothing, a crowd would form to see what they were observing.

When we begin to understand that there is a herd instinct within human nature, there is a lot that can change with behavioral economics. Suddenly, the always "rational" hypothesis no longer holds true. Every stock market crash in history has been followed by some investigation, instigated by the assumption there was a conspiracy to force it down by an individual or group who overpowers the market for sinister purposes. Never has anyone ever been found in 1907, 1929, 1987, 2008, and so on.

The Random Walk Theory

Every investigation of a stock market crash has begun with the presumption that some huge short position

42

overwhelmed the market. They base this on the supply side theory of a market. Behavioral economics needs to look not simply at some individual and rationalize why they will take some action. The Random Walk Theory was raised in 1973 by author Burton Malkiel in his book *A Random Walk Down Wall Street,* which was built upon the Efficient Market Hypothesis (EMH) of Eugene Fama. The Random Walk Theory maintains that it is impossible to outperform the market without assuming additional risk. Yet, technical analysis proves that there are patterns and statistics to prove that bullish trends are drawn out longer compared to bear markets that are typically panics. During the roaring '20s, the stock market took eight years to rally, but it only took from 1929 to 1932 to bottom. Simply put, it takes people a long time to believe in a trend, but they are very quick to panic.

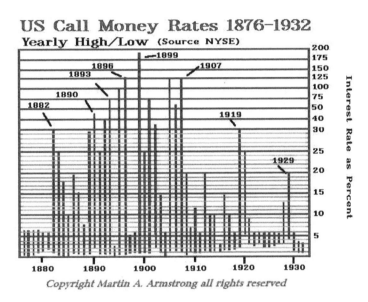

The Theory of Interest Rates

The central banks manipulate interest rates under the presumption that they can impact demand. Raise rates and people will stop buying; lower rates and people will buy more goods and services. A simple chart of call money rates from 1876 to 1932 illustrates how dead wrong this proposition has been. The stock market has never peaked with the same level of interest rates twice. The missing element never considered is expectations. If you believe the market will double by next year, you will pay 20% interest rates. If you believe the market will decline, you will not borrow even at 0.5%.

The decision-making process in behavioral economics is based solely upon what someone "believes" will happen tomorrow. A classic example took place in Japan when the government was going to raise the sales tax from 3% to 5% in April 1997. There was a mad rush of people buying things in March because they knew it would cost them more in April.

Therefore, attempting to adapt quantitative mathematical and statistical methodology to understand behavioral biases is by no means easy and will not offer consistency. The external factors to a domestic economy can alter the trend in the blink of an eye.

The Fish Bowl Economy

Markets trade on expectations ahead of economic numbers or central bank meetings concerning interest rates. The major surprises stem from what I call the Fish Bowl Economy analysis, which is confined to domestic policy objectives and information. The assumption is entirely parochial in that it attributes all actions to an isolated domestic economy. It fails to consider that capital flows around the world in a truly global sea of finance. Since ancient times and post-Dark Ages, people have been investing overseas, such as the notorious South Sea and Mississippi Bubbles of 1720.

When the British pound fell to near par against the dollar in 1985, Americans were in London buying whatever they could. The Brits thought they were mad. But when converted to dollars, it was like a 50% off sale for property at Harrods. Likewise, when the Japanese yen was strong, they were buying up American assets like Rockefeller Center post-G5 Plaza Accord in September 1985.

Buying Spree Sun., Sept. 21, 1986 — 1B

Japanese Investors Purchase U.S. Commercial Real Estate

'Certs' $3 Billion Farm Game

Francis Hutcheson
(1694–1746)

At the beginning of the study of economics, it was part philosophy. Adam Smith wrote *The Theory of Moral Sentiments*, which proposed psychological explanations of individual behavior, including concerns about fairness and justice. Jeremy Bentham wrote extensively on the psychological underpinnings of utility. These were part of philosophy that included ethics. Economics was not split into its own field until 1902 when Cambridge University began teaching the first course on the subject matter.

Xenophon (431–353 BC) wrote a book on how to manage your estate, wife, and slaves entitled *Okinomikos* (how to regulate the household) that gave birth to the term "economics" when translated by Francis Hutcheson (1694–1746; teacher of Adam Smith) who effectively copied his work.

We have clung to old theories and attempted to use them to manipulate society, despite the fact that there is no empirical evidence that they have ever worked. We continually try to manipulate society with the same old theories that are seriously incomplete and merely pray that they will at last work this time.

Clinging to Old Theories that no longer work

Governments and central banks have no other ideas or tools to use. This is why we now have people advocating the Modern Monetary Theory, which rests entirely upon the failure of Quantitative Easing. This theory believes that increasing the supply of money will force people to spend and therefore prices will rise, thereby stimulating the economy. Since that has failed, it does not justify adopting this Modern Monetary Theory while hoping for the best.

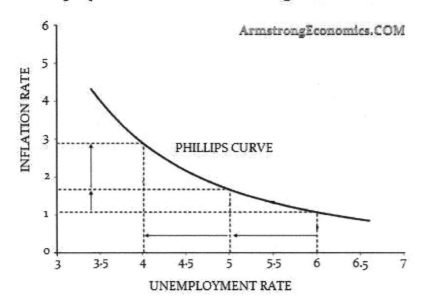

The Phillips Curve

Many are still married to the idea of the Phillips Curve, which represents the relationship between the rate of inflation and the unemployment rate. Alban William Housego Phillips first published his study in the magazine *Economica*. His study was carried out on the data of the United Kingdom from 1861 to 1957. It was hailed as a milestone in the development of macroeconomics.

Phillips argued that there was a consistent inverse relationship between inflation and unemployment. When unemployment was high, wages increased slowly; when unemployment was low, wages rose rapidly. What he failed to consider was simply the supply versus demand. It was not simply limited to a one-dimensional cause and effect. Additionally, the exceptions were war, but during such periods there was also a floating exchange rate with respect to the currency rather than a fixed gold standard.

The Phillips Curve has been modified several times since. Paul A. Samuelson and Robert Merton Solow in 1960 expanded the Phillips Curve. They created a link between unemployment and the change in the inflation rate, but this was again under Bretton Woods and a fixed exchange rate system.

The Phillips Curve assumptions are simply irrelevant today, and yet central banks have continued to try to manipulate society based upon these antiquated theories. Every assumption they make to manage the economy is dead wrong right down to the Quantity Theory of Money.

Edmund Phelps and Milton Friedman independently challenged the theoretical underpinnings of the Philips Curve. They argued that well-informed, rational employers and workers would pay attention only to real wages. Both Friedman and Phelps argued that the government could not permanently trade higher inflation for lower unemployment. The real wage is rather constant, for workers expect that their wages will increase at the same rate of price inflation to prevent the erosion of their purchasing power. At the same time, unemployment will tend to rise during a recession because workers' wages tend to be sticky and thereby do not move with the economy. This means workers will not expect or accept pay reductions. However, job loss becomes a risk for the employer's expenses to maintain workers are also sticky. Since rent and mortgages tend to remain fixed, workers are also unlikely to expect wages to decline in a recession. The management instead looks to reduce the number of people employed.

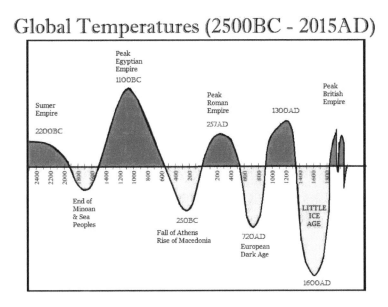

Global Temperatures (2500BC - 2015AD)

There are far more issues involved which prevent reducing everything to a single cause and effect to support various economic theories. The problem with the

Phillips Curve is similar to that of the data used in global warming. A mini Ice Age bottomed in the 1700s, and the data they have used begins in the 1850s. There were numerous periods of global warming followed by steep declines in temperature. It is part of the normal cycle of the planet. The advocates of global warming begin with the assumption that human activity must be the reason for the warming, ignoring the fact that such a period predates the Industrial Revolution.

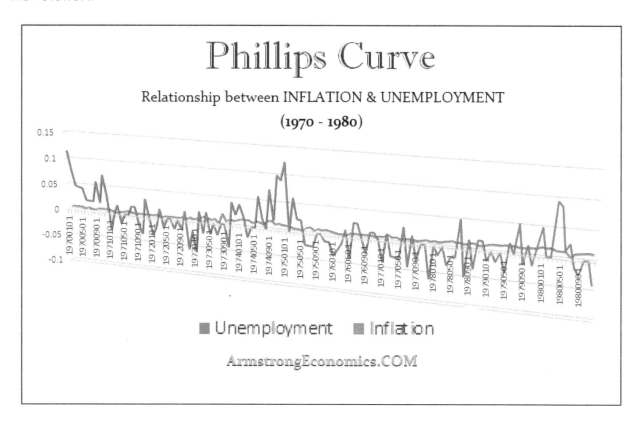

When we plot the annual rate of change in the CPI since the birth of the Floating Exchange Rate System (1971) into the first quarter of 2019 and overlay that with changes in the unemployment rate, we do not see a very strong correlation at all. In some instances, there was a complete opposite correlation. Focusing on the period of 1970 to 1980, which was the period of the OPEC Crisis that created stagflation[1], once again, the month over month rate of change for unemployment and inflation shows no correction.

Phillips conjectured that the lower the unemployment rate, the tighter the labor market and, therefore, the faster firms must raise wages to attract scarce labor. At higher rates of unemployment, the pressure abated. The Phillips "Curve"

---

[1] Stagflation refers to rising inflation caused externally with no real appreciable economic growth.

represented the average relationship between unemployment and wage behavior over the business cycle. It showed the rate of wage inflation that would result if a particular level of unemployment persisted for some time. But all of this was based upon a fixed exchange rate system constructed on the gold standard. Under a floating exchange rate system, capital flees for security reasons and not merely an investment opportunity.

The Obsession with Fixed Foreign Exchange Rates

There are some basic assumptions in economics that have been injecting serious problems in the way we try to manage the economy. I was giving a lecture in Chicago at a trading convention, and Milton Freidman came to listen to me. When I finished, Milton came up to shake my hand and said it was the best speech he had heard on foreign exchange. I was utterly flabbergasted. He said I was doing what he only dreamed about. Indeed, Milton had written a piece back in 1953 advocating a floating exchange rate system. He wrote:

"In principle there is no objection to a mixed system of fixed exchange rates within the sterling area and freely flexible rates between sterling and other countries, provided that the fixed rates within the sterling area can be maintained without trade restrictions." (Milton Friedman, *The Case for Flexible Exchange Rates*, Essays in Positive Economics, Chicago: University of Chicago Press, 1953, 193.)

Milton Friedman with President Nixon and Secretary of the Treasury Shultz in the Oval Office, June 1971 Box 115, Milton Friedman Papers, Hoover Institution Archives – Image credit: White House Photo

Milton advised President Nixon in 1971 when he abandoned the fixed rate currency system established in 1944 at Bretton Woods. Milton was an original thinker. He was someone who thought out of the box. More importantly, he understood that experience was everything. He came to the convention because we were not the academics. We were the people who actually lived and breathed the currency markets every single day. There are those who just theorize about the world economy, and then there are those of us who actually had to make decisions every day on the trends rather than theories.

As traders, we realized that the currency markets were really a vote made by international capital on the state of world politics. For example, even under the fixed exchange rate system of Bretton Woods, the dollar rose, and the pound fell during the October 1956 Suez Canal Crisis. The one

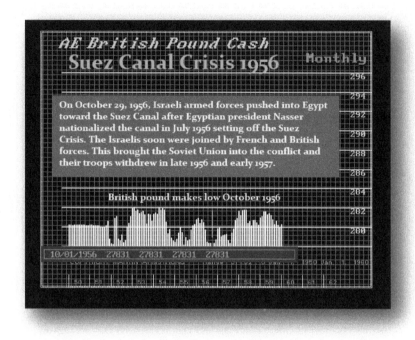

rule traders always learned was rather simple — sell the currency nearest the geopolitical conflict.

Some very basic things are seriously wrong. Politicians continually try to use theories that no longer work, and quite honestly, they have never worked because they were based upon a world of pre-1971 fixed exchange rates and just theory. Even universities still teach theories based upon the economic old world of fixed exchange rates among currencies. The entire movement to create the euro evolved into the idea of restoring fixed exchange rates, combined with the idea that governments stand isolated and can manipulate their domestic economy contrary to what is unfolding around the world. This has become the cornerstone of politics, "Vote for me, and I will give you x, y, z!" Politics has become all about bribing people for votes rather than properly managing the economy.

Believe it or not, traditional economists, politicians, and bankers have all failed to understand the role of money. They do not understand what has honestly happened over the centuries. There has been a complete ignorance of international capital flows and how this has impacted currency values. It seems that only those of us who have traded currencies even understand how they move as independent checks and balances against the follies of politicians. Then we have politicians starting trade wars and accusing other nations of deliberately devaluing their currencies for trade advantages. Many political issues from trade wars, protectionism, and civil unrest have all been centered around one thing — the failure to understand the role of money within society.

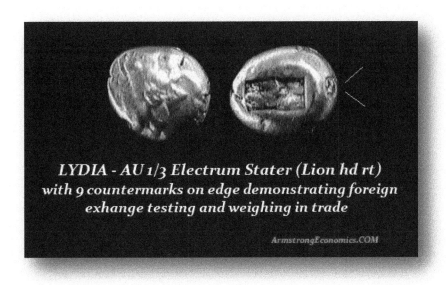

LYDIA - AU 1/3 Electrum Stater (Lion hd rt)
with 9 countermarks on edge demonstrating foreign
exhange testing and weighing in trade

ArmstrongEconomics.COM

Since gold was used in coins from the 7th century BC, there was an assumption that there was some sort of a fixed exchange rate. Here is a gold coin from Lydia where coins first began. There are nine banking/forex dealer counter stamps around the edge of this coin, which is rather worn, showing it indeed saw a fair amount of circulation. We find that the various city-states in Ionia at that period in time issued coins to varying standards of weight and fineness. Clearly, this coin serves as evidence that one of the earliest trades came from foreign exchange dealers. Each stamp on the edge of this coin confirmed that it had been inspected and approved by that foreign exchange dealer in ancient times.

Sir Thomas Gresham (1518-1579)

Most people have heard of Sir Thomas Gresham's (1518-1579) Law, which resulted from his observations following the debasement of the English coinage under Henry VIII (1509-1547). Gresham was also a trader. He acted on behalf of King Edward VI (1547-1553) and Edward's half-sisters, queens Mary I (1553-1558) and Elizabeth I (1558-1603) in the financial market, which was then in Antwerp and Amsterdam.

In 1544, Gresham left England for the Low Countries (Netherlands), where he worked for his family as a merchant. He would act in various matters as an agent for King Henry VIII, for that was the market where kings would borrow money. Gresham had a good "feel" for trading and became renowned for his skills in playing the market.

Henry VIII (b 1491; 1509 - 1547)
Debasement of the Gold Coinage

| Sovereign | Angel | Half-Angel |

Standard was 23 carats up to 1544, 22 carats in 1545, and 20 carats in 1546

ArmstrongEconomics.COM

The debasement of the coinage under Henry VIII impacted the gold coinage. The practice was causing massive economic problems and civil unrest in England. The velocity of money was declining as the old coinage was hoarded, giving rise to Sir Thomas Gresham's Law that bad money (debased) drives out good (undebased). As hoarding soared, so did inflation as expressed in terms of the debased coinage. Debasement actually caused the money supply to shrink, for all the old coinage was hoarded and withdrawn from circulation. Finally, in 1549, the silver content virtually doubled. Strangely enough, the higher silver content resulted in lighter weight coinage, which was still regarded as unacceptable. This resulted in a 25% reduction in silver content to increase the weight and "feel" of the coins. However, the shortage of cash led to further debasement, and the silver dropped by 50% to its lowest level in 1551. In 1551, another agent of the king, Sir William Dansell, created a serious crisis thanks to his mismanagement in the marketplace that created a collapse in confidence in the English government.

The authorities called Gresham for advice, and thereafter they deferred to Gresham who advocated some ingenious trading strategies that were arbitrary and unfair. Nevertheless, Gresham managed to create one of the earliest manipulations that raised the value of the pound sterling from 16s to 22s on the Antwerp bourse. A few years later, this maneuver allowed King Edward VI to discharge almost all his debts in the market. Thereafter, the English government would always seek Gresham's advice in all their financial difficulties. They even employed him in some diplomatic negotiations relying on his reputation with Charles V.

However, Gresham was a Protestant. He fell out of favor when Mary (1553–1554) came to the throne as a Catholic monarch. Mary introduced a new series of coins, the crown, half-crown, 6d and 3d, all back at the full silver standard. Mary restored the silver coinage to the full sterling standard and struck all her gold at 23 carats.

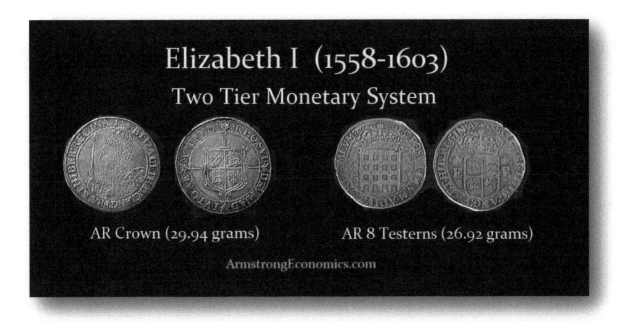

Then under Queen Elizabeth's reign (1558–1603), Gresham remained the financial agent of the crown in the marketplace, but he also acted as ambassador to Parma and governor of the Netherlands. It appears that Gresham understood that the fluctuation in international markets in the value of the pound could be sterilized with a two-tier monetary system. Under Elizabeth I, Spain was the financial capital of Europe thanks to the riches coming from America. It seems that Gresham advised the crown to employ a two-tier monetary system in England at that time. Elizabeth issued four denominations of Eight, Four, Two, and One silver Testern as they were known. They were also called "Portcullis Money." This was an attempt at producing a trade coinage sponsored by the newly formed East India Company to be used in overseas trade, principally in the Far East. In this manner, any debasement of the coinage for domestic use would not disrupt the value of the pound on the external foreign exchange markets.

The introduction of this two-tier monetary system came from the realization that there were separate and distinct factors that would influence the currency's value. Clearly, there was a major conflict between domestic policy objectives and international policy objectives. This is a lesson we still do not appreciate today. The Federal Reserve is often lobbied by the IMF (International Monetary Fund) and other central banks not to raise interest rates, for it would impact international markets.

Eventually, because of civil unrest evolving into the Dutch revolt, Gresham left Antwerp in 1567 and returned to London. His trading skills made him one of the richest men of his generation in England. In 1565, Gresham proposed to build, at his own expense, a bourse to compete with the Dutch, which would become the Royal Exchange.

Athenian Owl circa 449BC   Ancient Imitation

Not until the 19th century do we see an attempt to create a single currency or a fixed exchange rate. The misconception that there was some gold standard that existed since ancient times has seriously disrupted our understanding of the monetary system. It is true that many countries issued gold and silver coinage, but the coinage tended to trade based upon weight. Only in a few cases over the centuries do we see that the coinage of the dominant economy (financial capital) carries a sovereign premium. We see this with the Athenian Owls of circa 449 BC. Peripheral economies begin to imitate the Athenian Owls, demonstrating that they carried a premium over the silver content.

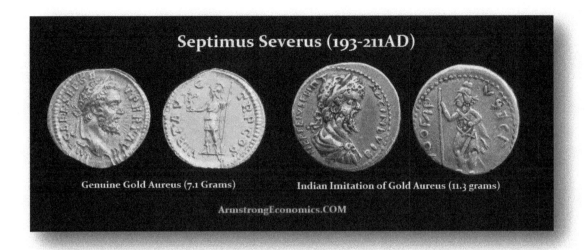

We find Roman gold coins commonly imitated in India from the time of Tiberius (14–37 AD) to as late as Gordian (238–244 AD). The gold content is not debased, and some are actually overweight, demonstrating that the gold carried a premium as a Roman coin.

Monetary System of the Republic of Florence

Fiorino d'Oro
1252-1303

Fiorino d'Argento
(Grosso), c. 1260

Even during the 13th century, other cities began to issue imitations of the gold florin of Florence, Italy. But there was also a two-tier monetary system, whereas gold was used only for international payments and silver was used for local trade, including wages. Obviously, there was a sovereign premium to the coinage that was issued by the dominant economy throughout the centuries. Even the silver Pillar Dollars (8 Reals) issued by Spain became the standard for the monetary system in Asia well into the 19th century.

Spanish 1768 *"Pillar Dollar"* 8 Reales

Single Currency of Napoleon 1808-1814

France 40 Francs   Italy 40 Lire

Spain 320 Reales

ArmstrongEconomics.COM

Therefore, the world was not on a pure fixed exchange rate system. Precious metals were used, but not at some fixed exchange rate. Napoleon first created a fixed exchange rate by the Monetary Ordinance of March 28, 1803. The 20–franc gold pieces, which he authorized in 1803, were the basis to standardize the monetary system according to a specific gold weight.

This Napoleonic model for a monetary system in Europe was truly this idea of creating Bretton Woods, and more recently the euro. This idea of a fixed exchange rate monetary system became the Latin Monetary Union, which prevailed in Europe from 1865 until 1914 and World War I. This eventually evolved into the idea that a fixed exchange rate monetary system had to be restored following World War II, which became Bretton Woods.

The downside of this monetary system was the simple fact that by creating a standard exchange value, which was fixed among nations, there was no understanding of a floating exchange rate system. Nothing along these lines was ever taught in universities, keeping the idea that money had to be standardized and fixed regardless of the business cycle and trends globally.

Latin Monetary Union 1865

France

Weight 6.4516g   Gold 0.1867 oz.   Fineness 90% gold   Diameter 21mm

Italy   Belgium

Switzerland

Copyright Martin Armstrong All Rights Reserved 2011

> During this new stage of the depression, the refugee gold and the foreign government reserve deposits were constantly driven by fear hither and yon over the world. We were to see currencies demoralized and governments embarrassed as fear drove the gold from one country to another. In fact, there was a mass of gold and short-term credit which behaved like a loose cannon on the deck of the world in a tempest-tossed era.

THE MEMOIRS OF Herbert Hoover - The Great Depression 1929-1941, id/p 67

ArmstrongEconomics.COM

Herbert Hoover
(1874 - 1964)
(President 1929 - 1933)

During the Great Depression, the spark which ignited the contagion began in Austria during May 1931 with a bank failure that spread to Britain by September 1931. President Herbert Hoover (1874-1964) wrote about the contagion in his memoirs. He wrote: "We were to see currencies demoralized and governments embarrassed as fear drove the gold from one country to another." He was describing what we still see today in modern times as he explained that capital "behaved like a loose cannon on the deck of the world in a tempest-tossed era."

The devaluation of the pound marked the end of the depression for Britain as prices began to rise. This was the reality observed by Warren and he began to understand that maintaining a strong currency meant that wages and prices declined.

In 1932, George Warren wrote *Wholesale Prices for 213 Years; 1720-1932*. Effectively, this work was a forerunner to Monetary Theory by making observations that prices rose with the gold discoveries and declined when supplies of gold declined. This work was a simplistic monetary view of the world that Franklin Roosevelt could understand. George Warren was approaching everything from the fringe, making truly a groundbreaking evolution in the concept of money, but that is where all major change comes from in every field. Only those with creative minds can think out of the box, whereas the field promotes conformity to gain the respect of the industry. This has always led to the simple maxim that the majority is always wrong.

George F. Warren (1874-1938)

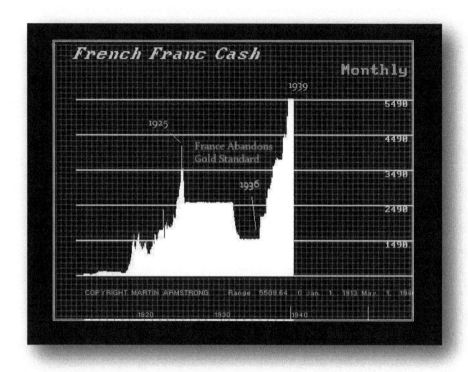

France, who worked so hard to gather gold, which they saw as the means to European dominance, was now left alone clinging to its gold reserves. They held the second largest in the world and the largest in Europe. France made its people endure hardship by austerity for the image of a future greater glory. Finally, in 1936, the Bank of France abandoned the gold standard only when it became so obvious that their economy was now becoming isolated, unable to export due to an overvalued currency plagued by deflation. The value of the French franc plummeted going into 1939 as Germany began to flex its muscles.

The traditional economic thought was that of austerity, and as such, they considered Warren a crackpot. The conventional wisdom simply failed to comprehend what constituted money or its role within the scope of our collective society. Money was fixed in value, except during periods of war. The traditional economic beliefs missed the entire point that money declines in purchasing power during economic booms and rises in purchasing power as assets decline during economic recessions and depressions. This also causes the cost of labor to rise and creates unemployment.

The assumption that money had to be tangible was just not correct for money rises and falls in value with economic booms (inflation) and recessions (deflation). The ultimate object of the medium of exchange is the exchange of one thing (object or labor) for another (object or labor). What constitutes "money" is simply the medium of exchange like words that relay concepts between two parties. At the core lies the perception of value, and that fluctuates according to demand and supply.

Therefore, Warren demonstrated that if you wanted prices to rise, the value of the dollar had to decline. Thus, the only way to do that was to abandon the gold standard, which was the fixed exchange rate system. Gold was merely one recognized object of value. Its advantage has simply been that it is movable compared to real estate. It is internationally accepted as a valuable object, and thus it is free of opinion regarding quality such as diamonds.

Consequently, George Warren saved the day and, contrary to the Brains Trust, moved toward creating inflation to end the austerity. The confiscation of gold was a different issue. This was primarily done to ensure that the government would make money on the revaluation of gold and not the public. It was also the idea of preventing the hoarding of money that was a serious issue at that point in time of the Great Depression, just as it has been in modern times under Quantitative Easing in Europe.

Bretton Woods

Following World War II, the United States ended up with 76% of the official world gold reserves. The assumption that there had to be some sort of fixed exchange rate was the primary belief. No one seemed to entertain anything different.

Bretton Woods Monetary Conference

The Bretton Woods system imposed an obligation on nations to adopt a monetary policy. This policy would maintain its external exchange rates within a 1% trading ban by tying its currency to gold and the ability of the IMF to bridge temporary imbalances of payments. By these steps, they hoped to end the competitive devaluation of currencies for trade purposes.

There were 730 delegates from all 44 Allied nations who gathered at the Mount Washington Hotel in Bretton Woods, New Hampshire. During most of the month of July 1944, the delegates deliberated and signed the Bretton Woods agreement on its final day of July 22. At this time, the International Monetary Fund (IMF) and the International Bank for Reconstruction and Development (IBRD), which today is part of the World Bank Group, were established. The United States' position insisted that the Bretton Woods system must rest on both gold and the U.S. dollar.

Bretton Woods fixed the price of gold at $35 per ounce in 1944, to which the dollar was pegged. The dollar became the derivative proxy for gold, and by fixing the peg, they thereby doomed the entire monetary system to collapse ultimately.

The Bretton Woods agreement completely failed because it did not take into account that there is a the business cycle. The economies would rise and fall according to their economic performance. The system was doomed, for it would not raise that value of gold in proportion to the creation of dollars. The supply of dollars increased dramatically, but the politicians never thought about readjusting the value of gold until it was too late in 1968.

Since the dollar was a representative currency and not the actual currency itself, this status eventually caused the monetary system to collapse in 1971. Foreign governments were exchanging dollars for gold since they could see that the quantity of dollars had increased, but the value of gold remained fixed.

The system of Bretton Woods was clearly under great stress, but as always, politicians refused to acknowledge the fact that they are incapable of managing any economy, no less a monetary system. First, silver had to be abandoned in 1965. Then in 1968, they were forced to create a two-tier gold market by allowing the private sector to trade gold in London, where they maintained a fixed conversion rate to gold.

On October 13, 1960, the third Kennedy–Nixon Presidential Debate took place. Kennedy set off a gold panic in 1960 when he made it clear that the United States was losing gold reserves because it was maintaining troops and bases overseas. He said:

> "Now on the question of gold. The difficulty, of course, is that we do have heavy obligations abroad, that we therefore have to maintain not only a favorable balance of trade but also send a good deal of our dollars overseas to pay our troops, maintain our bases, and sustain other economies. In other words, if we're going to continue to maintain our position in the sixties, we have to maintain a sound monetary and fiscal policy."

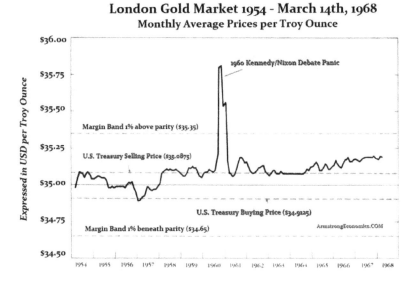

Kennedy indeed set off a gold panic. In London, gold rallied as high as almost $36, reaching nearly $40 for the first time in other forums. This was the first crack showing that the Bretton Woods System was indeed collapsing under a fixed rate system where the supply of dollars was not fixed.

The 1960 panic in gold shook the foundations of the monetary system. The London Gold Pool was thus established in response to that event to make sure no such panic would take place again. The idea was that the pooling of gold reserves by a group of eight central banks would be able to control the marketplace. This was to include the United States and seven European countries. The accord was reached on November 1, 1961, to cooperate in maintaining the Bretton Woods System of fixed rate convertible currencies and to defend a gold price of US$35 per troy ounce by interventions in the London gold market.

1964 / 1965 United States Silver Demonetization

This was the last year that silver was used to mint coinage in the United States whereby the silver content was 90% now valued at $2.1.

A blend of copper and nickel covering a copper core in this case. The value of the metal in this coin is now 2 cents.

Nevertheless, the 1960 Gold Panic was an early warning sign that confidence was beginning to erode in the fixed rate system of Bretton Woods. The long-term pressure of inflation was first felt in the silver market. President Kennedy issued Executive Order 11110 on June 4, 1963, which ended the use of silver as a domestic monetary instrument backing the domestic currency.

The fixed exchange rate system was clearly still under pressure. Politicians resisted recognizing this trend, but the free markets were applying the check and balance against a failed system. The 1960 Gold Panic exposed the fundamental problem for the first time. The government fixed the price of gold in dollars at $35, but they continued to create more dollars, as Kennedy pointed out, building all these military bases around the world. The economic pressure began to build once again in 1968, or about 3.14 years from the abandonment of silver in the coinage in 1965.

The pressure on the gold standard continued and culminated finally during 1968. By the end of February 1968, the demand for gold in both Zurich and London increased to very high levels. The demand for gold was not relieved by an announcement of the selling members of the London Gold Pool who met at the Bank for International Settlements in Basle on March 10, 1968. The public announcement said:

> "The central banks contributing to the London gold pool reaffirmed their determination to continue their support to the pool based on the fixed price of $35 per ounce of gold."

As typical, government tried manipulating the market again by scaring the traders with its statements. The public didn't buy it, and the demand for gold simply exploded, rising to a whole new level of panic proportions. At this time, the governments decided to close the London gold market on March 15, 1968, to stop the drain on official monetary reserves. That drastic event was taken as a confirmation that the central banks were weak and could not meet the demand.

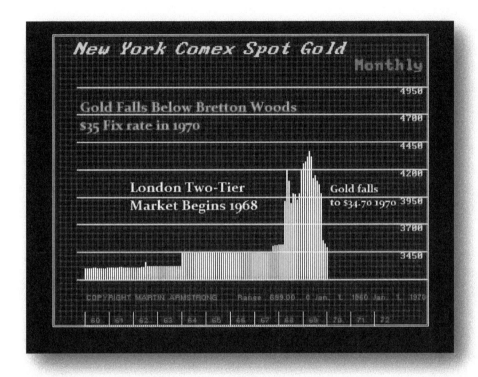

An urgent meeting took place in Washington on March 16 and 17, 1968, which I will refer to as the 1968 Washington Gold Panic Meeting. There, the London Gold Pool's selling members capitulated and decided to stop supplying gold from monetary reserves to the London gold market or any other gold market. The strings were cut, and the free market won. The London market remained closed until April 1, 1968, to allow the market to regain its stability in hopes that the panic would subside.

It became obvious to everyone but the politicians that the monetary system was failing.

The Gold Rush: What Price Money!

Cartoon from Newsweek 1972

65

The Europeans were seen as pushing gold ever higher, led by the French and the Swiss. Finally, in 1971 Richard Nixon was forced to close the gold window on August 15 that year.

Milton Friedman met with Richard Nixon and said he was one of the smartest presidents he ever met. Milton explained in an interview:

> "Nixon, as you know, had been in the price control organization during World War II and understood that price controls were a very bad idea, and so he was strongly opposed to price controls. And yet, in 1971, August 15, 1971, he adopted wage and price controls. And the reason he did it, in my opinion, was because of something else that was happening, and that had to do with the exchange rate; that had to do with Bretton Woods and the agreement to peg the price of gold.

**Nixon closes the Gold Window
August 15th, 1971 Beginning
the Floating Exchange Rate System**

> The United States had agreed in 1944, at the Bretton Woods Conference, on an international financial system under which other countries would link their currencies to the U.S. dollar, and the United States would link its currency to gold and keep the price of gold at $35 an ounce. And because of the policies that were followed by the Kennedy and Johnson administrations, it had become very difficult to do that. We had had inflationary policies, which led to a tendency for the gold to flow out, for the price of gold to go above $35 an ounce. And the situation had become very critical in 1971. Nixon had to do something about that. If he had done nothing but close the gold window, if he had said the United States is going off the gold standard and done nothing else, every headline in every newspaper would have been, "That negative Nixon again! Just a negative act." And so instead he dressed it up by making it part of a general economic policy, a recovery policy, in which wage and price controls, which the democrats had been urging all along, became a major element. And by putting together the combination of closing the gold window and at the same time having wage and price controls, he converted what would have been a negative from a political point of view to a political positive. And that was the political reason for which he did it."

Nixon's actual speech also imposed a 10% tariff on all imports rather than quotas as well as wage and price controls. The Watergate issue then served to distract everyone from the economic crisis of Bretton Woods collapsing. The Floating Exchange Rate System took hold as a default. Nixon's speech read in part as follows:

RICHARD NIXON

XXXVII *President of the United States: 1969-1974*

264 - Address to the Nation Outlining a New Economic Policy: "The Challenge of Peace."

August 15, 1971

I am today ordering a freeze on all prices and wages throughout the United States for a period of 90 days. In addition, I call upon corporations to extend the wage-price freeze to all dividends...

In recent weeks, the speculators have been waging an all-out war on the American dollar. The strength of a nation's currency is based on the strength of that nation's economy--and the American economy is by far the strongest in the world. Accordingly, I have directed the Secretary of the Treasury to take the action necessary to defend the dollar against the speculators.

I have directed Secretary Connally to suspend temporarily the convertibility of the dollar into gold or other reserve assets, except in amounts and conditions determined to be in the interest of monetary stability and in the best interests of the United States.

Now, what is this action--which is very technical--what does it mean for you?

Let me lay to rest the bugaboo of what is called devaluation.

If you want to buy a foreign car or take a trip abroad, market conditions may cause your dollar to buy slightly less. But if you are among the overwhelming majority of Americans who buy American-made products in America, your dollar will be worth just as much tomorrow as it is today.

The effect of this action, in other words, will be to stabilize the dollar.

Now, this action will not win us any friends among the international money traders. But our primary concern is with the American workers, and with fair competition around the world.

To our friends abroad, including the many responsible members of the international banking community who are dedicated to stability and the flow of trade, I give this assurance: The United States has always been, and will continue to be, a forward-looking and trustworthy trading partner. In full cooperation with the International Monetary Fund and those who trade with us, we will press for the necessary reforms to set up an urgently needed new international monetary system. Stability and equal treatment is in everybody's best interest. I am determined that the American dollar must never again be a hostage in the hands of international speculators.

I am taking one further step to protect the dollar, to improve our balance of payments, and to increase jobs for Americans. As a temporary measure, I am today imposing an additional tax of 10 percent on goods imported into the United States.2 This is a better solution for international trade than direct controls on the amount of imports.

This import tax is a temporary action. It isn't directed against any other country. It is an action to make certain that American products will not be at a disadvantage because of unfair exchange rates. When the unfair treatment is ended, the import tax will end as well.

REMARKS BY PAUL A. VOLCKER
AT THE ANNUAL MEETING OF THE BRETTON WOODS COMMITTEE
WASHINGTON, DC – MAY 21, 2014

A NEW BRETTON WOODS???

"The current travails of the Eurozone (the equivalent of an absolute fixed exchange rate regime) carry interesting lessons. A single currency with the free flows of funds among the member states simply could not substitute for the absence of a unified banking system and incentives for disciplined and complementary national economic policies.

That is all a long introduction to a plea – a plea for attention to the need for developing an international monetary and financial system worthy of our time. ...

What is the approach (or presumably combination of approaches) that can better reconcile reasonably free and open markets with independent national policies, maintaining in the process the stability in markets and economies that is in the common interest? ...

The creation of the G-20 at the exalted level of Presidents and Prime Ministers has been a political accomplishment. The agreed changes in IMF governing structure are important in achieving a sense of political legitimacy for its governing structure and decision-making. But that is not enough – it means little without substantive agreement on the need for monetary reform and practical approaches toward that end.

We are a long way from that. But what can be done now is to lay the intellectual ground work for approaches that can, for instance, identify and limit prolonged and ultimately unsustainable imbalances in national payments. We should be able, within a broad range, to manage exchange rates among major 6 currencies in a manner that discourages the extreme changes that are inconsistent with orderly adjustment. We can and should consider ways and means of encouraging – even insisting upon – needed balance of payments equilibrium.

Nor would I reject some re-assessment of the use of a single national currency as the dominant international reserve and trading vehicle. For instance, do we want to encourage or discourage so important a development as regional trade and currency areas?

A new Bretton Woods conference? We are long ways from that. But surely events have raised, whether we want to admit it or not, some fundamental questions that have been ignored for decades. ...

All that has happened reinforces what we typically affirm: a strong, innovative and stable financial system is fundamental to open trade and to the prosperity of all nations. Participation in such a beneficial system that has become truly international implies certain responsibilities. ...

Can we not, in approaching that challenge, restore something of the spirit and conviction that characterized the planning, the negotiation and the management of the Bretton Woods System that I once knew 50 years ago? Our host today, the Bretton Woods Committee lights the candle, but we have a long way to go.

Paul Volcker spoke at the annual meeting of the Bretton Woods Committee in Washington on May 21, 2014 (the meetings never died). His remarks offer a guide that behind the curtain, there are some who see the problems we face in the monetary system, albeit not yet that from a major perspective. There is still hope that balancing budgets will somehow lead to stability and returning to a fixed peg system among world currencies, although no backing of gold.

What is critical in his lecture is the fact that the need for monetary reform exists. Those who think the United Nations would step in I do not see as realistic, for there is way too much political distrust of that many nations being involved. Volcker is still willing to see either regional currencies or even a single currency for the reserve. Nevertheless, he speaks the truth insofar as the euro experiment has been a total disaster. He saw that the free flow of capital among the member states could not offset the lack of a central banking/bond system and the inability to control each member's fiscal spending. The failure to consolidate the debts just left the individual bond markets in the same manner as the currencies once did.

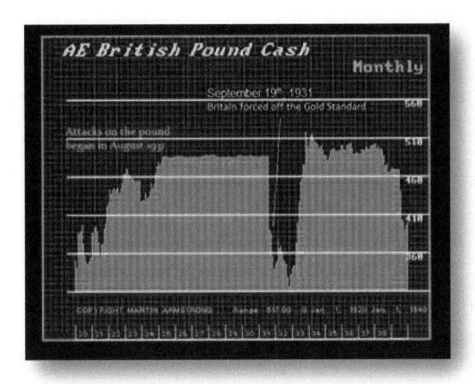

1992 Exchange Rate Mechanism (ERM) Crisis

Britain was forced to abandon the gold standard on September 19, 1931. The speculative attacks on the pound grew with intensity during August 1931. Britain tried to defend the pound, but no government is capable of such a move. This was not dissimilar to the 1992 ERM (European Exchange Rate Mechanism) Crisis, which was an attempt to take the pound into the euro. On Black Wednesday, September 16, 1992, the British Conservative government of John Major was forced to withdraw the pound sterling from the ERM after it was unable to keep the pound above its agreed fixed lower limit.

The ERM of 1992 was a prelude to the coming crash of the euro. While the 1992 ERM Crisis was still focused directly on currencies, what would unfold after the euro became the shift in trading instruments from currencies of individual nations to their bond markets. The failure to consolidate the debts of member states in Europe allowed the speculative forces to still target the bond and share markets of the individual members as if their currencies still traded.

The new government headed by John Major took the pound into the ERM the same month that German unification began. The monetary policies of Germany were starkly different from Britain's. I was called when the attack on the pound unfolded. They asked what our model said about the pound because they knew I was a friend of Margaret Thatcher. I relayed its analysis that the pound had to be devalued. I was told that was impossible because John Major had said just the week before that the pound would be maintained in the ERM. I then said that the pound must be suspended if not officially devalued. The

Sir John Major
(born 1943)
British Prime Minister (1990 – May 2, 1997)

pressure was intense. I explained that a fixed rate is a guaranteed trade. I can bet billions, and if wrong, nothing happens and I get my money back. That finally made the point.

The 1992/1993 collapse of the ERM was a system introduced by the European Economic Community on March 13, 1979, to which Thatcher was against. It was part of the European Monetary System (EMS), intended to reduce exchange rate variability and achieve monetary stability in Europe in the aftermath of the collapse of Bretton Woods in 1971. Only after the Plaza Accord in 1985, did the EMS prepare for the Economic and Monetary Union of Europe, which gave birth to the introduction of a single currency, the euro, which took place on January 1, 1999.

The Bundesbank finally began to reduce interest rates only when the 1992 Crisis emerged. They did not cut interest rates enough, and speculation continued, building tremendous pressure on the Italian lira and British pound. The clash between domestic policy in Germany was concerned that reunification could result in inflation with the economic recession external to Germany. This illustrates the problem that will always exist. Even within the United States, there were 12 branches of the Federal Reserve that all maintained a separate interest rate policy because there were regional differences. No matter the theory, a single currency will not promote a unified European economy, and more than the dollar creates that illusion within the USA.

The real value of the East German mark was worthless. The East German mark was officially valued by the East German government at parity with the (West German) Deutsche Mark. However, because it was not readily convertible and the GDR's export profile was restricted, it was practically worthless outside East Germany. The German government effectively bribed the East to join. East German marks were exchanged for West German

marks at a rate of 1:1 for the first 4,000 marks and 2:1 for larger amounts. Before reunification, each citizen of East Germany coming to West Germany was given Begrüßungsgeld (welcome money), a per capita allowance of DM 100 in cash.

Clearly, the tension within the ERM began to build up from mid-July 1992, concentrating initially on the Italian lira, then on sterling, and then on a variety of other currencies. The 1992-93 Exchange Rate Mechanism crisis created a huge strain between countries in the EU — both economic and political. The generally accepted belief was that there were four possible factors behind the crisis that included competitiveness problems, German unification, and inevitable policy shifts with the fourth pointing to self-fulfilling speculative attacks on the currencies. However, the speculative attacks on the currencies were not the cause of the crisis; they merely facilitated the events by acting on the weakness of the attempt to create a fixed exchange rate system once again.

The foreign exchange markets remained disturbed for the rest of the year, with a renewed outbreak of speculative pressures leading to the abandonment of Sweden's peg to the ECU, the devaluation of both the Portuguese escudo and the Spanish peseta in November, and the abandonment of Norway's ECU peg in December.

Thursday, July 2, 1992
Page B6

Economic reform

Pinch on Russians as ruble floated

• Government aims for stability and courts
Western aid in move that may boost import prices

However, also overlooked was the fact that in July 1992, the Russian ruble began trading for the first time. Meanwhile, the Bank of China required foreign visitors to China to conduct transactions with Foreign Exchange Certificates that were issued by the Bank of China between 1979 and 1994. Effectively, this was a two-tier monetary system (domestic v international).

Following the ERM Crisis of 1992, this two-tier system in China was abolished, and all transactions then took place in renminbi. The entire global foreign exchange system was changing. The biggest mistake people make looking at the British pound crisis of 1992, has been looking at it through a myopic perspective of isolation.

The pressure on the Finnish Markka was so strong at that time it was forced to abandon its peg with the ECU. Italy raised its interest rates to try to support its currency, but still, the lira had weakened repeatedly. The Bundesbank did not cut its interest rates enough, fearing inflation and speculation would continue, which put pressure on other European states.

On September 13, 1992, the Italians decided to devalue the lira by 7% (other currencies revalued at 3.5%; lira devalued 3.5%). The pressures on the lira led traders to look around and see that the British pound was also overvalued all relative to Germany.

Hence, the pound sterling became the next target during the ERM crisis of 1992. Black Wednesday, September 16, 1992, two days after the Italian devaluation, the UK Conservative government, which had thrown Margaret Thatcher out of power to take the pound into the coming euro, was forced to withdraw from the ERM as well. John Major was forced to withdraw the pound sterling from the European Exchange Rate Mechanism (ERM) after it was unable to keep the pound above its agreed lower limit in the ERM.

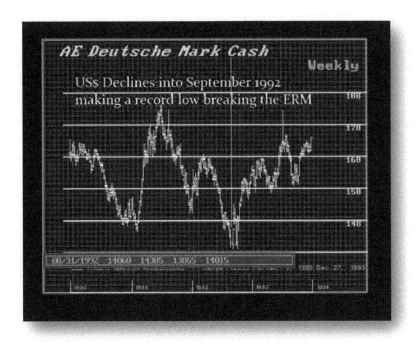

The day after the British crisis of Black Wednesday where they were forced to exit the ERM, the selling pressure against the ERM and thus the European single currency movement turned back upon Italy. The very next day, on September 17, 1992, Italy also withdrew from the ERM. The scheme to create the euro was proving to be a warning of what was to come in the decades that followed.

The Deutsche Mark was sent to significant highs even against the dollar in September 1992. The foreign exchange markets remained disturbed for the rest of that year. As mentioned, this led to a renewed outbreak of speculative pressures leading to the abandonment of Sweden's peg to the ECU, the devaluation of both the Portuguese escudo and the Spanish peseta in November 1992, and the abandonment of Norway's ECU peg in December 1992.

By January 1993, Ireland witnessed economic pressure due to the UK's sterling devaluation, which then compelled Ireland to devalue its currency by 10%. Germany finally reduced its interest rates in February, March, and April of 1993, trying to ease the economic pressure within the currencies that had not yet been realigned. The entire crisis of 1992–1994 was a prelude to the ultimate crisis that would hit the euro for similar reasons and Germany's fear of inflation that would impose austerity on the rest of Europe. It was Germany's high interest rates in 1992/1993 that broke the back of the ERM.

France was then presented with the problem of maintaining the franc at its existing parity. France wanted lower interest rates to relieve the recession, but it was influenced by the German concern for reunification inflation. France began to challenge the German economic policy of austerity. France was forced to maintain its interest rates high, abandoning its domestic policy objectives because of the Germans.

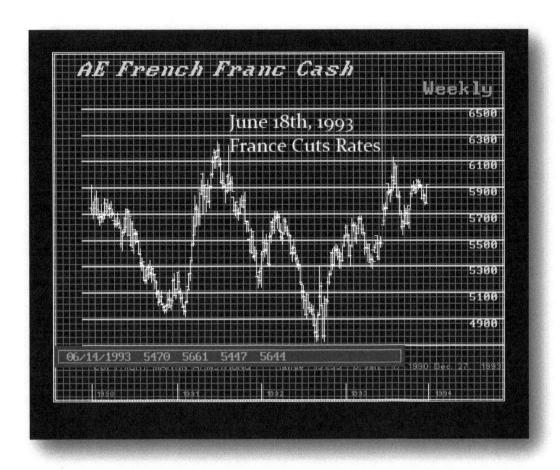

Finally, the economic pressures were building in France, and on June 18, 1993, the French money market intervention rate was dropped below German rates. The markets were concerned and became skeptical about the success of the entire scheme. The stress within the ERM was becoming obvious to professional traders, and the speculative positions began to increase. This time, traders now turned against the French franc during June 1993. The franc began to drop sharply against the U.S. dollar.

The Banque de France was forced to raise its interest rate to prevent the franc from falling through its ERM lower band. However, the Bundesbank did not lower its discount rate, and massive sales of the French franc, Belgian franc, Danish krone, Spanish peseta, and Portuguese escudo all took place in response. It was Germany's misunderstanding of its hyperinflation of the 1920s that once more dictated their response. Today, we have seen the price of German austerity upon the entire economic condition of Europe. While the ERM broke, today there is a full federalized government in Brussels attempting to maintain austerity and the same philosophies that broke the ERM during the 1992/1993 Crisis.

At this point in time, the ERM was in total crisis within Europe. One would think they learned from Bretton Woods, but politicians are blinded by their self-interest, which always comes before that of the people or country. A massive intervention was necessary to keep these currencies just above their ERM floor. On August 2, 1993, the European Commission monetary officials and finance ministers finally agreed that the ERM bands should be widened from 2.25% to 15% with the single exception being the Dutch-German trading band. They concluded that wider bands would make the system less vulnerable to speculation.

At the core of all of this was the German's complete misunderstanding of the hyperinflation and their attempt to impose austerity upon all of Europe, which is deflationary and anti-economic growth.

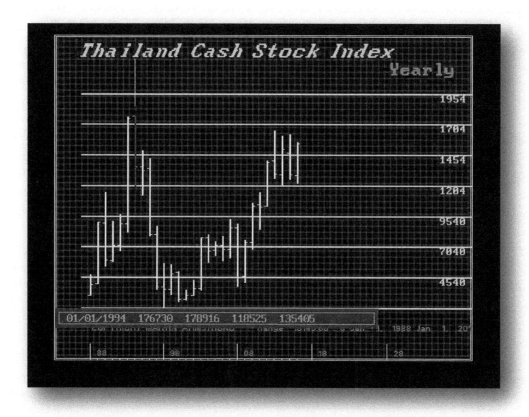

The ERM Crisis of 1992/1993 made George Soros famous, but it awakened international hedge fund traders to the currency markets. Traders then turned to the peripheral markets — Russia next and then South East Asia, which saw its share market peak in January 1994 and bottom in September 1998 (56 months).

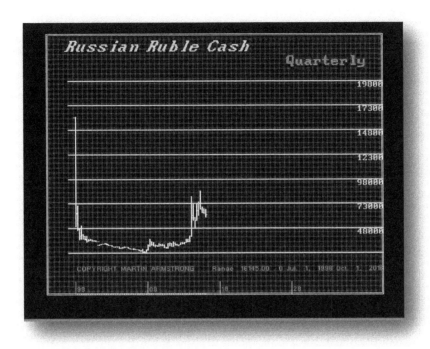

The Ruble Crisis of 1994

On October 11, 1994, the ruble tumbled in the Moscow interbank market by over 20% against the U.S. dollar. Black Tuesday became the first currency crisis in post-communist Russia, which politicians also caused. From July 1992, when the ruble first could be legally exchanged for United States dollars, to October 1995, the rate of exchange between the ruble and the dollar declined from 144 rubles per US$1 to around 5,000 per US$1. The float of the ruble in July 1992 started the shift in global capital flows and currency markets.

Politicians, for pride, artificially set the ruble's value too high against the dollar, reflecting past glories, which was the exact same mistake of the British entering the ERM. Rapid changes in the nominal rate of the Russian economy reflected the overall macroeconomic instability. After the ERM crisis, Forex traders then turned to emerging markets targeting Russia. This was Black Tuesday with a 27% collapse in the ruble's value against the dollar. Eventually, in July 1995, the Russian Central Bank announced its intention to maintain the ruble within a band of 4,300 to 4,900 per US$1 through October 1995. They later extended the period to June 1996. They attempted a "crawling band" exchange rate, which they introduced to allow the ruble to depreciate gradually through the end of 1996. This led to a further collapse from 5,000 to 6,100.

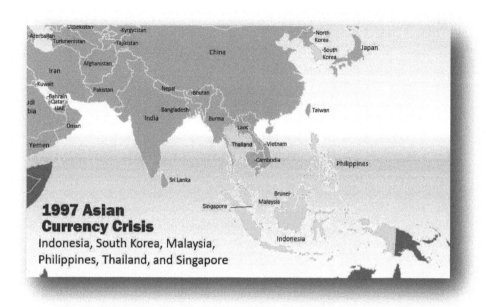

1997 Asian Currency Crisis

After the Russian introduction of the "crawling band," traders turned their attention to the emerging market in Southeast Asia with a more concerted force. This eventually manifested in the 1997 Asian Currency Crisis. The Asian financial crisis struck much of East and Southeast Asia beginning in July 1997. Once again, this involved the attempt to artificially create a peg between the Thai baht and the U.S. dollar. The Asian Currency Crisis raised fears of a worldwide economic meltdown due to a financial contagion. I myself flew to Beijing to meet with the central bank of China.

The crisis began in Thailand when the Forex traders looked around the world to see who had pegs that were questionable. The Thai baht was forced to float the currency due to a lack of foreign currency to support its currency peg to the U.S. dollar. Capital flight ensued, beginning an international chain reaction. Traders immediately looked around at what currency would be next.

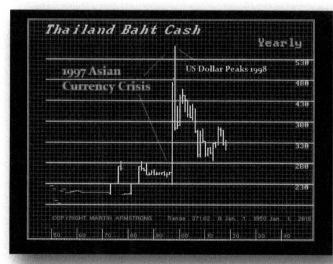

78

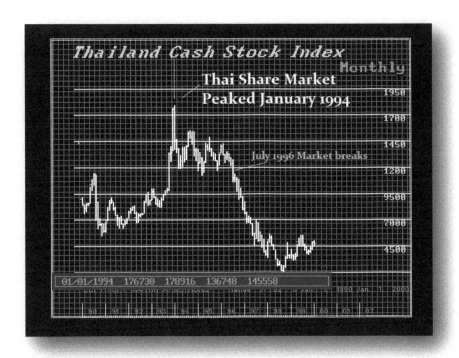

Many blamed the currency traders. Others pointed to the fact that Thailand had acquired a burden of foreign debt that made the country effectively bankrupt before the collapse of its currency. An overlooked fact was that its share market had already peaked in 1994. A capital flight began gradually in 1994 as international capital turned and began looking at the United States and Europe.

The real break came in July 1996. The international capital flows had shifted. There was excitement building in the United States which would become the Dot.com Bubble by 2000. But there was also great optimism to run back to Europe with the introduction of the euro coming in 1998. The shift in capital flows came first to which the currency traders responded in 1997.

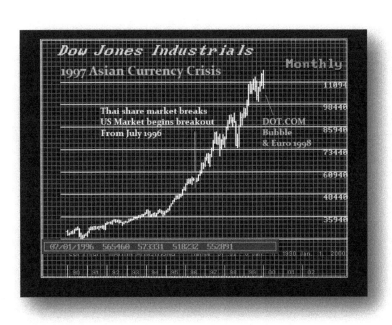

1998 Russian Financial Crisis

By now, there was "the club" where both hedge funds and New York bankers were banning together to make big bets on world markets. The Malaysian Prime Minister Mohamad Mahathir declared in October 1997: "Currency trading is unnecessary, unproductive and totally immoral." He further added, "It should be stopped." Noting that "the Jews are not happy to see the Muslims progress." Mahathir suggested that one of the world's leading currency speculators, George Soros, who is Jewish, was behind a conspiracy to bum rush the Malaysian currency, the ringgit. His comments did not help and instead of fostering any real investigation, attacking the Jews made it too hot of a topic to take seriously.

Nevertheless, after the Asian Currency Crisis, international investors were reluctant to lend to developing countries. The crude oil

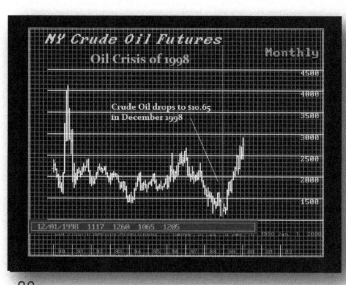

market also collapsed, reducing the price to a low of about $10.65 per barrel in December 1998. The drop in oil continued the financial contagion in emerging markets.

The reduction in oil revenue also contributed to the 1998 Russian Financial Crisis, which, in turn, caused Long-Term Capital Management (LTCM) in the United States to collapse after losing $4.6 billion in four months. The credit lines of the hedge fund now threatened to take down New York banks, which were also involved in the Russian play.

I have stated many times how I was invited to the IMF dinner put on by Edmond Safra in Washington. I was being pitched then to join "the club" and buy into Russia, for I was told they had the IMF in their pocket. The IMF would continue to guarantee Russian debt, so you could buy debt and earn five times the amount of interest. The IMF would eliminate the risk. My response was blunt, "No way, my computer warned Russia would collapse."

I gave a conference for our clients in London in June 1998. Barry Riley of the *London Financial Times* was there, and he reported the forecast on Russia I delivered that warned Russia would collapse by the end of the summer. He published that forecast on the front page of the second section on the 27th of June 1998. Of course, the bankers blamed me for that crisis. But once again, the capital flows were very clear, and Russia lost a fortune on the collapse in oil prices.

Alan Greenspan, former Chairman of the Federal Reserve in the United States, organized a $3.625 billion bailout. The entire crisis period between 1992 up to the 1998 Long-Term Capital Management Crisis was set in motion by politicians who attempted to fix currencies with domestic policies in opposition to international policy objectives.

Swiss Pegged to Euro

The Swiss Peg

The ERM failed in its attempt to fix the value of European currencies even with a trading band. Yet, government constantly attempts to freeze the value of currencies while failing to grasp that they are the hedge against governments. Currencies reflect capital flows both in and out.

On September 6, 2011, the Swiss National Bank (SNB) was aiming for a substantial and sustained weakening of the Swiss franc after Swiss companies threatened to leave because the rising franc reduced their exports. The SNB would no longer tolerate a EUR/CHF exchange rate below the minimum rate of CHF 1.20. The SNB set out to enforce this minimum rate with the utmost determination, and it began to buy euros in unlimited quantities.

Indeed, the peg lasted about 3.14 years (pi) before the pressure really built, and in 3.3 years, it cracked. Who is to blame? The Swiss? Does the blame belong to Brussels and stupid traders/investors who hopelessly believe whatever the government and press report without critical analysis?

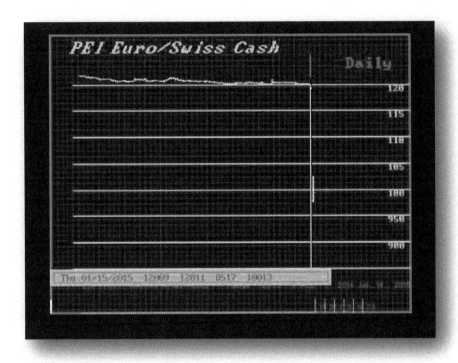

The euro collapsed against the Swiss, falling to 8517. This was a historical decline, and at first glance, one would think this was a bad tick gone way out of bounds. So how do we analyze such a new historical move? You cannot approach this with a view of the whole.

Here we have the euro/Swiss recreated back to 1984 before the G5 began in New York at the Plaza Accord. You always need a map even in markets. How can

you figure out where you are going if (1) you do not know where you have been, and (2) you do not know where you are right now? This pattern shows that we have broken the double bottom that I warned had to give way. That has now been accomplished. So yes, the euro/swiss collapsed to historic lows, and the Swiss ought to run out and buy whatever they can while their currency is strong.

83

The Swiss attempted in vain to stem the capital flows into the franc from the rising concerns about the euro. Indeed, Switzerland should have created a financial franc that could have easily been used to segregate capital inflows without altering the value of the domestic Swiss franc on international markets. What is abundantly clear is that the crisis building at the European Central Bank (ECB) is presenting a global contagion that is threatening the entire world economy. Draghi's policy of negative interest rates and Quantitative Easing have failed. With the ECB completely trapped, holding 40% of Eurozone government debt, the implications of rate hikes will be devastating.

The Swiss abandoned the peg, as was the case of Britain and others during the early ERM crisis. What the Swiss failed to comprehend is that being the target of capital inflows makes it impossible to prevent when capital is fleeing elsewhere without closing the currency markets to open trading.

This is also why pegs have always broken, as in the case of the Swiss peg to the euro in 2015. The Swiss National Bank (SNB) stunned markets when it abandoned its three-year-old peg of 1.20 Swiss francs per euro. In a chaotic few minutes after the central bank's announcement, the Swiss franc soared by around 30% in value against the euro. Any such peg is a guaranteed trade. If you are wrong, the government guarantees your money back at the fixed rate.

Trade Dollars with China

Spanish 8 Reals (Pillar Dollar)

China - Dragon Dollar | Japanese Dragon Trade Dollar

United Kingdom | United States

Trade dollars emerged due to the popularity of the silver Spanish dollar in China and East Asia. The establishment of the Spanish Philippines, led to China regarding these as the standard which led to the minting of the silver Chinese yuan imitating the Spanish coin. These trade dollars would approximate in specification, weight 7 mace and 2 candareens (approx. 27.2 grams) and fineness .900 (90%), the Spanish-Mexican coins so long trusted and valued in China. Britain minted Trade Dollars primarily in Hong Kong and we fine the United States also minted specific Trade Dollars 1873 to 1885

ArmstrongEconomics.COM

Two-Tier Monetary Systems

There have been countless two-tier monetary systems throughout history. There have been times when nations have minted two separate currencies; one for international trade and one domestically for circulation. These were known as trade dollars. China used a silver monetary system rather than gold built upon the acceptance of the Spanish pillar dollars. Japan, Britain, and the United States all minted coins according to the silver standard of China during the 19th century in order to carry out trade.

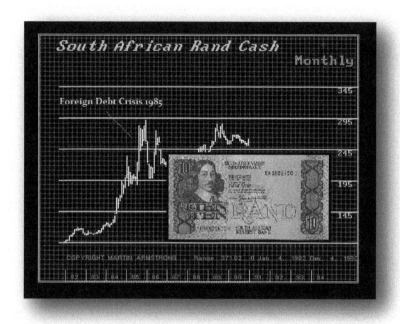

In some instances, a two-tier monetary system is officially established as a currency control. This was the case with the rand and financial rand in South Africa, which was finally abolished in 1995. During 1979, the South African government switched to a system that formally expressed parity against the dollar. The value of the rand followed changes in the balance of payments and moved roughly with sterling and other weaker currencies until 1985 when the dollar soared, and the birth of the Plaza Accord took place.

The foreign debt crisis of 1985 caused the rand to depreciate at a spectacular rate, and the dollar rose in value. The rand fell to an all-time low of fewer than 40 cents to the US$. The rand recovered somewhat in 1987, reaching 43 cents, but it declined steadily thereafter into 1998. The rand collapsed to about 26 cents against the US$ in late 1995. Between February 1, 1996, and May 1, 1996, the rand lost roughly 16% of its exchange value, falling from R3.7 to R4.33 to US$1, or a value of about 23 cents to the US$.

The government realized that its domestic policy objectives were incompatible with international investment. They then created a parallel currency to act as a two-tier currency unit they named the "financial rand." This hybrid currency was used exclusively for the movement of nonresident capital during the 1980s and early 1990s. The financial rand developed out of currency exchange controls instituted in the early 1960s, known as the "blocked rand." The financial rand was available only to foreigners for investment in South Africa and was created by the sale of nonresidents' assets in the country.

Series 1957 Silver Certificate   Series 1963 Federal Reserve Note

Even the fixed exchange rate system established under Bretton Woods was truly a two-tier monetary system in the United States. Gold was recognized as the backing of currency for international trade, and silver was used for the domestic backing of currency. The silver backing was abandoned in 1965, and the gold backing collapsed in 1971.

There are also emergency two-tier currency issues that have been private and exist alongside the official currency of the state, as took place during the American Civil War. Private tokens and postage stamps were encased postage stamps with advertising by various companies who made the coinage due to the shortage of metal during the war.

Civil War Encased Postage Currency

Austrian 20 Heller Privately issued Notgeld Currency Note
ArmstrongEconomics.COM

During this hyperinflation that raged both Germany and Austria, we find a wide variety of private currency issued known as notgeld meaning "emergency money" or "necessity money." These were indeed private issues of money issued by an institution in a time of economic or political crisis. The issuing institution was typically purely private, and their issues were without the central government's official sanction.

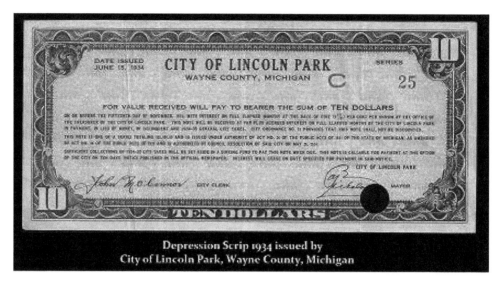

**Depression Scrip 1934 issued by
City of Lincoln Park, Wayne County, Michigan**

Once again, in the United States during the Great Depression, we find hundreds of cities issuing their own private currency because of the shortage of money. The Federal Reserve believed in austerity, as has Germany under the euro, and thus feared that the dollar would decline in value if they increased the money supply. This policy deepened the deflation and forced cities to issue their own currency known as Depression Scrip just to allow the economy to function.

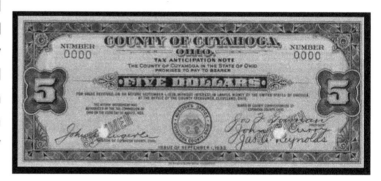

One example of private currency created in the middle of a financial panic due to a shortage of official currency issued by the state occurred during the 19th century when there was a need for "elastic money." The Panic of 1873 saw the government make a small gesture to try to calm the panic. The U.S. Treasury did the same thing with Quantitative Easing post-2007 (it failed then too).

The New York Clearing House was organized officially on October 4th, 1853

The U.S. Treasury injected cash by purchasing government bonds. It did nothing to help the economy. Why? When confidence crashes, people hoard money and will not spend it if they fear the future. The cash they injected was hoarded by the banks just as it has been post-2007. Quantitative Easing in this manner never produces inflation nor does it stimulate the economy. Those in government think they came up with a brilliant idea. No one bothers to look at history or ask, "Has this been tried before and did it work?"

The banks banded together to create their own "elastic money" using the New York Clearinghouse. Failing to increase the money supply means that the value of money in purchasing power rises and all assets decline. This is the hallmark of every recession or depression. During the Panic of 1873, the national banks of New York pooled their cash together and collateral into a common fund, which was placed in the hands of a trust committee at the New York Clearinghouse that was founded on October 4, 1853. The New York Clearinghouse then issued loan certificates that were receivable at the clearinghouse against this collateral. These certificates were absorbed like cash and could be used to pay off debt balances among members. Ten million dollars worth of these certificates were issued at first, but the sum subsequently doubled. This clearinghouse paper served its purpose admirably functioning as elastic money.

By October 3, 1873, confidence returned, and $1,000,000 of these certificates were called in to be canceled. The next day, another $1,500,000 more of these certificates were recalled. In the end, not much of this issue was outstanding very long. The clearinghouse scheme was also successfully applied in Boston, Philadelphia, Pittsburgh, and other large cities besides Chicago.

The tool of creating an elastic money supply was private in nature and was also used during the Panic of 1907 very successfully. This is where we begin to see small denomination notes in circulation that took the form of checks issued against certificates, and in some instances, banks issued bearer checks backed by the certificates.

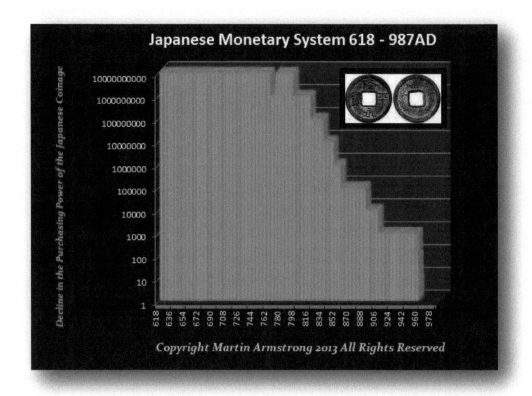

Japanese Monetary System 618 - 987AD

Decline in the Purchasing Power of the Japanese Coinage

Copyright Martin Armstrong 2013 All Rights Reserved

There are also instances throughout history where the people simply refused to accept the local currency and relied upon foreign currency. The progression of Japanese emperors devalued the outstanding money supply upon coming to the throne. The constant issue of a new coin with its value being decreed, as worth 10 times that of the old coinage in circulation, ruined the economy and undermined the state's integrity. This practice created the incentive to rely upon barter and Chinese coins in Japan.

Finally, the people just stopped accepting the emperor's coinage, and Japanese emperors lost the ability to create money as people simply refused to accept it in transactions. The state's assumption of the power to decree the value of coinage (fiat) only produced accumulative inflation during the Nara Period and early Heian Period that remains one of the highest in history. It would have been as if government printed a new one dollar bill and declared arbitrarily that all one dollar bills dated today are worth 10 dollars. This wiped out people's savings, and thus the people stopped hoarding Japanese coins and turned to Chinese coinage and bags of rice.

There are also instances where foreign currencies circulate against local currencies, as U.S. dollars did for years in Russia behind the Iron Curtain and in Asia. I personally went through Checkpoint Charlie in Berlin to see what East Germany was all about with a friend whose family had been trapped there. I was forced to exchange West German marks for East German marks at par. Once in East Berlin, everyone said the price was in West German marks. When I left, I had the same amount of East German marks, but I was forced to exchange them, and then they confiscated them at the border.

Tiberius (14-37AD)

Genuine AU Aureus   India Imitation
(7.82 grams)   (6.69 grams)

Pictured here is an Indian imitation of a Roman gold Aureus of Tiberius (14–37AD). This is not a counterfeit, for it is struck in gold and weighed approximately the same as the genuine coin. Imitations of Roman gold coins are found in India, demonstrating that gold in the form of a Roman coin was more valuable than just gold. There were no coins at this time in India that were official, so the coinage of Rome circulated there as payment in the spice trade.

We even find imitations of the ancient Greek coinage of Philip II (382–336 BC) among the Swiss tribe known as the Helvetii. In this case, the coin is underweight as a Stater but was probably used as a Half-Stater given that such foreign coins in Switzerland were highly prized.

Monetary System of the Republic of Florence

Fiorino d'Oro
1252-1303

Fiorino d'Argento
(Grosso), c. 1260

Two-tier monetary systems have also existed with the distinction between gold and silver, as was the case in the United States during the period of Bretton Woods. In Florence, Italy, the gold Florin, as it was known, was used in international trade. Domestically, wages were paid in silver. Merchants were required to maintain two sets of books; one for gold transactions in international trade, and the other calculated in silver for local expenses. Under Bretton Woods, gold was used by the United States in payment for international transactions, and silver was used domestically, just as was the case in Florence during the 14th century.

In ancient times, we do see large denomination coins both in silver and in gold, which were too high in value for circulation in day-to-day transactions. In Athens, they produced Decadrachms, which were equal to 10 drachms

Athens Decadrachm (c. 465-460 BC) 41.86 grams

of the Attic weight standard (roughly 4.3 grams), and as such tend to weigh between 42 and 43 grams. These are mostly discovered outside of Athens typically in trade ports.

Fixed Rate Summation

Economic theories based on false assumptions have given the field a bad reputation. Others presume government is all-powerful and can manipulate the economy at will. Since they fail to understand how the economy even functions, it would seem logical that any attempted manipulations would only create havoc.

Over the last few decades, economists have influenced every aspect of our lives, creating theories rather than offering proof as in hard science. Economists have dominated the central banks, even coming up with negative interest rates in a failed attempt to force people to spend money. They have argued that the business cycle is not inevitable, yet they cannot point to a single success. Their theories have underpinned all sorts of government policies right down to national debts, which they believe are perfectly fine because we are borrowing from ourselves. Of course, that is such an elitist perspective that ignores the history of debtor's prison. On average, one-third of national debts are held by foreign governments or investors. Throughout the postwar era, economists reigned for one simple reason — they advocated for the use of government power.

There are fundamental questions they have failed to address. What is money? What role does money play? Does the quantity of money in the system directly create inflation and deflation? The answers to these questions have led to the Quantitative Easing policies that have trapped central banks. The failure to create inflation after increasing the quantity of money has spawned the Modern Monetary Theory that purports to be able to create money at will without inflation.

The fate of the world economy lies in the answers to these critical questions. This is not something we can afford to rest solely upon opinion. We are entitled to some hard evidence. History offers a guide to the future. A common thread runs through history — human nature responds to the same problems time and time again.

The only academic to ask my opinion about currency movements was Milton Friedman. Forex traders are generally never asked how markets function. I did testify before Congress at the House Ways & Means Committee on July 18, 1996. They had to put me on a panel with economists. I told them to take me last. The economists all responded that "in theory" the dollar would not change on the Forex markets. I responded with the exact opposite.

The Western World Currency Standards
600BC - 1900 AD

Persian Gold Daric
(8.25 grams)

Athenian "Owl" Tetradracm
(17.18 grams)

Alexander the Great
Tetradrachm (17.0 grams)

Roman Silver Denarius
211BC (4.0 grams)

Byzantine Gold Solidus
(4.45 grams)

Charlemagne (768-814AD)
Silver Denier (1.7 grams)

15th Century Thaler
(28.8 grams)

Spanish 8 Reals (Pillar Dollar)
(26.4 grams)

British AR Crown
(92.5%, 28.29 g)

United States Dollar
(89.24%, 26.96 g)

Why the Euro Failed as a Reserve Currency

September 22nd, 1985 - Plaza Accord

From left: <u>Gerhard Stoltenberg</u> of West Germany, <u>Pierre Bérégovoy</u> of France, <u>James A. Baker III</u> of the United States, <u>Nigel Lawson</u> of Britain and <u>Noboru Takeshita</u> of Japan.

The birth of the euro actually goes back to the Plaza Accord in New York City in 1985 where the G5 (Group of 5; now the G20) was born. The entire idea resulted in a series of attempted economic manipulations. The dollar declined sharply into 1981 after the collapse of the fixed exchange rate system in August 1971. Former Chairman of the Federal Reserve Paul Volcker raised the discount interest rate (wholesale) into May 1981, reaching 14%. That action illustrates why governments are incapable of manipulating the economy. Volcker raised interest rates to reduce inflation by making it more costly for people to borrow, reducing demand.

The entire problem was the simple fact that the governments in all Western nations are the biggest borrowers. If the central banks attempt to curb the people from borrowing, the same applies to them. It is impossible to reduce inflation by raising interest rates, for it has no impact on reducing government spending.

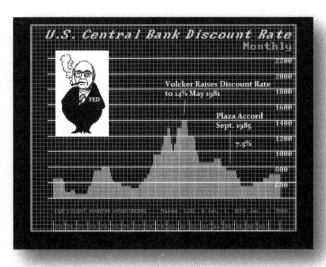

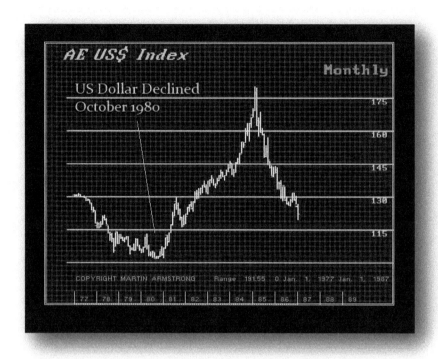

Raising interest rates to reduce inflation sent yields on U.S. government debt to astronomical levels. The U.S. dollar rose dramatically into 1985, forcing even the mighty British pound to collapse to $1.0520 on February 26, 1985. The national debt rose from 30.9% in 1980 to 56.03% by the end of 1990, thanks to an explosion in interest costs.

Since the dollar soared to such record highs, the U.S. argued that the problem stemmed from the fact that there was no alternative to the dollar in size within the world economy. They lobbied Europe to create a single currency in hopes that it would

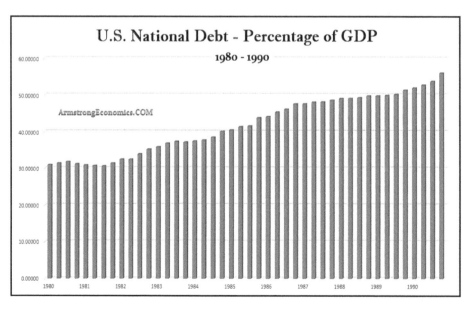

compete against the U.S. dollar. The Plaza Accord then announced that they wanted to see the dollar decline by 40%, and the G5 would manipulate the world economy to achieve that goal.

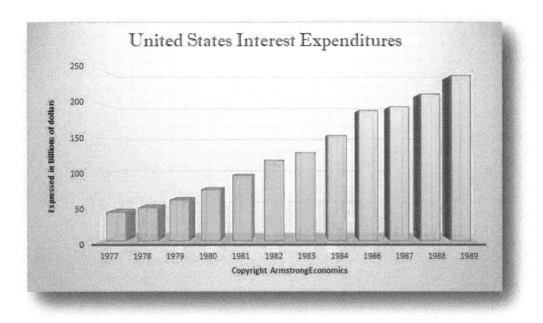

At the time, I met with people at the U.S. Treasury. I was young and naïve and assumed that there must be some mistake. Raising interest rates to fight inflation meant that the U.S. interest expenditures would explode. I showed them the simple calculations out for a decade. They acknowledged my findings but claimed they would pay the debt back with cheaper dollars. The interest expenditures alone exploded by 500% thanks to this insane attempt to curb inflation.

Raising interest rates to reduce consumer demand has no impact on government whatsoever. They will continue to spend regardless of the costs of interest to perpetually roll the national debts. This is true of all Western nations. Clearly, the idea that central banks can manipulate the economy with interest rates, as envisioned by John Maynard Keynes, would be possible only if the government was not borrowing money for its own survival each year.

John Maynard Keynes (1883-1946)

I wrote to the White House about this insane attempt to create a G5 to manipulate the dollar lower for trade purposes. The White House responded, but the mistake of creating a strong dollar was corrected by yet another manipulation that was also doomed to fail.

THE CHAIRMAN OF THE
COUNCIL OF ECONOMIC ADVISERS
WASHINGTON

November 8, 1985

Dear Mr. Armstrong

The President has asked me to respond to your letter of
October 25. It is important that concerned citizens such as
yourself express their views and we appreciate your efforts.
We share your concern about intervention into foreign
exchange markets. Numerous studies have failed to show that
sterilized intervention has a long-run impact on the exchange
rate, and unsterilized intervention affects the exchange rate
while at the same time increasing the risk of renewed
inflation. We agree that foreign exchange rate intervention
is not the appropriate means by which to influence the
exchange rate. We do not share, however, your concern over
exchange rate volatility.

Both the high value of the dollar and the volatility of
its value under the flexible exchange rate period have been
sources of concern for many. The first issue which needs to
be addressed is the reason behind the dollar's appreciation
and the implications for our economic performance. The
simultaneous existence of a current account deficit and a
high foreign exchange value of the dollar are often cited as
evidence that our international economic system is in
disarray. Modern exchange rate theory has demonstrated that
the exchange rate we observe need not be the one which
balances the current account in a world of capital mobility.
The exchange rate is instead influenced by both current and
expected trade and capital flows. Intervention which
attempts to force the exchange rate to a level thought to
achieve a current account balance of zero is therefore
misguided and may not be desirable.

In addition, one must remember that the exchange rate,
at the same time, both reflects and affects economic
variables. The exchange rate, for example, is affected by
the same variables which have led to the rise in the current
account deficit. One important factor driving the present
current account deficit is the difference in economic growth
rates between the U.S. and the rest of the world. This
economic growth which we now enjoy is therefore an important
factor driving the value of the dollar.

The volatility of the exchange rate is also cited as
evidence of disarray in international financial markets. We
do not believe this to be the case. The exchange rate is the
price of an asset which, like all assets, is determined by
the values of future economic variables as well as by their
current values. As is the case with many asset prices, day-
to-day fluctuations which reflect a reaction to news can be
large; however, the apparent volatility does not indicate

-2-

market imperfections or irrationality on the part of market participants. In addition, the empirical evidence does not support the hypothesis that exchange rate volatility is an impediment to trade. On the contrary, international trade has flourished in the floating-rate period, expanding much more rapidly than it did during the fixed-rate period.

The system you proposed to eliminate exchange rate volatility essentially implies a return to a fixed-exchange rate regime. We believe that such a system would suffer from many of the same problems encountered under the Bretton Woods System. Since there is no central international monetary authority, an SDR-based system would require that the monetary authorities of various nations intervene either directly or indirectly to maintain the par value of their currency with respect to other currencies included in the SDR currency basket. This would mean that nations relinquish the ability to use monetary policy to pursue domestic policy objectives, a very unpopular alternative. The proposed SDR-based system also suffers from the reality of portfolio preferences. Countries have failed to exhibit a demand for SDR's and have preferred to either let their currencies float or to fix their currency to a basket of their own choosing. It would be undesirable to force a country to accept a system which fixed their currency to other currencies which they do not desire to hold.

In conclusion, we believe that the attributes of a floating rate system have been misinterpreted as deficiencies. Exchange rate volatility has not been linked to a decline in economic growth and merely reflects a rational response to current or expected changes in economic conditions. The high value of the dollar does not imply an economy in turmoil; rather, the dollar reflects a healthy economy. The policies which are required to reduce our current account deficit and to reduce the uncertainty surrounding exchange rate movements are those which encourage economic growth and monetary stability at home and abroad. Actions which reduce fiscal deficits, ensure noninflationary monetary policies, and yield a worldwide reduction in barriers to trade will promise progress toward such goals.

Sincerely,

Beryl W. Sprinkel

Mr. Martin Armstrong
Chairman
Princeton Economics International
101 Carnegie Center, Suite 314
Princeton, New Jersey 08540

The dollar turned down, as did interest rates. It also collapsed as traders assumed the central banks were powerful, and the Federal Reserve finally realized that raising interest rates attracted capital to the dollar. The Fed lowered interest rates to 5.5%, reaching a temporary low about one year later during August 1986. The G5 became the G7 at the Louvre Accord in Paris in February 1987. Now they told the marketplace that the dollar had declined far enough. The Fed raised interest rates to 6% in September 1987 to stem the decline in the dollar. But the dollar continued to decline into December 1987, and the panic sell-off in the dollar unfolded, culminating in the 1987 Crash once the market players saw that the Louvre Accord failed to support the dollar. Confidence in the G7 crumbled to dust.

The Louvre Accord agreement, signed on February 22, 1987, in Paris, aimed to stabilize international currency markets and halt the continued decline of the U.S. dollar caused by the Plaza Accord. The agreement was signed by France, West Germany, Japan, Canada, the United States, and the United Kingdom. Italy declined to sign the agreement.

The G7 meeting of central bankers and finance ministers in Paris announced that the dollar was now "consistent with economic fundamentals." The announcement stated that they would only intervene when required to ensure foreign exchange stability. The objective was then to manage the floating currency system. Democrats gained control of Congress in 1986 and immediately called for protectionist measures. The dollar depreciation agreed upon in 1985 at the Plaza Accord failed to improve the trade perspective. In 1986, the trade deficit rose to approximately $166 billion, with exports at about $370 billion and imports at about $520 billion. The objective of manipulating currency to create jobs and alter trade flows proved to be completely ineffective.

The dollar's price action clearly proves that the central banks lacked the power to influence the markets. Once the marketplace realized they had no such power, the confidence in their ability collapsed.

Nevertheless, the idea that emerged from the Plaza Accord was for Europe to create a single currency to compete against the dollar. This was believed to solve the problem of trade deficits for the United States and support jobs.

Margaret Thatcher's Burges Speech took place on September 21, 1988. She stood up against the European Project, which went beyond creating a mere single currency as envision at the Plaza Accord. That project proposed the federalization of Europe and the surrender of national identity. *The Guardian* ran the story, "Thatcher Sets Face Against United Europe."

Thatcher's cabinet members, such as Nigel Lawson, had been at the Plaza Accord and were in favor of terminating the British pound for a single currency. Lawson was in favor of returning to a Bretton Woods system of fixed exchange rates and was joined by Geoffrey Howe (1926–2015), who was another cabinet member.

In June 1989, Geoffrey Howe and Nigel Lawson secretly threatened to resign over Thatcher's opposition to British membership in the Exchange Rate Mechanism (ERM) of the European monetary system. Both Howe and Lawson were sold on the ERM and the idea of the euro.

Thatcher's cabinet staged a coup and forced her to resign. Immediately, her cabinet plotted to take Britain into this new currency proposal. Under the new

Prime Minister John Major, Britain moved to place the pound in the temporary fixed exchange rate pre-euro known as the ERM (European Exchange Rate Mechanism). That resulted in Black Wednesday, September 16, 1992, when the British Conservative government of John Major was forced to withdraw the pound sterling from the ERM after it was unable to keep the pound above its agreed fixed lower limit. This was

Margaret Thatcher (October 13th, 1925 – April 8th, 2013)

"A single currency is about the politics of Europe. It is about a federal Europe by the back door." (Nov 22, 1990)

an early warning sign that the idea of creating a single currency in Europe would fail. On November 22, 1990, Margaret Thatcher stood up in Parliament and made it clear that the creation of the euro had become political and not economic.

The Great Disparity Among States When forming the US Dollar

Continental Currency	$40 for $1	April 1780
N.Y. & Conn	$40 for $1	April 1780
South Carolina	$52.50 for $1	May 1780
Mass., N,H. & R.I	$100 for $1	June 1781
New Jersey	$150 for $1	May 1781
Penn. & Delaware	$225 for $1	May 1781
Maryland	$280for $1	June 1781
North Carolina	$800 for $1	Dec 1782
Virginia	$1000 for $1	Jan 1782
Georgia	$1000 for $1	Feb 1785

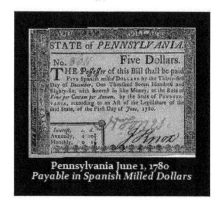

Pennsylvania June 1, 1780
Payable in Spanish Milled Dollars

When the U.S. dollar was formed, Alexander Hamilton (1755/1757—1804) consolidated the debts of all the states, arguing that they all contributed to the creation of the United States. That became the national debt. Thereafter, each state created its own debts, which were denominated in dollars and independent of the federal government. The rate at which each member state's currency would be absorbed was based upon free market values.

The structural crisis behind the euro has been the failure to consolidate all member states' debts from the outset, as Hamilton carried out. The German government wanted a single currency to increase their exports throughout Europe by eliminating currency fluctuations. However, the German government refused to allow any debt consolidation because they saw their fears of hyperinflation pass in front of their eyes.

It is also true that there were those who believed that this was an opportunity to create the United States of Europe to eliminate European war by creating one government. They remained silent about that goal, and the sales pitch was to stress the need for a single currency.

Helmut Kohl
(1930 – 2017)
ArmstrongEconomics.COM

Most people do not realize that creating the euro was never submitted to the German people to decide. Helmut Kohl (1930–2017), Germany's former chancellor, admitted that he acted like a "dictator" to create the euro.

> "I knew that I could never win a referendum in Germany," Kohl said. "We would have lost a referendum on the introduction of the euro. That's quite clear. I would have lost and by seven to three."

The refusal to consolidate the debts of the Eurozone members meant that the central government in Brussels would have supervisory power over member states' spending. That was starkly different from the structure in the United States. However, that also undermined the European banking system, for the banking system's reserves became the bonds of all member states. In the USA, only federal bonds are acceptable as reserves. If Illinois went bankrupt, for example, people would immediately start shorting banks that held Illinois debt. This became a serious structural crisis post–2010 once Greece fell economically.

Then there is the problem with bailing out banks. Chancellor Angela Merkel of Germany stated that there would be no bailout for Deutsche Bank — the biggest bank in Europe. She took that position because if a bank is in trouble in, say Italy, then funds from Germany might have to flow to Italy to save their bank. This very same position of refusing to consolidate debts led to abandoning the guarantees of socialism to protect depositors, which began to restore confidence out of the Great Depression.

The refusal to consolidate debts has resulted in the bail-in policy. When Spain's Banco Santander paid €1 to take over troubled rival Banco Popular, the deal resulted in all shareholder assets being confiscated in Europe's new system to rescue failing banks without burdening taxpayers or stressing markets. This was cheered as innovative. However, because the shareholders lost absolutely everything when the assets were valued at €1.6 billion but sold for €1, it suddenly introduced a whole new risk to buying bank shares. Where investing in any other type of company that goes bust, the shareholder gets something back from the bankruptcy proceeding. Here, an investor in a bank has their investment confiscated. This became a warning sign not to invest in European banks. That means that banks will find it more challenging to raise their capitalization if they cannot sell shares.

EUROZONE

The concept behind the Eurozone has been to pretend that Europe is one happy family. In reality, it is more like a family gathering, perhaps a wedding or funeral, where they do not want to lend money to the black sheep of the family who has always been highly questionable.

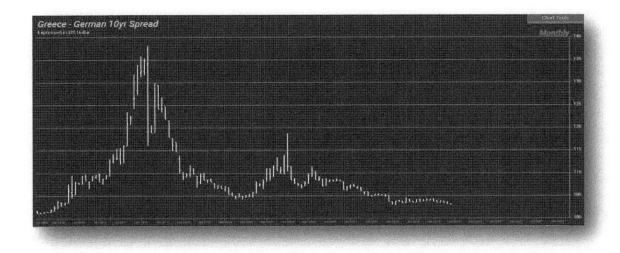

The refusal to consolidate the debts may have on the surface created the euro as a single currency, but it has simply transferred the currency risk and fluctuations from the Forex marketplace to the bond markets. Despite a single currency, the country risk has merely shown up in the differentials between member state interest rates. The promise that a single currency would result in a single interest rate, pointing to the USA, was a complete lie. They compared federal rates and ignored that each of the 50 states may issue debt in U.S. dollars, but they all pay interest rates based on their perceived credit risks.

Institutions must still choose which euro bonds to buy since there are no federal bonds pitting one state against another. This means that the Forex markets' volatility merely shifted to the bond markets, which is precisely what takes place in the United States. Capital invests in the euro still predicated upon the confidence within each member state.

4 BUSINESS 19 April 1998 **The Observer**

Emu crusader conquers Wall Street

Europe's currency soldier has found that most Americans are wary, says ANTHONY BROWNE in New York. But the financiers see a buck to be made

SITTING in the cavernous 11-storey atrium of the International Monetary Fund in Washington, the European Commissioner Yves-Thibault de Silguy was bemused. 'The most striking aspect in Washington is that the single currency is absent from the debate,' he said.

'What surprises me is that the impact of Emu on the international monetary system is not even discussed.'

The message had been the same the evening before in the bar of the city's swanky Four Seasons Hotel. John Lipsky of Chase Manhatten Bank, one of the top US economists, shared a Budweiser with the Commissioner for the Single Currency, and told him: 'There are three great economic developments at the moment — the unexpectedly good performance of the US economy, the conversion of the Asian miracle into the Asian débâcle, and Emu.

'Emu is by far the most important and historic, but it's virtually uncommented on.'

The euro will be the biggest change in the world financial system since the breakdown of the Bretton Woods agreement on fixed exchange rates a quarter of a century ago. It starts in only nine months, yet the world's largest economy could almost be accused of being involved in a conspiracy of silence.

Many Americans don't like the idea, many others are sceptical. Until recently, US pundits thought the euro was pie in the sky and wasted little thought on something that would never happen. Now that it's almost a certainty, attitudes are changing fast.

De Silguy spent last week on a whirlwind, five-day tour of the US to spread the euro gospel to academics, policymakers and financiers.

He flew on Concorde into the lion's den: leafy Boston, home of Harvard University and some of the most virulent anti-Emu criticism.

Opposition is almost universal among academic economists, whatever their politics. Professor Ben Friedman was typical: 'The single currency is a political, not an economic action. The economic benefits do not add up to much.

'It is easy to imagine a country finding it very difficult to live with a monetary policy that is right for the 11 as a whole, but is totally inappropriate for that particular country.'

Like others, he is concerned that the lack of labour mobility in Europe will prevent workers moving to find jobs when one country suffers a downturn.

They point out that US workers are always ready to drive to another state for work, but question whether people in Portugal will really move to Finland for a job. Without mobility, one part of the union could be going bust, while others are booming.

More extreme are the views of Professor Martin Feldstein, a former chairman of the President's Council of Economic Advisers, whose opinions are whispered in hushed tones even by Eurosceptics. He warned that the single currency could lead to war: 'It will change the political character of Europe in ways that could lead to conflicts in Europe and confrontations with the US.'

One European academic based at Harvard, who is in favour of the single currency, reckoned that around 80 per cent of his colleagues were opposed. But, he dismissed their views as a gut reaction: 'They may be intellectual economists, but in the last analysis, they're Americans. They're scared. They're concerned about the dollar losing its position as the world's reserve currency.'

Despite the academic doubts, de Silguy was spared a confrontation. In a room at the Harvard Faculty Club, dripping New England Establishment from the gilt frames of the portraits, he addressed a lunchtime gathering and received a polite reception. He stressed that the single currency was not a leap in the dark, that it was an evolution in Europe, not a revolution.

It seems those most opposed to his project didn't want to talk. 'We invited the sceptics,' said the organiser, 'but they didn't come.'

After lunch, de Silguy went to convert the next generation of America's business leaders, packed into a pine-panelled lecture hall at Harvard Business School. His joke on the earlier unpopularity of Emu had them rolling in the aisles, but all the questions afterwards came from Europeans. The American students, it seemed, weren't interested enough, or didn't feel sufficiently knowledgeable, to ask anything.

Next stop: the self-styled capital of the free world. Washington was buzzing with finance ministers and their retinues, attending the interminable spring meetings of the IMF, the World Bank and the G7. Six months ago de Silguy thought this round of meetings would be dominated by Emu, but it was hardly mentioned. 'They would discuss it if there was a problem, but there are none,' he said.

Policymakers in Washington have been puzzled about the single currency, and hedging their bets on it. Since the Second World War, the Americans have been in favour of greater integration in Europe, and supported anything that promoted it. But they have doubts that the single currency is the best means to achieve this.

Ever-diplomatic, they have said nothing openly critical. A year ago, when they didn't think it would happen, they are reported to have briefed journalists against single currency. Now the official position is 'what is good for Europe is good for America'.

At the IMF meeting the US Treasury Secretary Robert Rubin was probably his most positive yet, but fell short of an outright endorsement of the plan: 'Whether the single currency is good or bad for Europe is something the Europeans are best-equipped to judge, and they clearly have made the judgment that it is good.'

De Silguy said now that the euro was a certainty, policymakers had come round to the idea and were now very positive: 'Everywhere I go, I am congratulated on the achievement and progress that Europe has made. Many didn't think we would be able to do it.' His roadshow, he implied, is more a triumphal march.

But not everyone is convinced that the positiveness is heartfelt. One observer said: 'The officials still have doubts, but they are being diplomatic.' In a meeting behind closed doors, Larry Summers, the US Deputy Treasury Secretary, was also said to be positive. The Americans are now wondering who will represent the single currency on the world stage at meetings such as the G7 and IMF. It's a technical subject but a very touchy one: the Americans feel Europe is over-represented already and want to deal with just one person, not a crowd.

Alan Greenspan, chairman of the Federal Reserve, and the world's most powerful central banker, also congratulated de Silguy. However, he was concerned that the row between France and Germany over who should head the European Central Bank, due to start in July, could harm its credibility.

After seeing the academics in Boston and the policymakers in Washington, de Silguy and his entourage flew to meet the financiers in New York. Perched on the 36th floor of the Swiss Bank Tower, with panoramic views of fog-shrouded skyscrapers, he addressed a conference of bankers and brokers.

Wall Street is possibly more important to the euro than Washington. The world's biggest economic project needs the world's largest financial market on its side. Europe needs Wall Street to be confident enough about the euro to invest there, and it needs the huge American banks to have their systems ready when the euro launches.

In some parts of Wall Street there is still a pervasive scepticism. Mickey Levy, chief economist of NationsBank, did not think it would increase the economic performance and living standards of Europe, at least not directly. 'It doesn't solve Europe's economic problems, but it does make Europe's economic policymakers act more responsibly,' he said.

He did not know whether it would last, and had the common US distaste for anything smacking of big government: 'It's based on historical, socio-political reasons and just creates a super-government that will impose a single regime on a diverse group.'

Other Wall Street economists are far more positive. Lipsky of Chase Manhatten said all informed Wall Street opinion was in favour of the single currency. 'Many people don't understand it. The idea that you should have a single currency controlled by a central bank that doesn't correspond to a government has little historical precedent.

'The critics haven't spent enough time in Europe, and don't appreciate that the single currency is a vehicle for economic and financial reform.'

He is particularly dismissive of the frequently voiced concern that Europe lacks labour mobility: 'Most of the people who say that have European surnames and they, or their ancestors, came over here. People who are supposed not to be able to cross the street came over to America. I don't think that the Europeans have a gene that means they can't move for a job.'

Such enthusiasm is shared by William McDonough, president of the New York Federal Reserve Bank, who has responsibility for supervising Wall Street banks, as well as implementing US exchange rate policy. He cheerfully admits that *of all US* top officials, he is just about the most keen on the euro.

As he sat in his oak-panelled office in the heart of the financial district, he said the financiers were coming round to his way of thinking: 'Wall Street is still somewhat sceptical, but its knowledge is growing. People now realise it is going to happen. The arguments against it are increasingly being seen as unrealistic.'

In Wall Street more than anywhere, it's the bottom line that counts. If there's a buck in it, they'll believe in it. And Wall Street seems to have decided there's money to be made.

When the single currency is launched next year, the academics may furrow their brows, the policymakers may bite their lips, the great American public may shrug their shoulders — but Wall Street will be holding out its hand.

Yves-Thibault de Silguy. Photograph by Yves Herman/Reuters

'What surprises me is the impact of Emu on the international monetary system is not even discussed here in Washington'

Baby euro ready to challenge dollar domination

THE MIGHTY US dollar has been the world's foremost currency since it saw off sterling two generations ago. Now for the first time it is facing a rival that could have just as much muscle.

Although the US accounts for a fifth of world economic output (GDP), half of global trade is done in dollars, two thirds of foreign reserves held by governments are in dollars and a massive 83 per cent of foreign exchange transactions involve the dollar.

But such dominance could be threatened by the euro — which will enjoy similar economic backing. The European Union's economy is similar in size to the US, and accounts for a slightly larger proportion of world trade. And the euro is being given a boost by Europe's current account surplus, in sharp contrast to the US current account deficit.

'The dollar will have its first real competitor since it surpassed the pound as the world's dominant currency in the inter-war period,' said Fred Bergsten, a former US presidential adviser and director of the Institute for International Economics.

He expects that once the new currency is established, central banks and investment funds will want to hold a greater proportion of their assets in it. 'It is likely to produce the biggest shift in portfolio investment in history, with anything from $500 billion to $1 trillion being shifted into it. We should expect the euro to move up alongside the dollar as key currencies.' He sees the change coming in the next 10 years or so.

Professor Richard Portes of London Business School believes countries that do a large part of their trade with Europe will quickly start invoicing their goods in the euro — particularly central and eastern Europe, the Middle East and north Africa.

However, most Americans play down any threat to the dollar. Larry Summers, the US Deputy Treasury Secretary, said last year that 'the dollar will remain the primary reserve currency for the forseeable future ... We expect the impact of the euro on the monetary system to be quite limited initially'.

Barry Eichengreen, Professor of Economics at the University of California and an adviser to the International Monetary Fund, said: 'The euro will not challenge the dollar as a reserve currency in our lifetime. There is tremendous inertia — people use the currency everyone else uses.'

The key question is whether the US will suffer from the dollar sharing its limelight with the euro. The US gains widespread benefits from the dollar's supremacy, although the size of these is a matter of considerable debate.

The US can borrow without limit in its own currency and run huge current account deficits without facing currency crises. With trade and commodities priced in dollars, American companies export much of their foreign exchange risk. Printing the world's currency is worth up to $10bn a year.

Portes claims the demand for dollars allows the US government to borrow at lower cost, saving it up to $10bn a year.

The privileges of the dollar have caused diplomatic tension. Former US Treasury secretary John Connally, accused of letting the dollar devalue, said in the Seventies: 'The dollar is our currency but your problem.' Charles De Gaulle once complained bitterly that the power of the dollar 'enabled the United States to be indebted to foreign countries free of charge'.

Many Americans now insist that such benefits are small, and losing them would make little difference.

The European Commissioner for the Single Currency, Yves-Thibault de Silguy is diplomatic, saying: 'The euro will create the opportunity for a more balanced international monetary system. It would be wrong to see re-balancing as a zero sum game, where Europe gains at the expense of others.'

But that's exactly the conclusion of a report by Portes out this week. The report, published by the Centre for Economic Policy Research, concludes that the potential benefits for the euro area are at the cost of the US. 'Europe would gain by promoting the use of the Euro as a rival international currency to the dollar, but such a policy would go against the interests of both Japan and the US.'

THE most likely result is a bi-polar world, with the euro enjoying a similar position to the dollar. But it's not clear how such a global financial system would behave. De Silguy says it will be more balanced than the current one and therefore more stable.

But Bergsten reckons it will be inherently unstable. He forecasts that the euro will rapidly appreciate by 15 to 20 per cent against the dollar, with a risk of over-shooting. 'Volatility of the world's key currencies will increase substantially, requiring new forms of international cooperation if severe costs for the economy are to be avoided.'

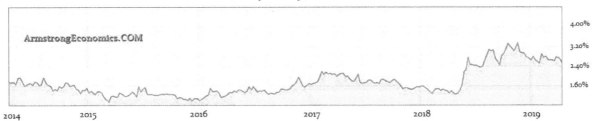

ITALY-GERMANY 10-YEAR BOND SPREAD
(2014 - 2019)

The dream that the euro would provide a single interest rate was never realized. Each state within the USA pays a different interest rate according to its own credit ratings. The very same pattern emerged in Europe despite the political promises that there would be a convergence of interest rates when the euro was created. All the press back in 1998 only spoke of invoicing goods in euros. They claimed that Europe had a current account surplus, so the euro would defeat the dollar and become a major player.

There was never any serious discussion of the details about how the euro was going to be structured. There were some critics who warned that losing the flexibility of the floating currency would introduce tremendous risks to member states that would introduce a gradual decline in competitiveness within Europe. Nations would surrender the ability to devalue their currency to bring costs in line to stimulate the economy. In reality, no one would listen.

When we look at these structural flaws, we can see that without the debt consolidation, each state would retain its central bank and surrender control over their interest rate policy. Between the loss of any currency to offset costs and the loss of interest rate policies for their domestic economy, there was a serious question as to how this pretend structure would truly function.

The failure to consolidate member states' debts would be no different from any country issuing debt denominated in U.S. dollars. Here, they issued their debt in euros but lacked the control to adjust their currency or local interest rates. This was economically no different than Hong Kong pegging their currency to the U.S. dollar. They import U.S. inflation or deflation with no control over interest rates or the value of the dollar that is set in motion by confidence within the United States. Here, all nations would suffer the pains of the euro that were beyond their local domestic control.

The Quantity Theory of Money & Its Failure

Milton Friedman
(1912–2006)

John Maynard Keynes
(1883-1946)

Perhaps there is no other theory in economics that has caused more turmoil than the Quantity Theory of Money (QTM). Both Milton Friedman and John Maynard Keynes developed their ideas based upon the interpretation of the German hyperinflation as the result of an increase in the supply of money. Nevertheless, their theories were predicated upon a strikingly different system from today, for it was the era of gold standards and fixed exchange rates that ended in 1971.

Keynes suggested that the government could stimulate economic demand by lowering taxes and increasing spending even into deficits. The governments love to keep deficit spending going without end, but the fight to lower taxes seems to be a dragged-out bloody fight. Keynes never advocated perpetual deficit spending indefinitely. Few presidents have ever lowered taxes. Some who did were John F. Kennedy, Ronald Reagan, and Donald Trump.

Milton Friedman argued that the Fed was following austerity. The Fed refused to monetize the gold, which reached twice the required backing, and raised rates to support the dollar during 1931. Milton Friedman and Anna Jacobson Schwartz wrote:

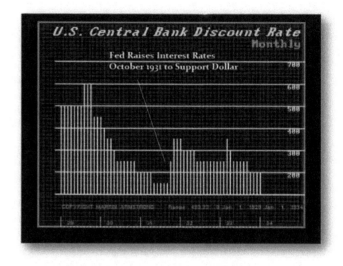

> "The Federal Reserve System reacted vigorously and promptly to the external drain...On October 9 [1931], the Reserve Bank of New York raised its rediscount rate to 2-1/2 per cent, and on October 16, to 3-1/2 per cent–the sharpest rise within so brief a period in the whole history of the System, before or since."

Milton and Anna's premise was that the Fed was doing what Germany is doing today — austerity. They were trying to support the currency to retain confidence in the bond market rather than stimulating the economy. The gold flows to the USA were excessive, and the gold backing of the dollar reached double the requirement. The Fed saw this as refugee gold and declined to increase the money supply. Instead, they believed that austerity was the best policy to maintain confidence in government debt. As mentioned, the Bank of France engaged in the very same policy.

In theory, Milton makes sense in stating that one should expect higher inflation if the money supply expands instead of contracts. Nevertheless, there are a lot of assumptions in that statement that simply do not hold up with time.

Money is only a medium of exchange. It is not a store of wealth. There is no perfect store of wealth because the business cycle exists, and at times assets rise in value. This means that the purchasing power of money declines (inflation), and when asset values decline, as in a recession or depression, the purchasing power of

the currency rises (deflation). The terms in and of themselves are designed to shift the blame away from government in the first place. When assets rise, the blame is often placed on private sector greed. When assets decline, they call it deflation in the value of assets when, in fact, it is the rise in the purchasing power of money.

Therefore, while interesting, this argument that the Great Depression was caused in part by the Federal Reserve and Bank of France refusing to expand the money supply in fear of creating inflation is one slice of the pie. There is a lot more going on here. This theory has been behind the entire philosophy of Quantitative Easing (QE). Expanding the money supply was supposed to create inflation, yet it too has failed to do so post-2007.

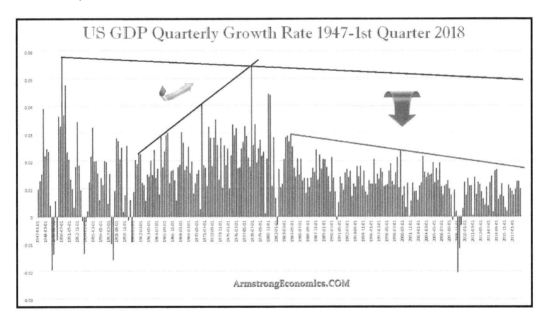

Indeed, taking the Quantity Theory of Money (QTM) as the foundation for economics has been disproven. We can see this by looking at 10 years of QE by the European Central Bank, which has failed to create inflation or stimulate the economy. Additionally, the money supply has expanded dramatically since the

1970s, yet economic growth has been steadily contracting. Each high is lower than the previous since the 1950s.

These economic theories have completely failed to grasp the economy's full scope and how it functions, leaving us with a strange paradox. If we cannot restore economic growth and stimulate the economy with QE, then where does this leave us? Sure, the Fed may try the 1941–1951 peg, but that cannot prevent the crisis.

Now Modern Monetary Theory (MMT) is rising, which assumes we can just expand the money supply indefinitely without causing inflation because QE proves there will be no inflation even after 10 years. They are ignoring the clash between fiscal policy carried out by government enforcing taxes (deflationary) and monetary policy in the hands of the central banks, who are expanding the money supply (inflationary).

Interest Rates & their Failure as a Monetary Tool

John Maynard Keynes criticized the QTM in *The General Theory of Employment, Interest and Money.* Keynes had originally been a proponent of the QTM, but he presented an alternative in the *General Theory.* Keynes argued that the price level was not strictly determined by the money supply. Changes in the money supply could have effects on real variables like output.

It was Keynes who viewed the Great Depression as a contraction in demand. His solution was to manipulate interest rates to "stimulate" demand. Again, this has proven false since the European Central Bank (ECB) even took interest rates negative. People simply bought safes and moved their money out of banks. They will not spend until they believe in the future. You cannot "stimulate" demand even at 0.1% interest rates if the people do not believe they will make 0.2%.

Supply-side economic theory aims to increase the supply of goods and services available to consumers by keeping corporate taxes down. The theory alleges that this will create jobs and entice businesses to spend on research and development, thereby creating new innovations. Apple's i-series products are an example of creating demand by producing an innovative supply of new goods and services. Some argue that this presents a greater danger because tax cuts will reduce government revenue by creating higher deficits that will weigh heavily on the future economy. But this is only enhancing because government continually borrows with no intention of paying off the debt they create.

Conversely, demand-side economic theory is all about increasing consumer demand. This has been referred to as Keynesian economics. The idea here is that the quickest way to spur demand is to increase the relative wealth of the people who want to make purchases. This theory is mostly espoused by liberal Democrats who want to redistribute wealth by taking extra income taxes from corporations and the rich to redistribute it to the middle class and poor. This mainly becomes socialism under the name of demand-side economics.

The economic view regarding demand-side economic theory maintains that the economy can increase in two primary ways. First, it will create jobs and raise minimum wages. Tax rebates and cuts are another way to increase discretionary funds to drive consumer spending. Of course, government hates cutting taxes. They do regard the danger of producing inflation through too much consumer demand.

What Keynes ignored was the mere fact that there can be a shortage at times, let's say of wheat due to weather, which will result in prices rising irrespective of a change in the supply of money. The 1970s produced stagflation because the costs were forcibly raised by the OPEC oil embargo whereby prices rose, but there was no economic growth. Keynes never quite took this potential into consideration, which we can call cost-push inflation rather than pure demand.

In 1978, former Chairman of the Federal Reserve Paul Volcker made it clear that Keynesianism failed in light of stagflation and the economic recession of 1974-1976. His lecture was republished in a publication, *the Charles C. Moskowitz Memorial Lectures.* Volcker said:

> "The Rediscovery of the Business Cycle – is a sign of the times. Not much more than a decade ago, in what now seems a more innocent age, the 'New Economics' had become orthodoxy. Its basic tenet, repeated in similar words in speech after speech, in article after article, was described by one of its leaders as 'the conviction that business cycles were not inevitable, that government policy could and should keep the economy close to a path of steady real growth at a constant target rate of unemployment.

> Of course, some minor fluctuations in economic activity were not ruled out. But the impression was conveyed that they were more the consequence of misguided political judgments, of practical men beguiled by the mythology of the old orthodoxy of balanced budgets, and of occasional errors in forecasting than of deficiency in our basic knowledge of how the economy worked, or in the adequacy of the tools of policy. The avant-garde of the profession began to look elsewhere – to problems of welfare economics and income distribution – for new challenges.

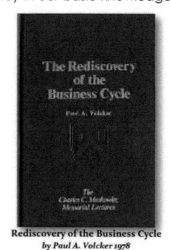

Rediscovery of the Business Cycle
by Paul A. Volcker 1978

> Of course, the handling of the economic consequences of the Vietnam War was an obvious blot on the record – but that, after all, reflected more political than economic judgments. By the early 1970s, the persistence of inflationary pressures, even in the face of mild recession, began to flash some danger signals; the responses of the economy to the twisting of the dials of monetary and fiscal policy no longer seemed quite so predictable. But it was not until the events of 1974 and 1975, when a recession sprung on an unsuspecting world with an intensity unmatched in the post-World War II period, that the lessons of the 'New Economics' were seriously challenged."

The mere fact that prices could rise in the middle of a recession (cost–push inflation) was something outside of economic theories. It has still not been incorporated into any of the tools employed by central banks in their attempt to manage the economy using demand-side economics.

Obviously, the price of something can also rise simply because of popular demand, as is the case when some new toy becomes the craze for Christmas. Neither of these types of demand/cost–driven price rises will ever be impacted by manipulating interest rates.

Ludwig von Mises
(1881 – 1973)

Ludwig von Mises agreed that there was a core of truth in the Quantity Theory of Money (QTM), but he criticized its focus on the supply of money without adequately explaining the demand for money. He said the theory "fails to explain the mechanism of variations in the value of money." Of course, von Mises lived through the hyperinflations in Germany and Austria. He became too focused on the QTM, yet he understood there was something else lurking behind QTM by itself.

Time Magazine - March 1982

Mises maintained that all economic phenomena must be traced back to individual decision-making. Otherwise, the analysis would lead to wrong conclusions. Von Mises believed that decisions had to be traced back to the individual rather than the community view. Yet, he still fell into the same trap as so many do by attempting to reduce the effect to one cause.

The Austrian theory of money is constructed on the ideas of Ludwig von Mises's work, *Theory of Money and Credit*, published in 1912. Mises took the marginal utility theory, which examines the increase in satisfaction consumers gain from consuming an extra unit of a good or service. The marginal utility theory is the idea that people get a certain level of satisfaction/happiness/utility from consuming goods and services. This has been the academic explanation of consumer demand, which sets the basis for the market price. Mises took the position that no longer did the theory of money need to be separated from the general economic theory of individual action and utility, supply, demand, and price. Consequently, he concluded that monetary theory should not be confined in isolation in a context of "velocities of circulation," "price levels," and "equations of exchange."

Defining Money

Von Mises did not develop a proper definition of what constitutes the money supply. In current mainstream economics, there are at least four competing definitions, ranging from M1 to M4. However, the broad definition of the money supply has excluded assets that are not redeemable on demand at par in legal tender money. Therefore, anything that has a time liability, such as savings certificates, certificates of deposit (CDs), whether negotiable or nonnegotiable, and government bonds are normally excluded. Only debt instruments redeemable at par are money substitutes under this definition. Therefore, the very definition of what constitutes the total supply of money to this day seriously impacts everything that surrounds the core economy.

Commercial bank reserves are excluded from the outstanding supply of money definition on the theory that they are not available for use in the economy. This leads to the argument that those types of demand deposits that function as reserves for the deposits of these other financial institutions must be excluded as well.

These definitions only confuse the entire analysis. If you wish to trade futures, you can put your money in the account and direct that it be kept in T–Bills — paper dated 90 days or less. There is a time element. However, it is acceptable collateral for instant trading because it is liquid and can be sold at any moment. When it was illegal to borrow against government bonds, such as savings bonds during the

1960s, then there was a critical distinction between debt and money. Zero–coupon debt is not acceptable for collateral.

ACCEPTABLE COLLATERAL FOR 31 CFR PART 225
(Acceptance of Bonds Secured by Government Obligations
in Lieu of Bonds with Sureties)
Effective: March 26, 2018

Acceptable collateral is currently limited to only public debt obligations of the United States Government whose principal and interest are unconditionally guaranteed by the United States Government (excluding stripped components).

The following classes of transferable securities are acceptable as collateral to secure obligations in lieu of a surety bond or to secure deposits of bankrupt estates under the jurisdiction of the U.S. Executive Office of Trustees or a bankruptcy court or judge. Zero-coupon obligations included in these classes, such as stripped principal and interest components, are currently not acceptable.

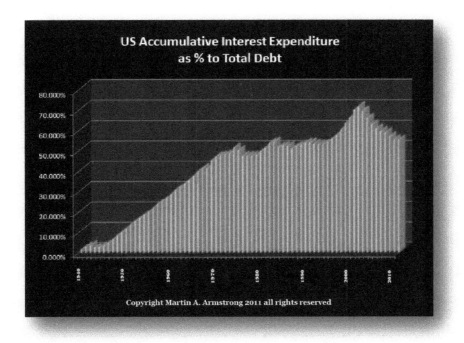

The evolution of the definition of what constitutes money is also what plagues our current situation and future. Because debt was not considered part of the money supply, it was believed that if governments borrowed rather than created money, this would not be inflationary since the supply did not increase.

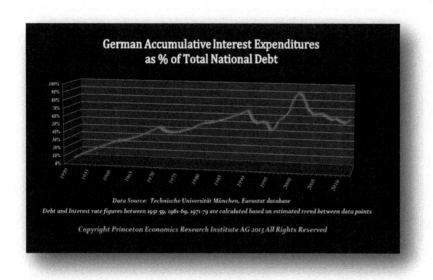

German Accumulative Interest Expenditures as % of Total National Debt

Data Source: Technische Universität München, Eurostat database
Debt and Interest rate figures between 1951-59, 1961-69, 1971-79 are calculated based on estimated trend between data points

Copyright Princeton Economics Research Institute AG 2013 All Rights Reserved

When we look at the national debts of all major Western powers, we are confronted with a shocking realization. This distinction that debt is not money is propelling us into a complete economic meltdown. At times, up to 70% of the entire national debt is composed of accumulated interest expenditure. Since the government never pays down its debt, but constantly issues new debt to retire the old debt, the level of interest it takes to keep the Ponzi scheme rolling crowds out all other spending. In the USA, interest expenditures are destined to exceed military expenditures.

Banks and the Creation of Money

Then there is the external factor that creates money outside the ability of government to control. The majority of money is created as book-entries by banks. I deposit $100 in my account, and the bank lends you $100. We now both have bank statements that clearly show we both have $100 in cash. In this manner, lending creates money. Obviously, the money supply can be increased domestically simply through lending.

On June 10, 2018, Switzerland's electorate voted on a referendum calling for the country's commercial banks to be banned from creating money. The referendum proposed that commercial banks in Switzerland should no longer be allowed to create money out of thin air by lending, and that in the future only the Swiss central bank should have the power to create money. The very idea of

introducing a "*vollgeld*" or "real money" system convinced voters to reject the proposals. The outcome would have created an economic disaster. Switzerland would have committed suicide and entered a complete Dark Age unto itself. What about mortgages? The housing market would collapse under such an idea of preventing bank lending.

Capital Flows & the Creation of Money

Money is also created by simple capital flows. If I owned a skyscraper in New York and sold it to another American, the transaction is neutral domestically with respect to the money supply. Even if both of us have mortgages, obviously, there would be no real increase in the money supply except perhaps my profit. If I owned the building outright, then obtaining a mortgage would increase the money supply, for I would then be monetizing that asset.

However, let us now introduce a foreign buyer. I sell the building to a Chinese investor. They bring cash into the USA (yuan) and convert it to dollars to purchase the building. Now the domestic money supply has increased, for I have the cash to spend domestically, and they have the non-liquid asset that is not part of the actual money supply.

The same is true when a foreign government buys U.S. government debt. The payment increases the domestic money supply. If a foreign investor buys Dow Jones Industrial shares, they bring in their currency, such as the euro, and convert it at banks to book-entry dollars. There is no creation of dollars formally by the U.S. Treasury. Therefore, countries such as Japan had capital controls. You cannot issue a bond in Japanese yen without the permission of the Japanese government. That is not the case under the U.S. dollar.

External Creation of Money

There is also the creation of money that is entirely external to the domestic economy. Foreign governments can issue debt in another nation's currency to eliminate currency risk when a currency is free without controls. This is the case with the U.S. dollar. Even two private parties in a foreign country can create a private loan in terms of dollars without asking the United States for permission. As a result, lending externally to the United States can also blindly increase the world economy's supply of dollars.

Emerging markets have introduced another problem. To sell their debt to American institutions seeking higher yields, they issued their debt denominated in U.S. dollars. The sovereign forex-denominated debt burdens vary relative to GDP.

The Treasury and Finance Ministry of Turkey announced that the country's net external debt stock totaled $286.2 billion going into the end of the third quarter of 2018. The country's net external debt stock to its gross domestic product (GDP) ratio was 34.4% at the end of the third quarter of 2018. However, Turkey's gross external debt stock amounted to $448.4 billion at the end of the 3rd quarter, bringing the debt/GDP ratio to 53.8%, according to the official figures.

Interestingly, because of the fear of the Turkish lira, Turkish corporations have been often compelled to borrow in dollars. Therefore, the private sector's share in the country's gross external debt stock was 68.2% ($305.9 billion), while some $215.9 billion of this amount consisted of long-term debts with a maturity of more than one year. The Turkish public sector's share of this debt was 30.6% in the country's total foreign debt, which is about $21.4 billion short-term (under one year) with $115.7 billion in the long-term (over one year). The banking sector's (lenders and the central bank) external debt stock was $176.99 billion at the end of the third quarter.

When we break this down further, 58.5% of the total gross external debt is denominated in U.S. dollars, and only 32.3% was denominated in euros. The amount denominated in Turkish lira among the external debt stock was a trifling 5.9%. This illustrates the crisis that will emerge with a change in the currency values.

The problem with issuing debt in a foreign currency is that there is never any professional risk analysis or management. The dollar debt rises exponentially in the cost to service that debt as the currency declines irrespective of interest rates. That very relationship sent Germany into hyperinflation during the 1920s. If you look closely, Turkey's external debt has grown 10% just in the past year alone as its currency has declined and interest rates have risen.

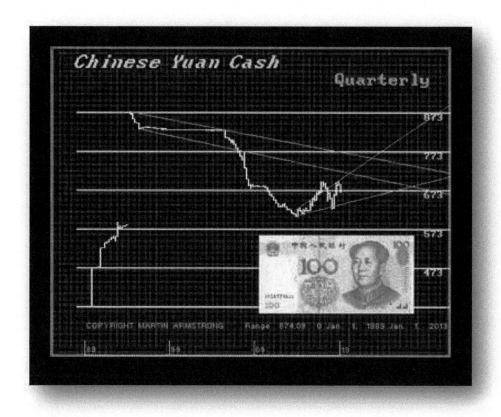

Then we have rising interest rates that add to the crisis, further undermining the economy. The interest must be paid in terms of the foreign currency. Also, keep in mind that they have also issued external debt in euros.

The third dimension of the Emerging Market Crisis is private debt. Many private companies have also borrowed in dollars. This is true in Turkey, but also for China, which includes local municipalities and provinces.

China has previously underestimated its US$3 trillion-dollar debt and how this poses a major threat to creating a Chinese financial crisis. Property developers, other mainland companies, and investors have borrowed dollar-denominated debt at low U.S. interest rates, mainly through Hong Kong. Once again, the risk of a rising dollar overwhelms any interest rate risk.

In many cases, this debt crisis differs significantly in a very critical manner looking at Turkey on one side and China on the other — private debt is overlooked. Focusing only on government debt, we cannot ignore the private sector and municipality level of debt that does not impact the sovereign nation. Much of corporation's private debt has also borrowed in dollars and euros, exposing them to FX risk.

Summation

Clearly, defining precisely what money is within the system has never been a simple question.

Money can be created in five distinct ways:

(1) the direct creation of money printed by the government

(2) government debt that is acceptable collateral for loans, making it currency that pays interest

(3) banks creating money through lending

(4) capital flows and the creation of money when fixed, immovable assets like real estate domestically are sold to foreigners

(5) the external creation of money when other nations issue their debt in terms of a foreign currency

All these aspects combine to alter the money supply dynamically, which is far beyond the control of purely a central bank. The fiscal side of the equation being debt is a major factor in creating money that is traditionally just ignored.

The Velocity of Money

When we simply introduce the velocity of money to test the Quantity Theory of Money, we reveal another problem. The velocity of money is defined as how many times the outstanding supply of money changes hands. Suddenly, we see that you can increase the supply of money, yet the velocity declines, meaning people are not spending the money supply increase.

This interaction between the velocity of money and the Quantity Theory of Money has produced the reality that after 10 years of Quantitative Easing in Europe by the European Central Bank (ECB), inflation failed to materialize. In the United States, the velocity of money peaked during the third quarter of 1997. The debt to GDP ratio stood at 62.48:1 back in 1997 and rose to 105.23:1 at the end of August 2018. One would expect the velocity to rise with the quantity of money, but that did not unfold.

Consequently, after the Fed created $4 trillion of Quantitative Easing and Obama ran trillion-dollar deficits every year, the velocity of money declined, yet the debt rose dramatically. This led to so many analysts screaming that gold would take off, and we were heading into hyperinflation. Again, nothing happened. Why?

There have been arguments that the QTM fails to work because the velocity of money is not stable, and in the short-run, prices are sticky. What they mean by that is that prices and wages do not tend to decline in proportion to the changes in the money supply. The argument remains that there is no direct or constant relationship between money supply and price levels. Wages are indeed far "stickier" than prices, meaning people are less likely to accept a cut in wages during a recession, and thus companies simply lay off workers instead. Stores will offer sales to reduce inventory, but employees do not easily accept a decline in wages during a recession. Alternative theories include the real bills doctrine and the more recent fiscal theory of the price level.

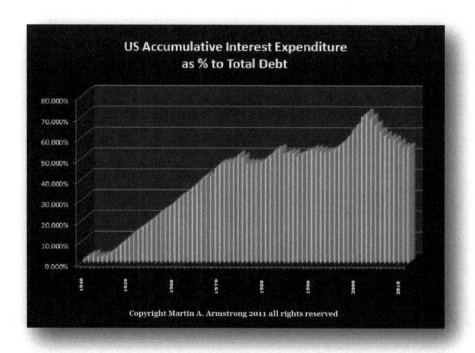

It is by no means a one-dimensional economy. The economy is global; we are all connected. The overlooked aspect here is that the size of government has drastically changed from the time Keynes lived and Milton published his book. The size of government has grown to consume nearly 40% of GDP on average. It is no longer the incidental observer. Government can no longer raise and lower interest rates to control demand when the government is the lion's share of that demand and competes against the private sector. Volcker raised interest rates into 1981 to fight inflation and succeeded in costing the government vast amounts of interest thereafter. Raising rates to curb demand may stop the private sector, but it has no influence upon government. You cannot stop a Ponzi Scheme once it begins.

In Europe, increasing the money supply has had zero inflationary impact and has not stimulated the economy in the least. There is no one-to-one relationship. It is far more complex, and it becomes a balancing act. They have been sterilizing any impact of increasing the money supply by raising taxes. The monetary increase is only coming from buying government bonds. It is not supporting the private sector. Instead, it has subsidized the government sector.

The Three Faces of Inflation

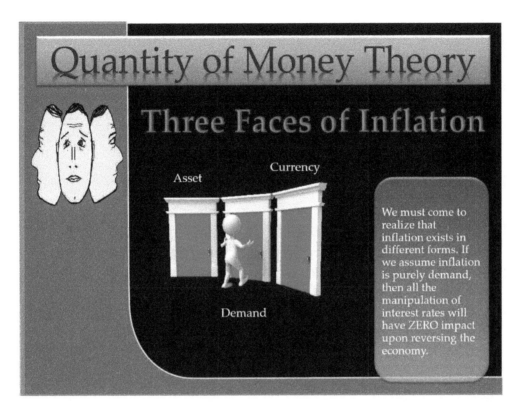

There are three major categories of inflation that unfold. First, there can be asset inflation that is not a general inflation experienced throughout the entire economy. Asset inflation can unfold from two main sources such as cost-push inflation where there is a shortage in a particular asset, such as the oil embargo of the 1970s or a weather event that creates a shortage in something like wheat or corn. Asset inflation can also be caused by a shift in sentiment where people no longer trust government and seek to move their assets out of government assets, such as bonds, and shift to any type of tangible asset that is short of hyperinflation. We can also see asset inflation by observing the Dow Jones Industrial Index, which rose from 1,000 in 1985 to 26,000 by 2019, far in advance of prices or wages in basic living items.

Secondly, there is currency inflation. The decline in a currency will result in a corresponding rise in the prices of imported goods. This is what we saw with OPEC during the 1970s, and the rise in the dollar from 1980 into the 1985 all-time high that correspondingly produced deflation. The extreme of currency inflation is hyperinflation scenarios where people effectively abandon the local currency and begin to rely upon foreign currencies and commodities. As I have mentioned with buying a Ferrari in London in 1985 when the pound fell to par, the car in dollars lost about $30,000. The Italians could not sell the cars for that amount, so they raised the price to about £50,000, and the pound rallied to nearly $2. Suddenly, the car was now $100,000. People misread the appreciation, thinking the car was a great investment rather than merely a currency play.

Finally, there is the standard demand inflation which is what economists focus on. Since under Bretton Woods the world functioned on a fixed exchange rate, they never considered currency inflation as part of an economic model. This took place recently in Europe as butter prices soared 300% because of shortages.

Only demand inflation was dealt with by Keynes, and it was assumed that by utilizing interest rates, one could impact demand. Friedman believed that increasing the money supply would then relieve the deflation and stimulate the economy. Today, central banks employ both theories in setting their monetary policies without success.

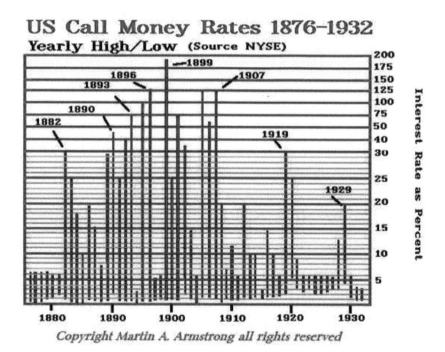

US Call Money Rates 1876–1932
Yearly High/Low (Source NYSE)

A close analysis of interest rates reveals that the economy has never peaked or bottomed with the same level of interest rates twice. The missing element in these theories is expectation. People will pay 20% rates of interest if they believe they will double their money in the same period of time. However, they will not pay 1% if they do not believe that they will make even 2%.

Any close study of market behavior exposes the truth behind the fiction. The old saying among traders is to buy the rumor and sell the news. People will act on the anticipation of something regardless of whether it ever materializes. It is like a herd of wild animals, such as the example used earlier of a herd of zebras. One may think he sees a lion in the bush and begin to run. The rest of the herd saw nothing, but there must be a reason if one is running. This is the essence of a financial panic. People sell, not because they believe something will occur, but because everyone else is selling. Far too often, there has been a rumor that moves the market, and it is later found to be untrue.

The human emotional aspect of the economy turns on anticipation and belief. As they always do, a central bank can lower interest rates, and it will never support the market. Unless people believe there is an opportunity, they will never borrow if they do not see the potential to make a profit.

Consequently, there is no one-to-one relationship between raising interest rates and stopping inflation or asset inflation or conversely lowering interest rates to support a market in a freefall. The stock market has never peaked with the same level of interest rates twice in history. We have watched the European Central Bank lower interest rates to negative to punish people for not spending without success. It boils down to the simple realization that people respond to the anticipation of further expectations, not to theory.

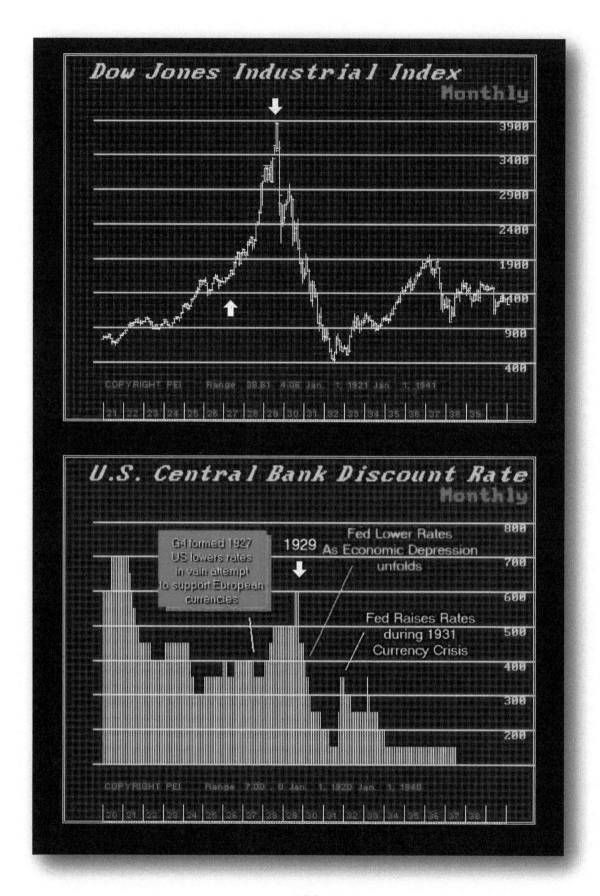

The bull market in 1929 witnessed the Federal Reserve attempt to discourage demand by raising interest rates from 3.5% to 6% without success. Yet, the rally into 1919 saw interest rates peak at 7%. Likewise, the Fed dropped interest rates rapidly from 6% to 1.5% with no success in preventing the Great Depression.

Attempts to employ monetary theory to artificially control demand has had zero success. Nevertheless, central banks still use these tools, knowing they fail to work only because they are expected to do something.

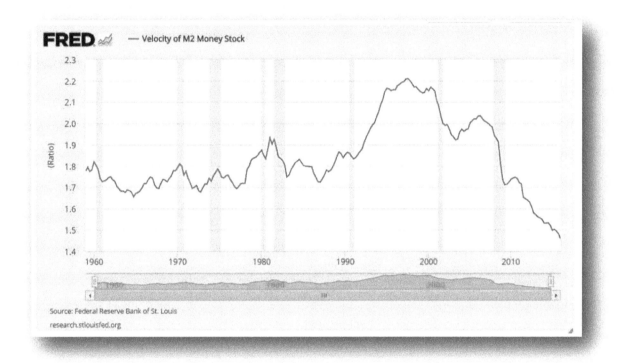

It comes down to a complex formula driven by confidence. People are hoarding cash even though the quantity has increased in theory, so the velocity of money has declined. The higher the tax rate, the lower the economic growth as people hoard money (save), which produces the decline in the velocity of money.

Lowering interest rates does nothing to stimulate the economy when the banks do not lend anyway and would prefer to park money at the Fed in excess reserves, which are sterilizing and behind the idea of Quantitative Easing. If the QTM theory worked, then the central banks' stimulation through QE should have worked. It failed. There is a lot more to this than a simple one-to-one relationship.

Even in ancient times, QTM did not hold up. There was no central bank in the Roman Empire, and there was no public debt. The state funded itself by simply creating new coinage to cover expenses. Inflation was minimal during the empire and even during the Republican period before 27 BC except in times of war.

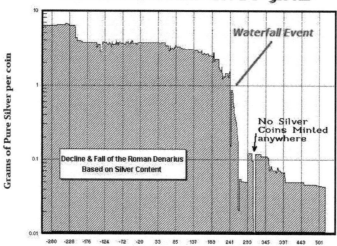

Collapse of the Roman Silver Monetary System
Silver Denarius Basis - 280 BC - 518 AD

The narrow neo-classical economic theory maintains that hyperinflation is rooted in the increase in the money supply. This does not hold up historically. The entire monetary crisis in the Roman Empire took place between 260 AD and 268 AD when the silver content of the coinage collapsed to virtually zero. This took place only when the Roman Emperor Valerian I (253-260 AD) was captured by the Persians and turned into a royal slave.

That single event shocked the Romans, and they suddenly saw their empire as vulnerable. Other barbarian tribes began to invade. People contracted and began hoarding money.

A bas relief at Naghsh-e Rostam, Shiraz, Iran with Shapur I on horseback showing Roman Emperor Valerian held captive chained to the wall who he eventually had stuffed as a trophy

Historically, the human response to an uncertain future is always the same — contract spending and save for a rainy day. When people have no concerns about the future, they spend and the velocity of money increases. When they are faced with a debased currency, then they hoard the old and spend the new. Hence, Gresham's Law observed the debasement of the English coinage under Henry VIII (1509–1547).

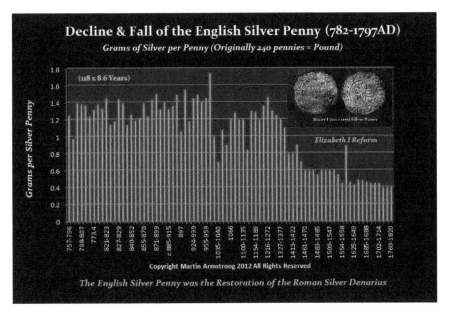

Gresham was an advisor to Henry's daughter, Elizabeth I. He represented England in the financial markets, which were in Amsterdam at that point in time. As coinage was debased, people hoarded the older, higher quality coins, and thus his maxim — bad money drives out good money. As debasement unfolds, the money supply shrinks and this, in turn, compels the state to produce even more money to keep the economy afloat and meet expenses. This has led to the erroneous assumption that hyperinflation is caused by an increase in the money supply, rather than in response to hoarding money.

Conversely, if the money supply contracts, you must understand that assets must decline, for they are merely expressed in the current purchasing power of money. An example of this was the Great Depression and how both the Federal Reserve and the Bank of France refused to increase the money supply, hoarding gold themselves.

In 1920, Britain legislated a return to the gold standard at the prewar parity to take effect at the end of a five-year period. That took place in 1925. Britain based its decision in part on the assumption that gold flowing to the United States would raise price levels in Britain and limit the domestic deflation needed to reestablish the prewar parity. This was their goal — a strong British pound.

Indeed, the United States sterilized gold inflows as did the Bank of France, to prevent a rise in domestic prices. In the 1920s, the Federal Reserve held almost twice the amount of gold required to back its note issue. Britain then had to deflate to return to gold at the prewar parity when the pound was $4.86.

When Britain was forced back off the gold standard, the deflation immediately ended. It then became clear that the way out of the Great Depression required the end of central bank gold hoarding, which would be the same human response of an individual during a period of financial crisis.

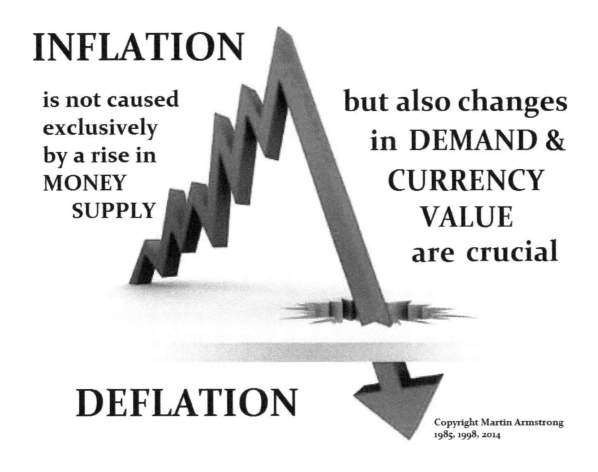

INFLATION

is not caused
exclusively
by a rise in
MONEY
SUPPLY

but also changes
in DEMAND &
CURRENCY
VALUE
are crucial

DEFLATION

Copyright Martin Armstrong
1985, 1998, 2014

Milton Friedman saw this deliberate deflation and how the Fed failed to monetize the refugee gold inflows fearing it would lead to inflation. So, we had the opposite roles back then. This predates the income tax being applied to everyone, so there was no hunt for taxes on the part of the political government. The scale tipped because the Fed was imposing intentional deflation by sterilizing the gold inflows.

Conversely, after World War I, France had counted unrealistically on German reparations to balance its budget. When reparations did not materialize, France used inflation as a tax to finance expenditures. In 1926, France pulled back from the brink of hyperinflation. Unlike Britain, in France inflation had put the old parity hopelessly out of reach.

Clearly, inflation is by no means one-dimensional. The causes of inflation vary, and the main driving force behind it may be demand. Yet, demand is a human emotion inspired by everything from the anticipation of the future to cost-push inflation and the belief in a stable political government.

What is the Value of Money?

There is something very curious lying at the core of MMT. Is the value of money simply the fact that it is legal tender and accepted by government for taxes, fees, and fines? Naturally, pointing to countries that experienced hyperinflation invokes rebukes that it is not a fair comparison. Yet, to test a theory, one must apply it to all situations throughout history, not just the periods supporting one's theory.

We cannot simply accept MMT as a solution by pointing to QTM and arguing it failed. This is how politicians may campaign, "Vote for me because the other guy is worse than me!" That may be a common political tactic, but it ignores any positive justification for a vote. This becomes merely a vote for the better of two evils.

When it comes to economics, we are talking about impacting society as a whole. This is not something to experiment with lightly. All major revolutions begin with corruption or taxes — no taxation without representation. Claiming that taxation is a tool to prevent inflation, justifying class warfare, is fooling around with the same principles that have led to civil wars and revolutions.

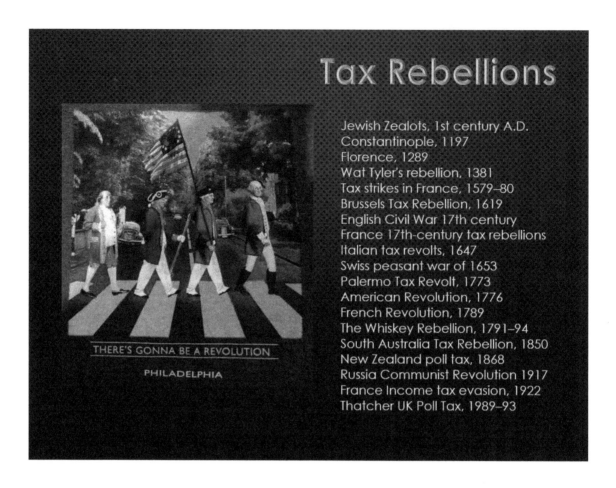

A simple list of the top major tax rebellions throughout history should be a warning. The idea that MMT can create money without limits and rely on taxing the people to reduce net disposable income to curb inflation presents a very serious social problem. Such a policy's failure will warn that the cost will be rising civil unrest as a price for the denial of equal protection of the law.

Additionally, we must answer why some countries have gone into hyperinflation, which becomes the argument behind the QTM. If we do not address that issue, it is impossible to accept MMT as any possible valid solution, even ignoring the proposition that inflation can be controlled by using taxation as a monetary tool.

The proposition that money can be created merely because it is legal tender is never addressed in depth, for it centers upon the degree of confidence the people have in government. It merely assumes that people will remain confident in accepting the currency because of the power of government.

Obviously, there is an assumption here that government in its present form will last forever. There is a further assumption that all governments that came before the age of Marxism were somehow primitive and unworthy of our study. There should be no need to investigate the past because they did not possess the technology we do today. Such assumptions are arrogant, to say the least, and lethally adopted without investigation. Are all societies that existed before us merely primitive and not worth investigation?

> "[T]he different forms of government make law democratical, aristocratical, tyrannical, with a view to their several interests; and these laws, which are made by them for their own interests, are the justice which they deliver to subjects, and him who transgresses them they punish as a breaker of the law, and unjust. And that is what I mean when I say that in all states there is the same principle of justice, which is the interest of the government; and as the government must be supposed to have power, the only reasonable conclusion as, that everywhere there is one principle of justice, which is the interest of the stronger."

Thrasymachus (Θρασύμαχος)
(ca. 459-400 BC)

Many governments have come before us in various forms from empires, nations, and city-states with monarchies, tyrannies, republics, and democracies. Not a single one has survived. Thrasymachus (459–400 BC) argued against Socrates that justice was the same in all forms of government, for they all have acted in their own self-interest. Indeed, Socrates was sentenced to death even in a democracy for that was the exercise of the self-interest of those in power. There is never any difference in justice. Now we have MMT arguing that the state can increase the money supply and appease the masses by confiscating the wealth of one class to maintain their power. Attacking the upper class in any republican form of government becomes bribing the masses for their vote at the exploitation of the minority. Hitler accomplished that same goal by stereotyping the Jews.

Those supporting MMT ignore history, claiming it lacks anything worthwhile as a lesson for the future as anything to the contrary would be against the self-interest of those supporting MMT. They ignore any possible common themes that history exposes, which results in the demise of all forms of governments that came before us. The proposition that class warfare ignores the same arguments was used to justify the American Civil War because the slaves were human.

Ignoring the past to avoid criticism puts our entire future at risk as a modern society. For example, we know some mushrooms are poisonous because someone before us ate them and died. Should we ignore the lessons of the past and just eat any mushrooms that we find? Economics is no different. Suppose we do not explore the history of how previous economies functioned and the links to the rise and fall of empires, nations, and city-states. In that case, we indeed risk the fragmentation of society and separatist movements that arise from clashes in economics and culture.

Discovering the Existence of the Business Cycle

William Stanley Jevons (1835-1882)

When I was in school, the economics teacher stated bluntly that there may be a business cycle, but it was not definitive or inevitable, and the government could smooth out the wrinkles. The very debate about the existence of a business cycle attempts to shut down any investigation that might expose the fact that economists and governments cannot manipulate the cycle.

The discovery of the business cycle was made during the 19th century. The understanding that cyclical activity was the cornerstone of everything in nature, from how sunlight and sound traveled to the beat of your heart, was beginning to dawn on the minds of people in other fields. William Stanley Jevons (1835–1882) was an accidental economist. He was studying natural science at the University College in London. He left school in 1854 and took an exciting job as an assayer in Sydney, Australia, as the big gold rush developed in 1851. Jevons thus was exposed to the real world, and this experience in the bullion field with wildly fluctuating prices exposed him to trends that were not yet discussed in moral philosophy. There was no course on economics until Marshall in 1903 at Cambridge.

The gold discoveries in Australia in 1851 in Victoria set off a gold rush following the California discoveries in 1849. This dramatically increased the quantity of money

143

by creating an inflationary boom. Since gold was fixed, prices rose in response to the increase in supply. This led to the Panic of 1857, which produced a global contagion that caused Jevons to return to England in 1859.

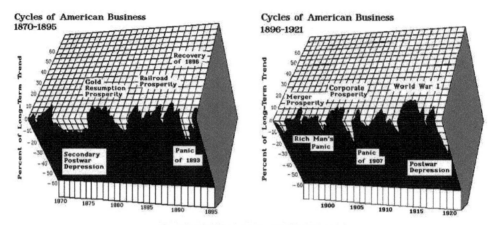

Jevons began to see the world economy in terms of a cycle with its booms and busts. He wrote his observations in 1862, *A General Mathematical Theory of Political Economy*, which he followed up the next year with *A Serious Fall in the Value of Gold (1863)*. It was Jevons who created indexes and mapped out inflation. This was the first quantitative analysis of money and prices.

Since Jevons was in the real world, he saw firsthand what was taking place. He caught a glimpse of cyclical behavior in markets, which was not so dissimilar to the debate in science between one group who saw sudden climate changes and those who preferred a steady uniform movement. This debate emerged in 1772 with the discovery of a frozen animal in Russia with food still in its stomach.

A few years later, Jevons wrote *The Coal Question* in 1865. In this work, he provided a forecast that the supplies of coal in England would decline and that prices would undergo a dramatic price rise. He was obviously looking at cycles in supply and demand.

Jevons became fascinated by the rise and fall of economies and markets. He witnessed firsthand the first real global contagion in 1857. He thus saw a world that was interconnected even back then. It was also a period of turmoil in science.

Jevons' *A Serious Fall in the Value of Gold* (1863) and *The Coal Question* (1865) placed him in the front rank as an economic writer and statistician. His other writings, *Money and the Mechanism of Exchange* (1875), were written for the general public describing the economy rather than merely offering theory. This was followed by a *Primer on Political Economy* (1878), *The State in Relation to Labour* (1882), and two later works that were published after his death, *Methods of Social Reform,* and *Investigations in Currency and Finance.* It was this last volume where Jevons reveals his quest to understand the driving force behind the cyclical patterns within the economy.

Jevons speculated on the connection between the economic and commercial crises and sunspots. Sir Frederick Herschel's (1738–1822) investigation of sunspots and their connection with wheat prices back in 1801 was certainly logical since crops are directly impacted by weather. During this period of the 19th century, agriculture accounted for 70% of employment of the civil work force around 1860. This would decline with the rise of the Industrial Revolution, dropping to about 40% by 1900. Without question, Jevons logically considered the possible influence of sunspots upon the economy. He was indeed preparing a large treatise on economics and had drawn up a table of contents and completed some chapters and parts of chapters. This fragment was published in 1905 under the title of *The Principles of Economics.*

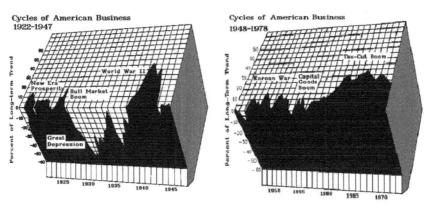

In his work entitled *The Coal Question,* Jevons covered an interesting aspect of market prices and their relation to supply and demand. For example, he explained that improving energy efficiency would typically reduce energy costs. However, paradoxically, this leads only to an increase rather than a decrease in energy use and in turn creates a counterbalance within the entire system. *The Coal Question* was a brilliant observation of how markets truly function.

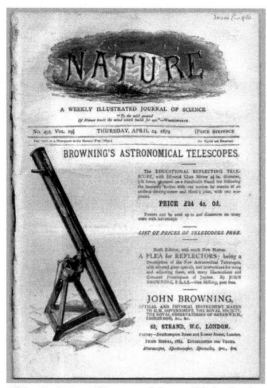

William Stanley Jevons "Sun-spots and Commercial Crises." London: Nature, April 24, 1879. 1st edition. Jevons article occupies only 588-590 it contains some 3000 words and was a densely-printed journal

ArmstrongEconomics.COM

Jevons, in an overlooked minor work, *Commercial Crises and Sun-Spots,* analyzes the business cycle and proposes that crises in the economy might not be random events at all. In fact, they might be based on discernible prior causes. To clarify the concept, Jevons presented a statistical study relating business cycles to sunspots. His reasoning was that sunspots affected the weather, which in turn affected crops. Crop changes could then be expected to cause economic changes given the high concentration of agriculture within the civil workforce during the mid-19th century.

Jevons correlated business patterns with occurrences of sunspots, theorizing that changes on the sun would cause changes on the Earth via weather and thus impact patterns in farming production. This is a very early example of statistical interpretation in economic research. Jevons became a professor of logic at Owens College, in Manchester, England, in 1866, and in 1876 at University College in London. He was one of the three economists to put forward a marginal utility theory in the 1870s. He argued that one commodity would exchange for another such that the ratio of the prices of the two commodities traded equally at the ratio of their marginal utilities.

Francis Edgeworth (1845 – 1926) criticized the way Jevons developed these ideas. Edgeworth invented the indifference curve, a graph that claimed a combination of two goods that give a consumer equal satisfaction and utility renders the consumer indifferent in their choice. This was in itself questionable.

Still, Jevons also made an important contribution to the theory of capital, many aspects of which were taken up by the Austrian school. He superimposed on the classical economic theory the idea that capital should be measured in terms of time and quantity. An increase in the amount invested is the same as an increase in the time period in which it is employed. Output can increase by extending the period in which the investment is available by, for instance, reinvesting the output instead of consuming it at the end of the production period. With given levels of labor and capital, the output becomes a function of time only. He derived from this a definition of the rate of interest the ratio of the output gained by an increase in the time capital invested divided by the amount invested (i.e., the internal rate of return). Jevons was also one of the founders of econometrics, for he invented moving averages.

The theory that light itself moves in cyclical waves was first established by Christiaan Huygens (1629–1695). This was overshadowed by Sir Issac Newton (1642–1695), who was making a comeback thanks to Thomas Young (1773–1829), who rescued Huygens' work. By 1850, it was then Huygens who was accepted as being correct, not Newton. This created a vibrant world of inquiry and debate regarding the sun. Jevons' theory of a link between sunspots influencing the behaviors of man was then considered possible rather than Herschel's exploration of the impact of sunspots on wheat prices.

Jevons was the first to consider that there was a cyclical aspect to the economy. His work foreshadowed several developments of the 20th century that looked at things from a cyclical perspective. Jevons effectively created the marginal revolution in economic theory by shifting the focus from classical to neoclassical economics. He was certainly the first economist to construct index numbers that greatly influenced the development of empirical mathematical methods and statistics, giving rise to econometrics in the social sciences. However, the field ignored his cyclical perspective and thus economics, which began as a separate

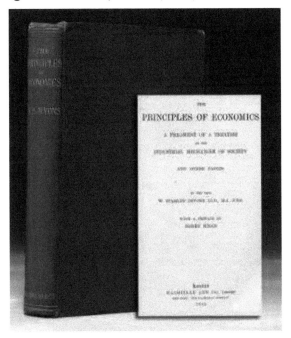

course taught at Cambridge University in 1902. Jevons' philosophy was a precursor to the development of logical empiricism, but because of his cyclical vision of the economy, he remains largely overlooked as many took what they liked and ignored the essence of his insight. As mentioned, he was indeed preparing a large treatise on economics. This fragment was published in 1905 under the title of *The Principles of Economics*. Jevons begins this work with a defense of new theories.

"The contents of the following pages can hardly meet with ready acceptance among those who regard the Science of Political Economy as having already acquired a nearly perfect form. I believe it is generally supposed that Adam Smith laid the foundations of this science; that Malthus, Anderson, and Senior added important doctrines; that Ricardo systematised [sic] the whole; and, finally, that Mr. J. S. Mill filled in the details and completely expounded this branch of knowledge. Mr. Mill appears to have had a similar notion; for he distinctly asserts that there was nothing in the Laws of Value which remained for himself or any future writer to clear up. Doubtless it is difficult to help feeling that opinions adopted and confirmed by such eminent men have much weight of probability in their favour. Yet, in the other sciences this weight of authority has not been allowed to restrict the free examination of new opinions and theories; and it has often been v vi THE THEORY OF POLITICAL ECONOMY ultimately proved that authority was on the wrong side."

The mathematical and deductive economic aspects of Jevons' work were incorporated by many. Jevons maintained that market prices within the economy were derived directly from a series of fundamental motive forces, such as "the mechanics of utility and self-interest," which integrates Adam Smith's invisible hand. Markets were perfectly rational in the most abstract fashion and were thus predictable if one possessed all the information. Jevons saw the role of anticipation in market prices, concluding that a rational human being would anticipate the future and include that in his expectation of future prices. Jevons perhaps went too far in this line of thought by attributing variations to "the intellectual standing of the race, or the character of the individual." (Jevons 1879, 34). Foresight in markets depended upon the state of civilization, or basically upon experience and intelligence. This line of thought appears to be driven by British colonialism.

Therefore, this idea that market behavior is determined by information on the participants' part emerged from Jevons. His ideas are indeterminate in cases where more information is required. Even wages he saw varying according to knowledge. Behavior was everything to Jevons. He viewed Irish laborers as responsible for the higher mortality rates because they were more easily subject to drunkenness. Jevons believed the proper place for women was in the home. Clearly, the British Victorian-era middle-class was used as a standard for his evaluation.

Jevons concluded his *Principles of Economics* by stating very humbly:

> "I trust that the theory now given may prove accurate; but, however this may be, it will not be useless if it cause inquiry to be directed into the true basis and form of a science which touches so directly the material welfare of the human race."

As the 20th century dawned, the idea of a business cycle was emerging in academia. Wesley Clair Mitchell (1874–1948) was an American economist known for his empirical work on business cycles and for guiding the National Bureau of Economic Research in its first decades.

Mitchell began the first chapter by stating that the idea that there was a cycle to the economy emerged after the Panic of 1825, which was a very serious crisis that began with the Bank of England arising out of speculative investments made in Latin America after the South Sea Bubble of 1720. This time it concerned an imaginary country that did not even exist called Poyais. This crisis originated in England involving the concept of emerging markets with unlimited opportunity and the potential to strike it rich. The Panic of 1825 led to the closing of six London banks, which now included the failure of the bank formed by Henry Thorton (1760–1815), who had defended the issue of paper money by the

Wesley Clair Mitchell (1874–1948)

Bank of England in his 1802 publication, *Enquiry into the Nature and Effects of the Paper Credit of Great Britain.*

Thorton had defended the Bank of England against charges that the excessive issue of paper money caused inflation. In 1810, he published his *Bullion Report* that inquired into the high price of gold and the depressed currency exchange that, again, he argued was not caused by an excess of paper currency. Nevertheless, while denying the supply of money did not cause inflation, he did advocate a reduction of its supply. He did, however, oppose a rigid contraction. At this time, he was a member of the Bullion Committee and advocated a flexible or managed contraction in the supply of money.

Mitchell in his 1913 treatise, *Business Cycles,* seriously derailed the investigation of the business cycle because of his unfamiliarity with how to define cycles or how they functioned. He thus wrote in chapter I:

> "Serious efforts to frame the theory of business cycles began with contemporary discussions of the economic crisis of 1825. Differences of opinion promptly appeared regarding the cause of this widespread dislocation of trade-differences which multiply as the crises of later years brought new materials and new man into the discussion. Presently crises the

cane one of the accredited topics economic theory and systemic writers began to develop explanations based on their doctrines production distribution and exchange. Before the end of the 19th century there had accumulated a body of observation and speculation sufficient to justify the compile Asian of histories of the theories of crises.

Inevitably, the early efforts to account for the exceedingly complex phenomenon of crises were crude and superficial but the problem commanded so much attention that the character of the treatment rapidly improved. Each reoccurring crises, indeed, produced a fresh crop of ill-considered explanations; but meanwhile other writers were steadily using and bettering the work of their predecessors. In this process of elaboration, however, the early differences of opinion did not disappear. Instead they became standardized into several distinct types of theory, each represented in the growing literature a number of variants."

Mitchell's main teacher was James Laurence Laughlin (1850–1933), who supervised his dissertation. Laughlin's chief interest was what had become the "currency question" during the 19th century. Laughlin was a strong opponent of the Quantity Theory of Money, which today we call Monetarism thanks to the Chicago School and Milton Friedman. The currency question of the 19th century came to a head during the 1890s when there was a choice between alternative monetary systems

James Laurence Laughlin
(1850-1933)

— inconvertible paper money, the gold standard, and the gold/silver bimetallism standard. Laughlin also assisted in setting up the Federal Reserve.

Mitchell published his thesis in *A History of Greenbacks*, where he considered the consequences of the inconvertible paper monetary system during the American Civil War. Nonetheless, Mitchell examined the Quantity Theory of Money, which he followed up with *Gold Prices and Wages under the Greenback Standard*. Mitchell then embarked upon his desire to define the business cycle in 1913. The preface begins:

"This book offers an analytic description of the complicated processes by which seasons of business prosperity, crisis, depression, and revival come about in the modern world. The materials used consist chiefly of market reports and statistics concerning the business cycles which have run their course since 1890 in the United States, England, Germany and France."

Mitchell spent the next 30 years trying to define the business cycle and he published *Measuring Business Cycles* with Arthur Burns (1904–1987). However, Mitchell never made the connection with other scientific areas of cyclical behavior, and thus did not truly progress from the methods of analyzing the business cycles that he originally adopted in 1913. Milton Friedman believed, "Mitchell is generally considered primarily an empirical scientist rather than a theorist." In effect, Mitchell believed that the business cycle was created purely by the internal dynamics of capitalism. He did not ever quite grasp that cycles need not be symmetrical.

> "If the years between one crises and the next be taken at the length of a business cycle the English, French, and German cycles beginning in 1890 lasted ten years and those beginning in 1900 lasted seven years. The contemporaneous American cycles have shown wider variations: three years from 1890 to '93; 10 years from 1893 to 1903 and four years from 1903 to '07. In view of these diverse cities the notion that crises have a regular. A reoccurrence is plainly mistaken."

Two Dutch economists also explored the cyclical aspect of the economy by building upon the revelations from natural science and the door opened by Jevons. Jacob Van Gelderen (1891–1940) took a job after school at the Office of Statistics of the Municipality of Amsterdam. He became engrossed in Marxism for the Industrial Revolution was creating factory work, and in the early stages, there was no real experience with worker safety. In the United States, on March 25, 1911, a fire broke out at the Triangle Shirtwaist Factory in New York City. The employer had locked the doors to ensure the workers could not leave early unnoticed. However, when the fire broke out, this policy created a death trap. Within 18 minutes, 146 people died. This certainly was a profound tragedy that contributed greatly to the trend toward safe working conditions and illustrated some of the support behind Marxism at this point in time.

1911 Triangle Shirtwaist Factory fire killing 146 workers

Van Gelderen was a member of *The Weekly,* edited by F.M. Wibaut and H. Roland Holst. He also published under a pseudonym of economic commentary in *The People*. It was 1913 in *The New Age* where he published his observations *Spring Flood,* in which he discusses a new theory that has become known as Long Wave Cyclical Theory in the economy. Van Gelderen explains an average ten-year cycle in the fluctuations of the overall general price level in several countries that

Jacob van Gelderen (1891-1940)

he investigated. He also referenced a larger cyclical wave movement spanning several decades.

He was still a Marxist and published under a pseudonym a brochure on class struggle, embracing the fight of the people. He covered topics such as social democracy and national defense (Amsterdam, 1915). In 1916 and 1919, he published with B.H. Sajet some medical statistical studies, and in 1918 he published his first demographic article concerning the impact of war upon the Amsterdam population movements. In 1919, Van Gelderen traveled to India in the service of the Ministry of Agriculture, Industry and Trade, constructing a new statistical database. He actually argued in 1923 against a progressive rate of corporation tax. In 1925, he became the Director of the Central Office of Statistics in Batavia, where he remained until 1932. In 1928, Van Gelderen was appointed extraordinary professor of political economy at the Law School in Batavia.

Van Gelderen was now abandoning Marx. His understanding of cycles was leading him to see that Marxism could not create a sustainable economic system. He began to criticize the work of Karl Marx, writing, "The labor theory of value can be no satisfactory, complete system of building economic analysis." Van Gelderen further realized that Marx underestimated the importance of agriculture. Clearly, Van Gelderen was beginning to see the dynamic structure and that agriculture is not driven simply by greed. Nature has a lot to do with it, as the Dust Bowl would demonstrate.

His rejection of Marxism as an economic-theoretical system is articulated in an article series entitled *Deepening of Marxism?* published in *The Socialist Guide* in 1930. This is a critical review of a book published in 1929 by another Dutch economist, Salomon De Wolff, who wrote, *The Economic Tide.* Van Gelderen was more of a socialist rather than a communist. Following the Great Depression, he became a professor of sociology at the Faculty of Law at the University of Utrecht where he advocated government intervention and international economic and political cooperation.

Salomon (Samuel) de Wolff (1878-1960) was an economist and politician who became a Socialist in 1898 and supported the Marxist philosophy. In 1921, after the war, he was elected to the City Council in Amsterdam. However, the work of Wolff is more radical than that of Van Gelderen, although both were investigating cycles. Van Gelderen saw the cycles as more dynamic and turned against Marxism as the cure for the business cycle.

Salomon de Wolff (1878-1960)

Wolff began with a concept of historical materialism influenced by Marx that appeared in an article in 1906 in *The New Era.* The sixteenth-century urban working population's central role at the beginning of the revolt against Spain deeply colored his thoughts. Not only did he develop the anachronistic concept of proletariat, but he was limited to the iconoclasm of 1566. Thus, what escaped him was the important military role of the peasantry.

In 1913, Wolff returned to the Social Democratic Labour Party (SDAP). Wolff began to write his cyclical economic theory in support of Marxism. In 1915, he wrote a series of articles, *The Accumulation and Crisis,* in *The New Era* in response to Rosa Luxemburg's book, *The Accumulation of Capital* (1913). Rosa Luxemburg (1871-1919) was also a member of the SDAP, albeit far left-leaning. Her book, *Capital Accumulation*, disagreed with Marx's view that capital could function alone due to economic underconsumption. Luxemburg stated that the proletariat could not increase the demand for commodities as they could not afford what they produced. She argued that capitalism could not prosper in a closed-capitalist system, which often led to those nations absorbing non-capitalistic nations in order to offload their surplus and increase demand. In 1919, Rosa Luxemburg was captured in Berlin and killed for her Communist ideas.

Salomon (Samuel) de Wolff (1878-1960)

Group photograph of the SDP, Department Rotterdam, Congress, 1911, with Sam de Wolff, Willem van Ravesteyn, Herman Gorter, David Jozef Wijnkoop, Louis de Visser, Gerrit Mannoury and Jan Ceton

Social Democratic Party of the Netherlands was founded on March 14, 1909, after splitting from the Dutch Social Democratic Workers' Party

The plea of Wolff's former fellow student, J. van der Wijk, was expressed in his series of articles *Laws of Nature and Society* (1921) and called for the sciences to derive a mathematical approach to the political economy by following the footsteps of Jevons, which was now in the direction of Wolff. Wolff wrote a preliminary study, *Prosperities and Depression Periods,* in *The Socialist Guide* (1921). The eventual result was his 1929 Amsterdam publication, *The Economic Tide (Contribution to the explanation of the cyclical phenomenon).* Building on such considerations of Jacob Van Gelderen, he developed the theory of a double wave in the capitalist economic cycle. These were long ascending and descending waves of an average of twenty-five years. Within these waves, he saw shorter periods of about five cycles that he saw as the business cycle characteristics. Wolff further developed his original theory, involving what he termed "cyclical phenomenon" (*cunjunctuur verschijnsel*) to support Marx's ideas about the value and the reproduction of capital.

The theory of sunspots put forth by William Stanley Jevons in *The Theory of Political Economy* (1871) was developed to explain the cyclical movement within the economy. This stood in contrast to Wolff, who preferred to see a highly developed capitalist economy overall driven by man rather than nature. According to Wolff, the economy had developed its own internal laws, regardless of what was happening in nature.

The average lifespan of the long and short waves had its special interest. Despite the fact that critics argued about his calculations, Wolff achieved remarkably accurate economic forecasting movements in 1920 about the crisis of 1921, and in 1928 that of 1929. He also forecast a revival in 1932 and an impending depression in 1937. The *New York Times* on December 27, 1931, included the reassuring message that Wolff, "[A] man who predicted the present world crisis a year before its outbreak...now sees the end of the depression in 1932."

Economists refusing to consider cycles met his Dutch book with more criticism than approval. Wolff was largely ignored because of his Marxist views. He maintained that the coming of socialism would first be expected in the most developed capitalist countries. Strangely enough, Wolff was correct in that developed countries would become socialistic. After World War II, socialism dominated Europe and the United States despite the protestations against Marx and communism.

Nikolai Dmyitriyevich Kondratieff (1892–1938) was a Russian economist. Following the 1917 Russian Revolution, Kondratieff was an economics professor who was called upon by the new government to create the first Soviet Five-Year-Plan. Kondratieff was thus given the opportunity to draw the economic plan for Russia, he assumed, upon a blank slate. Kondratieff explored the past to gather empirical data upon which to construct the new economy. What he observed was the cyclical nature of society through its booms and busts, and that knowledge would later cost him his life.

Nikolai Dmyitriyevkh Kondratieff
(1892 - 1938)

In 1926, Kondratieff published his conclusions after investigating history and entitled his work, *Long Waves in Economic Life*. Kondratieff discovered that there were progressive wave formations running the span of 50 to 60 years in length. He was reviewing the time span beginning with 1789 up to the date of his publication in 1926. He described three great waves with highs of about 1820, 1864, and 1920 that were closely linked to wars. However, we must also keep in mind that the economy, even in the United States, was about 70% agrarian during this time period. Even by 1929, the United States was still about 40% agrarian. This naturally provided an undertone to his work.

Even without war, adding the maximum time frame of 60 years to 1920 brings us to 1980, the peak in OPEC oil and gold. Kondratieff effectively reached his conclusion that the economy was driven by cyclical activity, and thus this was implicitly against Hegel and Marx insofar as the new government would not be able to reach some perfect state of synthesis. For this reason, Kondratieff's work was seen as a criticism of Stalin's goals. He was arrested in July 1930 and accused of being a member of a non-existent Peasants' Labour Party. Kondratieff was sent to prison for eight years. Stalin wanted him dead and expressed that in a letter dated August 1930. When his eight-year sentence was complete, he was put on trial again with new charges during the Great Purge and sentenced to ten years in prison.

However, upon his sentencing on September 17, 1938, he was taken outside and shot to death at the age of 46. Kondratieff died a political prisoner, for his research was something that the government did its best to destroy to prevent it from influencing anyone.

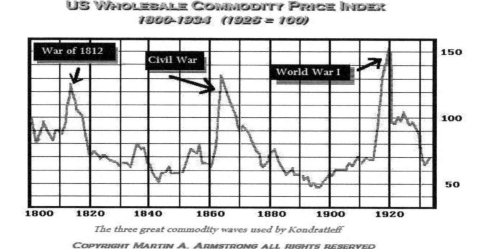

US WHOLESALE COMMODITY PRICE INDEX
1800-1934 (1926 = 100)

The three great commodity waves used by Kondratieff

Kondratieff's work was compelling and contributed greatly to the Austrian School of Economics that first began to develop the concept of a business cycle. The general central principle of the Austrian business cycle theory is concerned with a period of sustained low interest rates and excessive credit creation, which results in a volatile and unstable imbalance between savings and investment. Within this context, the theory supposes that the business cycle unfolds whereby low rates of interest stimulate borrowing from the banking sector, resulting in the expansion of the money supply. In turn, that causes an unsustainable credit source boom that leads to a diminished opportunity for investment by competition. Therefore, at the top, this causes speculative misallocation of resources that manifests into a bubble top. The decline unfolds as a credit-crunch, creating the speculative bust and recession. This contraction in credit shrinks the money supply, completing the cycle to return to its prior state.

The usual criticism of Kondratieff's work has been the absence of any empirical cycle that is symmetrical. This was the criticism of Mitchell, who argued that since economic crises did not appear with clockwork regularity, then any "reoccurrence is plainly mistaken." It is true that the cycle discovered by Kondratieff was by no means symmetrical when there were only three waves that varied from 50 to 60 years. However, this expectation of rhythmic perfection illustrates the lack of understanding of cyclical wave structures. Such perfect waves with regular intervals are known as transverse waves, whereas waves that differ in wavelength (distance between peaks) are known as longitudinal waves. We will examine these two types of waves later on. It is sufficient to state at this time that these are two fundamentally different wave structures.

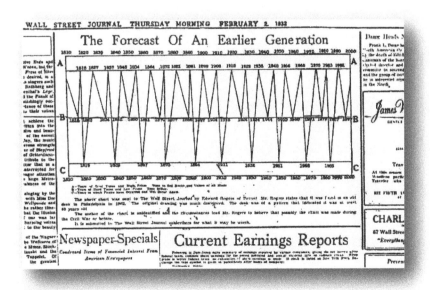

The Wall Street Journal published a chart on February 2, 1932, based on the work of Samuel Benner (1832–1913), who was a prosperous farmer. Benner was wiped out financially during the Panic of 1873 and a hog cholera epidemic. In retirement, he set to establish the causes and timing of the market and economic fluctuations. Perhaps because farmers are in tune with the cycles of nature, Samuel saw the world in a cyclical manner. In 1875, Samuel published his business and commodity price forecasts for the period of 1876 up to 1904 entitled *Benner's Prophecies – Future Ups and Downs in Prices.*

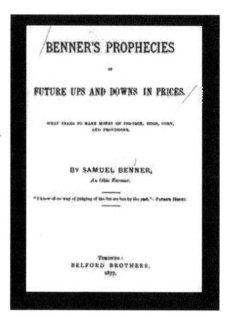

Benner's work's most fascinating aspect is that he saw the far more complex cyclical structure, which is not a symmetrical transverse wave as expected by Mitchell, but the longitudinal wave structure that is a repetitive pattern rather than one of a constant wavelength. Mitchell was unaware of this structure and assumed if a cycle was not a transverse wave, then there was no business cycle.

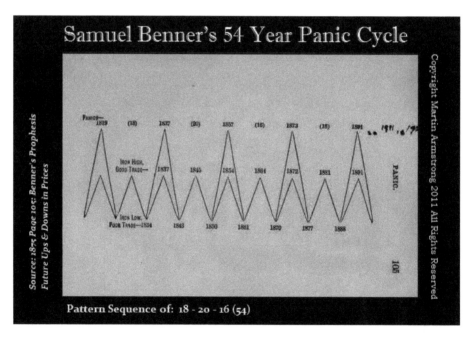

Benner's 54–Year Panic Cycle is interesting for it emerges from a sequence of 18, 20, and 16 years that repeats and forms groups of 54 years. According to Benner, "It takes panics 54 years in their order to make a revolution or to return to the same order." The key years were 1819, 1837, 1857, 1873, and 1891. Extending his series would give us 1911(20), 1927(16), 1945(18), 1965(20), 1981(16), 1999(18), 2019(20), and 2035(16). Benner's approach to cyclical behavior was truly intuitive based upon what he saw in nature rather than a perfect transverse wave of a constant duration.

The 8-9-10 (27) year and the 16-18-20 (54) year Benner cyclical sequences are based on the interval of 9 years and its regular deviations. Benner indeed believed the driving force was nature, stating, "The cause producing the periodicity and length of these cycles may be found in our solar system." Benner never actually fully explained the basis of his cyclical research. Benner clearly made the connection with nature. He may have been aware of the earlier work on sunspots by Herschel, who related his work to wheat prices, and Jevons applied his work to economics.

Joseph Schumpeter
(1883-1950)

Kondratieff did not quite have Benner's instinct of adopting a longitudinal wave structure. Nonetheless, he had a huge impact upon others investigating the cause of the business cycle among academics. One such person was Joseph Alois Schumpeter (1883–1950). In his 1942 work, *Capitalism, Socialism and Democracy*, Schumpeter asked the question: "Can capitalism survive? No. I do not think it can."

Certainly, at first glance, it would appear that Schumpeter was a Marxist. To the contrary, Marx believed capitalism would be destroyed by its enemies, who he called the "proletariat," because of their exploitation by the bourgeois. However, Schumpeter believed that capitalism would be destroyed by its friends rather than by its enemies. He believed capitalism and its successes would nurture a new vast intellectual class that made its living by attacking the very bourgeois system of private property and freedom. To a large degree, he is correct, for that has taken place by the aggressive trading investment banks like a lion hunting a zebra from the herd. Schumpeter did not relish the thought of the destruction of capitalism. He wrote, "If a doctor predicts that his patient will die presently, this does not mean that he desires it."

Schumpeter is best known for his theory of creative destruction, in which he argues that there is an economic force of obliteration where the old makes way for the entrepreneurial new. This groundbreaking analysis made him an early champion of free markets and entrepreneurial profit that lay the foundation for the business cycle. Schumpeter wrote extensively on the subject of capital and capitalism, earning the nickname of the "bourgeois Marx." He wrote that most ideas fade with varying degrees between "after-dinner and a generation. Some, however, do not. They suffer eclipses but they come back again, and they come back not as unrecognizable elements of cultural inheritance, but in their individual garb...These we may well call the great ones – it is no disadvantage of this definition that it links greatness to vitality."

Marxism, he noted, had become a religion.

> "Analyzing business cycles means neither more nor less than analyzing the economic process of the capitalist era....Cycles are not like tonsils, separate things that might be treated by themselves, but are, like the best of the heart, of the essence of the organism that displays them."

Schumpeter did not stay in an ivory tower. He also studied law, handled an Egyptian princess's financial affairs in Cairo, became the youngest full professor at the University of Graz at the age of 28, and served as Austria's finance minister. He was famous for telling his students that he had three goals in life. First, to become the greatest horseman; second, to become the greatest lover; and third, to become the greatest economist. He would then inform the class that he fulfilled only two of his life's goals, leaving them to decide what remained.

Indeed, Schumpeter wrote *The Theory of Economic Development* in 1911, followed by *Business Cycles* in 1939, and in 1942, his more controversial work, *Capitalism, Socialism, and Democracy.* He disputed Marx, arguing that the attempt to redistribute income would destroy the business cycle by eliminating innovation driven by entrepreneurs. In this respect, he correctly forecasts the collapse of communism precisely due to central planning that sought to eliminate the business cycle. Schumpeter sought to explain Kondratieff waves in terms of innovation that would lead to spurts of economic expansion. He did see that big business would also reduce entrepreneurs who are free to make the decisions to risk their capital. This observation was correct

insofar as big companies buy startup companies, but they are incapable of creating new technology and are thus forced to acquire innovation. Corporations merely become mini-governments insofar as they reject the creative individual, such as Steve Jobs, and embrace bureaucratic administers.

In 1935, a trader by the name of William Delbert Gann (1878–1955) also embarked upon trying to ascertain time in price movements of markets. Perhaps Gann's most important trading technique was to determine market timing using fractions of a circle. Gann would divide a circle (the perfect cycle) into quarters, eighths, and thirds to count the number of days, weeks, and months between highs and lows. For example, a circle has 360 degrees, with 90 being one quarter, 45 one eighth, and so on. He thus determined important numbers to count between highs and lows are therefore 30, 45, 60, 90, 135, (90 + 45), 150, 180, 210, 225, 270, 315, 330 and 360. He then rounded up one-eighth of 90 being 11, two-eighths was 22, and three-eighths was 33. Therefore, he arrived at 45, 56, 67, 78, and 90. These are other numbers to direct attention. Gann wrote:

> "The Great Time Cycles are most important because they record the periods of extreme high or low prices. The cycles are 90-Years, 82 to 84 Years, 60 Years, 45 Years, and 20 Years."

Most of Gann's cycles appear to have relationships to planetary cyclical movements. Gann states the 82 to 84-year cycle relates to one-half of an orbit of Neptune and an orbit of

William Delbert Gann
(1878–1955)

Uranus. The 60-year cycle relates to two orbits of Saturn or three cycles of Jupiter and Saturn appearing at the same place in the sky. The 45-year cycle relates to a cycle of Saturn and Uranus. Gann's 90-year cycle is two cycles of Saturn–Uranus and so on. Of course, there is no empirical evidence that planetary movements exert an actual influence. Merely correlating such events to the markets does not prove that this is the actual source.

Elliott Wave

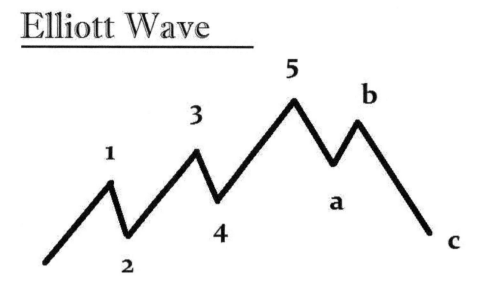

An American accountant by the name Ralph Nelson Elliott (1871–1948) was an investor. During the Great Depression, there was a growing sense that some mysterious force had laid waste to the economy. No one could put their finger on it, but there was a sense of some predetermined fate, as in the Bible that there was a time "to be born, and a time to die." (Ecclesiastes 3:1–8).

Elliott took a different approach in trying to ascertain rules based upon patterns. He studied the stock market data, which led him to develop what has become known as the Elliott Wave Principle, a form of technical analysis that looks at patterns rather than cyclical analysis. It seeks to identify trends within the financial markets by trying to understand how market prices unfold in specific patterns.

During the Great Depression, Elliott began his study of stock market data by observing patterns from annual down to half-hour intervals. Finally, in August 1938, he detailed the results of his studies by publishing his third book which he wrote in collaboration with Charles J. Collins that was entitled simply, *The Wave Principle*. Elliott had observed repetitive patterns within stock market prices that may appear random at first glance but actually followed predictable paths. Soon after the publication of *The Wave Principle*, *Financial World* magazine commissioned Elliott to write 12 articles describing his new method of market forecasting. Elliott came to believe that the patterns were a natural law of how things functioned, which he published in June 1946.

Yet, Elliott's approach was one of pattern recognition rather than a cyclical measurement of time. He observed the cyclical nature of how energy is transmitted but sought to study the shape of the wave rather than actually focus on the repetitive nature from a timing perspective. He could see the sidewinding snake but did not focus on when the snake will appear at points A and B. He saw the essence of the shape of the wave rather than time.

Arthur Burns (1904–1987) was an American economist who became chairman of the Federal Reserve from 1970 to 1978. He served as Fed chairman from February 1970 until the end of January 1978, and was wrongly blamed for the inflation of the period that set the stage for Paul Volcker. However, this was the period when the floating exchange rate system was born on August 15, 1971, as a temporary bargaining chip. The inflation was caused by an across the board decline in the dollar on world markets and the birth of OPEC. Burns also had a reputation of being overly influenced by political pressure when it came to monetary policy decisions while at the Fed. He

Arthur Burns (1904-1987)

also attempted to comply with the Fed's political demands to maintain an unemployment rate of around 4 percent. The political demands were unrealistic and assumed that the Fed and government could control the economy.

> "For well over a century business cycles have run an unceasing round. They have persisted through vast economic and social changes; they have withstood countless experiments in industry, agriculture, banking, industrial relations, and public policy; they have confounded forecasters without number, belied repeated prophecies of a 'new era of prosperity' and outlived repeated forebodings of 'chronic depression'"

The idea that cycles exist was springing from every sector and field. The essence of time was emerging, yet some could not see the shape of cyclical waves while others saw the shape but not the element of regular time. Still, the one thing that was becoming clear was that there was a hidden interconnectivity that tied everything together.

Source of Discoverying the 8.6 Year Business Cycle

LISTING OF INTERNATIONAL FINANCE PANICS 1683-1907

1683							
1711	1720	1731	1745	1763	1772	1783	1792
1814	1818	1825	1857	1866	1869	1871	1872
	1873	1884	1890	1893	1895	1896	1899
1901	1903	1907					

224/26events = 8.615

Martin Armstrong
ArmstrongEconomics.COM

When I began my research, I did not even believe that cycles existed. Never in school had anyone ever mentioned the cyclical nature of the universe. There was no possible formal educational training one could study to learn about cycles. I was merely a kid, unfettered by formal tradition and with no career to jeopardize as an academic bucking the establishment. I was untainted by tradition and free to roam where perhaps no one dared to go.

What set me in motion was effectively the 1966 Stock Market Crash. That was a watershed event where no one understood what was truly afoot. While in high school, at the age of 13, I began working for a bullion dealer. Gold in those days traded in coin form since bullion was not legalized until 1975. I struck lucky, and by chance picked up some rare Canadian pennies in 1965. I had several bags, and there were four varieties. The one I had soared in price to the point where a roll of 50 would bring in over $1,000. For a brief and shining moment, I had become a millionaire on paper. I held back, wrongly thinking the price would go higher. What I witnessed in the Crash of 1966 changed my life forever.

It is part of my family history. My father's relative made a fortune in the 1920s and lost a fortune in the stock market crash that began in 1929. So, my father, a conservative man, became upset seeing his son making a lot of money before he could even drive. My father feared I would become a speculator and perhaps go down the same path as a previous ancestor.

He attempted to shape me by handing me my first book assignment, which was Aristotle. I was given the summer to read and understand the book well enough for a discussion by the end of the season. I was told that Aristotle was the teacher of Alexander the Great. He said if Aristotle was good enough to teach Alexander, then he was someone I should learn from in life. My father died in 1983. I handed my son Aristotle at the age of 12 to keep the family tradition alive.

The Boston Globe—Saturday, August 13, 1966   **11**

Fidelity Trend Assets at $29.91

NEW YORK—Fidelity Trend Fund Reorted net assets were $958,105',389, or $29.91 a share, on June 30, compared with $307,505,664 or $19.28, on June 30, 1965.

On June 30 Fidelity Trend had 32,033,490 shares outstanding compared with 15,953,152 shares June 30, 1965.

Fidelity Trend Fund was a net buyer of stocks during the latest quarter.

I recall my father arranging a meeting with an insurance broker who came over one night to sell me a Fidelity Trend mutual fund. He said this option was more conservative, and I should not speculate in commodities. It peaked at almost $31 on February 10, 1966, and crashed to $23.26 by October 10, 1966. I asked my father if this was the way rich people made their money.

1964 / 1965 United States Silver Demonetization

This was the last year that silver was used to mint coinage in the United States whereby the silver content was 90% now valued at $2.1.

A blend of copper and nickel covering a copper core in this case. The value of the metal in this coin is now 2 cents.

Back in 1964, that was the last year silver coins were issued. President John F. Kennedy had signed an Executive Order 11110 on June 4, 1963, which ended both the use of silver in coinage as well as the issuing of silver certificates. This executive order delegated to the secretary of the Treasury the president's authority to issue silver certificates under the Thomas Amendment of the Agricultural Adjustment Act, as amended by the Gold Reserve Act. The order allowed the secretary to issue silver certificates, if any were needed, during the transitionary period under President Kennedy's plan to eliminate silver certificates.

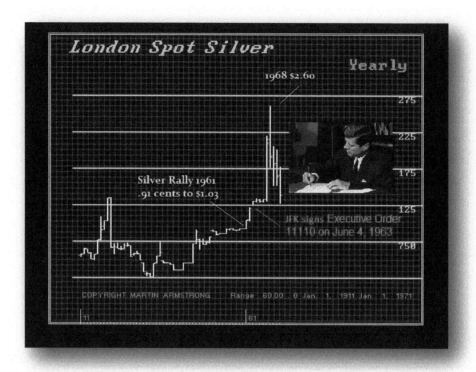

On November 28, 1961, President Kennedy halted sales of silver by the Treasury Department. Silver had been rising steadily since the low made back in 1932. In 1961, silver rallied sharply, jumping from 91 cents a troy ounce to $1.03. The increasing demand of silver as an industrial metal had led to an increase in the market price of silver above the United States government's fixed price. This led to a decline in the government's excess silver reserves by over 80% during 1961. President Kennedy also called upon Congress to phase out silver certificates in favor of Federal Reserve notes.

There was a conspiracy theory about JFK's Executive Order 11110 as the motive for his assassination since it removed the Federal Reserve's authority to issue money and transfer that money to the Treasury. In his book *Crossfire*, Jim Marrs presented the theory, stating that Kennedy was trying to reign in the power of the Federal Reserve, and forces opposed to such action might have played at least some part in his assassination.

1957 Silver Certificate   1963 Federal Reserve Note

The theory truly was off the wall since Kennedy's Executive Order had the opposite effect of handing exclusive power to the Federal Reserve to print currency. The 1957 issue was the last of the silver certificates issued by the U.S. Treasury. The 1963 series began the "Legal Tender" issue, omitting any reference to silver, which had been defined as "lawful money" and it expressly states it was issued by the Federal Reserve. So much for Kennedy being assassinated for taking power away from the Federal Reserve.

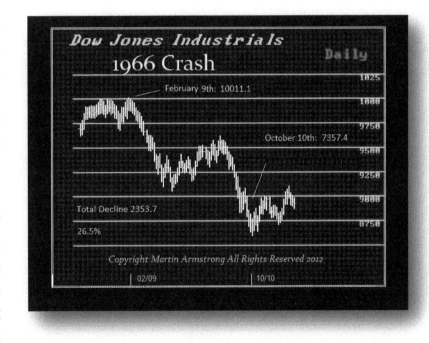

The rise of silver from 1961 reflected the sentiment of the period as inflationary. When the crash came in 1966, it was far more than just a collapse in stock prices. It was a contagion that I did not understand at the time, but I watched it in a very active way. The stock market boomed before the crash, as did rare coins and just about everything else. The permanent Kennedy tax cuts in 1964 created a huge consumer-buying binge that hit nearly every sector domestically. I did not understand this at the time, but the seeds of contagion had been set in motion. The stock market correction spared nothing.

This watershed event is what got me interested. I saw everything rise to excessive levels and then crash and burn. It was not a cycle I was exploring but a contagion that I did not yet understand. I subsequently identified this as a pure "Phase Transition," the sudden exponential move that marks a departure from normal

trading, even to an explosive move, wiping out both sides. That resonated in my mind from physics class. It reminded me of how water boiled in a pot. It does not occur in a steady linear progression. Instead, it suddenly bursts into a boil.

I believe I was in 9th grade when my history professor brought in an old black and white film for us to watch in class. Had I not gotten a part-time job in that coin store where I bought my first Roman coin for $10, the movie may not have resonated with me. Back then, people bought and sold gold coins, which was legal as long as they were dated before 1948. Austria, Hungary, and Mexico issued restrikes, which were coins still dated pre-1948, so they could sell gold in the U.S. retail marketplace. As a result, I was well aware that the value of gold was $35 an ounce.

Film Toast of New York
1869 Character Jim Fisk Reading the Ticker-Tape as Gold hits $162

The film, *The Toast of New York*, was about the Panic of 1869 and Jim Fisk's attempt to corner the gold market. There was a scene where Jim Fisk is at the ticker tape where he turns and quotes gold at $162. Now, I knew from working that gold was $35. Suddenly, I was confronted with an anomaly. I was taught that everything was linear. How was it possible for gold to be $162 in 1869 and $35 today in the 1960s?

At first, I assumed it was just a movie. But it bothered me. There was a question in the back of my mind that I could not answer. I just could not imagine how the price of gold fell from $162 in 1869 to $35 in 1960. I was simply compelled to understand something that was against everything I was told in school.

follows disaster. Before 11 o'clock, the price again sprang up five per cent. further at a single leap, and, in less than half an hour, amid the hottest excitement of the masses that surged to and fro, inside and outside of the Gold Room, it leaped up to 160, and then, for a few seconds, touched 164. The shouts and cries of the hundreds of active operators seemed here like the outpourings of maniacs, and for a short time a pallor seemed to overspread the faces, and a tremor to overcome the persons of the mass, which had been wrought up to a point beyond human endurance. The majority felt the

I went to the library and looked up the price of gold in the microfilm copies of *The New York Times* for September 24, 1869, and it changed my life. There it was in black and white. *The New York Times* reported on Saturday, September 25, 1989: "It leaped up to 160, and then, for a few seconds, touched 164." It was real. It profoundly shook my belief system to the very foundation.

I was still unaware of cyclical theory in economics. A nonlinear fact from history

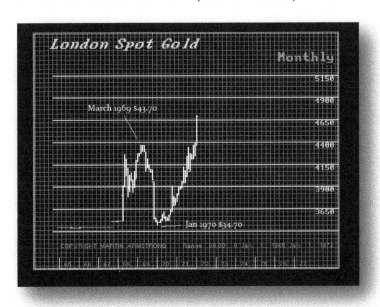

suddenly confronted me. As I began to read in libraries on my own, I kept looking in microfilms to ascertain these sudden bursts of price movement. Meanwhile, I had observed booms and busts in various sectors in 1966, 1968, and then in 1970, for a brief moment, gold fell below the $35 fixed value set at Bretton Woods. I was now confronted by the realization that not even pegs would hold.

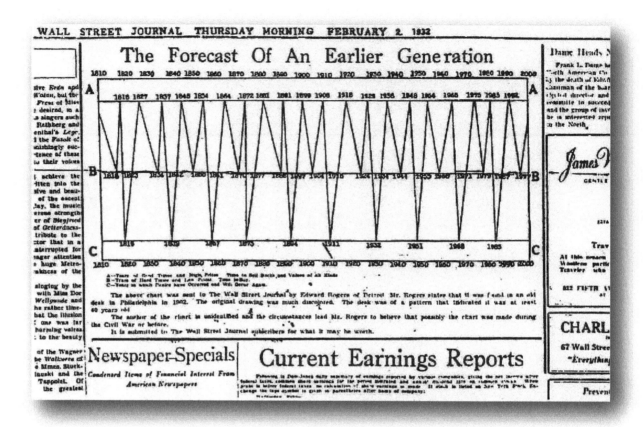

I eventually came upon a chart of the business cycle published in the *Wall Street Journal* back on February 2, 1932. It began to resonate in my mind that the booms and busts I had been personally witnessing in the late 1960s to early 1970s were a type of waveform. The caption accompanying the chart read:

> "The above chart was sent to the Wall Street Journal by Edward Rogers of Detroit. Mr. Rogers states that it was found in an old desk in Philadelphia in 1902. The original drawing was much discolored. The desk was of a pattern that indicated it was at least 40 years old.
>
> The author of the chart is unidentified and the circumstances lead Mr. Rogers to believe that possibly the chart was made during the Civil War or before. It is submitted to Wall Street Journal subscribers for what it may be worth."

Energy waves pass through the water, which is the medium. The bottle moves up and down as the energy waves pass through the water. The water itself is not actually moving.

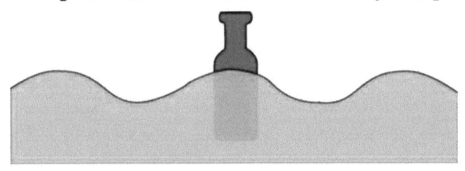

I suddenly remembered from physics class that the waves in the oceans are actually energy passing through the water rather than the water moving. I had always loved the ocean, and noticed that a floating bottle would move up and down as the energy passed through the water. It would move only with the current until it reached the shore.

LISTING OF YEARS IN WHICH PANICS TOOK PLACE

INTERNATIONALLY

1683							
1711	1720	1731	1745	1763	1772	1783	1792
1814	1818	1825	1857	1866	1869	1871	1872
	1873	1884	1890	1893	1895	1896	1899
1901	1903	1907					

I went to the Firestone Library at Princeton University to search old newspapers on microfilm. I then came upon a list of panics from 1683 to 1907 during my research before the Great Depression. I hadn't realized at that moment that this was a list of international panics rather than just domestic events in the United States. That would later prove to be crucial, but at that instant, I did not pay attention.

I just naturally added the total number of years (224) and divided it by the number of events (26). This generated 8.615384615, which was just an average, nothing more. I began to investigate history to see how it lined up with events.

Battle of Vienna, September 12th, 1683

One of the first things that jumped out at me was that there were differences between the events with respect to intensity. It appeared that there were groups of waves that would build in volatility and significance. It appeared that the groups were forming clusters of 51.6-year intervals. Additionally, I noticed that 1683 was not a panic that was concentrated in the United States. I know my history, and that was the date when the Ottoman Empire laid siege to Vienna. At the time, Vienna was the capital of the Holy Roman Empire in Europe and thus the financial capital of Europe, which was on the decline.

In 1655, Leopold I was chosen as the king of Hungary; the following year, in 1656, he became the king of Bohemia. Then in 1657, he became the king of Croatia. In July 1658, more than a year after his father's death, he was elected emperor at Frankfurt in spite of the intrigues of Jules Cardinal Mazarin, who wished to place Ferdinand Maria on the imperial throne, the elector of Bavaria, or some other prince whose elevation would break the Habsburg succession. In governing his own lands, Leopold found his chief difficulties in Hungary, where unrest was caused partly by his desire to crush Protestantism. A rising was suppressed in 1671, and for some years, Hungary was treated with great severity. In 1681, after another uprising, some grievances were removed and a less repressive policy was adopted, but this did not deter the Hungarians from revolting again.

1683 Liberation of Vienna
ArmstrongEconomics.COM

The Sultan of the Ottoman Empire used the Hungarian rebels as an excuse to invade. The Sultan sent an enormous army into Austria early in 1683, which advanced with hardly any resistance from Vienna. The Sultan laid siege from July to September 1683. Leopold took refuge at Passau. The leaders finally realized the gravity of the situation; this was really an invasion by the Ottoman Empire to take Europe. Eventually, the German princes, including Saxony and Bavaria, led their contingent troops to Vienna under the leadership of Charles, Duke of Lorraine. The king of Poland, John Sobieski, joined the campaign. The Turks particularly feared him. Sobieski came with 20,000 troops and led the troops himself. He drove the Turks back to the Raab, and thereby freed Hungary in the process. By leading the decisive Polish cavalry charge himself, Sobieski was acclaimed the hero of Christendom. On September 12, 1683, the allied army fell upon the enemy, who was utterly routed, and Vienna was saved.

The Austrian silver Thalers were not resumed and did not reappear until 1692. However, they did strike a silver medal celebrating the liberation of Vienna and the saving of Christendom.

Of course, the Panic of 1711 was due to widespread war throughout Europe. The French defeated a combined Dutch–Austrian force in the Battle of Denain. Sweden defeated Denmark and Saxony in the Battle of Gadebusch. In Switzerland, there was a civil war between the Protestants and the Catholics. The Catholic cantons were defeated in the Battle of Villmergen, and eventually, the Treaty of

Aargau was signed establishing Protestant dominance in Switzerland, but they preserved the rights of Catholics. There was also a slave rebellion in New York City during April 6 and 7, where they killed nine whites. This resulted in 21 slaves and others being convicted and executed.

Peter the Great wanted access to the Baltic Sea and Baltic trade. In 1700, he began the Northern War with Sweden, which lasted for 21 years. In the course of the war, St. Petersburg was founded in 1703. Peter moved the capital from Moscow to St. Petersburg in 1711, and by the end of the war, Russia's victory gained him vast lands on the Baltic coast that opened up access to European trade. When the Northern War ended in 1721, Peter the Great proclaimed himself emperor and Russia an Empire.

The next target was 1720, which was the famous South Sea Bubble in Britain and the Mississippi Bubble in France. Both focused internationally on emerging markets.

The Economic Confidence Model

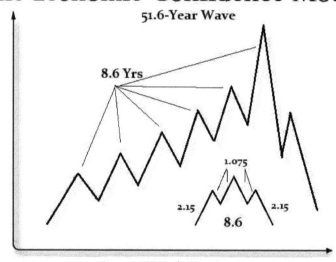

Copyright Martin Armstrong, 1979

The shape of the business cycle appeared in groups of six waves of 8.6 years. They built up into waves of 51.6 years. I began to read others who had investigated the cyclical activity. I began to understand that this wave structure was the international business cycle and not limited to simply one country. There were events that were obviously global contagions, others that began as domestic events, and others that were due to investing in emerging markets internationally.

I was also familiar with the history of the Roman Empire and that of Athens. I knew the coinage of the Romans could be dated to specific years thanks to the practice of recording successive titles each year. I was able to reconstruct Rome's entire monetary history to backtest this business cycle into ancient times. To my shock, I found the same intervals that were present in ancient data, such as the 52-year decline in the Roman follis before reform.

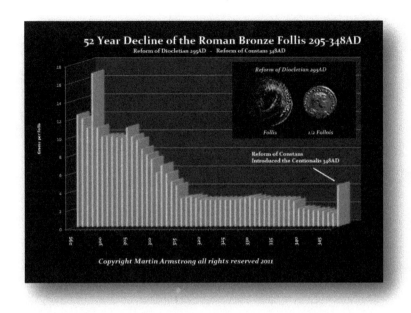

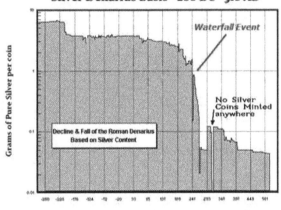

©Martin Armstrong - All Rights Reserved 2012

I reconstructed the Roman Empire's monetary system to see how this cycle performed throughout thousands of years. I was attempting to answer a question no academic ever seemed to address — how did Rome fall? Was it like a 747 plane coming for a nice gradual landing or was it abrupt? When I put it all together, the answer was startling — a violent collapse in just 8.6 years.

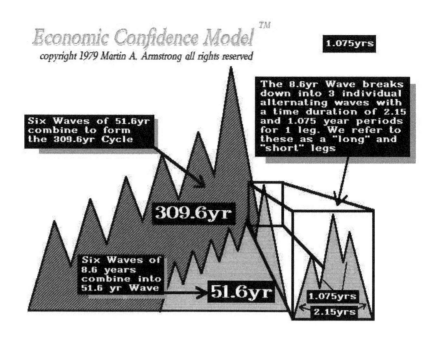

Economic Confidence Model ™
copyright 1979 Martin A. Armstrong all rights reserved

Six Waves of 51.6yr combine to form the 309.6yr Cycle

The 8.6yr Wave breaks down into 3 individual alternating waves with a time duration of 2.15 and 1.075 year periods for 1 leg. We refer to these as a "long" and "short" legs

1.075yrs

309.6yr

Six Waves of 8.6 years combine into 51.6 yr Wave

51.6yr

1.075yrs

2.15yrs

Backtesting this cyclical wave through the centuries revealed that it was actually fractal. Not only did six waves of 8.6 years build into major waves of 51.6 years that appeared similar to Kondratieff's work of long-waves, but I discovered that six waves of 51.6 years built up into major waves of 309.6 years. The structure of the business cycle was taking shape.

All historians agreed that the peak of the Roman Empire took place during the reign of Marcus Aurelius. His death began the decline and fall, but 51.6 years from his death, we arrive

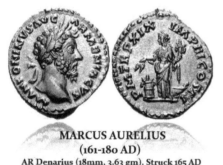

MARCUS AURELIUS
(161-180 AD)
AR Denarius (18mm, 3.63 gm). Struck 165 AD
Annona standing left, holding grain-ears and cornucopiae; modius at feet to left; prow at feet to right illustrating importation of grain and ample food supply

at the last of the Severan Dynasty emperors — Severus Alexander. His assassination began the final decline and fall of the Roman Empire during the 3rd century AD.

Indeed, it was Severus Alexander who refurbished the Colosseum. He proudly announced his achievements on his coinage.

Severus Alexander
(222-235AD)
celebrating restoration of Colosseum

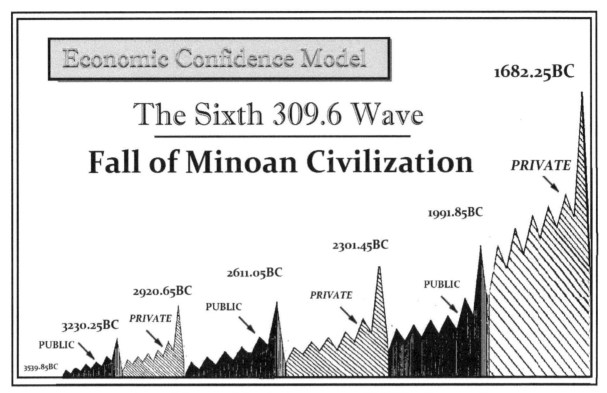

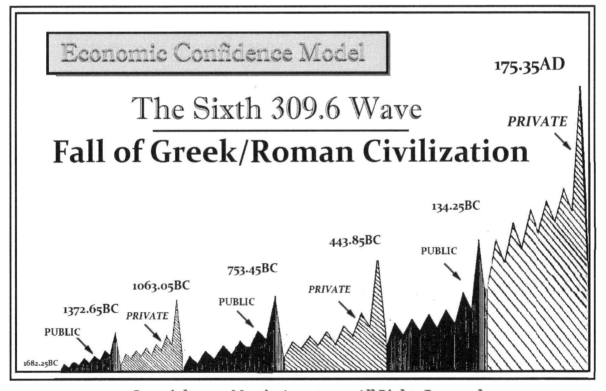

It was rather shocking to discover how the same timing dominated in ancient times. Even taking 1929.75 and successively scrolling back through time arrives at 31 BC. That was the Battle of Actium where the decisive confrontation of the Roman Republic's Final War defeated Mark Antony and Cleopatra on September 2, 31 BC. It also marks the beginning of Octavian's rise to become the first emperor of Rome, thereby ending the Republic. The 1929.75 event was more than the Great Depression. It also marked the rise of socialism.

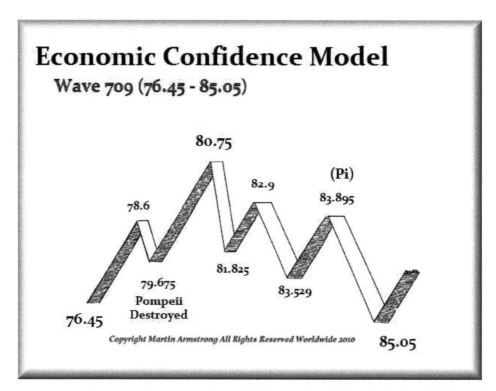

Yet, there was still something in the background. What was emerging was more than merely a business cycle. There was a link to nature. Major disasters would alter society dramatically. The Minoan Age was brought to an end by the volcanic eruption of Thera. So many other events were also linked to natural disasters. Even the destruction of Pompeii took place on a turning point. The 1906 San Francisco earthquake set in motion the Panic of 1907.

What was emerging was that the business cycle was not simply a one-dimensional cyclical wave. It was the composite of everything from planetary weather, volcanoes, earthquakes, and wars. Julius Caesar's assassination (100–44 BC) took place when the 8.6–year wave #694 ended and just began (52.55 BC–43.95 BC).

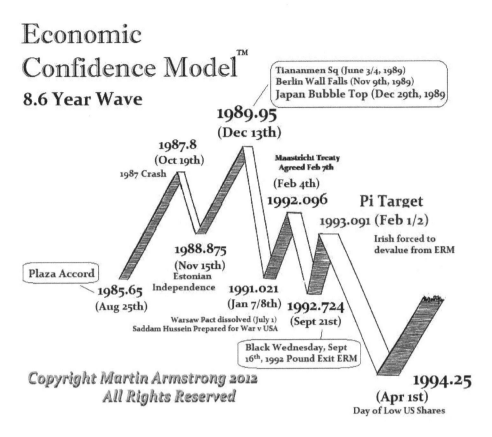

Economic Confidence Model™

8.6 Year Wave

Tiananmen Sq (June 3/4, 1989)
Berlin Wall Falls (Nov 9th, 1989)
Japan Bubble Top (Dec 29th, 1989)

1989.95
(Dec 13th)

1987.8
(Oct 19th)
1987 Crash

Maastricht Treaty
Agreed Feb 7th
(Feb 4th)
1992.096

Pi Target
1993.091 (Feb 1/2)
Irish forced to
devalue from ERM

1988.875
(Nov 15th)
Estonian
Independence

Plaza Accord
1985.65
(Aug 25th)

1991.021
(Jan 7/8th)
Warsaw Pact dissolved (July 1)
Saddam Hussein Prepared for War v USA

1992.724
(Sept 21st)

Black Wednesday, Sept
16th, 1992 Pound Exit ERM

*Copyright Martin Armstrong 2012
All Rights Reserved*

1994.25
(Apr 1st)
Day of Low US Shares

I called this the Economic Confidence Model (ECM) because it was a question of confidence that would make people spend or hoard their wealth in times of uncertainty. The startling confrontation was that events would take place on the precise day of the ECM. The mere fact that events would happen precisely to the day seemed impossible. The turning point was 1987.8, which was October 19 (.8 x 365).

Naturally, I first assumed this had to be just a coincidence. I began to explore events and their relationship to this ECM. To my shock, it was no coincidence. There were other targets unfolding precisely to the day or within 24 hours thereof.

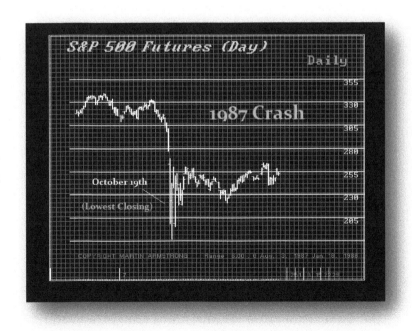

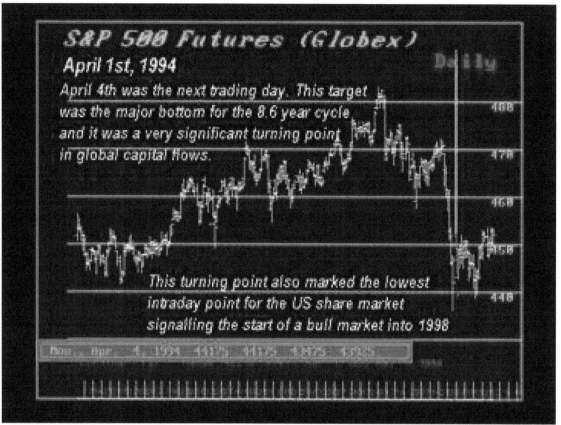

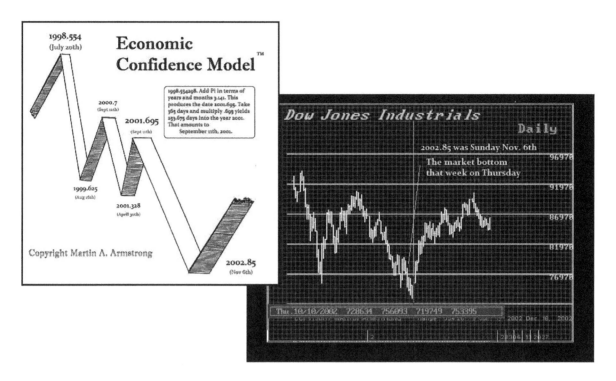

In some cases, it was not precisely to the day but to the week, such as on Thursday the 10th. The Nasdaq, where all the action was during the Dot.com Bubble in 2000, bottomed that same week but on Tuesday 8th. In both cases, the ECM target picked the week.

The pi target from the high of each 8.6–year cycle wave also tends to be rather

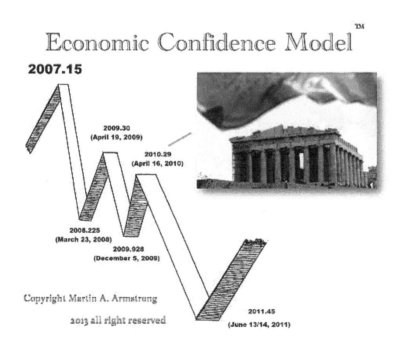

important. In the case of the turning point of April 16, 2010, this target produced the precise day that Greece petitioned the IMF for a bailout, beginning the Eurozone debt crisis. The chaos that unleashed was huge. For the first time, traders began to look closely at all the member states and began to attack the various bond markets in Europe.

181

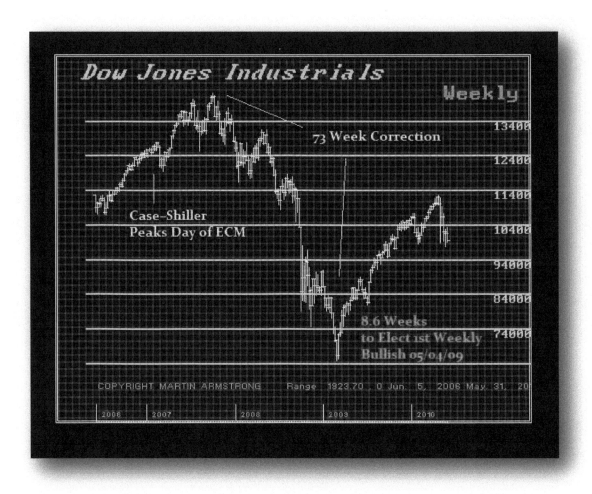

When we look at the 2007.15 turning point, which was February 24, 2007, this ended up being the peak in the real estate market. There was an initial break in the market.

Even when we look at the Dow Jones Real Estate Index, we see a February high here too. While the stock market continued into October for a high after making an initial correction on the February target, it was clear that the ECM had picked the high in the underlying market that ultimate was responsible for the crash — mortgages.

THE MORNING CALL

THURSDAY, OCTOBER 1, 2015 NEWS 11

NATION & WORLD

Russia launches airstrikes in Syria

U.S. mulls Putin's claim aerial attacks targeted militants

BY PATRICK J. McDONNELL, W.J. HENNIGAN AND NABIH BULOS
Tribune Newspapers

BEIRUT — Russian warplanes launched their first airstrikes Wednesday against opposition targets in Syria, signaling a new and uncertain turn in the long conflict there.

Russian officials said the attacks in support of President Bashar Assad's government targeted positions of the Islamic State, the al-Qaida breakaway faction that has seized control of vast areas in Syria and neighboring Iraq.

ca and the Middle East, causing militants to temporarily set aside their differences to fight together against the Assad government and its Russian backer.

"There's no doubt extremists will look to amplify their recruiting pitches to would-be foreign fighters by capitalizing on Russia's expanded role in Syria," a U.S. counterterrorism official said, speaking on condition of anonymity in discussing internal assessments.

"Depending on the scope of Moscow's actions in Syria, it could also help energize jihadi efforts both inside and outside Syria."

Despite or perhaps because of such concerns, Russian officials insisted Wednesday that their airstrikes hit Islamic militants.

A video shows billowing smoke after airstrikes hit the Syrian town of Talbiseh on Wednesday, the same day Russia's military carried out aerial attacks in the country for the first time, targeting what Moscow said were terrorist positions.

HOMS MEDIA CENTRE

We warned that the 2015.75 turning point would be the peak in confidence in government. This also marked a critical geopolitical event that took place precisely on the day of the turning point. Russia sent in troops to Syria precisely on the target 2015.75. On September 30, 2015 (2015.75), Russia gave the U.S. one-hour notice before they began bombing both ISIS and rebels who were seeking to overthrow the Syrian government. *The Washington Times* wrote on September 10, 2015, "Angela Merkel welcomes refugees to Germany despite rising anti-immigrant movement." Merkel created the entire refugee crisis as a diversion because Germany was being viewed as the harsh enforcer of loans to Greece. The Russian invasion really sent the refugees pouring into Europe.

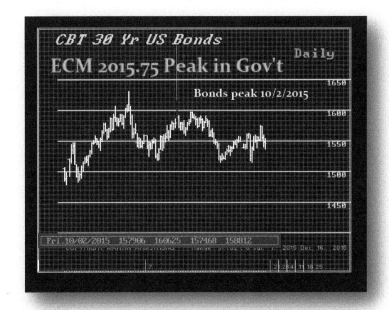

Indeed, even politically, things were changing. The forecast my computer made was that in 2016 the establishment would lose, and indeed Trump was elected.

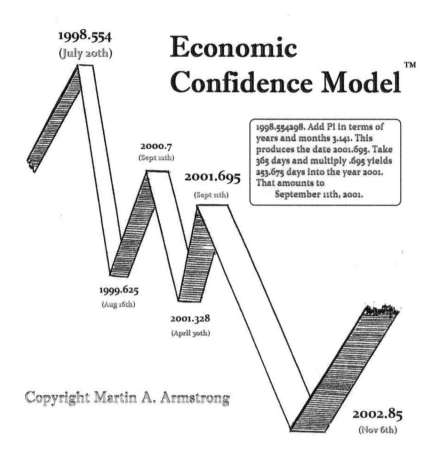

1998.554
(July 20th)

Economic Confidence Model™

2000.7
(Sept 12th)

2001.695
(Sept 11th)

1998.554298. Add Pi in terms of years and months 3.141. This produces the date 2001.695. Take 365 days and multiply .695 yields 253.675 days into the year 2001. That amounts to September 11th, 2001.

1999.625
(Aug 16th)

2001.328
(April 30th)

Copyright Martin A. Armstrong

2002.85
(Nov 6th)

The same pi calculation from the 1998.54 peak in the 8.6-year wave of the Economic Confidence Model was 1998.554298 to be precise. This produced the pi target date of 2001.695. Taking 365 days and multiplying that by .695 yields 253.675 days in the year 2001. This translates to precisely September 11, 2001. How geopolitical events will unfold on precise targets is just amazing.

Many people have asked me over the years how it is possible to forecast. The computer program I wrote takes into account absolutely everything globally from weather, markets, commodities, debts, to international capital flows. It will also identify regions and historically how and where wars are chronic problems. Cyclical trends for each region determine that, yet at times it is augmented by a combination of capital flows. Picking things like the fall of communism back in 1989 when the Berlin Wall fell were based cyclically on that trend's outcome. That was 72 years from the Russian Revolution of 1917. That was the perfect target for the volatility models within the ECM. Both converged, so it made it really a piece of cake, statistically.

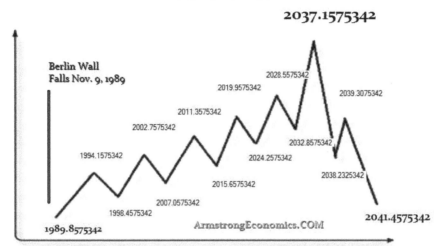

Collapse of Socialism/Communism
(1989 - 2041)

2037.1575342

Berlin Wall
Falls Nov. 9, 1989

2028.5575342

2019.9575342

2039.3075342

2011.3575342

2002.7575342

1994.1575342

2032.8575342

2024.2575342

2015.6575342

2038.2325342

2007.0575342

1998.4575342

ArmstrongEconomics.COM

1989.8575342

2041.4575342

The collapse of the Soviet Union came in 1991. That was a simple two-year reactionary process all within a cyclical forecast from the turning point in 1989. However, the collapse of the Russian bond market that set in motion a major contagion and the Long-Term Capital Management debacle in 1998 was determined from a capital flow and cyclical perspective given the ECM peaked July 20, 1998. That came 8.6 years following the fall of the Berlin Wall. I delivered

that forecast in London and it made the front page of the second section of the *London Financial Times*. After that forecast, just about every intelligence agency began paying attention to our models.

The above chart is calculated from the day the Berlin Wall fell – November 9, 1989. Our forecast for the fall of the Russian financial system in 1998 was 8.6 years from the fall of the Berlin Wall. But look at the dates beyond that time. In 2002 we saw the low in the U.S. market post–Dot.com Bubble. In 2007, it was the peak in the world economy and start of

185

the real estate meltdown. In 2015, Russia invaded Syria, refugees were welcomed into Europe by Merkel, and it marked the rise in interest rates at the Fed. The dates to come are 2024, 2028, and 2037.

Clearly, life is a journey to acquire knowledge. So much research is bogus because it begins with a predetermined conclusion and goes off in pursuit of data that supports the conclusion. That is no way to conduct research.

Planetary Movements

	Venus	Earth	Mars	Jupiter
Period, d	224	365.25	687.00	4332.00
Period, y	0.61	1.00	1.88	11.86
Orbits 7	4.3	16	4	
Pi Cycles	1.0	1.0	7.0	11.0

Further unbiased investigation revealed that there was perhaps a reason why such a cycle would be accurate rather than just an average approximation. It turned out that 8.615 years converted to days turned out to be pi — 3,141 days. Suddenly something was running through everything that was extraordinarily precise. Pi was the perfect cycle. The fractal nature of the entire structure was incredible. Three times 8.6 was 25.8. The precession of the equinox was about 25,800 years. The Venus orbital cycle is 224.7 days. Seven orbits of Venus complete in 4.3 years, or two 2.15-year cycles (224.7*7/365.25 = 4.3). So, each 2.15-year cycle traces 3.5 orbits of Venus. Indeed, some planets also seem to line up with the pi frequency.

I have never been someone who looks at the stars. I confess I do not pay attention to astrology. Nonetheless, everything is connected. The word "lunatic" refers to people who tend to be affected by changes of the moon, which was said to cause intermittent insanity. There is even folklore of a werewolf who would be affected by a full moon. Of course, these are exaggerations, but some people are affected by the moon. People with schizophrenia generally exhibit 1.8% of increased violent or aggressive episodes during full moons. An analysis of mental health data found a significant effect of moon phases, but only on schizophrenic patients.

There have been at least 40 published studies on the purported lunar-lunacy connection. There are also at least 20 published studies on the purported lunar-birthrate connection that claim births increase during a full moon. There have also been studies that show the incidence of crimes committed on full moon days is much higher than on all other days (*Full Moon and Crime*, P. Thakur and D Sharma). So obviously, we cannot simply dismiss the correlations with anything at this stage in our investigation. It is just that nothing can be reduced to a single cause and effect.

Public v Private

I conducted my research by reading newspapers in the library. I found that the only way to do such research was going directly to contemporary sources. I knew that the great danger in research was that people interpret history according to their current belief system. The funniest example of failing to understand the thinking process at any point in time is when they named the city of Philadelphia. The slogan has always been "The City of Brotherly Love." The problem is that they looked at the Greek translation of "brotherly love" in the view of Christianity. In truth, Ptolemy II of Egypt is known as Philadelphus, which meant "brotherly love" but incest — he married his sister. So, it was obviously correct to translate Philadelphus as "brotherly love," but it was by no means Christian.

Ptolemy I and Berenice I (left)
Ptolemy II Philadelphus & sister-wife Arsinoe II (right)

ArmstrongEconomics.COM

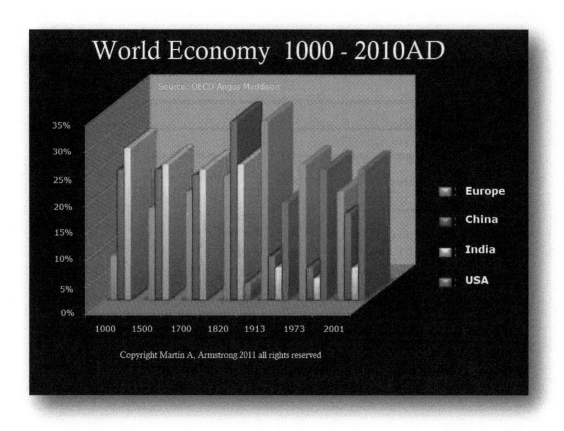

Understanding that I cannot judge things by what my current understanding might be, it was essential to read the newspapers of the day and contemporary writers to comprehend the actual thinking process during the period of investigation. I understood that there were events throughout history where capital migrated from region to region, both for trade and investment purposes as well as for security. After all, even the financial capital would migrate. The Persians conquered Babylon and were defeated by the Greeks giving rise to Athens as the ancient world's second financial capital. Athens fell to Alexander the Great of Macedonia, who then created the first world currency that standardized the monetary system.

The Greeks fell to the Romans, who then acquired the new financial capital of the world. When Rome fell, that title migrated to India, who then lost it to China. Spain bumped into America when trying to get to India, thanks to Columbus in 1492. The Italian cities lost their capital when Spain defaulted seven times on their debts. The financial capital migrated to the Dutch, and then they lost it to Britain. The British sought to capture the wealth of Asia, looking to conquer India and China. The British lost the title to the United States who will lose it to China, most likely after 2032.

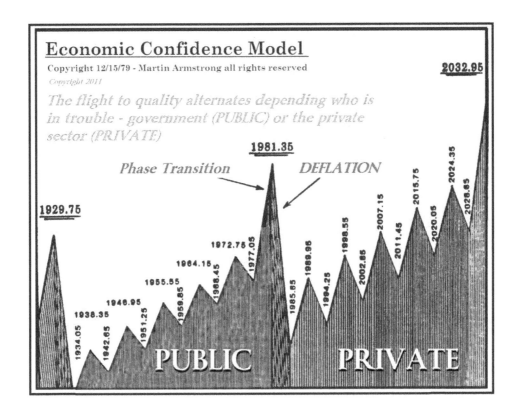

What also began to emerge from reading contemporary news articles was that the thinking process was strikingly different pre-1929. It became clear that capital moved distinctly differently in one 51.6-year wave when compared to another. This difference followed an oscillating trend that moved back and forth from one 51.6-year wave to the next. In studying how capital reacted, it became clear that the capital moved back and forth between government and private sector investments. It boiled down to who you trusted.

For example, during the 1929 wave, capital investment was quite intense in the private sector. It was obvious that the prevailing atmosphere was one in which

investments were focused on new innovations and advancements during the rise of the Industrial Revolution. Capital was investing in the railroad up until 1907. Then as the combustion engine revolutionized agriculture, it also eliminated the need for tracks. The rally into 1919 was focused on World War I, so that was a raw commodity cycle. The next wave was investment in industry, with the lead sector being the automobile.

But trains, planes, and automobiles also meant that remote real estate regions were suddenly an opportunity. This led to the Florida Land Boom, which turned into a bubble that burst in 1927. Capital shifted its focus and steered into equities, and that culminated into yet another bubble in 1929. This is a private wave of investment looking for the next innovation and opportunity.

Virtually every 8.6-year turning point became known as the "panic" of something or other depending on the nation under study. One could state that capital appeared to be more "confident" in the private investment sector as opposed to that of the public sector represented by government bonds. However, the higher levels of volatility also reflected a greater level of uncertainty about government.

Andrew Mellon
(1855-1937)

"This market will end when 'Gentlemen prefer bonds.'"
1929

This quote is sometimes on occasion attributed to Andrew Carnegie, but appears to belong to Andrew Mellon former US Treasury Sec..

Indeed, when the stock market began to crash, Andrew Mellon (1855–1937) made his famous statement, "Gentlemen prefer bonds." Of course, they would make a film and change the words in 1953 to "Gentlemen Prefer Blonds."

However, the following 51.6-year wave, which peaked in 1981, was a period of high public governmental confidence on the part of capital. Here we find a completely different psychology behind capital investments and a tremendous concentration of capital in government bond markets.

Creative Destruction

Continuing the research through the various groups of 51.6-year waves revealed this perpetual oscillation in capital movement. The human's actual thought process, relative to their economic philosophy, was actually shifting back and forth between each 51.6-year wave formation. This constant oscillation in capital movement between the private and public sector paved the way for the foundation of economic shifts.

Indeed, I read Schumpeter's theory of innovation that sought to explain the business cycle. Schumpeter studied how the capitalist system was affected by market innovations. In his book *Capitalism, Socialism and Democracy,* he described a process which has been best described as the forces of creative destruction:

> "... the opening up of new markets, foreign or domestic, and the organizational development [...] illustrate the same process of industrial mutation, that incessantly revolutionizes the economic structure from within, incessantly destroying the old one, incessantly creating a new one."

(Schumpeter 1942, 83)

Indeed, Schumpeter's observation of creative destruction was right on point and we still face this process today as robots and Artificial Intelligence begin to replace jobs. The railroads created a distribution network that gave birth to mail orders, which allowed companies like Sears and Roebuck & Co. to expand. The introduction of the combustion engine was also a wave of creative destruction. They competed with the railroads and eliminated jobs in that field. Tracks were no longer necessary to provide a means to distribute goods. This created the trucking industry. Insofar as agriculture was concerned, the tractor replaced field hands. That sector expanded in production but contracted in employment, dropping 41% of the civil workforce in 1900 to just 3% by 1980 — hence, creative destruction.

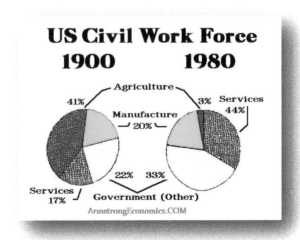

191

Port of New York City - 19th Century

The idea of a universal guaranteed basic income has been floating around since the 1960s. The driving force behind it is always the displacement of jobs due to technological advancements that result in creative destruction. The resistance mentioned by the horse and buggy industry paying off British politicians to restrict the development of automobiles is an example of the core issue behind the process of creative destruction.

The entire Labor Union Movement of the 19th and 20th centuries attempted to manipulate the economy by preventing the evolution of technology, which produces the wave of creative destruction. Instead of adopting new technologies and improving skills, labor unions fought hard to stop the cycle in its tracks. They kept demanding higher wages for the same work and became very militant. New York City was the largest port in the United States. The labor unions overpriced themselves to the point that no ships dock in New York City today.

The Japanese and German auto industries made headway into the U.S. marketplace because the quality of American cars declined as labor unions saw it as a war against management to do as little as possible. The political involvement turned to tariffs to appease the unions because they courted their votes. Nobody looked at it from the consumer's perspective.

Willis C. Hawley (left) and Reed Smoot (right)
Hawley Republican Congressman from Oregon
Chairman of the House Ways and Means Committee
Smoot Republican Senator from Utah
Chairman of the Senate Finance Committee

When we examine the infamous Smoot–Hawley Protectionist Act, which many claim created the Great Depression, we find that it was in response to the wave of creative destruction that was impacting agriculture. The introduction of the combustion engine drastically altered agriculture by increasing yield and reducing required labor.

By the late 1920s, the United States economy had changed remarkably. There were exceptional gains in productivity due to electrification, which increased the production of goods, and the combustion engine profoundly altered agricultural production. With tractors replacing horses and mules, previously, up to 25% of the agricultural land had been used to feed horses and mules. This land suddenly became available to produce crops. The ability to produce food soared and exceeded market demand, creating an overproduction of wheat as well as underconsumption since the price declined for 14 years following World War I as they no longer needed to feed troops and Europe.

Senator Reed Smoot (1862–1941), a Republican from Utah and the chairman of the Senate Finance Committee, and Congressman Willis C. Hawley (1864–1941), who was a Republican from Oregon and chairman of the House Ways and Means Committee, were focused on listening to farmers who wanted high

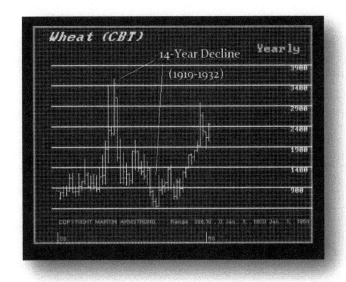

tariffs to prevent competition. Neither Utah nor Oregon were industrial states. The Smoot–Hawley Act was to protect farmers from falling prices. The Silver Democrats did the same for silver miners during the second half of the 19th century.

The imposition of tariffs to protect jobs means that the consumer is expected to reduce their standard of living to support overpaid jobs. The answer is never to manipulate the economy to alter what someone does not like but to live with the cycle and understand that there are always such waves of creative destruction.

Many universities still teach economics under antiquated theories of Marx and Keynes that were based upon fixed exchange rate systems. You cannot go to school to get a degree in hedge fund management or even how to hedge currency to protect a company in international trade. Many schools do not teach high-end programming. All these skill sets are usually learned by people interested in the field who are self-taught. Ernst & Young stopped requiring degrees to be an accountant. Google, Apple, and many other large companies no longer require employees to have a college degree in the United States.

The careers that are rapidly moving into not requiring college degrees are Marketing Designer, Publicity Assistant, Senior Manager of Finance, Production Assistant, Senior Editor, Production Editor, Art Director, and more. Even at IBM, they no longer require a college degree for positions as a Financial Blockchain Engineer, Lead Recruiter, Contract & Negotiations Professional, Product Manager, Entry-Level System Services Representative, Research Staff Member, and Client Solution Executive. Formal education is far behind the technology curve and is becoming antiquated. The original way education worked for thousands of years was simple. You learned the basics, reading, writing, arithmetic, but for jobs, you then applied for an apprenticeship in the field that interested you. You learned from real people actually doing the job.

Back in 2014, *Forbes Magazine* reported on April 21 that college degrees are not becoming more valuable — their glut confines people without them to a shrinking, low-pay sector of the market. Back on March 1, 2012, *Forbes* reported that sixty percent of U.S. college graduates could not find a full-time job in their chosen profession for which they paid dearly for a degree.

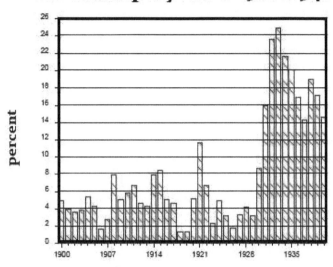

US Unemployment 1900-1940

Copyright Martin A. Armstrong 2011

Every facet of the economy is always undergoing a cyclical trend of creative destruction. Instead of looking to create some sort of guaranteed income, address the problem of education. The solution will be to encourage what life is all about — a journey of enlightenment and learning. Nothing lasts forever. Every trade or field is evolving, and that requires retraining. High unemployment occurred during the Great Depression, reaching nearly 25% in 1933 during the Dust Bowl. That was the direct result of the collapse of employment in agriculture. The farmhands became the hobo or unskilled labor. "Hobo" was a very distinctive term, for they were unlike a "tramp," who worked only when forced to do so to stay alive. The classic "bum" was a term reserved for those who did not work at all. Thus, the "hobo" became a distinctive term for a traveling worker who would do odd jobs. World War II solved that problem by taking in the unemployed and giving them new skills.

Universal Basic Guaranteed Income

There are cries for universal basic income touted by Elon Musk and Mark Zuckerberg in recent times. Others such as Milton Freidman have made the same plea, but with a different twist. The danger this idea creates is the failure to understand human nature. Milton's version took notice of human nature and thus sought to address the danger of providing basic income where people prefer not to work. Milton warned that such a system could never provide someone who does not work with the same basic income. This would only create a disincentive for those who work. When students were asked if they would support reducing their grade by 70% to 50% and handing the 20% to someone who scored less, their immediate answer was, "No way!" So, what is the answer?

We must first recognize that the economy is constantly evolving and growing like a child as it moves through these periods of creative destruction. I once had an office in a shared arrangement where the receptionist worked for several companies in the building. She was in her 50s and insinuated that the two girls who worked for me were hired simply because they were in their 20s. After enduring her passive slurs too often, "Marty and the girls..." I asked her if she knew how to edit videos or what podcasts were. She had no reply. I said bluntly, "Sorry, but the younger generation has skills that the older generations do not." It had nothing to do with this assumption that men prefer younger women. That seems to be a great excuse for avoiding self-reflection.

Now, even teenagers run circles around 30-year-olds when it comes to technology. Major computer companies like Google are hiring kids out of high school, for they have grown up with technology that even a 30-year-old is not so familiar with using.

Perhaps the key is keeping up with the Joneses, not materially, but rather through skill sets. I have been in programming all my adult life. I stay on top of every new twist and have been involved in Artificial Intelligence since the 1970s. I have kept up with the evolving technology. This is so important in every field to survive the long-term.

Creating universal basic income because people do not keep pace with technology's evolution is not a very good idea. We should be encouraging development instead of suppressing it. Of course, there are those who are disadvantaged mentally or physically who cannot be expected to function within society fully. They are not a class that should even be in this discussion.

Nevertheless, we must also respect the fact that governments are driving the trend toward automation by taxes and the refusal to deal with the healthcare crisis. The greater the social regulation imposed upon business, the greater the incentive to replace workers with machines. Bill Gates called for imposing income tax on robots back in 2017 because they have an unfair advantage over human workers. He was acknowledging that taxation and rising healthcare costs were creating a trend to replace workers wherever possible. The answer is not to tax robots, for then the companies will move offshore.

The answer is to address the issue of taxation and address the healthcare crisis. Obama forced the youth to buy insurance they did not need to increase the premiums collected by insurance companies in hopes that would reduce costs for elderly people. It completely failed and resulted in rising healthcare costs, creating an unfair advantage for healthcare imposing it by law.

Even the argument to raise the minimum wage is seriously flawed. The minimum wage was something the kids relied on for part-time jobs. Doubling the minimum wage will only reduce the jobs available that the youth need to get started in life. Simply define wages by age. Those still in school should be at the minimum wage.

They should not be subjected to healthcare when they are covered by other means. If not, they can apply for subsistence.

We must distinguish between non-students working for a living and those just getting started. One size does not fit all. If you want to raise the minimum wage, then simply raise the minimum tax level. As an example, somebody under the age of 65 filing as a single taxpayer will only be required to file if his or her income is $10,400 or more. Why $10,400? That was the value of the standard deduction for a single taxpayer (including one exemption) in 2017. In other words, that is the amount of money that a single filer would have deducted from his or her income anyway. So, if that individual did not reach the $10,400 threshold, he or she would effectively have no taxable income, and there would be no reason to file.

Employees covered under the federal Fair Labor Standards Act are subject to the federal minimum wage of $7.25. Many states have minimum wages greater than that, with some over $10. If someone worked 40 hours a week for 52 weeks at $7.25, they would earn $15,080 gross. Advocating a $15 minimum wage would mean the annual income would be $31,200. The tax bracket would be 12% between $9,526 to $38,700 and 10% applied below that level. That means after taxes, that person would be earning a net of $6.91 per hour. If we raised the minimum tax bracket to $30,000 and made that 0%, the only tax paid would be $1,200 starting at 10%, so they would pay only $120.

This would encourage many more people to work, making the unskilled labor jobs more affordable to compete with robots. Milton Freidman's proposal was a negative income tax. Under the current tax system, if they did not pay taxes under $10,400 and someone only earns $8,000 working full-time and is a non-student, the maximum basic income would be $2,400 annually. If they earned $20,000 and we used the $38,700 tax bracket, their basic income supplement would be 12% on $18,700 or $2,244. This way, they are not rewarded for not seeking a higher-paying job or working more. They should not be handed the same amount of money as someone who works.

A LOOK AT THE VA HEALTH CARE SCANDAL

Many Veterans Affairs medical facilities are under investigation for concealing long wait times. A recent USA TODAY poll found Americans are not confident in the medical care provided to our veterans. According to data USA TODAY obtained from the VA, the average new patient waits 27 days for an appointment.

Healthcare Crisis

We also hear a lot about free healthcare or at least reform. The advocates point to Europe or the UK as examples. What they fail to explain is that the doctors work for the government. The Veterans Health Administration scandal of 2014 was a reported pattern of negligent treatment of United States military veterans. Governments are not capable of managing even a bubble gum machine.

That said, the only way to solve the healthcare crisis is to address the abuse in billing, which drives up the costs and tort reform. First, people should be exempt from lawsuits if they cannot afford medical care. Stop subsidizing the high cost of healthcare. It should be treated as a public utility by fixing prices for specific procedures. Then criminalize overbilling. The Office of Inspector General reports countless frauds in the medical industry against Medicare and Medicaid. The same should apply to lawsuits against doctors. They should be restricted to specific amounts for specific injuries. That will reduce the cost of litigation. Make the lawyers also subject to criminal prosecution if they fail to ensure the person they represent is not submitting a fraudulent claim

The government should establish clinics for those who cannot afford to pay, but they should be privately managed. Even the VA should be outsourced, for government is not competent to manage any type of healthcare facility.

The Obama approach of forcing the youth to buy healthcare they do not need only subsidized the inefficiencies of insurance companies and hospitals. Only when hospitals compete will they ever bring down costs. According to the U.S. Bureau of Labor Statistics, the average American household spent $4,928 on healthcare in 2017. This represents 8% of the total average household expenditure of $60,060. Out of this total expenditure for healthcare, almost 70% ($3,414) was spent on health insurance. This was about 6% of total household expenditures. Healthcare costs are disrupting employment and contributing to robotic automation.

The Decline & Fall of the Utopian Economics

Boom & Bust - The Credit Cycle

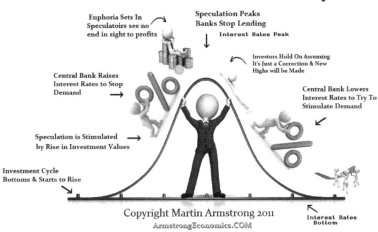

Copyright Martin Armstrong 2011
ArmstrongEconomics.COM

Wesley Clair Mitchell (1874–1948) was an American economist known for his empirical work on business cycles and guiding the National Bureau of Economic Research in its first decades. He then embarked upon his desire to define the business cycle. He failed to comprehend that the business cycle has existed since ancient times, and it is not created purely by the internal dynamics of capitalism as he believed. Nature plays a major role, for there has always been a cycle to climate from ice ages to periods of warming when society historically expands. Mitchell failed to comprehend that the business cycle is not just global in nature; it is the sum of everything which extends beyond simply human nature. We are all connected, and one government's folly spreads like a contagion throughout the world impacting everyone.

The entire theory of how central banks have been charged with managing the economy is what we call demand-side economics. This refers to the manipulation of interest rates in hopes of if altering our economic behavior. Raise rates and we will stop borrowing. Lower rates and we will borrow, thereby stimulating the economy. But this simplistic concept is not validated by history. There is far more behind the economy than meets this superficial observation.

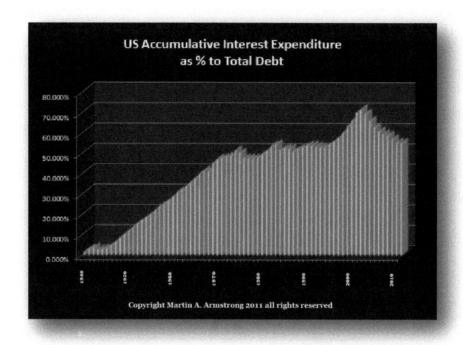

Curiously, central banks strive to manage the economy, steering it to achieve utopian economics by eliminating recessions and smoothing out the business cycle. However, using interest rates to manipulate the private sector's demand has no impact upon government, which is the biggest borrower within the economy. Because governments borrow with no intention of paying anything off, they must keep paying interest to roll the debt perpetually. That suppresses the economy, for it nullifies manipulating interest rates that will have no impact upon government curtailing its expenditure. Moreover, government then competes with the private sector for capital, suppressing economic growth and expansion. It is a contributing factor to why 80% of small businesses get turned down for loans to expand the economy.

As shown here, the accumulative interest expenditures eventually exceed 70% of the total debt, so the money never funded anything such as schools, roads, or social programs. Eventually, the interest expenditures will exceed all other expenditures, including military, within just a few years.

Today, the Federal Reserve raises interest rates to slow our spending, yet it increases government spending. The economic theories of Keynes and Marx cannot function when government is the single greatest borrower. Our current economic system is doomed. No rational person would ever create such a completely flawed monetary system.

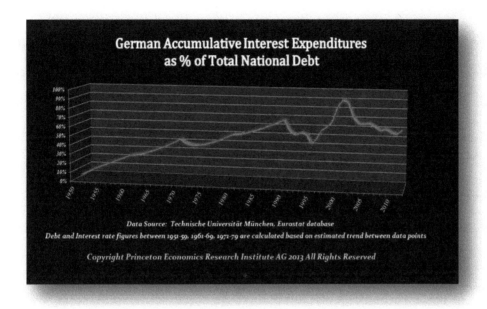

While many people only look at the U.S. national debt and preach that the dollar is going to crash, what they fail to comprehend is that this crisis in debt engulfs all nations post-World War II. No government even thinks about paying off its debt. The policy is always to borrow more each year for the overall inflation reduces the real value of what must be repaid. Governments always find it easy to separate a fool from their money.

If we look at Germany, the most conservative European nation, we see that the accumulative interest rates have also consumed a large portion of the national debt. It becomes impossible for the central bank to escape the fact that manipulating interest rates to stimulate the economy cannot work.

What has emerged is that Quantitative Easing (QE) is dead. The central banks are now trapped. They cannot sell what they have purchased, and they have maintained interest rates so low without success that government is being kept on life support. Raising interest rates now will blow out the budgets of all governments and create an economic nightmare. China has come out and stated publicly that they would not engage in QE.

We are witnessing the gradual situation of a major crisis brewing. How this will play out does not bode well for a happy ending. We are looking at a major financial crisis created by the economy's failed manipulation that never realized that

Economic Research Division
Federal Reserve Bank of St. Louis
U.S. Fiscal Deficit
Millions of Dollars (Annual, Not
Seasonally Adjusted)
Frequency: Annual, Fiscal Year

Year	FYFSD
2006	-248181
2007	-160701
2008	-458553
2009	-1412688
2010	-1294373
2011	-1299599
2012	-1076573
2013	-679775
2014	-484793
2015	-441960
2016	-584651
2017	-665446
2018	-779137
2019	-984388
2020	-3131917

government itself was the biggest borrower. It simply became impossible to use these tools exclusively against the private sector while ignoring the public sector.

The central banks cannot neutralize the fiscal spending of government. This is deeply entrenched. Just look at the table above concerning the Federal budget illustrating the perpetual annual deficits since 2007. This has increased about 364% since the 2007 crisis began.

Government has become addicted to cheap interest rates. If rates go back just to 5%, we are looking at a fiscal deficit explosion the Fed cannot overcome. Therefore, the central banks are trapped. They are in a position that makes it impossible to allow the economy to be restored to pre-2007.

John Kenneth Galbraith
(1908–2006)

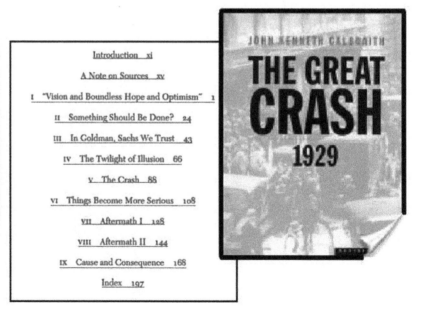

Whatever I learned in school quickly became irrelevant when I read the memoirs of President Hoover. The economic history books such as the *Great Crash* by John Kenneth Galbraith (1908–2006) never spoke of government defaults. It was also never fully mentioned how badly corporations acted. The spin on the Great

Depression was geared to create a new socialist form of government regardless of the truth.

World War II really began during 1931 in the financial markets. On May 11, 1931, the Credit-Anstalt Bank (Kredit Anstalt) failed in Austria, in part, edged onward by the French. This was the oldest and most widely respected banking house in Austria. Its losses exceeded its total capitalization.

Herbert Hoover
(1874 - 1964)
(President 1929 - 1933)

During this new stage of the depression, the refugee gold and the foreign government reserve deposits were constantly driven by fear hither and yon over the world. We were to see currencies demoralized and governments embarrassed as fear drove the gold from one country to another. In fact, there was a mass of gold and short-term credit which behaved like a loose cannon on the deck of the world in a tempest-tossed era.

THE MEMOIRS OF Herbert Hoover - The Great Depression 1929-1941, id/p 67

ArmstrongEconomics.COM

President Herbert Hoover wrote of the Sovereign Debt Crisis of 1931. He explained a situation similar to the 2010 crisis. Greece could not pay its debts; capital quickly looked around and began attacking other countries' bond markets it suspected were also weak. Hoover wrote that capital "behaved like a loose cannon on the deck of the world in a tempest-tossed era." He explained that the Forex markets erupted with volatility. Indeed, capital would flee from one currency to the next in fear of defaults.

Germany could not meet its reparation payments, and the French were adamant about punishing Germany for their previous loss to Germany in 1871. Germany and Austria announced their agreement on March 21, 1931, to merge in order to restore their economies. This led France to declare a financial war. France was perhaps the strongest European nation as a result of its intentional undervaluation of the franc in 1928 that gave rise to substantial flows of gold into France. France was a heavily commodity-oriented nation that had imposed substantial tariffs to protect its economy both from the U.S. (prior to Smoot-Hawley) and its European neighbors. Therefore, France suffered least among the Western nations from the ills of depression. France protested the German-Austrian customs agreement, calling it a violation of the Versailles Treaty. Britain agreed with France and protested in fear that this was the resurrection.

After the formal protesting period had lapsed, France immediately turned. The Bank of France, accompanied by many other French banks, presented short-term Austrian bills that they held for redemption. They did the same with their German holdings. It was estimated that France held some $300 million worth of these bills at the time. This was the final straw that broke the back of the European economic system.

Credit Anstalt - 1931 Austria

On May 11, 1931, the Credit-Anstalt Bank (*Kredit Anstalt*) failed in Austria, in part, edged onward by the French. This was the oldest and most widely respected banking house in Austria. Its losses exceeded its total capitalization. The failure of Credit-Anstalt had severe repercussions throughout Austria. Numerous banks turned to the National Bank of Austria, which quickly ran out of foreign currency reserves. Austria then had no other choice but to appeal to other nations. France, being the strongest, set the price as the dissolution of the German-Austrian customs agreement, which was a price Austria felt was too high. Toward the end of May, the Austrians turned to Britain and the United States for help when the Austrian National Bank, their equivalent of the U.S. Federal Reserve, was on the verge of collapsing. The French would not cooperate at all.

The failure of the Credit-Anstalt had severe repercussions throughout Austria, and as panic spread, the National Bank of Austria quickly ran out of foreign currency reserves. The French demanded the dissolution of the German-Austrian customs agreement, which was a price Austria felt was too high. In May 1931, the Austrians turned to Britain and the United States for help. The French would not cooperate at all.

Since the Rothschilds partly owned Credit-Anstalt Bank, this sent a massive wave of withdrawals from banks in Germany. Riots broke out in front of Austria's Credit-Anstalt, and bank runs were reported throughout Hungary as well. Britain came to the aid of Austria gallantly with an advance of 4.5 million pounds. However, the French became a bit annoyed with the British rescue of Austria and began selling the pound through the liquidation of their sterling holdings. The warfare had taken on a new front, with France waging a financial war that resulted in European monetary systems' wholesale collapse. This drove capital to the United States and sent the dollar to record highs.

The problems that developed in Austria spread, resulting in massive withdrawals of funds in Germany. Riots broke out in front of Austria's Credit-Anstalt, and bank runs were reported throughout Hungary as well. By the end of May, these pressures mounted against the Austrian National Bank.

Germany had nowhere to turn. France would not come to its aid and still expected reparation payments. The various payments on reparations and war loans between nations amounted to about $1 billion of which the U.S. received only $250 million annually.

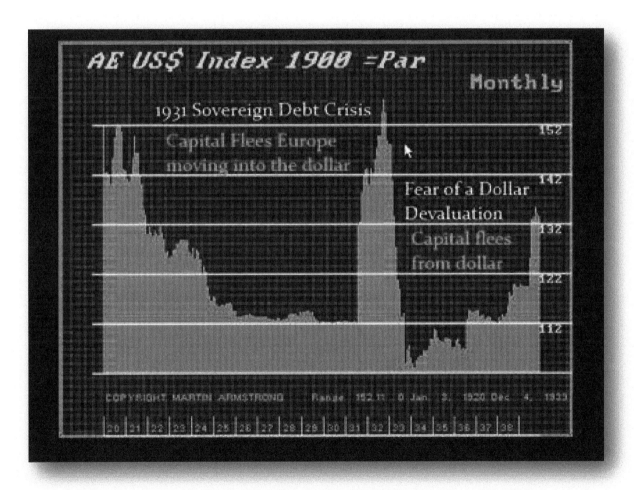

As European banking failures spread along with the quiet financial war that was raging in the foreign exchange markets, the Federal Reserve got into the act by reducing the discount rate to 1.5% in hopes of making it less attractive for foreign capital. Yet, capital was pouring into New York to get away from the chaos that reigned throughout Europe. The dollar began to strengthen as "smart" money set sail, once again, for the United States.

BIS Original Building in former Hotel Savoy-Univers Basel Switzerland (1930-1977)

On January 20, 1930, the BIS was created under the Young Plan at the Hague Conference agreed on by Belgium, France, Germany, Italy, Japan, United Kingdom, and Switzerland. The BIS was intended to settle the reparation payments imposed on Germany by the Treaty of Versailles. Therefore, the BIS was appointed agent to the trustees for the German government international loans of 1924 and 1930. Additionally, the BIS was intended to promote central bank cooperation, which was clearly ignored during 1931.

The Austrian and then the German financial and banking crisis of the summer of 1931 led first to a one-year suspension on reparation payments under the Hoover Moratorium of July 1931 and subsequently to their complete cancellation after the Lausanne Agreement of July 1932. The BIS focused its activities on the technical cooperation between central banks, including reserve management, foreign exchange transactions, international postal payments, gold deposit, and swap facilities. They did provide a forum for regular meetings of central bank governors and officials.

The Fed's actions were not by any means domestically oriented. Britain had been losing gold to the United States as capital fled the financial war zone. As a speculator, it was an easy bet. You essentially could short the pound by transferring it into dollars. The downside was perhaps a penny at best, and the upside was perhaps a return to the $3.20 level that had been seen following the Panic of 1920.

Throughout the European community, the problems had emerged into a financial war that replaced guns with capital controls, tariffs, restrictions, quotas, and interest rate manipulations. Central European states raised their interest rates in an attempt to attract foreign capital, which was the opposite move of the Federal Reserve. That attempt failed because confidence was far from present, and no exorbitant rates of interest would suffice in restoring stability. A decree followed this that capital was not permitted to leave the country. As Turkey attempted in 2019, these capital controls may have solved the immediate flight of capital, but at the cost of a complete collapse in confidence in Europe as a whole. It also brought international trade to a halt. If capital could not be exported, then commerce could not buy any goods. This was far more drastic than protectionism with tariffs.

Some increased their restrictions on imports and tried to stimulate their own exports. Yet, this failed as diverse approaches continued to disrupt trade, which only heightened the urge for capital to flee to the United States. In effect, this was the first crack in the gold standard. Although no one officially went off the gold standard in May of 1931, no gold payments were made since the exportation of capital was prohibited. Thus, the same result of abandoning the gold standard transpired among the Central European states.

14

MONDAY, JUNE 1, 1931
THE MANCHESTER GUARDIAN

Austrian Banking: A Triple Assistance

LONDON, SATURDAY.

Can the financial stability of Austria be maintained in the next few years through the united efforts of Austrians and of those outside Austria to whom this is a serious question? The authorities of the Bank of England, who are among this number, have been working late hours and at high pressure in the past week to safeguard the results of the international financial reconstruction of Austria which has been claimed as the best achievement in European politics since the war. Less than three weeks ago Austria was relatively a secure country in the view of bankers and investors. The Vienna banks were receiving short loans from London and New York banks on more advantageous terms than the German banks. The biggest of the Vienna institutions was reported in the private records of London houses to be credit-worthy for any customary amount. Suddenly losses of rather over £4,000,000 were announced as the result of that bank's operations in the year 1930. That this loss could have been so suddenly ascertained few will believe, and another explanation must be given of the brusque announcement. A single member of the managing directorate of the bank (a committee of three bankers—Messrs. Deutsch, Hojdu and Pollak) is reported to have stood out for a frank balance-sheet, and when he insisted his colleagues decided—in order to avert later troubles—to place on every asset of the institution the lowest and safest valuation. From these figures was composed a balance sheet revealing the maximum loss of 140,000,000 schillings. However, as soon as the news was known, the shares of many companies controlled and financed by the Credit Anstalt—half the big business of Austria—were sold and marked down on the Vienna Bourse many points. Thus, the shares of the Steyr Motor Company, one of the prosperous undertakings in the Credit Anstalt, were at once marked down from 212 to 190, and later to 177. The Credit Anstalt must be assumed thus to have lost further very considerable sums in the sales value of its assets, since the declaration.

Large sums were withdrawn from deposit with the Bank; 500,000,000 schillings, or over £14,000,000, is an estimate. Was the whole of this withdrawn after the announcement of the loss? According to a Vienna report, the troubles were precipitated by a previous sudden cancellation of credits by the Guaranty Trust Company and the Irving Trust Company of New York. New York banks are also accused of adding to the difficulties by cancellations after the announcement. The Austrian Government at once sought to allay anxiety by arranging, together with the Austrian National Bank, to take over the big mass of the Credit Anstalt's losses. It was blamed by the Socialists for not obtaining in return for this subsidy a complete control of the bank, yet the law enabling the Government and National Bank to undertake the operation was passed. This is known as Law No. 1. Immediately after, a further measure, known as the Credit Anstalt Law No. 2, was seen to be required to check deposit withdrawals. By this the State is made responsible for the security of all new engagements incurred by the bank in replacement of cancelled credits or withdrawn deposits. This law also is approved by a majority of the Austrian Parliament.

The Austrian State is thus engaged to make up the bulk of the losses of the chief commercial bank in the country in 1930 and to guarantee its solvency for a further two years. The National Bank of the country is called in to second the action of the State. And this has to be done within the terms of the agreements by which Austrian finances were internationally restored in 1922 and subsequent years. Legislative enactments are necessary in Austria to authorise the State and the National Bank to spend money on supporting the Credit Anstalt. Consent of the International Commission of Control, representing the States which participated in the reconstruction scheme of 1921, has to be obtained to authorise the State to raise the necessary funds by borrowing and to pledge itself in the future.

As reported in the *Guardian* on June 1, 1932, there was an effort to help Austria. This confirms what Herbert Hoover wrote about in his memoirs. On June 5, 1931, there was a panic in the German markets as rumors spread that Germany would suspend payments on foreign loans. Then the European press began to point the finger at the United States. They tried to assert that the economic policies of the U.S. were attracting the world's gold, creating the flight from European stock markets and the foreign exchange markets as well. The U.S. gold reserves had climbed by $600 million despite the Fed's cut in the discount rate.

Clearly, those charges by the European press were totally unfounded. Although Europeans sought to point the finger at the U.S. for causing their economic difficulties, the problems originated in Europe. Despite the depression in the U.S., it was viewed by world capital as the safest place at that point.

Financial warfare in Europe created a massacre within the banking industry. The Federal Reserve's textbook attempt to lower U.S. interest rates to stem the influx of capital and provide an incentive for capital to flow toward Britain failed. Confidence was not restored, and higher rates of interest were not among the concerns of nervous capital. Outright fear of loss dominated the free markets.

With economic conditions tightly strained throughout Europe, President Hoover believed that these intergovernmental payments were adding pressure that weakened confidence. This perhaps was evident when one considers the intentional actions on the part of France at this time. As early as May 11, Hoover had proposed to Secretaries Stimson and Mellon that they should study these intergovernmental payments and report their recommendations if any action should be taken. On June 5, Hoover called Mills to the White House and proposed that a moratorium of one year on all intergovernmental payments should be implemented.

On June 7, 1931, the German finance minister publicly stated that the Austrian banking crisis would spread to Germany in about 60 days. Of course, after making such a definite public statement, the panic began to spread immediately. Virtually every German bank was under siege, and foreign banks began wholesale demands for the immediate redemption of German trade bills and bankers' acceptances.

The situation was obviously becoming much more serious. After arriving in Europe on June 18, 1931, Andrew Mellon had "frantically" telephoned President Hoover, according to Hoover's memoirs, reversing his former opposition to a moratorium on intergovernmental payments. Mellon then advocated quick action, fearing that the American financial system was in grave danger from the events transpiring in Europe.

Paul von Hindenburg
(1847–1934)

President von Hindenberg of Germany sent an urgent letter of appeal to Hoover that warned that Germany was in danger of collapsing. The letter read as follows:

Mr. President:

The need of the German people which has reached a climax compels me to adopt the unusual step of addressing you personally.

The German people have lived through years of great hardship culminating in the past winter, and the economic recovery hoped for in the Spring of this year has not taken place. I have, therefore, now taken steps, in virtue of the extraordinary powers conferred upon me by the German Constitution, to insure [sic] the carrying out of the most urgent tasks confronting the Government and to secure the necessary means of subsistence for the unemployed. These measures radically affect all economic and social conditions and entail the greatest sacrifices on the part of all classes of the population. All possibilities of improving the situation by domestic measures without relief from abroad are exhausted. The economic crisis from which the whole world is suffering hits particularly hard the German nation which has been deprived of its reserves by the consequences of the war. As the developments of the last few days show, the whole world lacks confidence in the ability of the German economic system to work under the existing burdens. Large credits received by us from foreign countries have been withdrawn. Even in the course of the last few days the Reichsbank has had to hand over to foreign countries one third of its reserves of gold and foreign currency. The inevitable consequence of these developments must be further serious restriction of economic life and an increase in the numbers of unemployed who already amount to more than one third of the total number of industrial workers. The efficiency, will to work, and discipline of the German people justify confidence in the strict observance of the great fixed private obligations and loans with which Germany is burdened. But in order to maintain its course and the confidence of the world in its capacity, Germany has urgent need of relief. The relief must come at once if we are to avoid serious misfortune for ourselves and others. The German people must continue to have the possibility of working under tolerable living conditions. Such relief would be to the benefit of all countries in its material and moral effect on the whole crisis. It would improve the situation in other countries and materially reduce the danger to Germany due to internal and external tension caused by distress and despair.

You, Mr. President, as the representative of the great American people, are in a position to take the steps by which an immediate change in the situation threatening Germany and the rest of the world could be brought about.

—Von Hindenberg

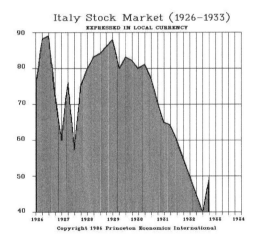

Italy Stock Market (1926-1933)
EXPRESSED IN LOCAL CURRENCY

Copyright 1986 Princeton Economics International

MONDAY, JUNE 29, 1931
THE MANCHESTER
GUARDIAN

Italy's Experience

The depression in Italy has been in some ways peculiarly severe. The lira was stabilised in 1927 at a notably difficult moment, when the balance of payments was being affected by the rapid decrease of emigrants' remittances. Money was also being drawn to the United States for use in the Wall Street boom. Imports were encouraged, exports discouraged by the stabilisation of the lira at a high level, and this was only gradually righted. In the years 1927-9 Italy was parsing through a local depression, due to the "valorisation" of the lira. From March, 1928, the gold and exchange reserves of the Bank of Italy were being rapidly depleted, from a total of 12,516,000,000 lire at the end of that month to 10,005,000,000 thirteen months later. Italy was caught by the world depression after some years of local depression.

Consequences of the world depression were (according to Professor Mortara) reduced demand for Italian goods abroad—between December, 1929 and December, 1930, there was a decline of 108 points in the export price index and only of 85 points in the import price index.—reduced tourist expenditure, reduced remittances from emigrants, and diminished shipping receipts. The reserves of the Bank of Italy were again, especially after August, 1930, resorted to for the stability of the currency. The next two Budgets are expected to close with large deficits, and Professor Mortara advocates a generous international policy— for example, in the matter of disarmament—as the best hope for his country's financial stability.

Even the situation in Italy had turned grave. They were arguing simply from a mercantilist perspective that the cause of the depression in Italy was the decline in exports. Still, a simple look at the share market reveals it never made new highs in 1929. What is very clear is that the attribution of blame for the Great Depression being assigned to the private sector was intended to create the new age of socialism by ignoring the role of government mismanagement.

Karl Heinrich Marx
(1818-1883)

John Maynard Keynes
(1883-1946)

People sometimes forget that Karl Marx and John Maynard Keynes have a lot in common. Marx was the first to advocate government intervention to eliminate the business cycle. Keynes followed Marx in advocating a government role, and the analysis put forth from the Great Depression ignored the role of governments in creating that event. The belief that government economic intervention could temper, control, and eliminate the business cycle became the norm post–Great Depression. That is what has completely failed, and the central banks are now trapped by Keynesian-Monetarism and the never-ending borrowing by governments with no intention of paying anything off.

Paul Volcker, the former Chairman of the Federal Reserve under Carter and Reagan, came out and stated bluntly that the economic theories that government could manipulate the business cycle to eliminate depressions and recessions were seriously flawed. He called it:

"The Rediscovery of the Business Cycle – is a sign of the times. Not much more than a decade ago, in what now seems a more innocent age, the 'New Economics' had become orthodoxy. Its basic tenet, repeated in similar words in speech after speech, in article after article, was described by one of its leaders as 'the conviction that business cycles were not inevitable, that government policy could and should keep the economy close to a path of steady real growth at a constant target rate of unemployment.'"

Paul Adolph Volcker, Jr.
(born September 5, 1927)

Paul Volcker, *Rediscovering the Business Cycle* (1979)

Prior to Marx, the dominant theory was laissez-faire, which was the abstention by governments from interfering in the workings of the free market. It was clearly understood after Adam Smith that collectively there is an invisible hand that creates society. Smith wrote in his 1776, *Wealth of Nations*:

Adam Smith
(1723-1790)

"It is not from the benevolence of the butcher, the brewer, or the baker that we expect out dinner, but from their regard to their own interest."

Smith's invisible hand was precisely why Marx's dream of utopian economics and eliminating the business cycle failed. Only the individual can provide the innovation to create the next advancement in technology that reshapes the economy. Communism failed because it usurped that innovation from the individual and installed it within the bureaucracy of government which cannot create. Centralized government is simply incapable of advancing society; it is the individual who sees an opportunity and creates something out of their own self-interest. Hence, for thousands of years, human society advanced from creating plows and ships to devising math and science without government intervention or domination.

Government intervention began with Karl Marx. Since then, all major economic theories are constructed on this proposition that government has the authority, power, and knowledge to manipulate society to smooth out the business cycle. Of course, they have never been able to prevent a single economic recession. This is what Paul Volcker called the 'New Economics,' which has completely failed. The question that is staring us dead in the eyes — what comes next?

The Industrial Revolution began in Great Britain with the invention of steam power. In 1770, Nicolas-Joseph Cugnot (1725–1804) demonstrated his *fardier à vapeur* ("steam dray"), an experimental steam-driven artillery tractor, but it proved to be impractical. However, by 1784, William Murdoch (1754–1839) had built a working model of a steam carriage (automobile), which was probably the first steam locomotive without tracks.

The problem with government has always been the abuse of its power. In a representative form of government, it has historically been subjected to bribes. The Industrial Revolution may have begun in Great Britain, but it was also stopped there by the corruption of the business establishment who controlled Parliament and did not want any competition.

These early attempts showed the potential for mass transit until a backlash unfolded. The horse and buggy industry lobbied to impose very low speed limits and other restrictions on the use of locomotives and motorcars on UK public highways. They bribed the politicians to enact the Locomotive Act (1865), which required self-propelled vehicles on public roads in the United Kingdom to be preceded by a man on foot waving a red flag and blowing a horn with speed limits. It was eventually repealed in 1895, but speed limits were retained to prevent these new gadgets from delivering anything faster than a horse. What they did was send the innovation of the automobile to Germany and the United States.

Clearly, these early attempts in the newfangled field of automobiles would have made Britain the leader in the auto field. Yet, it was effectively killed by legislation orchestrated by the establishment bribing the English Parliament. Britain would not regain that status as the Industrial Revolution shifted to America and continental Europe. Government proved it was not the creator of innovation, but often its direct enemy.

To circumvent the restrictions on steam carriages, this gave way to the idea to create trains where these inventions would travel on tracks rather than a road. This eliminated the need for a man on foot waving a red flag to warn people of your approach. The earliest railways actually employed horses to draw carts along rail tracks. After William Murdoch's 1784 steam carriage, a full-scale rail steam locomotive was proposed by William Reynolds around 1787, merging Murdock's idea with the horse-drawn carts on rails.

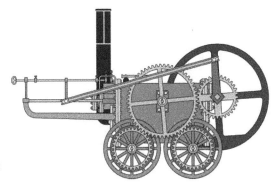

An early working model of a steam rail locomotive was designed and constructed by steamboat pioneer John Fitch in the U.S. during 1794. Clearly, the English regulations against steam carriages forced the evolution of steam engines into railways, and retarded the British economy during the Industrial Revolution.

In 1801 Richard Trevithick (1771–1833) built a full-sized functioning road locomotive known as the "Puffing Devil" that operated on the road. These early vehicles came at the dawn of the Industrial Revolution. Inventors and engineers abandoned the idea of creating automobiles and turned to build railway locomotives that traveled on tracks instead. There had been such use of rails with the wagon pulled by horses.

The British did eventually remove the restrictions and finally went on to abolish the law entirely in 1896 due to the fact that automobiles were becoming far more common in America and Germany. This left Britain behind in the Stone Age. Similarly, President George Bush, Jr. banned stem cell experimentation that led to such developments leaving the United States. In this case, the religious right stopped the innovation. It is always the oligarchy that influences government to support their status quo.

In 1802, Trevithick's Coalbrookdale locomotive was invented. It was constructed for the Coalbrookdale ironworks in Shropshire in the United Kingdom to haul goods on rails, thereby replacing horses. Then on February 21, 1804, the first recorded steam-hauled railway journey took place as another of Trevithick's locomotives hauled a train along the 4 ft 4 in (1,321 mm) tramway from the Pen-y-darren ironworks, near Merthyr Tydfil, to Abercynon in South Wales.

Eventually, replacing horses to haul carts on rails became the next innovation that gave birth to the railway system. By 1869, the United States had connected the East with California, thereby allowing trains to cross the United States. This innovation began the new wave of the Railroad Era.

John Maynard Keynes (1883-1946)

Before Keynes died, in 1946 he told Henry Clay, a professor of social economics, that he hoped Adam Smith's invisible hand would help Britain. "I find myself more and more relying for a solution of our problems on the invisible hand which I tried to eject from economic thinking twenty years ago."

Socialism Violates the Ten Commandments

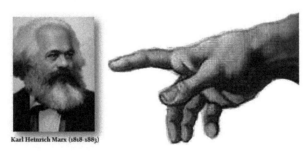

Karl Heinrich Marx (1818-1883)

You shall not covet your neighbor's house. You shall not covet your neighbor's wife, or his manservant or maidservant, his ox or donkey, or anything that belongs to your neighbor.

Exodus 20:17

Nevertheless, the very ideas put forth by Karl Marx, which have been adopted by most economists post-1950, are in direct conflict with the equal protection of the law and our right to the freedom of religion. Socialism is constantly being preached as class warfare. The political mantra is always about taking from the "rich" to give to the "poor," but as all charities go, the administration costs consume most of that money. Raising the taxes on the rich never lowers them for anyone else.

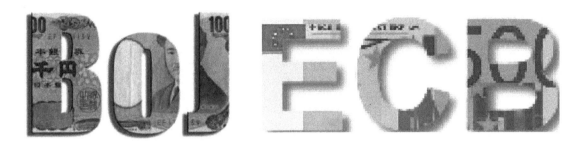

The central banks have sought to manipulate the business cycle by employing over 10 years of Quantitative Easing and pushing short-term rates to negative. The European Central Bank (ECB) owns 40% of the national debts in the EU, and it can neither sell them nor stop buying without creating a panic in interest rates.

Likewise, the Bank of Japan (BoJ) owns between 70% to 80% of the ETF bond market in Japan. The BoJ confirmed it is ending free market determination of interest rates for the municipal level and that they "will not require any procedures such as auction as the method of determining lending conditions." The BoJ announced it may introduce a lending facility for its exchange-traded fund buying program, allowing it to lend ETFs to market participants temporarily.

> 4. Introduction of Exchange-Traded Fund (ETF) Lending Facility

> "The Bank will consider the introduction of ETF Lending Facility, which will make it possible to temporarily lend ETFs that the Bank holds to market participants."

The statement at the end of the announcement on its monetary policy has left traders in shock. It appears that the BoJ realizes that it effectively destroyed its bond market and that this is not only the end of a free market, but there is a contagion surrounding the lack of liquidity.

We have never before in the history of human society ever witnessed such a major financial crisis. The BoJ makes it clear it will continue its policy of Quantitative Easing. It stated plainly:

"The Bank will continue with "Quantitative and Qualitative Monetary Easing (QQE) with Yield Curve Control," aiming to achieve the price stability target of 2 percent, as long as it is necessary for maintaining that target in a stable manner."

Both the ECB and the BoJ are completely trapped. They have destroyed their respective bond markets, meaning they can no longer tolerate a free market with respect to interest rates. They cannot stop buying government debt, for there is no bid at these insanely low rates.

We are far beyond every economic theory ever contemplated. The idea that central banks can use Keynesian Economics to save the day has vanished into thin air. Central banks cannot allow interest rates to rise, for the cost of rolling the various national debts will explode. They have no other economic theory to attempt. They cannot allow the free market to function, for the fiscal budgets will collapse. Add in the pension crisis where most funds are required to own government bonds, and some, like the U.S. Social Security system, only contain government debt. Artificially low interest rates will only propel the pension crisis into a catastrophic meltdown. Never before in the history of civilization have we faced such an intricately interconnected complex crisis.

How we deal with this government-created financial crisis will be extremely interesting. This is where opinion will just not suffice. There is no reference in history to turn to. Governments have always defaulted on their debts. This time, we have all Western governments together in a debt cycle that can be catastrophic if we do not comprehend that this one is far worse than anything that has come before us in history.

In 2011, Carmen M. Reinhart and Kenneth S. Rogoff wrote a book entitled, *This Time Is Different: Eight Centuries of Financial Folly Paperback*. They explain that governments have been lending, borrowing, and crashing. Each time, the experts have chimed, "This time is different!" and put forth countless excuses as to why history no longer applies. They reviewed sixty-six countries across five continents, covering various financial crises, including government defaults and banking panics.

"Stock prices have reached what looks like a permanently high plateau. I do not feel there will be soon if ever a 50 or 60 point break from present levels, such as they have predicted. I expect to see the stock market a good deal higher within a few months."

Dr. Irving Fisher, Professor of Economics at Yale University, October 17, 1929

Irving Fisher (1867-1947)

Perhaps the most famous statement along those lines took place on October 17, 1929 by Irving Fisher who was the most quoted economist of the time. The Sovereign Debt Defaults of 1931 took down most of Europe, South America, and even China. The government defaults were clearly anticipated by capital, as shown by the capital flows. Fisher lost his reputation because his focus was purely domestic.

British Hoard Discovered 2007
Containing 52,000 Roman Coins

When governments defaulted, people were able to hoard their wealth in tangible assets and coins of neighboring states. This time, there are no coins for everything is merely book-entries with less than 10% of the money supply in paper currency. Still, people are hoarding paper currency today just as they hoarded even debased coinage during the decline and fall of the Roman Empire during the 3rd century.

Indeed, we are all connected and what takes place in one government spreads like a contagion throughout the world, impacting everyone. What is most critical is confidence. When that is lost, then everything comes into question. We cannot manage our economy under any economic theory in total isolation of external factors.

Direct v Indirect Taxation

It is imperative that we understand why the Founding Fathers of the U.S. prohibited direct taxation that requires the individual to report to government. The income tax is an outcrop of Marxism. Instead of outright confiscating all property, they demand a pound of flesh. There is nothing more important than eliminating the income tax. It is a purely Marxist development that is destroying the world economy and has become such a tyranny that our liberty, freedom of movement, and world economic growth are all at great risk. Never before in the history of human civilization do we find an income tax. It is true that Ben Franklin once said that the two certainties in life are death and taxes, and it is equally true that taxes, in general, have been around since the beginning of civilization. We do know that the earliest recorded tax was implemented in Mesopotamia over 4,500 years ago. People paid taxes throughout the year in the form of livestock, which was the preferred currency at the time. The ancient world also had inheritance taxes, also known as estate taxes or death taxes. The earliest recorded evidence of a death tax came from ancient Egypt in 700 BC, where they charged a 10% tax on property transferred at the time of death.

The most serious crisis we face is that with the dawn of Marxism (communism/socialism), the way we pay taxes has changed significantly. Yet, one for the record took place in 2006, when China eliminated what was once the oldest existing tax in history. The agricultural tax was created 2,600 years ago and was eliminated in 2006 to help improve rural farmers' well-being in China.

Second Issue 1801-1802 US Embossed Tax Stamp Scott no. RM263a. 25 cents

Tax Stamp on 1769 Colonial Newspaper

Taxation in the United States can be traced to the colonists when they were heavily taxed by Great Britain on many things from tea to newspapers and legal and business documents that were required to display a stamp tax. Most colonists objected to this form of taxation, since they had no political input about the creation of new taxes, giving rise to the term "taxation without representation." After the American Revolution, the new government of the United States passed the Stamp Act of July 6, 1797, which levied taxes on wills, personal estates, and the infamous death taxes — the transfer of possessions of the deceased. The death tax only lasted five years and was abolished in 1802.

The first issue of the U.S. tax stamps of July 1, 1798, had the name of the state incorporated in the design. This issue lasted until February 28, 1801. The highest denomination was $10. The second issue was authorized by the Act of April 23,

1801, and lasted from March 1, 1801, to June 30, 1802, and also carried denominations up to $10. The third federal issue was imposed by the Act of August 2, 1813, and was in effect from January 1, 1814, to December 31, 1817.

The Revenue Act of July 1, 1862 imposed a 2 cent tax on all checks and sight drafts. This continued until July 1, 1883, and all other war taxes ended on October 1, 1872

ArmstrongEconomics.COM

By the American Civil War, embossed tax stamps were replaced by printed tax

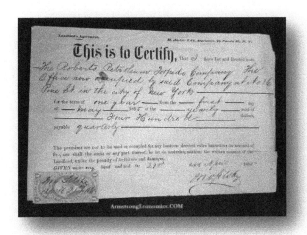

stamps. Because of the demands on the government to fund the Civil War, Congress passed the Revenue Act of 1862, which put taxes on boxes or packages of matches, perfumery, playing cards, documents, and then medicines. There was also an issue of paper printed by private firms under the government's supervision with the tax stamp in place that lasted from 1862 into 1883.

The government even allowed the manufacturers to create their own stamps at their own expense. The government allowed various companies to add 5% to 10% premiums on their products if they covered the costs of manufacturing the tax stamps. This private tax stamp system was in use until July 1, 1883, when the Act of March 3, 1883, took effect.

The first income tax was created in 1861 during the Civil War as a mechanism to finance the war effort. In addition, Congress passed the Internal Revenue Act in 1862 that created the Bureau of Internal Revenue, an eventual predecessor to the IRS. The Bureau of Internal Revenue placed excise taxes on everything from tobacco to jewelry. However, the income tax did not last and was not renewed in 1872 when Congress allowed it to expire. In Springer v. United States 102 US 586 (1881), the Supreme Court upheld the income tax in force.

Justice Swayne wrote the opinion of the court. The central and controlling question in the case was whether the tax, which was levied on income, gains, and profits was Constitutional since it forbids any direct taxation. The court played games with the words to uphold the government. It wrote, "Our conclusions are, that direct taxes, within the meaning of the Constitution, are only capitation taxes, as expressed in that instrument, and taxes on real estate; and that the tax of which the plaintiff in error complains is within the category of an excise or duty." A capitation tax is an assessment levied by the government upon a person at a fixed rate regardless of the property, business, or other circumstances. The reasoning used was clearly overruled later, which necessitated amending the Constitution in 1913.

Moreover, the Revenue Act of 1862 created a federal estate and gift tax system. Following the end of the Civil War, those taxes were rolled back, but the War Revenue Act of 1898 created another death tax to raise revenue for the Spanish–American War.

Melville Weston Fuller
(1833 – 1910)
8th Chief Justice (1888-1910)

An 1894 statute was ruled unconstitutional in the case of Pollock v. Farmers' Loan and Trust Company 157 U.S. 429 (1895) delivered by Chief Justice Fuller. It was held that taxes upon rents, profits of real estate, and returns from investments of personal property were direct taxes upon the property from which such income arose imposed by reason of ownership. It held that Congress could not impose such taxes without apportioning them among the states according to population, as required by article 1, 2, cl. 3, and section 9, cl. 4, of the original Constitution.

William Howard Taft
(1857 – 1930)
27th president (1909–1913)

The origin of the current income tax is generally cited as the passage of the 16th Amendment, passed by Congress on July 2, 1909, and ratified February 3, 1913. On June 16, 1909, President William Howard Taft, a Republican, in an address to the Sixty-first Congress, proposed a 2% federal income tax on corporations by way of an excise tax and a constitutional amendment to allow the previously enacted income tax. Once this Marxist concept of direct taxation was created, the government decided it must know everything we do. Government tracks us, for it assumes we all cheat and lie, and in the process, it is hunting money globally to the point that world economic growth has been declining.

Teddy Roosevelt (1858–1919) was the 26th president of the United States from 1901 to 1909. He previously served as vice president to the 25th president, William McKinley, and became president upon McKinley's assassination. Roosevelt pledged not to run for reelection. However, he became frustrated with William Taft's conservatism and tried to win the 1912 Republican nomination but failed. Teddy then founded a third party, the Progressive "Bull Moose" Party, which called for wide-ranging progressive reforms that gave rise to socialism constructed upon Marx's theories.

Theodore *"Teddy"* Roosevelt
(1858–1919)

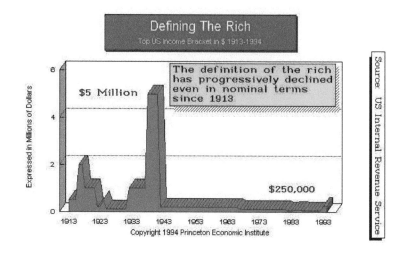

Ever since the income tax passed, the problem has been systemic. The original income tax was installed as a 2% federal income tax. It was to apply only to the rich. With World War I, the definition of the rich was raised to $2 million, which was a lot of money considering cars were less than $500. The definition of the rich was raised to $5 million for World War II.

In 1916, Congress amended the income tax law to remove the ambiguous question of what taxing "lawful" income meant by substituting the phrase "from whatever source derived." The Revenue Act of 1916 stated that all income was taxable even if it was earned by illegal means. This new language also became the basis on which the taxation of overseas sourced income was justified.

Then during 1917, due to the expense of World War I, the federal budget was almost equal to the total U.S. budget for all the years between 1791 and 1916. Congress enacted new tax provisions under the War Revenue Act of 1917 to lower exemptions and increase taxes. The amount of tax to be collected increased fourfold from $809 million in 1917 to $3.6 billion in 1918.

The following year in 1918, efforts were made in the House of Representatives to exempt foreign source income from U.S. taxation because of alleged competitive disadvantages suffered by American corporations operating branches abroad (Hearings Before the House Committee on Ways and Means on the Revenue Act of 1918, 65th Congress, 2nd Session 648 (1918)). This was unsuccessful.

A new revenue act was passed that increased taxes on incomes in excess of $1 million per year to a rate of 77%. The new act also introduced estate taxes (death taxes) and excess profits taxes. Still, only 5% of the population had to pay income taxes. Nevertheless, Americans working abroad were allowed to reduce their federal income tax liability with a tax credit equal to the amount of any foreign income taxes paid. Until 1918, all foreign taxes were treated as deductible expenses in the same manner as state and local taxes (Revenue Act of 1918).

After the war in 1921, Congress enacted a new tax law that was held to also apply to overseas Americans. Treasury Regulation No. 62 applied the tax to overseas Americans under Article III of the Act, codified in Treasury Regulations, Section 1.1-I(b), T.D. 7332, 1975-1 C.B. 205,207 (Revenue Act of 1921).

A determined effort was once again made to exempt foreign income from U.S. taxes in the case of U.S. Corporations that derive 80% of their income from foreign sources. The Treasury, Commerce and State Departments favored the exemption, but it ran into determined opposition in Congress. The provision finally passed in the House but was defeated in the Senate (61 Congressional Record 7023, 7026 (1921)). Congress amended the tax law to provide for an exemption for corporate income earned in a U.S. possession but not remitted to the United States (Revenue Act of 1921, Chapter 262, 42 Stat. 271 (1921)).

Americans officially transformed into economic slaves in 1924. The decision came in Cook v Tait, 265 US 47 (1924) after the Supreme Court upheld the constitutionality of the taxation of Americans on their foreign earned income. The court stated:

> "The principle was declared that the government, by its very nature, benefits the citizen and his property wherever found and, therefore, has the power to make the benefit complete. Or to express it another way, the basis of the power to tax was not and cannot be made dependent upon the situs of the property in all cases, if being in or out of the United States, and was not and cannot be made dependent upon the domicile of the citizen, that being in or out of the United States, but upon his relation as citizen to the United States and the relation of the latter to him as citizen. The consequence of the relations is that the native citizen who is taxed may have domicile, and the property from which his income is derived may have situs, in a foreign country and the tax be legal – the government having power to impose the tax."

(Cook v. Tait, 265 U.S. 47 (1924))

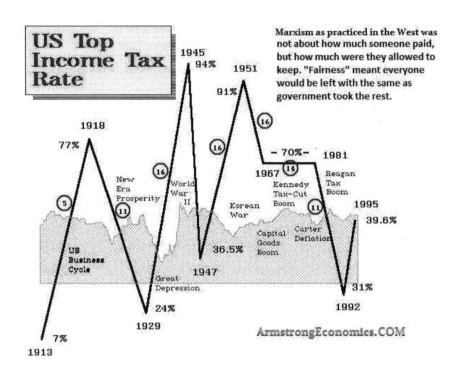

What emerged has become a serious political problem. The top tax rate constantly moves up and down depending on which party wins an election. The top tax rate went to 94% in 1945 and collapsed back to 36.5%, only to rise again to 91% for the Korean War.

The economic destruction that has taken place because of the income tax has altered society. Corporations were left to establish stable economic bases outside the USA just to get tax deals that did not change with each election. The payroll tax was imposed for World War II, and no longer was it only for the rich. Ever since the income tax implementation, it now takes two wage earners to support a family.

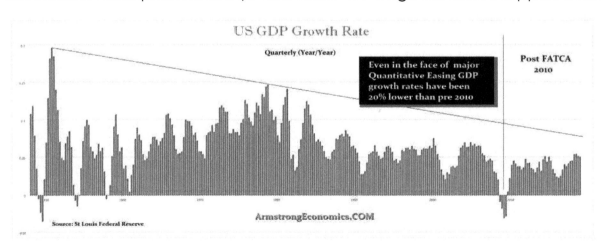

Obama pushed FATCA (Foreign Account Tax Compliance Act), which requires all foreign entities to report on anything they do with Americans outside the USA or their assets will be confiscated in the USA. The FATCA legislation was passed into law in 2010 as part of the unrelated jobs legislation known as the HIRE law. FATCA is a broad, complex set of rules designed to increase tax compliance by Americans with financial assets held outside the United States. Consequently, no American can have a bank account outside the USA, for banks will no longer accept the risk that an American failed to pay their taxes. Prior to FATCA, growth rates were generally greater than 6% reaching 7% in 2004 annually. Since then, the highest growth rate was 5.4% in 2018.

A German computer scientist in Switzerland was sentenced to three years in prison for stealing the data of 2,700 German and Dutch bank customers while working at Bank Julius Baer in Zurich. Germany had been bribing employees of Swiss banks for names of German clients with accounts in Switzerland.

The Guardian reported that the hunt for money was indeed in full swing. Germany handed Greece the names of more than 10,000 Greeks who they said were dodging taxes with holdings in Swiss banks. They obtained this data by bribing employees in Swiss banks and then demanded they be prosecuted to make payments to Germany.

Switzerland caved in entirely and sealed its own demise. Everything that made Switzerland the place to be, from religion to economic freedom, is becoming lost thanks to bureaucrats. Switzerland began as a tax revolt; William Tell would be rolling over in his grave if he knew what this country has just done. The Swiss began banking secrecy when Adolf Hitler came to power in 1933 and declared it illegal for a German to have an account outside of Germany. The USA is doing the same with FATCA indirectly. Not even Hitler violated the sovereignty of Switzerland, but those in government today are far more financially ruthless and threaten other nations with ultimatums. This is all about their greed for taxes.

The European Union and Switzerland signed a major accord that will end banking secrecy for EU residents, preventing them from hiding undeclared income in Swiss banks. All the Swiss will be left with is chocolate and watches. They fail to grasp that what made the country great was its respect for freedom against Hitler. The Swiss bureaucrats are committing treason against their own people. There is no reason for anyone to bother having an account in Switzerland, and these bureaucrats cannot figure out the net effect.

All countries are now hunting taxes and destroying world economic growth. The tax dispute UBS is in with France will occupy them for years to come. At the end of February 2019, a Paris-based criminal court ordered UBS to pay 5 billion Swiss francs in damages because the big bank helped wealthy French citizens hide their money from the tax authorities between 2004 and 2012. UBS has moved on. It will take years to reach a final decision.

The Swiss bureaucrats have forgotten the origins of Switzerland. The country began as a tax revolt against the Hapsburg Empire, whose tax collectors allegedly made William Tell shoot an apple off his son's head. Switzerland was a refuge for the French fleeing the revolution and the guillotine. They were the refuge for those who were religiously discriminated against. The long historical birth of Switzerland and what it stood for has been abandoned. This seems to be in line with the 26-year peak in real estate expected during 2020. The worldwide asset tax, the peg, and the loss of Switzerland's financial base are setting the stage for a serious shift in direction for Switzerland. If William Tell were alive today, he would be leading an army in revolution against the current government.

The entire direct taxation is what the Founding Fathers in the U.S. forbid. We are now witnessing the destruction of the world economy as governments hunt down everyone for taxes. The Common Reporting Standard (CRS) is an information standard for the automatic exchange of tax and financial information on a global level. It was put together by the Organisation for Economic Co-operation and Development (OECD) back in 2014. Its purpose was to hunt down tax evasion primarily for the European Union. They took the concept from the US Foreign Account Tax Compliance Act (FATCA), which imposes liabilities on foreign institutions if they do not report what Americans do outside the country.

The legal basis of the CRS is the Convention on Mutual Administrative Assistance in Tax Matters. In 2016, 83 countries signed an agreement to implement it into law. The first reporting took place in September 2017. The CRS has many loopholes as countries must sign the agreement. This has omitted the United States as well as most developing countries. Note that countries that are included are China, Singapore, Switzerland, Canada, Australia, New Zealand, and most tax havens.

It is abundantly clear that we must eliminate the income tax, for this Marxist idea is destroying the world economy by converting republican governments into tyrannical entities that only exert their self-interest. As governments hunt taxes globally, they are reducing world economic growth. There is no longer a viable future, for revolutions are always born from tax revolts.

As of 2018, the signing nations to avoid are:

Albania, Andorra, Antigua and Barbuda, Aruba, Australia, Austria, The Bahamas, Bahrain, Belize, Brazil, Brunei Darussalam, Canada, Chile, China, Cook Islands, Costa Rica, Dominica, Ghana, Grenada, Hong Kong (China), Indonesia, Israel, Japan, Kuwait, Lebanon, Marshall Islands, Macao (China), Malaysia, Mauritius, Monaco, Nauru, New Zealand, Pakistan, Panama, Qatar, Russia, Saint Kitts and Nevis, Samoa, Saint Lucia, Saint Vincent and the Grenadines, Saudi Arabia, Singapore, Sint Maarten, Switzerland, Turkey, United Arab Emirates, Uruguay, Vanuatu

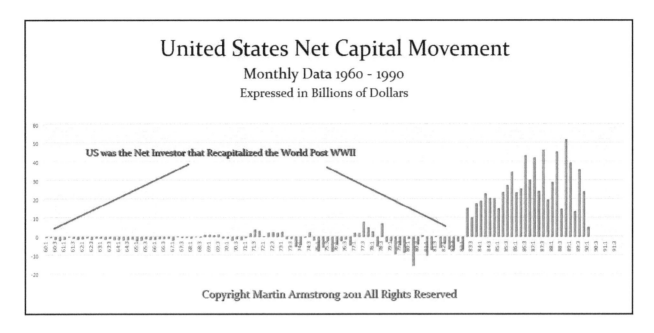

What rebuilt the world economy after World War II was the free flow of capital and overseas investment. The USA had 76% of the total world capital, and investment outside the USA restored the world economy. These politicians are now reversing the process and destroying everything by raising taxes and hunting anyone with money outside their own country. This is precisely the reverse position of what created the world economy, and now we are in a contraction mode that no amount of QE will reverse. Net capital outflow weakened the dollar, but it rebuilt

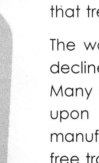

the world economy. We have now completely reversed that trend, and this is part of the deflation.

The world economy has been in a prolonged economic decline as taxes have risen, and regulation has expanded. Many economies, such as Germany's, are still constructed upon old mercantilist principles. They focus on manufacturing cars and products to export. That requires a free trade market. By hunting taxes on a global scale, they are impacting world trade simultaneously. When we open the doors to see the future, we are coming up against a brick wall.

235

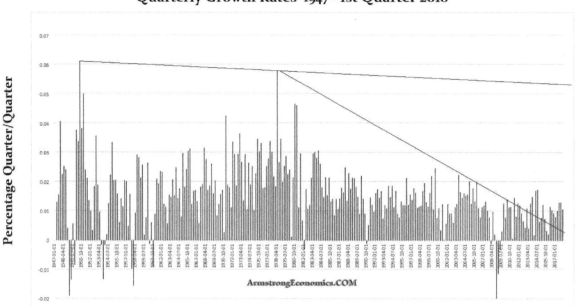

United States Economic Growth Rate Gross Domestic Product
Quarterly Growth Rates 1947 - 1st Quarter 2018

Global debt grew over 12% after adding $27 trillion since 2016 and reaching $244 trillion in total or 318% of world GDP going into the end of 2018. Most people have no idea that China's debt is 250% of GDP compared to the USA at 103%. All the focus on the collapse of the dollar has caused many people to take their eyes off the real time bomb ticking away.

It is laughable how so many pretend analysts never bother to do the research. They are clueless as to how the world monetary system could even collapse. All they do is constantly talk about the Fed, U.S. national debt, and the dollar as they remain oblivious to anything taking place around the world.

We can see that GDP peaked during the 1970s after it made a second rally to retest the highs immediately following the war. We are watching the economy gradually decline in terms of real growth, confirming that we have a serious crisis. As central banks have engaged in Quantitative Easing to "stimulate" the economy, the legislative and executive branches of governments have been increasing their taxes and the enforcement of taxes. This conflict between fiscal and monetary policy has resulted in the failure of utopian economics (Keynesian Economics) to act as a tool to manage the business cycle.

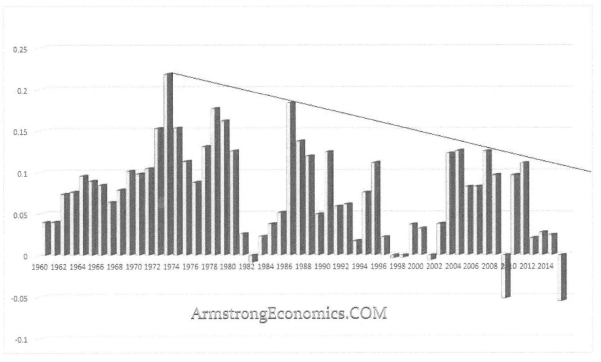

WORLD GDP GROWTH 1960-2015

Global GDP growth has been steadily declining since the 1970s — the greater the tax burden and enforcement, the lower the economic growth. We are moving into a crisis of monumental proportions. There has been a serious fundamental problem infecting economic policy on a global scale. This conflict has been between monetary and fiscal policy. While central banks engaged in Quantitative Easing, governments have done nothing but reap the benefits of low interest rates.

This is the problem we have with career politicians who people vote for because they are a woman, black, or smile nicely. There is never any emphasis upon qualification. Every other job in life you must be qualified to obtain. Would you put someone in charge of a hospital, making life and death decisions, because they smile nicely?

Economic growth has been declining year-over-year, and we are in the middle of a situation involving low productivity expansion with high and rapidly rising budget deficits that benefit no one besides government employees. Once upon a time, 8% growth was average, then 6%, and 4% before 2015.75. Now 3% is considered to be fantastic. Private debt at least must be backed by something, whereas escalating public debt is completely unsecured. The ECB wanted to increase the criteria for bad loans, yet if those

same criteria were applied to government, no one would lend them a dime.

Monetary policy, after too long a phase of low interest rates and Quantitative Easing, has created governments addicted to low interest rates. They have expanded their spending and deficits for the central banks to keep the government on life support and not actually stimulate the private sector. Governments have pursued higher taxes and more efficient tax collections. They have attacked the global economy, assuming anyone doing business offshore was just hiding taxes.

The combination of fiscal policy and monetary policy around the world has produced the most irresponsible economic mismanagement in history. This assumption that government can manipulate the economy is extremely dangerous for we remain clueless about how the global economy even functions. This entire Marxist/Keynesian proposition that governments are capable of managing the economy has implemented various miserably conceived theories that will lead to a budget crash and a debt crisis for every reasonably rational contemporary society. Historically, there were debt jubilees mentioned in the Bible.

"You shall then sound a ram's horn abroad on the tenth day of the seventh month; on the day of atonement, you shall sound a horn all through your land. You shall thus consecrate the fiftieth year and proclaim a release through the land to all its inhabitants. It shall be a jubilee for you." (Leviticus 25:1-4, 8-10, NASB).

Tommaso Portinari
(1428-1501)

The Rise & Decline of the Medici Bank

The Medici has entered a directive that the bank would not engage in sovereign loans stating *"to deal as little as possible with the court of the Duke of Burgundy and of other princes and lords, especially in granting credit and accommodating them with money, because it involves more risk than profit."* Their downfall was Portinari who in 1470 began to lead the bank into the business of sovereign loans and then were bankrupted by the defaults of the princes of Europe.

Raymond de Roover The Rise and Decline of the Medici Bank (1966) (id/ p 343)

ArmstrongEconomics.COM

Religion aside, the Medici were major bankers even to the Popes. Raymond de Roover, who became a professor of history at Brooklyn College, wrote, *The Rise and Decline of the Medici Bank*, which was first published in 1966. It remains the seminal work on this period. He had access to contracts and internal documents. A special clause was entered into the core contract of the Medici bank "to deal as little as possible with the court of the Duke of Burgundy and of other princes and lords, especially in granting credit and accommodating them with money, because it involves more risk than profit."

Obviously, Raymond de Roover makes it clear that the Medici did not wish to lend to the princes of Europe, for there was no way to collect a debt from a sovereign. The contract continued by warning that "many merchants in this way fared badly…our fathers have always been wary of such involvements and stayed aloof, unless it was a matter of a small sum lent to make or to keep friends." The Medici policy was "to preserve their wealth and credit rather than enrich themselves by risky ventures."

Indeed, later generations ignored this command, and once they lent to government that was the end of the Medici. The Fugger's were the German bankers who were wiped out by Spain's default. That was rather stupid since they had previously defaulted after wiping out the Italian bankers.

Governments are desperate to retain power. They are becoming aggressive in collecting taxes, and in the process, are reducing economic growth. This conflict between fiscal policy and monetary policy will finally become obvious to everyone as we head into 2021–2022.

The Emergence of Banks

Minoan Brone Ingot - Used as Money in Trade

While the use of money predates recorded history, transactions clearly began as just barter, whereas all commodities had a value. Barter was inconvenient for someone who had carrots or perhaps too many potatoes to be interested in the trade. Eventually, a common unit of exchange emerged from seashells in some places to cattle or bronze. Precious metals eventually emerged simply because they were once the symbol of royalty. The metals had no actual value, as was the case with bronze which was the monetary unit of the Minoans.

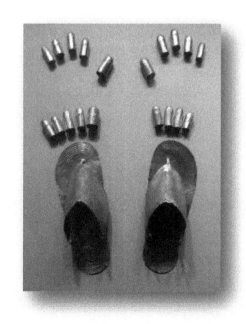

Gold was first believed to be the tears of the sun and was reserved for royalty. This can be seen in the gold coffin of King Tutankhamen, surviving jewelry, drinking cups, and even gold sandals, all used by royalty from Egypt to Greece.

241

Spectacular golden objects were discovered in Greece at Mycenae, including a death mask believed to belong to Agamemnon. Eventually, gold was discovered in Anatolia (modern Turkey). Its quantity rose, and its availability expanded first among aristocrats and then in trade as a medium of exchange for the more common merchant. For gold to acquire a value, there had to be enough of it to go around. Thus, only as gold mining expanded do we begin to find it becoming a valuable commodity beyond the wealth or pleasure of the sovereign.

Mining did exist in the Stone Age, but it was limited to practical ventures such as digging primarily for flint to be used for arrowheads and axes. Copper mining is known to date back to 4500 BC in Serbia. While the Egyptians were mining turquoise in the Sinai for luxury around 2600 BC, it was the wealth of the famed King Solomon that came from mining. It was not gold but copper mines in the 9th century BC that made King Solomon a very wealthy man.

The Greek historian Siculus Diodorus (1st century BC) of Agyrium, Sicily, wrote a 40-volume work of universal history known as the *Biblioteca Historica*. The information inside is invaluable since no other continuous historical reference has survived. It informs us that Egyptian gold mines in Nubia were manned by those declared to be criminals or dissidents who were sentenced to work there until they died.

Before coins began to circulate in ancient Egypt after its conquest by Alexander the Great in 334 BC, there was perhaps the first monetary system in the world where a form of paper money emerged. There was a unit of account based on weights of gold, silver,

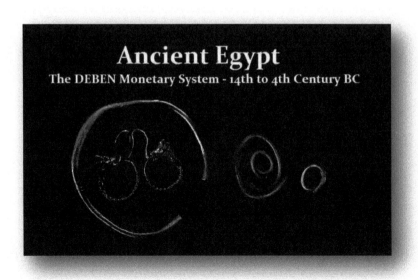

Southern Bulgaria
Oldest Gold Object

A Gold bead - 4 mm (1/8 inch) in diameter - found at a pre-historic settlement in Southern Bulgaria, dates back to 4,500-4,600 BC is probably the world's - oldest gold artifact.

and copper, whereby they were measured in units of weight known as deben (around 90 grams). Deben was used to settle bills and trade internationally. Records from the Eighteenth Dynasty (1550–1295 BC) show that often the actual metal, however, did not change hands. Instead, metal formed only a unit of account rather than a medium of exchange by which everything was valued for exchange.

In 1972, a gold ring was discovered at a prehistoric settlement in southern Bulgaria dating back to 4500–4600 BC. Archaeologists reported that this discovery predates jewelry from the Copper Age by at least 200 years. The necropolis in the Bulgarian Black Sea city of Varna predates Egypt, and the total find was 13 pounds of gold artifacts. The Varna cache is a mystery, for the inhabitants of the region were believed to be farmers who migrated out of the Anatolia just a few centuries prior. How were they able to master the smelting of copper and gold? "I have no doubt that it is older than the Varna gold," commented Yavor Boyadzhiev, a professor at the Bulgarian Academy of Science in charge of the dig.

Pharaoh Thutmose III, around 1450 BC, is said to have made an offering at the Temple of Amen in Thebes of some 13.5 tons of gold. You may have seen the exhibit of Tutankhamen with his solid gold death mask and solid gold casket. This amount of pure gold is simply breathtaking.

Egypt had no easily accessible source of silver, yet curiously the Egyptian word for silver, *hedj* came to mean something close to "money." Gold existed in northern Africa, and Turkey had a natural alloy of gold and silver known as electrum. The Greeks had silver but little gold, and in Italy, they had copper.

The Bible tells us that gold and silver were weighed. Clearly, metal was being exchanged as we discussed with the Romans using lumps of bronze that required weighing for each transaction. These ingots and metal rings date from the

fourteenth century BC and were found at el-Amarna. They give us rare archaeological evidence for Egypt's earliest money system. The complete ingots weigh around 3 asset-backed (265–286 grams).

However, banking also predates the creation of formal money. The invention of banking preceded that of coinage by several thousand years. Banking appears to have originated in ancient Mesopotamia. Receipts in the form of clay tablets were used to record transfers between parties. Some of the earliest recorded laws (e.g., Code of Hammurabi) pertain to the banking industry regulation in Mesopotamia.

The development of banking in Mesopotamia is quite interesting. It illustrates that all the modern practices such as deposits, interest, loans, and letters of credit existed from the time of the first great civilizations on Earth. In effect, these clay tablets were the forerunner of our more modern paper money systems that emerged in China by 900 AD and in Western culture by the 18th century. The distinction appears to be that these clay tablets were more of a bank draft or money order issued by the private sector rather than by the state. In that respect, they were a function of the banking system that facilitated the development of an officially sanctioned form of a standardized monetary system.

Egyptian sources also show that a vibrant banking industry emerged whereby the state provided warehouses in which farmers deposited their grain. In turn, the farmer would receive a "deposit receipt"

Ancient Babylonian Economic Receipts
(circa 1500BC)
ArmstrongEconomics.COM

reflecting how much wealth was held by the bank in question. Egypt never invented coinage, but they used this receipt monetary system that one could call the first paper money. Such written receipts eventually were used as a general method of making debt payments to third parties even during the Ptolemy era, including payments in trade, taxes, and donations to the Gods.

Anatolia (Ionia) Weight Standards

Miletos. Before 575 BC
Electrum Stater (13.99 gm)

Mysia, Kyzikos Circa 500-450 BC
Electrum Stater (16.15 gm)

Ephesos circa 625-600 BC
Electrum Trite (Third Stater) (4.66 gm)

Eventually, gold began to trade by a specific weight and was the forerunner to coinage during the 8th century BC. Moneychangers emerged because there was no universal standard. There were coins based on a 17.2 grams weight that we call the Euboic standard of Euboea. Phokaia used a 16.1 grams Phokaic standard, and in Miletus, they used the 14.1 grams Milesian standard. Eventually, most adopted the Phokaic standard. Kyzikos, which was a Milesian colony on the sea of Marmara, adopted the Phokaic standard of 16.1 grams, probably for trade purposes.

During the 6th century BC, the invention of coinage spread from Anatolia to Greece. Athens developed the Attic standard based on a silver didrachm of 8.6 grams. Corinth created a silver stater, but the weight was also 8.6 grams. The island of Aegina was probably the first to issue coins, and their Aiginetic standard was 12.3 grams for a stater. There were other standards, such as that of the Achaean, which was fixed at 8 grams for a silver stater, and the Euboic standard for a stater of 17.2 grams. In Syria, the Levant, the shekel was 7 grams of the Phoenicians. It was the bronze standard of Sicily from which our monetary system has emerged. The bronze litra was divided into twelve onkiai, which translates in Latin to "uncia" or an ounce, meaning 12 ounces to a pound which we use in precious metals to this day.

Gradually, they would apply geometric designs to certify it had not been shaved down. Then during the 7ᵗʰ century BC, in the city of Sardis, Lydia (modern Turkey), we find the first design of a lion applied which was the symbol of the king who assumed authority over the coinage. It was the king who was creating the monetary standard and the unit of account. When Lydia faced Cyrus the Great (600 – 530 BC) in war from Persia, we see the first signs of inflation as the king began to reduce the weight of the coinage to fund the war effort which he lost.

Even in the aftermath of the metallic monetary system introduced in Egypt by Alexander the Great in 332 BC, grain banks continued to serve as a medium of exchange in Egypt. Precious metals were used in international trade or military conquests more so than in local transactions during

the early centuries. Naturally, grain deposited in a bank in Egypt would provide little use to a third party in Asia Minor. Eventually, the metallic monetary system displaced the use of grain as a medium of exchange by the Roman era.

Banking emerged in virtually every city of the ancient world. In Athens, as in most cities, banking had been conducted exclusively on a cash basis. The first offshore banking industry emerged in the tiny and remote island of Delos. Here the islanders had few natural resources. Their two greatest assets were the natural harbor, and it had a position as a holy sanctuary for a millennium before Olympian Greek mythology made it the birthplace of Apollo and Artemis.

To buy favor with the Gods, people would donate money to the Temple of Apollo in Delos. Since Gods cannot spend money, its wealth grew in size and fame. This was the beginning of the closest thing to an ancient central bank.

In Delos, cash transactions were replaced by an actual system of credit receipts and payments. Accounts were maintained for individual clients who could send instructions to make

Temple of Apollo - Delos

payment to another's account. Due to the rise of Rome, Delos' competitors were eliminated, namely Carthage and Corinth. This allowed the tiny island to prosper in its banking industry, thus providing a model system for the Romans to imitate. Yet, Rome never had a central bank nor a national debt.

The first such sovereign debt default on record took place at least in the 4th century BC when ten out of thirteen Greek municipalities in the Attic Maritime Association defaulted on loans from the Delos Temple of Apollo. In times of war, various city-states would borrow money from Delos. This sovereign default was on the Gods' property, but the kings seemed unphased by that technicality.

Government control of the monetary system first appeared in the ancient Egyptian economy, dating back into the third millennium BC (2750–2150 BC). The Egyptians measured the value of goods with a central unit but kept accounts. In many ways, they began with a paper money system, but they did not produce coinage until they were conquered by Alexander the Great in 334 BC. Banking and money changing (Forex) were closely centered around temples. Often, great temples served as treasuries holding vast sums of wealth donated by its followers. At times, various rulers would borrow from these treasuries at a prescribed rate of interest. Thus, temples provided a center for civilization to grow through their interactions.

The banking industry was needed for safekeeping as well as money changing. As the standardization of coinage began to take hold among the Greek city-states, the variety in weight standards created a demand for foreign exchange transactions thus creating the profession of moneychangers. The famous episode from the Bible (New Testament) where Christ overturns the tables of the moneychangers in the Temple of Jerusalem (Matthew 21:12) demonstrates how widespread the banking industry and foreign exchange dealers had become by the 1st century BC. The tables utilized by the money-changing traders were trapezium in shape and usually marked with a series of lines and squares used in calculations. This is the origin of the word "*trapezitai*" or the name used for Greek bankers. The word "bank" owes its heritage to the Italian word "*banca*," meaning bench or counter.

This need to store wealth greatly increased the ability to borrow, thus allowing modern-day credit foundations to emerge. The development of the banking industry was a milestone in the evolution of civilization. Both the banking industry and the monetary system fostered interaction among the peoples of the world, thus allowing international trade. This new age of interaction is the foundation of civilization. It is important in forming primitive societies to hunt and gather food in a cooperative manner to foster the need to develop language. The emergence of the banking system was an integral part of the development of civilization. The monetary system gravitated toward a one-world metallic form during the Hellenistic era when Alexander the Great standardized the coinage system, much like the euro, and eliminated money changing (Forex).

Indeed, banking had come a long way since the Babylonians first invented a monetary system's basic function to transfer wealth among individuals and collect

Alexander III the Great
(336-323BC)
AR Tetradrachm Babylon Mint

taxes. The Ptolemies of Egypt developed the two-tier monetary system using precious metals for international trade and grain for local monetary transactions. The Romans institutionalized banking, building upon the Delos model, and attempted to standardize the world's monetary system based upon a single world currency under Alexander the Great. But the Romans never created a central bank.

However, in the aftermath of the fall of the Roman Empire, banking disappeared in the chaos of barbarian invasions. The collapse of Rome ushered in the Dark Ages. The absence of banking led to the breakdown of trade and organization. Civilization had been dealt with a severe deathblow in Europe. It would take several centuries to pass before general prosperity and a rise in culture and living standards would reemerge once again out of necessity.

Historically, most fiscal crises were resolved through either war, where the loser's debt evaporates (e.g., Germany after WWII or the Confederate states in the USA), or by currency debasement by inflation or devaluation. This is demonstrated by numerous city debasements or a reduction in weight of gold and silver coinage. One of the earliest debasements was during 404 BC in Athens during the war with Sparta. The silver coinage was reduced to bronze and silver-plated to fund the Peloponnesian War with Sparta.

Banking has existed from the earliest of times. It has taken many forms from safe deposit storage, moneychangers, merchants with the ability to move money internationally, moneylenders, and governments to fund wars.

The Rise of Ancient Banking

Throughout the financial history of civilization, there have always been bank failures. They take place for two primary reasons: fraud and structural flaws that are exposed during a crisis when banks borrow short-term and lend long-term, which some argue is fractional banking. The former has been around since ancient times. We find that regulations were put in place due to financial panics that go back to the legal code of Hammurabi in 1750 BC. Not only did he require all transactions to be documented by a contract, but he also established specific wages and prices.

Even corruption between governments and bankers is nothing new. During the 4th century BC in the ancient Greek world, money that was donated to the Gods became the temple Treasury. Typically, the government would borrow from this hoard of cash, and thus temples emerged as bankers. In Athens, one of the early banking crisis events involved who we would call the secretary of the Treasury, so to speak, and his banking friends. While there may be some parallels to U.S. Treasury Secretary Hank Paulson helping Goldman Sachs during the crisis of 2007–2009, the events that took place are different, while the ethics are probably very similar.

Athenian Crisis 354 BC

Demosthenes
(384-322BC)

The temple kept its donations in the Opisthodomos and was not earning interest on its hoard of cash. The treasurer agreed to lend the money to personal banking friends who would then pay the treasurer interest that he could personally put in his pocket. When the banking crisis hit and there was a liquidity problem, the banks could not repay the loans to the temple.

Demosthenes (384–322 BC) tells us that banking transactions were completely confidential in Athens. He tells us that the rich could "conceal [their] wealth in order that [t]he[y] might obtain secret returns through the bank." (Dem 45.66). The banker Aristolochos was said to have taken substantial deposits and owed many a significant amount of funds (Dem 46.50). The bankers Sosinomos and Timodemos failed along with many others and were unable to meet demands for withdrawals (Dem 36.50). With a banking crisis in full bloom, the treasurer was exposed. In an attempt to cover up the scandal, they set fire to the Opisthodomos. Nevertheless, the scheme was detected, and the treasurers of Athens were seized and imprisoned around 377–376 BC.

In 1989, government ministers of Crete pulled the same scam. They were depositing government funds in the Bank of Crete and diverting interest into their own pockets. The Bank of Crete's failure exposed the scam.

Aristolochos' bank failed, it appears, due to real estate prices collapsing. Then the bankers failed, and all of their funds and properties were seized. Interestingly, Demosthenes warns his fellow Athenians of all of Attica's dire consequences should the banker Phormion be forced into bankruptcy. "Don't throw [him] away! Don't allow this piece of filth to bankrupt him!" In the midst of one of the earliest banking crises in history, Demosthenes saw that lending money was clearly the leverage that supported the entire economy. The drop in real estate in ancient Athens is not unlike that of the 2007 crisis. The deep corruption on the part of the treasurer is something that sets off a public crisis in the collapse of confidence in banking.

Demosthenes does make it clear that the people should be angry at the bankers who failed. Reading between the lines implies he is trying to counsel the people that they should not panic and withdraw their funds from all bankers. They should be justly concerned and outraged by the bankers who have failed, but they should not by any means attribute that to all bankers. These are words that have been repeated countless times in the midst of every panic throughout every century. They are being repeated once again today, with huge record bailouts. Demosthenes focused on the individual and tried to dispel the contagion that was spreading throughout the Athenian economy.

The second period of a banking failure occurred around 336 BC and involved a banker by the name of Herakleides. The 370 BC decade was one of a major Athenian banking crisis that seems to have involved government officials, which should come as no surprise.

Aristotle, in his *Politics,* argued against the idea of supply and demand insofar as he saw the problem from the demand side disconnected from the supply. Aristotle thus saw the problem that demand would rise and fall and sometimes exceed the supply without just cause.

Athens was transitioning from a predominantly agrarian society to one of trade that included manufacture and finance. He called this the "monied mode of acquisition" that drove the economy fed by businessmen concerned purely with profit, who he described as "making money from one another." The predominant economy was the villa that produced and consumed what it planted. Thus, his *Politics* was describing the changing economy as Athens was rising as an economic power.

Aristotle (384-322BC)

Roman Financial Crisis 33 AD

Tiberius
(14-37AD)

Augustus (27BC–14 AD) was very liberal in his spending. He is said to have been the richest man in all of history by a handsome margin. Because of this policy, there had been much real estate speculation. He had boasted that he found Rome made of brick but would leave it in marble.

When Tiberius came to power in 14 AD, he was intent upon ending the liberal spending habits of Augustus. He imposed limitations on credit to curtail real estate speculation. He required that two-thirds of every loan be invested in Italian land to reduce the speculation in the provinces that had become the emerging markets. Additionally, Tiberius decreed that two-thirds of every loan be repaid. Tiberius was imposing massive deleveraging within the economy, which would have been tremendously deflationary. The Senate was also deeply involved in real estate speculation. To protect their own self-interests, the senators implemented an 18-month stay to allow those impacted by these laws to settle their affairs before final judgment.

Restricting loans to Italian land and then ordering the repayment of two-thirds of such debts set in motion the collapse in real estate, especially in the provinces. Loans were now called in to be paid in full. Debtors were forced to sell, and the market was flooded with real estate as prices collapsed. Combined with Tiberius' contraction in new money, what developed was a tremendous shortage of money.

During the reign of Tiberius, we see a host of tokens privately produced to compensate for the shortage of coinage. We saw precisely the same response during the American Civil War, the German hyperinflation with private issues of Notgeld, and Depression Scrip of the 1930s. Over 200 American cities issued their own private money to allow commerce to take place.

Roman Tokens Time of Tiberius

probably issued during Massive Deflation 29-33AD
Copyright Martin Armstrong All Rights Reserved Worldwide 1998

Tiberius also set in motion a contagion of banking failures as people could not pay off their loans as prices collapsed. The banking firm Seuthes and Son of Alexandria faced difficulties after the loss of three richly laden ships in a Red Sea storm. This was followed by a fall in the value of ostrich feathers and ivory on top of the collapse in real estate values. At nearly the same time, the house of Malchus and Co. of Tyre with branches at Antioch and Ephesus suddenly became bankrupt as a result of a strike among their Phoenician workmen and the embezzlement of a freedman manager. These two failures also affected the Roman banking house Quintus Maximus and Lucious Vibo operating in the Roman Forum.

Roman Wall Street in the Forum - Via Sacra

These events set in motion bank runs, which then impacted another major Roman banking house of the Brothers Pittius. Via Sacra was the Wall Street of the day in the Roman Forum. It erupted in panic as the collapse impacted merchants in banking and the money supply. There was also a rebellion among the people of Northern Gaul, so now the emerging markets went into crisis as well. Money was contracting as no one would lend and hoarding soared. Tiberius' austerity created a major financial crisis.

When Publius Spencer, a wealthy nobleman, requested 30 million sesterces from his banker Balbus Ollius, the firm was unable to fulfill his request and closed its doors. Over the next few days, prominent banks in Corinth, Carthage, Lyons, and Byzantium all announced they had to also "rearrange their accounts." The banking panic and the closure of several banks along the Via Sacra in Rome devasted the economy because of Tiberius' austerity policy.

As the crisis spread throughout the empire, banks began calling in their loans on everyone to raise capital. When debtors could not meet their creditors' demands, they were forced to sell their homes and possessions. With money unavailable even at the legal limit of 12% interest, the economy tumbled down into deflation. The prices of real estate and other goods completely collapsed in a downward spiral of deflation. A full-scale financial panic was sweeping the entire Roman Empire. It has been argued that the crucifixion of Jesus was also in the midst of this financial crisis which played a role in Pontius Pilate's judgment since he was appointed by Tiberius in 26/27 AD and served until 36/37 AD.

The Financial Panic of 33 AD became so severe that Emperor Tiberius implemented what we would call Quantitative Easing. Eventually, the decrees which had precipitated the problem were suspended. Then 100 million sesterces were to be taken from the imperial treasury and distributed among reliable bankers to loan to the neediest debtors. A loaf of bread sold for half a sestertius, and soldiers earned around 1,000 sesterces annually. Therefore, this financial crisis sent the purchasing power of money drastically higher.

**Archelaus, (Caesarea, Cappadocia)
(36 BC - 17 AD)**
AR Drachm (3.78 grams) Year 22 (15/14 BC)

Tiberius responded by making loans interest-free. Furthermore, no interest was to be collected for three years. Security was to be offered at double the value in real property. This enabled many people to avoid selling their estates at distressed prices. It arrested the contraction in prices and ensured that the lack of liquidity would be addressed, but many banks never survived.

Cappadocia was a province in Turkey that remained an important and trusted eastern client kingdom under Emperor Augustus' reign. Tiberius' policy towards Cappadocia changed for personal reasons. Tiberius set about a change in Rome's eastern policy, for he felt slighted by Archelaus (36 BC–17 AD), the client king. Tiberius wanted direct access to Cappadocia's resources with the added advantage of reducing Archelaus who Augustus had placed in power over the kingdom. Tiberius summoned Archelaus to Rome, and upon his arrival, he threw him in prison where he died of natural causes. It is true that Tiberius provided aid to the cities in the East in the face of a major devastating earthquake. Tacitus tells us:

> "[T]welve noble cities of Asia were overturned by an earthquake: the ruin happened in the night, and the more dreadful as its warnings were unobserved; neither availed the usual sanctuary against such calamities, namely, a flight to the fields, since those who fled, the gaping earth devoured. It is reported 'that mighty mountains subsided, plains were heaved into high hills: and that with flashes and eruptions of fire, the mighty devastation was everywhere accompanied.'"

We have found that with the passage of time, nothing changes. History will always repeat, not because governments are the same or the level of technology may vary, but because the passions of human beings never change. The policies imposed by Tiberius are no different from the policies imposed by the U.S. Congress when the Democrats came into power and changed the laws to stop real estate speculation. Those misguided regulations led to the S&L Crisis as property values collapsed and banks failed.

The same frugal policies of Tiberius that led to a massive financial crisis during 33 AD have been employed in Germany and exported to the European Union. We must understand that when assets rise in value, that means the currency is declining in purchasing power. When the assets decline, this means there is a shortage of money, and its purchasing power then rises in value. You cannot have assets rise without the currency declining — plain and simple!

Julius Caesar & the Debt Crisis

In the late Roman Republic that pitted Julius Caesar against Pompey the Great, the entire Civil War was not due to Caesar desiring to be dictator for life. He was a member of the Populares, which was a party of the people against the oligarchy party by the name the Optimates. The core issue was a debt crisis where the Senate and the moneylenders abused the people. The people hoped for the cancelation of all debt, and they cheered Caesar when he crossed the Rubicon. Pompey and the corrupt senators fled to Asia, for they knew they did not have the people's support.

Julius Caesar (100-44BC)

Caesar showed remarkable insight into understanding the core nature of a debt crisis that modern politicians and economists lack. The historian Suetonius informs us on this subject that Caesar did not do what the people had expected of him. Even Mark Antony had bought Pompey's estate at auction on credit, assuming that Caesar would cancel all debts and he would end up with that property for free. Caesar refused to cancel all debts, for he saw such a measure would indeed wipe out the economy. In fact, it would have been a move akin to Marxism. Suetonius tells us:

> "He disappointed popular agitators by cancelling no debts, but in the end decreed that every debtor should have his property assessed according to pre-war valuation and, after deducting the interest already paid directly, or by way of a banker's guarantee, should satisfy his creditors with whatever sum that might represent. Since prices has risen steeply, this left debtors with perhaps a fourth part of their property."

Suetonius' Latin text:

> "De pecuniis mutuis disiecta novarum tabularum expectatione, quae crebro movebatur, decrevit tandem, ut debitores creditoribus satis facerent per aestimationem possessionum, quanti quasque ante civile bellum comparassent, deducto summae aeris alieni, si quid usurae nomine numeratum aut perscriptum fuisset; qua condicione quarta pars fere crediti deperibat."

Despite the desperate self-serving arguments of the Optimates that Caesar was seeking only personal power, his actions speak far beyond their biased words. This was truly a man who acted with incredible speed, making decisions in the remarkable short time he had as the economic reformer of Rome. He understood that the value of money was merely a commodity. This is a reality that nobody seems to pay attention to in governments.

ArmstrongEconomics.COM

The purchasing power of money rises and falls against all things tangible. This is effectively no different than the price of common stock of a corporation. People will spend feverishly when they believe delaying a purchase will cost them more. Likewise, central banks cannot stimulate the economy as long as people have no faith in the future, and they will hoard their money if they perceive their assets will remain the same in price or even decline.

Julius Caesar was confronted by a collapse in real estate values probably as a percentage far greater than we have seen during the 2007–2009 mortgage crisis. The people hoped that Caesar would just cancel all debts and end the crisis. That would have been a solution that only benefited the debtor. But such a policy would have wiped out the capital formation of the economy and caused serious harm to future economic growth that comes only from capital investment.

During the early Roman Republic, there was the nexum which was a contract whereby a free man became a bond slave, or nexus, until he could pay off his debt to the creditor. Therefore, it was not a simple act of handing back the property on which you had a mortgage. People became slaves to their mortgage, which extended to their children in the event of their death. It is likely that the terms of the nexum may have varied depending upon the lender. Still, the critical issue was that this was a debt bondage that existed during the Roman Republic. In some instances, people who had lost everything by some other means would also sell themselves into bondage to survive.

Nevertheless, nexum contracts were a preferable alternative to slavery for debtors since slaves could be sold or killed by their masters at will. This was more akin to indentured servitude, which expired with the termination of the contract. Creditors valued a nexum contract more so than a slave from a foreign land, for the person would generally be more motivated and still had human rights.

Roman historian Livy tells us of the abolishment of nexum contracts because of abusive Lucius Papirius. In 326 BC, a young boy named Gaius Publilius was the guarantor to his father's debt or contracted the debt to pay for his funeral. The lender desired the boy sexually, and when he refused, he was stripped and flogged. The boy ran out into the streets, and this incident is said to have prompted reform perhaps around 326 to 313 BC.

Cicero, an opponent of Caesar and a member of the Optimate Oligarchy, wrote about 300 years later that the abolishment of nexum was a political move to appease the plebeian masses temporarily. He wrote:

> "When the plebeians have been so weakened by the expenditures brought on by a public calamity that they give way under their burden, some relief or remedy has been sought for the difficulties of this class, for the sake of the safety of the whole body of citizens."

> (Cicero. *The Republic II. Trans. Clinton W. Keyes. On the Republic. On the Laws.* Cambridge, Massachusetts: Harvard University Press, 1928. 171)

Nevertheless, while the nexum as a legal contract was abolished, there still remained debt bondage where a borrower who defaulted the courts would still grant creditors the right to take insolvent debtors as bond slaves (*Social Conflicts in the Roman Republic.* Chatto & Windus Ltd. London: 1971. pp 56–57). This was clearly an issue behind the Civil War and why the people cheered Caesar.

The debt crisis that Julius Caesar faced was widespread, but the implications of an actual default by a debtor would not resolve the problem. If someone was unable to pay, it was not a question of just walking away and letting the lenders repossess the property. The lenders would refuse to accept a simple return of the original asset to settle the debt.

Consequently, this debt crisis faced by Julius Caesar was much more difficult to solve. There was no central bank or government bonds to buy to inject cash into the system, which fails to work anyhow. Caesar had to truly understand the problem and come up with a solution that would not destroy the economy as the majority of the Populares had been advocating.

Julius Caesar dealt with this extraordinary situation in a truly astonishing manner. Caesar realized that assets and money are on opposite sides of the scale. If the assets rise, then the purchasing power of money declines. Likewise, during an economic crisis when assets decline, the purchasing power of money rises. During the Civil War, bronze coinage virtually disappeared. About 95% of all coinage issued was silver with some gold and a tiny issue of bronze. After the rise of Augustus and the assassination of Caesar, bronze coinage was standardized and reintroduced.

Caesar understood that as the value of property rose, the measurement was money or the unit of account. When property declined in value, it was also measured in the same unit of account. Therefore, he realized that there was no constant relationship or ratio between money and assets. To this day, politicians try to pass laws to freeze the value of assets. This is also why Bretton Woods collapsed, for they fixed the value of money to gold but failed to restrict the quantity of money.

Athens (545 - 515BC)
Monetary System

Athens (Circa 545-525/15 BC) AR Didrachm (18.5mm, 8.49 grams)
"Wappenmünzen" series Facing gorgoneion

Athens (Circa 515-510 BC) AR Drachm (14mm, 3.76 grams)
"Wappenmünzen" series Wheel with four spokes

Athens (Circa 515-510 BC) AR Obol (8mm, 0.55 grams)
"Wappenmünzen" series Four-spoked wheel

Athens (Circa 561-546 BC) AR Hemiobol (6mm, 0.31 grams)
"Wappenmünzen" series Apple

ArmstrongEconomics.COM

The same human response in Athens may have inspired the Democratic Revolution in 508 BC, which was also instigated by a debt crisis. While there are no written sources identifying why there was civil unrest in Rome to overthrow their king and begin the Roman Republic in 509 BC, the answer may lie in a contagion from Athens' debt crisis.

Farmers were threatening rebellion in Athens (Attica), and a debtor not only risked personal slavery but that of his entire family as well. Once a slave, creditors could do with them as they saw fit. Many families were broken up and sold in overseas markets. The debt crisis was indeed severe, and the widespread personal slavery became a major problem that threatened to destroy the Greek Empire.

The Laws of Solon were the first major reform to the legal code of Hammurabi from 1792–1750 BC, which appears to have been custom in the ancient world. Although the Greeks lifted all maximum limitations on the legal rate of interest a moneylender might charge, personal slavery was banned entirely. All those who had been enslaved for debt were freed, and those sold into slavery in foreign lands were brought back at the expense of the state. Many debts were canceled, and others were secured by land when possible.

Solon
630-560BC

Athens - AR Tetradrachm
510-505BC (17.35 grams)

The issue of inflation was dealt with by devaluing the drachma by 25%, and weights and measures increased in size. Archaic Owls were the first owls issued c. 510 BC, at about the same time as the establishment of Athenian democracy, which was clearly linked to a debt crisis. Political power shifted from landowners to capitalists and this was reappointed once again back into the hands of the property owners.

Citizenship had been granted to immigrants who were skilled, which is similar to what we still do to this day. The influx of people created speculation, much as we witnessed with the Chinese migration to Vancouver, Canada. No doubt, there were stories that Athens was the place to make your fortune, similar to stories that the streets in America were paved in gold to inspire the great European migration to America. There is always an attraction in the early development of a city that draws in the population. The same has taken place throughout the centuries from Rome, London, New York, and Hollywood.

In modern times, the bankers donated to the Clintons to create similar laws to benefit lenders whereby student loans cannot be extinguished in bankruptcy. While students cannot be sold into slavery, they are burdened with the abuse the Democrats enacted that prevents them from applying for a house loan.

The Laws of Solon in 594 BC were indeed a major reform that dealt directly with the issues of a major debt crisis. Over the following 100 years, the laws of Solon had helped insofar as avoiding massive debtor slavery, but interest rates were still free to float without legal limitation. The customary rate on secured loans tended to move back and forth between 16% and 20% per annum. The scarcity of precious metals also aided in creating somewhat of a digression atmosphere at times. This may have been a contributing factor to the widespread political upheavals that came in 508 BC. The birth of democracy in Athens and the birth of the Roman Republic happened in 509 BC.

Money Can Never be a Constant

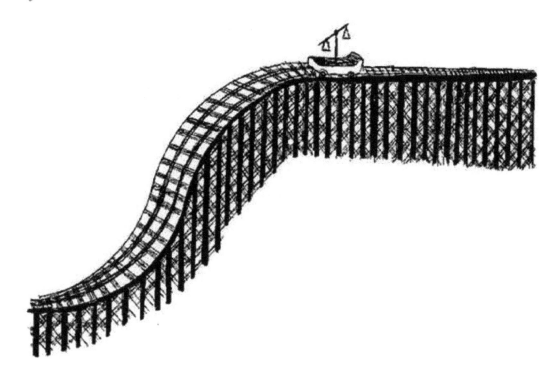

Our greatest problem has been this failure to grasp the fact that the value of money cannot be constant. The boom-bust of the business cycle has inspired Marxist philosophies from socialism to communism, all in hopes of smoothing out the business cycle and creating the economic land of Utopia.

The problem we face is the balance with assets on one side and money on the other. Picture it as a cart attached to a ride on a rollercoaster. The value of money moves up and down against assets, but then it also rises and falls based upon international confidence in a country on the world's foreign exchange markets. So, it is in a cart on a rollercoaster where domestic policy objectives cannot be controlled because of international policy realities. We may think we are making or losing money, but are we if money itself cannot be a constant? We are taxed based only on one side of the scale without understanding that often the net true wealth may have never changed.

Albert Einstein was seen as a genius. He was asked how he thought. People just assumed that his brain was some sort of a fluke. He replied, "A new idea comes suddenly and in a rather intuitive way," and his thoughts, he exclaimed, moved in a "wildly speculative way." He was also asked if he thought in words. Einstein replied, "I rarely think in words at all. A thought comes and I may try to express it in words afterward…I have no doubt that our thinking goes on for the most part without the use of signs and, furthermore, largely unconsciously."

Most people assume that they think only in words. But they are wrong. People assumed that Einstein was just a genius and did not listen to what he was saying. He visualized relationships, and that leads to concepts. The concepts flow so fast that there is no time to bother forming words. The comprehension suddenly appears, and then you try to rationalize the idea in words.

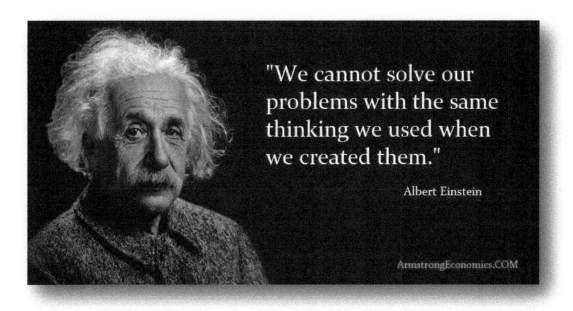

Government appears to be incapable of thinking in concepts. They always try to reduce everything to a single cause and effect. We cannot solve the problem we face with the same thinking process that created this mess. Those of us who can see the patterns throughout history are condemned to watch history repeat, as society constantly makes the same mistakes over and over again.

When we are children, our parents tell us not to stick our finger in the flame of a candle because it will hurt. We all do it because we must experience it for ourselves. If we are not totally stupid, we learn after one attempt and never do it again. History repeats because society is incapable of acquiring such knowledge so we attempt the same stupid solutions and get the same disastrous results. Nobody simply asks, "Has this been attempted before? Did it work?"

The Structural Flaw that Always Dooms Banking

It appears that most people are unaware of the actual model upon which banking takes place today post-slavery and debtors' prison. For if you look closely, you will understand why banks fail in the middle of a financial crisis. This is created by the fact that banks borrow on-demand short-term, but they lend long-term. When a financial crisis hits, the banks cannot raise cash fast enough to meet the demands of people wanting to withdraw their money from the bank because the bulk of it has been lent out long-term on loans such as mortgages.

The business model is inherently flawed. They borrow short-term on-demand and lend long-term. They take your demand deposits in your checking account and lend for mortgages out 30 years. Some just book the loans and then resell them. Nevertheless, there will always be bank failures because the business model is simply unsound. The way to correct the problem is simple — long-term lending must be matched only with term deposits and never with demand deposits. However, traditionally, long-term interest rates are higher than short-term. The central bank can regulate the short-term rates, but not the long-term without draconian measures.

Jay Cooke (1821 - 1905)

Back during the U.S. Civil War, the U.S. federal government suddenly needed to borrow money. They turned to Jay Cooke (1821–1905) who became the first "Primary Dealer" to sell government debt for the Civil War. Cooke was the real financier of the Civil War. He is considered to be the first major investment banker in the United States. Cooke embraced technology by adopting the telegraph and thereby establishing the first wire house firm. He used the railroads to distribute bonds to people around the nation.

John Pierpont Morgan
(1837-1913)

The Panic of 1873 ended Jay Cooke & Company with his losses in the railroads. With the collapse of Jay Cooke & Company, the investment banking field opened. The next man to fill that role was none other than J.P. Morgan (1837–1913), who also began in Philadelphia. J.P. Morgan moved the financial capital of the United States to New York City. New York and Wall Street became the primary financial center of the United States.

There was always rivalry between Philadelphia and New York City. In fact, New York did not sign the Declaration of Independence on July 4th with other states. On July 15, New York's delegates finally received permission from their convention to agree to sign the Declaration. New York was the first capital of the United States since that is where Washington was sworn in on April 30, 1789, on Wall Street.

Since the government turned to Jay Cooke to sell the bonds for them during the American Civil War, the system of relying on bankers, known as Primary Dealers, to sell the government debt left them with extraordinary power. No matter what they have done to create financial disasters, many now regard them as the untouchables, for they can engage in crimes and fraud, and no one will ever be prosecuted. The government needs them to sell their debt, and thus they have become the exception to legal prosecution.

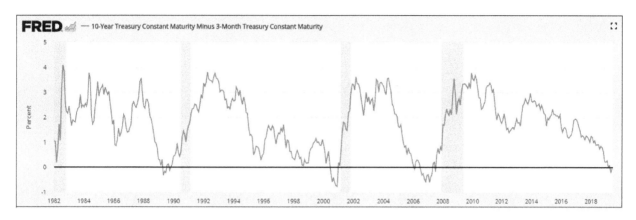

Since the business model is to borrow short-term and lend long-term, we can see that the majority of the time long-term interest rates are above that of short-term rates. This is the way banks make money in general.

However, during an economic crisis, a liquidity crisis emerges since assets are overvalued relative to the supply of money. People then rush for cash, and tangible assets decline in value against cash. Suddenly, short-term rates will invert and rise above long-term. This is when banks fail. If the banks try to foreclose on long-term loans and take back property, they are confronted with losses, for the value of the property declines as the purchasing power of money rises.

During economic booms, tangible assets rise in value, and the purchasing value of money declines. When the economic boom is over, then the value of cash rises, and tangible assets fall. This is merely the reality of the business cycle. People demand that government create a solution by creating some law that could never work. Human emotions drive the business cycle. It cannot be eliminated and governments will typically enact a solution which only becomes the very cause of the next business cycle event.

There is little doubt that banking crises appear throughout history. There were some 9,000 bank failures during the Great Depression which had a common theme. The very structural design upon which the banking system operates is flawed. Banks take deposits on-demand but will lend money out long-term as in mortgages on real estate. When there is a banking crisis, it is driven by fears of losing assets which materialize in bank runs. Because the banks borrow on-demand with short-term customer deposits and lend long-

term, they are unable to recall their loans to get cash to meet the withdrawal of demand deposits. This is what we call a liquidity crisis. They cannot liquidate the long-term assets at the values they once were to meet the demand for withdrawals on short-term cash.

The problem with banking is the model fails every time, thanks to the business cycle. The business model of banking is simply to borrow on-demand and lend long-term. In a panic, the demand wants its cash now, and that cash is tied up long-term. Hence, there is a liquidity crisis, and the bank will fail.

Many banks have adopted the idea of securitization. Goldman Sachs, for example, packaged mortgages into pools and sold them to investors. The banks make the loans and then sell them in bundled lots (asset-backed securities) rather than tying up their cash long-term. This structure went bust in 2007 and caused a major financial crisis during 2007-2009, which was profound and the worst since the Great Depression. This event destroyed two investment banks, Lehman and Bear Stearns.

We must understand the nature of the banking system. It is this flaw of borrowing short-term and lending long-term that works only when all things are equal. If the public's confidence is suddenly shaken, then we end up with a banking crisis that fuels the event of a financial panic.

Relationship v Transactional Banking

Relationship v Transactional Banking

With the dawn of modern banking, there has been a shift from relationship banking to what has become transactional banking. Banks are trying to escape the business cycle, and inevitable banking crises emerge in the aftermath of liquidity crises between short and long-term capital.

The Clintons drastically altered banking and created the crisis of 2007-2009 with the collapse of mortgage-backed securities. The Clintons allowed banks to depart from the age-old establishment of relationship banking with one-on-one lending to embark on the securitization of debt to resell loans. This removed the binding element that created civilization — relationships. They spread the risk from banks to the entire economy for the incentive shifted to create products that could be sold rather than offer valid contracts that would expand economic growth and create jobs.

The Clinton Administration opened the door to the dawn of transactional banking and aligned itself with the investment banks. Post-1993, Goldman Sachs and Solomon Brothers were caught manipulating the U.S. government Treasury auctions. In 1991, I believe Goldman Sachs' strategy turned to infiltrate government to secure immunity for the future. Glass-Steagall of the 1930s emerged after about 9,000 banks failed during the Great Depression. The main investment banks had one common theme. They were speculating and trading while selling products to customers, be it foreign government bonds or pools for investing in stocks, as Goldman Sachs did.

William Jefferson Clinton (born 1946)
42nd President of the United States (1993 - 2001)

Interstate banking was prohibited in 1927 under the McFadden Act. The act sought to give national banks competitive equality with state-chartered banks by letting national banks branch to the extent permitted by state law. The McFadden Act specifically prohibited interstate branching by allowing each national bank to branch only within the state in which it was situated. This was intended in part to prevent the collapse of one bank, which could create a national contagion.

Louis Thomas McFadden
(1876 - 1936)

The interstate banking prohibition of the provision of the McFadden Act was then repealed by the Riegle-Neal Interstate Banking and Branching Efficiency Act of 1994, which declared that state law continued to control intrastate branching, or branching within a state's borders, for both state and national banks, but not outside the state. Clearly, the Clinton Administration altered the entire banking structure in 1994. The Clintons repealed this safeguard that had been put in place after the experience of the Great Depression.

However, the Bank Holding Company Act of 1956 (12 U.S.C. §1841, et seq.) regulated the actions of bank holding companies. Originally, the Federal Reserve Board of Governors had to approve the establishment of a bank holding company and prohibited bank holding companies headquartered in one state from acquiring a bank in another state. The law was intended to regulate and control banks, preventing them from owning both banking and non-banking businesses and circumventing Glass-

Steagall. The law generally prohibited a bank holding company from engaging in most non-banking activities or acquiring voting securities of certain companies that were not banks.

The Bank Holding Company Act (1956)
Clintons Repealed in 1994 under the
Riegle-Neal Interstate Banking and Branching Efficiency Act of 1994 (IBBEA)

ArmstrongEconomics.COM

The Clintons also repealed the Bank Holding Company Act under the Riegle-Neal Interstate Banking and Branching Efficiency Act of 1994 (IBBEA). The IBBEA then allowed interstate mergers between "adequately capitalized and managed banks, subject to concentration limits, state laws and Community Reinvestment Act (CRA) evaluations." Other restrictions that prohibited bank holding companies from owning other financial institutions were all repealed in 1999 by the Gramm-Leach-Bliley Act, which ended Glass-Steagall. In the United States, financial holding companies continue to be prohibited from owning non-financial corporations in contrast to Japan and continental Europe where this arrangement is common.

Private equity firms that solicit funds but are not classified as banks, and are thus outside the Federal Deposit Insurance Corporation (FDIC), were suddenly allowed to acquire large ownership positions in a number of non-bank corporations. However, private equity firms could also profitably invest in banks by injecting reasonable capital, engaging experienced, professional bank management, and prudently investing the bank's funds in loans and other investments that make economic sense. The Clintons opened Pandora's box entirely.

Goldman Sachs' U.S. Secretaries of Treasury

Robert Edward Rubin (born 1938)
70th US Secretary of the Treasury
during the Clinton administration
*(Was at Goldman Sachs for 26 years
before entering government)*

Henry Merritt "Hank" Paulson, Jr. (born 1946)
74th United States Secretary of the Treasury
*(He had served as the Chairman and Chief Executive
Officer of Goldman Sachs which he joined in 1974)*

Robert Rubin, the former chairman of Goldman Sachs, was the first to take a government job in the White House after Solomon Brothers had been caught manipulating the U.S. Treasury auctions in 1991. Hank Paulson, former Chairman of Goldman Sachs, took the post under George Bush Jr. and protected Goldman Sachs during the 2007–2009 crisis. Rubin became the first director of the National Economic Council on January 25, 1993, which was a post he kept until January 11, 1995, when he became the 70th United States secretary of the treasury until July 2, 1999.

Roosevelt signs Glass-Steagall Act (June 16, 1933)

Clinton signs Gramm-Leach-Bliley Act, repealing key aspects of Glass-Steagall Act (November 12, 1999)

Rubin held that position of treasury secretary until he managed to get Glass-Steagall in the cue to be repealed. It certainly appears that the entire purpose of

Glass–Steagall separating banks, brokers, and insurance was the last straw to be repealed by the Clinton Administration who did the bidding on behalf of the New York investment banking firms. Robert Rubin worked from the inside during the Clinton Administration to repeal all restrictions on banking. This enabled the creation of mortgage-backed securities that the banks created and sold to investors, thereby blowing up the world economy. Rubin cut the chains that bound the bankers and opened the gates to unsound finance by blending trading, banking, and insurance, culminating in the 2007–2009 crisis. The world economy has been unable to recover from that crisis even with more than 10 years of Quantitative Easing.

These regulations were put in place because of the Great Depression, and it was Goldman Sachs who had the worst track record back then as well. Goldman Sachs was under Waddill Catchings' leadership (1879–1967) who influenced many policymakers, including Herbert Hoover.

Waddill Catchings
(1879 – 1967)

Catchings graduated from Harvard and replaced Henry Goldman as senior partner of Goldman Sachs in 1918. He transformed the brokerage house into an investment trust, establishing the Goldman Sachs Trading Corporation (effectively, a hedge fund). He nurtured its meteoric rise during the boom years of the 1920s to the point where it reached nearly a half-billion dollars in assets.

Catchings saw that a giant fund could maximize profits by buying and selling stocks to generate commissions for the firm. He promoted this as a business model that was professional and the way to the future.

Catchings named this company Goldman Sachs Trading Corporation. The deal was that Goldman Sachs would be paid 20% of the profit, offering stocks at $104 per share. The stock jumped to $226 per share — twice its book value. He expanded the leverage going right into the eye of the storm.

During the summer of 1929, Goldman Sachs launched two more trusts: Shenandoah and the memorable Blue Ridge. The shares were over-subscribed. Shenandoah began at just $17.80 and closed on the first trading day at $36 per share. Blue Ridge was leveraged even more, and the partners at Goldman Sachs put pressure on everyone to buy as a sign of support. The leverage was astonishing; with just about $25 million in capital, there was more than $500 million at stake.

By 1931, Catchings had nearly bankrupt Goldman Sachs. The floating of its Shenandoah & Blue Ridge investment trusts were nearly wiped out during the crash of 1929. Catchings left the firm in 1930 in shambles. The disaster was monumental. Goldman Sachs Trading Company, whose shares had stood at $326 at their peak, fell during the Great Depression to $1.75. They fell to less than 1% of their high. The loss suffered at Goldman Sachs on a percentage basis was far worse than at any other trust. In fact, of the top trusts,

Marcus Goldman
(1821-1904)

Samuel Sachs
(1851-1935)

Goldman Sachs had lost about 70% of the entire trust market.

Goldman Sachs was awash with lawsuits and became the target of jokes in Vaudeville. This would fuel the anti-Jewish feeling in New York for decades to

Sidney James Weinberg
(1891–1969)

come. Samuel Sachs (1851–1935) died in 1935 at the age of 84. He was devastated, for what he had worked for was to build the firm's reputation. That is what broke the family in two.

Catchings' No. 2 at Goldman Sachs Trading was Sidney Weinberg (1891–1969), who would have to unwind the worst fund management in history. The share price of Goldman Sachs Trading dropped from $326 to $1.75. Weinberg reorganized the firm and lifted it from oblivion. He eventually became known as "Mr. Wall Street," a title given to him by the *New York Times*.

Against the historical backdrop, Robert Rubin managed to sell the idea of transactional banking once again. He argued that allowing investment banks to create products and resell them would make the banks stronger. The loans would not sit on the books of the banks. They would create the loans and repackage them, thereby creating transactional banking. This resulted in the complete abandonment of relationship banking, where the bank knew the borrower and was there to verify the security.

With transactional banking restored, banks could now package loans and resell them. They could not care less about the quality of the loans or the traditional relationship banking structure to secure debts. This transformation of banking from the historical relationship banking to transactional banking undermines civilization itself. This is at the heart of everything that is turning society

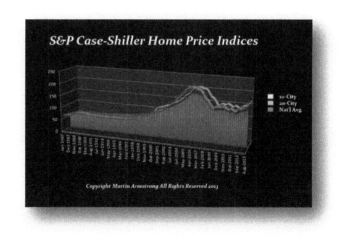

down. About 80% of small businesses cannot get loans, and this is where relationship banking counts, for that is the type of lending that creates jobs and expands the economy.

The Economic Confidence Model (ECM) peaked in 2007.15 (February 26, 2007). That turning point marked the very day of the high in the Case-Shiller Real Estate Index. However, it also marked the precise day of the infamous sale at the top of Goldman Sachs' notorious ABACUS 2007–AC1 $2 billion Synthetic CDO.

The *New York Times* reported on November 9, 2009, that the chief executive of Goldman Sachs, Lloyd Blankfein, had responded to "widespread media attention over the size of its staff bonuses, says he believes banks serve a social purpose and are 'doing God's work.'"

On April 27, 2010, during the Senate's permanent subcommittee on investigating Wall Street's latest crisis, the most memorable moment burst onto the scene. Democratic Senator Carl Levin of Michigan held up an e-mail that had been written almost three years before by two of Goldman Sachs' most senior traders. The dramatic event emerged as the e-mail described a Goldman CDO

(collateralized debt obligation) as "one shitty deal." Lloyd Blankfein was testifying. Levin interrogated him, demanding to know if it was ethical for Goldman to sell a security that its traders believed was a "shitty deal" for the client when Goldman Sachs was betting against the success of that security and their own client.

Blankfein was noticeably uncomfortable yet defended Goldman's conduct, replying:

> "In the context of market-making, that is not a conflict. What the clients are buying, or customers are buying, is—they are buying an exposure. The thing that we are selling to them is supposed to give them the risk they want."

Blankfein was stating that it did not matter what Goldman thought of a deal. Clients "are not coming to us to represent what our views are." However, when Goldman is designing the instrument, a different perspective emerges as they know what is inside that product. This takes on a whole different ethical connotation.

Levin indeed had dug through the 900 pages of additional Goldman documents that were released that same day. Another three-year-old e-mail popped out. This one was written by Craig Broderick, who was Goldman's chief risk officer and a top player in the firm, relied upon by Blankfein.

The Broderick Memo of May 11, 2007, as it became known, revealed that Goldman planned to keep the firm profitable while many other banks went under by marking down the prices on its portfolio of CDOs and synthetic CDOs. Short the market first and then mark down the products to force others to do the same. It was a brilliant scheme — the ultimate inside trade. Broderick's memo stated that Goldman's decision to mark down the prices on its portfolio of derivatives such as CDOs and synthetic CDOs "will potentially have a big [profit and loss] impact on us, but also to our clients....We need to survey our clients and take a shot at determining the most vulnerable clients, knock on implications, etc. This is getting lots of 30th floor attention right now."

Goldman was net short on the mortgage market by May 2007, and such a markdown would be profitable to the firm and devastating to the marketplace. Goldman's decision to mark down the CDOs aggressively indeed set off a chain reaction of events that led to the failure of Lehman and Bear. Goldman's most profitable year to date was 2007, posting earnings of $17.6 billion pretax.

"So what happened to us? ... In market risk – you saw in our 2nd and 3rd qtr results that we made money despite our inherently long cash positions. – because starting early in '07 our mortgage trading desk started putting on big short positions ... and did so in enough quantity that we were net short, and made money (substantial $$ in the 3rd quarter) as the subprime market weakened."
-- Goldman Sachs, Tax Department Presentation by Craig Broderick, Chief Risk Officer, 10/29/07, GS MBS-E-010018512, Exhibit 48

Broderick's subsequent email on October 29, 2007, confirmed that Goldman was trading against its clients. Originally, investment bankers were supposed to bring new companies to market and expand the economy by creating jobs. But Goldman Sachs, I believe, saw how Solomon Brothers was taken down and was the biggest primary dealer in government bonds. It was after that 1991 incident when suddenly Goldman's staff began to enter politics. This provided immunity to prosecution. With the crash of 2007–2009, the people and press outside of New York City began to question why no New York banker ever went to jail for what they did. The Securities Exchange Commission (SEC) then at least tried to pretend they were unbiased by charging Goldman Sachs, but nobody was ever prosecuted. This led to the term "Government Sachs" who are "untouchables."

6A   Saturday, April 17, 2010   Montgomery Advertiser

Goldman Sachs faces charges of defrauding clients

By Marcy Gordon
The Associated Press

WASHINGTON — The government on Friday accused Wall Street's most powerful firm of fraud, saying Goldman Sachs & Co. sold mortgage investments without telling the buyers that the securities were crafted with input from a client who was betting on them to fail.

And fail they did. The securities cost investors close to $1 billion while helping Goldman client Paulson & Co. capitalize on the housing bust. The Goldman executive accused of shepherding the deal allegedly boasted about the "exotic trades" he created "without necessarily understanding all of the implications of those monstrosities!!!"

The civil charges filed by the Securities and Exchange Commission are the government's most significant legal action related to the mortgage meltdown that ignited the financial crisis and helped plunge the country into recession.

The news sent Goldman Sachs shares and the stock market reeling as the SEC said other financial deals related to the meltdown continue to be investigated. It was a blow to the reputation of a financial giant that had emerged relatively unscathed from the economic crisis.

Goldman Sachs denied the allegations. In a statement, it called the SEC's charges "com-pletely unfounded in law and fact" and said it will contest them.

The SEC said Paulson paid Goldman roughly $15 million in 2007 to devise an investment tied to mortgage-related securities that the hedge fund viewed as likely to decline in value. Separately, Paulson took out a form of insurance that allowed it to make a huge profit when those securities' value plunged.

The fraud allegations focus on how Goldman sold the securities.

Goldman told investors that a third party, ACA Management LLC, had selected the pools of subprime mortgages it used to create the securities. The securities are known as synthetic collateralized debt obligations.

The SEC alleges that Goldman misled investors by failing to disclose that Paulson & Co. also played a role in selecting the mortgage pools and stood to profit from their decline in value.

"Goldman wrongly permitted a client that was betting against the mortgage market to heavily influence which mortgage securities to include in an investment portfolio, while telling other investors that the securities were selected by an independent, objective third party," SEC Enforcement Director Robert Khuzami said in a statement.

But Goldman said in a state-ment that it never mischaracterized Paulson's strategy in the transaction. It added that it wasn't obliged to "disclose the identities of a buyer to a seller and vice versa."

The charges name Goldman and one executive, Fabrice Tourre, who was a vice president in his late 20s when the alleged fraud was orchestrated in 2007. Tourre, the SEC said, boasted to a friend that he was able to put such deals together as the mortgage market was unraveling in early 2007.

In an e-mail to the friend, he described himself as "the fabulous Fab standing in the middle of all these complex, highly leveraged, exotic trades he created without necessarily understanding all of the implications of those monstrosities!!!"

Tourre, 31, has since been promoted to executive director of Goldman Sachs International in London. A call to a lawyer for Tourre, Pamela Chepiga at Allen & Overy LLP, wasn't returned.

Two European banks that bought the securities lost nearly $1 billion, the SEC said. The agency is seeking restitution and unspecified fines from Goldman Sachs and Tourre.

Asked why the SEC did not also pursue a case against Paulson, Khuzami said: "It was Goldman that made the representations to investors. Paulson did not."

Paulson & Co. is run by John Paulson, who reaped billions by betting against subprime mortgage securities. He is not related to former Treasury Secretary Henry Paulson, a former Goldman CEO.

John Paulson was among the first on Wall Street to bet heavily against subprime mortgages. His firm earned more than $15 billion in 2007, and he pocketed $3.7 billion. He has since earned billions more, largely by betting against bank stocks and then buying them back after their shares plunged.

In a statement, Paulson & Co. said: "As the SEC said at its press conference, Paulson is not the subject of this complaint, made no misrepresentations and is not the subject of any charges."

Goldman, founded more than 140 years ago, built a reputation as a trusted adviser to investment banking clients and for sending top executives into presidential Cabinet posts.

In recent years, it shifted toward taking more risks with its clients' money and its own. Goldman's trading allowed the firm to weather the financial crisis better than most other big banks. It earned a record $4.79 billion in the last quarter of 2009.

The complaint filed in federal court in Manhattan "undermines their brand," said Simon Johnson, a professor at the Massachusetts Institute of Technology and a Goldman critic. "It undermines their political clout. I don't think anybody really values being connected to Goldman at this point."

He continued: "There are many people who — until this morning — thought Goldman Sachs was well-run."

The SEC's enforcement chief said the agency is investigating a wide range of practices related to the crisis. The prospect of possible legal jeopardy for other major financial players roiled the stock market.

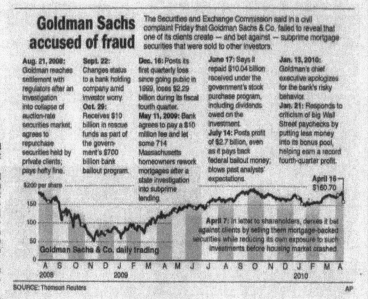

Goldman Sachs accused of fraud

The Securities and Exchange Commission said in a civil complaint Friday that Goldman Sachs & Co. failed to reveal that one of its clients create — and bet against — subprime mortgage securities that were sold to other investors.

Aug. 21, 2008: Goldman reaches settlement with regulators after an investigation into collapse of auction-rate securities market; agrees to repurchase securities held by private clients; pays hefty fine.

Sept. 22: Changes status to a bank holding company amid investor worry. **Oct. 29:** Receives $10 billion in rescue funds as part of the government's $700 billion bank bailout program.

Dec. 16: Posts its first quarterly loss since going public in 1999, loses $2.29 billion during its fiscal fourth quarter. **May 11, 2009:** Bank agrees to pay a $10 million fee and let some 714 Massachusetts homeowners rework mortgages after a state investigation into subprime lending.

June 17: Says it repaid $10.04 billion received under the government's stock purchase program, including dividends owed on the investment. **July 14:** Posts profit of $2.7 billion, even as it pays back federal bailout money; blows past analysts' expectations.

Jan. 13, 2010: Goldman's chief executive apologizes for the bank's risky behavior. **Jan. 21:** Responds to criticism of big Wall Street paychecks by putting less money into its bonus pool, helping earn a record fourth-quarter profit.

Goldman Sachs & Co. daily trading

April 7: In letter to shareholders, denies it bet against clients by selling them mortgage-backed securities while reducing its own exposure to such investments before housing market crashed.

April 16: $160.70

SOURCE: Thomson Reuters   AP

STOCKS OF LOCAL INTEREST						
NAME	SYMBOL	DIV	PE	DAILY CLOSE	DAILY CHG	YTD %CHG
AT&T Inc	T	1.68	12	25.93	-.31	-7.5
BB&T Cp	BBT	.60	29	33.76	-.42	+33.1

Indeed, Goldman Sachs was later charged with fraud by the SEC. Goldman Sachs was formally charged to make a show that Goldman Sachs did not buy the government. But the fine was minor compared to the role the company played in the 2007 mortgage scandal.

The Wall Street firm agreed to only a civil settlement of up to $5 billion with federal prosecutors and regulators arising from its marketing and selling of known faulty mortgage securities to investors. Goldman Sachs announced:

> "Under the terms of the agreement in principle, the firm will pay a $2.385 billion civil monetary penalty, make $875 million in cash payments and provide $1.8 billion in consumer relief. The consumer relief will be in the form of principal forgiveness for underwater homeowners and distressed borrowers; financing for construction, rehabilitation and preservation of affordable housing; and support for debt restructuring, foreclosure prevention and housing quality improvement programs, as well as land banks."

February of 2007 was the peak of the U.S. Real Estate Bubble. Even the Wilshire U.S. Real Estate Investment Trust (REIT) Total Market Index set a record high of 6,501.40 at the time. Taking this index and creating a ratio to GDP illustrated that the Wilshire US REIT/GDP Ratio stood at 45.7% in 2007 and crashed to 13.32% by 2009. The high-end real estate recovered as people tried to move money out of banks and bonds by 2013 into 2018. However, the low-end of the market where the mortgage-backed securities were created has still not recovered by the middle of 2019.

Thanks to the Clintons leading the Democrats to eliminate all bank regulations from the Great Depression, the real crisis emerged. The Democrats allowed investment banking and proprietary trading to expand into the entire financial system, converting relationship banking into transactional banking. Small business was now routinely denied access to funding with the rejection rate running at about 80%.

The Washington Times

Reliable Reporting. The Right Opinion.

News · Policy · Investigations · Opinion · Sports · Special Reports · Games ·

Clinton says she has 'both a public and a private position' on Wall Street: WikiLeaks release

She also admitted she was 'kind of far removed' from the middle class

Hillary Clinton told top banking executives that she has "both a public and a private position" on Wall Street reform and is reliant on wealthy donors to fund her campaign, leaked excerpts of the former first lady's speeches seem to show, fueling claims of hypocrisy on the part of Mrs. Clinton at a crucial moment in the presidential campaign.

The release by WikiLeaks, which the Clinton campaign has said it will not confirm, appears to show Mrs. Clinton discussing how she seeks to "balance" her public rhetoric on Wall Street reform with her actual positions, and with the reality that wealthy bankers and investors must partner with government to enact change. The documents also show the former secretary of state admitting that she's out of touch with average Americans and is "kind of far removed" from the lives of the middle class.

She also claims it's an "oversimplification" to say that the banking sector was responsible for the 2008 financial meltdown.

The bombshell revelations, which came less than 48 hours before Mrs. Clinton's next debate against Republican Donald Trump, led top progressives to publicly call on Mrs. Clinton to redouble her vows to crack down on Wall Street. Leading liberals, including Sen. Bernard Sanders, long have called on Mrs. Clinton to release transcripts of the speeches, which she delivered after her four years as secretary of state.

During the presidential campaign of 2016, it was revealed that Hillary Clinton told the bankers whatever promises she made to the public were irrelevant, for she was on the side of the bankers. The Democrats even came out and demanded that she "redouble her vows to crack down on Wall Street," but of course, the bankers were donating to Hillary — not Trump. The Clintons did everything in their power to remove all restrictions on the bankers, and they completely altered society by shifting finance from the relationship banking ethical way of doing business to packaged products and transactional banking where they even trade against their own clients.

Fractional Banking

There are those who blame fractional banking for everything, arguing that banks are creating money by lending out of thin air. They argue if a bank lends, say $100, then two accounts would show $100 each despite the original amount of $100 created by the government. On Sunday, June 10, 2018, Switzerland's electorate voted on a referendum calling for the country's commercial banks to be banned from creating money by lending. They have no understanding of the world economy and would have gone as far as destroying the value of their own homes since no one could buy under those terms unless they paid cash.

This referendum was known as the "sovereign money" proposal that commercial banks in Switzerland should no longer be allowed to create money out of thin air. They argued that only the Swiss central bank should have the power to create money. Sovereign money was a concept where they referred to money issued or created by a state or central bank exclusively.

They tried to tell the people that the bulk of all money in today's global financial system was created, not by central banks, but by commercial banks. They argued that these commercial banks create money without restriction, which is untrue, and in unlimited amounts (also untrue). When they lend money, they provide credit and create debt, which they then call an 'asset' on the asset side of their balance sheets.

The popular argument was that commercial banks create money via lending on the asset side of their balance sheets and creating deposits. As liabilities of a commercial bank, these deposits are only fractionally backed by the bank's assets, hence the term fractional-reserve banking.

These arguments all assume:

(1) the validity of the Quantity Theory of Money, and

(2) that the Business Cycle with its booms and busts are caused, at least impart, by the Fractional Banking issue

These groups who target fractional banking as the cause of booms and busts further allege that this would solve all the world's evils if it were eliminated. Such a proposal would flatline the business cycle, and by no means would it create a financial Utopia. Effectively, that was the world that existed under communism. However, they fail to take into account the fact that government is the biggest borrower. All lending in this respect creates "leverage" in the entire economic system.

1860 Gosbank Russia

Banking in the Soviet Union was provided by a state-run and owned bank, Gosbank (Literally, "The State Bank"). Gosbank was originally a Tsarist Russia State Bank, the central bank owned and operated by the government. Tsarist Russia also had private banks that were used to improve the Russian economy by loaning money at low rates to industrialists and facilitating foreign investment in Russia. They also provided support to the landed class and industrialists by providing modern banking practices and facilities.

The concept of a bank was the target of the Russian revolutionaries. Lenin himself was in favor of a single banking entity and eliminating all lesser private banks. Lenin saw that a single state-controlled bank entity was to be integrated into the centrally planned economy of the Soviet Union. It was to control the economy, providing a stable currency and foreign exchange.

Lenin's view was that the bank would be essential to maintain accounting of production and distribution of goods. It would also provide the infrastructure needed to create a Socialist society. Obviously, after the Revolution and Civil War, the existing state bank collapsed, and the modern Gosbank did not arise until about a decade later during the early 1930s. Gosbank was then joined by Sperbank ("Savings Bank"), the sole bank for household savings deposits, which earned a positive but very low rate of interest. Then there was the Stroibank ("Investment Bank"), which was responsible for disbursing funds to enterprises for long-term investment in accordance with the dictates of the central plan and the Vneshtorgbank ("Foreign Trade Bank") that handled all transactions involving imports and exports.

Gosbank operated a book-entry accounting system whereby when one state enterprise shipped its goods to another state enterprise, the Gosbank account of the "output-enterprise" would be credited, while that of the "input-enterprise" would be debited.

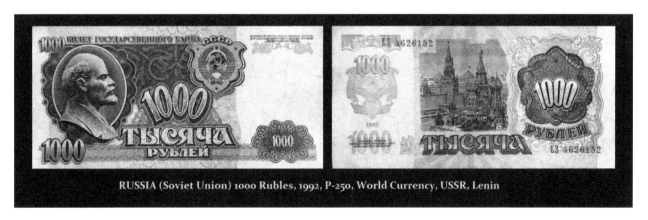

RUSSIA (Soviet Union) 1000 Rubles, 1992, P-250, World Currency, USSR, Lenin

For ordinary workers, there was cash, which was used for only two purposes. First, the state industries paid their workers with cash provided by Gosbank (the account of the state enterprise would be debited), then workers purchased goods with cash, which was then turned over to Gosbank (the account of the store would be credited). If a farm produced milk and it was delivered to the cheese factory, each would report to Gosbank that the commodity was transferred. When the cheese factory shipped the product to the store, each would report the transfer of the product. The accounting was in commodities rather than money. In this manner, Gosbank kept track of production and consumption in the Soviet Union.

Gosbank was in control of the communist planned economy rather than private enterprise. There were no credit lines or fractional banking. Credit was simply not allowed. There was no account receivable among the state enterprises. Moreover, there were no new inventions. Gosbank could only be used to pay for the type of goods specified in the communist plan. Gosbank would not allow any deviations from the central production plan.

Black markets did emerge when the plan could not be flexible to accommodate an increase in demand for food, for example. In order to meet demand, sources of supply began to bypass Gosbank, where cash and bartering came into play.

The black market in the Soviet Union would emerge with excess production that would be traded for other commodities or cash. State enterprises were actually forbidden to hold cash for any purpose other than payment of wages. The retail stores that accepted cash were required by law to deposit it with the Gosbank.

Insofar as any exports were concerned, only Vneshtorgbank was allowed to sell goods for export. Their supplier would only receive a book-entry credit but never cash. The Vneshtorgbank would then export the goods and receive foreign currency. They, in turn, would use foreign currency to pay for any imports. The state enterprises they shipped the imports to would only again receive book-entry credits. In this manner, foreign currency was monitored and restricted from entering the economy.

It was the Stroibank that provided financing to state enterprises for capital investments and expansion. Again, Stroibank provided book-entry credits within the central planning limitation. Any new expansion or construction projects had to be authorized by the political government, allowing for the expansion of these book-entry credits.

Stroibank did loan book-entry credits to individuals for residential construction. The individual would be debited for the new equipment or work over and above their allowed allotment of income, and the state enterprise that provided the equipment or work would be credited in this cashless transaction. The individual would need to go to the bank with a list of everything required, generally for repairs, and the bank would review their list. If approved, they would issue the bank-entry credit. You were also not simply allowed to move.

Those who advocate the end of fractional banking need only look at the Middle Ages prior to banks and the history of the Soviet Union to see if their idea works. If there is no fractional banking, then the value of property would collapse, and the maximum value of normal middle-class homes would rapidly fall to the point where people could afford to buy in cash.

Even during the Great Depression, mortgages were generally for five-year periods. Under the New Deal, Franklin D. Roosevelt created the 30-year mortgage to facilitate real estate transactions that would otherwise have been impossible in that depressed economic state.

The Central Bank Conspiracies

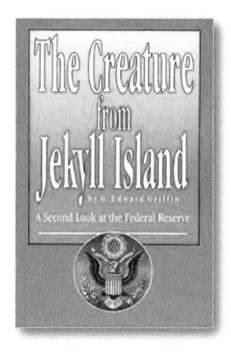

G. Edward Griffin
(born November 7, 1931)

I. WHAT CREATURE IS THIS? 1

What is the Federal Reserve System? The answer may surprise you. It is not federal and there are no reserves. Furthermore, the Federal Reserve Banks are not even banks. The key to this riddle is to be found, not at the beginning of the story, but in the middle. Since this is not a textbook, we are not confined to a chronological structure. The subject matter is not a curriculum to be mastered but a mystery to be solved. So let us start where the action is.

The United States created the Federal Reserve (commonly referred to as "the Fed") in 1913, and many have judged the world of central banking based upon the powers of the Federal Reserve and its structure. Countless conspiracy theorists have been focused on who owns the Fed, and many have wrongly assumed that all interest paid on the national debt in its entirety goes into the Fed's pocket. The false conspiracies have clouded the role of the Fed and hidden from view the critical risks we face with respect to central banks. Some even question if it is possible for central banks to collapse into bankruptcy.

Much of the conspiracy theories have emerged from a book, which is certainly not authoritative. *The Creature of Jekyll Island* by Edward Griffin, in my opinion, is very biased. The book mentions a quote from Mayer Amschel Rothschild (1744 – 1812) that I cannot verify in any other source whatsoever.

"Let me issue and control a nation's money and I care not who writes the laws."

This popular quote, I believe, is fake. This quote has convinced many that the Rothschilds were an evil family who is still somehow secretly in charge of the world.

I believe this is a fake quote because it is intended to support the proposition that the Federal Reserve creates the money.

1799 British Gold Guinea of George III
Last to be issued until 1813 and the defeat of Napoleon

ArmstrongEconomics.COM

The problem with this quote is that there were gold shortages in the 18th century

Nathan Mayer von Rothschild
(1777–1836)

caused by the Seven Years' War and the war with Revolutionary France. Both events began to affect the supply of gold bullion reserves. This led to what became known as the "Restriction Period" where the Bank of England could not pay out gold for its notes due to hoard during times of war. Parliament passed the Bank Restriction Act of 1797, authorizing £1 and £2 notes in place of gold guineas. There is no basis for the belief that the Rothschilds were in control of the money supply.

Another unattributed quote involves Nathan Rothschild. He supposedly said:

> "I care not what puppet is placed on the throne of England to rule the Empire...The man that controls Britain's money supply controls the British Empire. And I control the money supply."

During the Napoleonic Wars, the Rothschild's London bank took a leading part in managing and financing the subsidies of the British government. The Rothschilds were set up in Europe which enabled them to provide transfers of funds to British allies during that war effort. Through the creation of a network of agents, couriers, and shippers, the Rothschilds bank provided funds to the Duke of Wellington's armies in Portugal and Spain, therefore funding the war.

In 1818, the Rothschild bank also arranged a £5 million loan to the Prussian government and issued bonds for government loans. They became investment bankers at that moment in time, underwriting the bond issue. N. M. Rothschild & Sons' financial strength in the city of London began to rise from obscurity. By 1825/1826, the bank was able to supply enough coin to the Bank of England to enable it to avert a liquidity crisis at that point in time.

During the summer of 1846, a political pamphlet bearing the ominous signature "Satan" swept across Europe. This anti-semitic pamphlet fabricated the story that the Rothschilds made a fortune on the war.

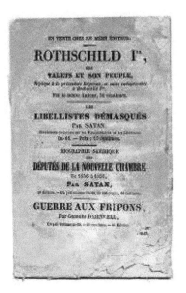

The pamphlet claimed that their vast fortune was built upon the bloodshed of the Battle of Waterloo. It claimed that Nathan Rothschild, the founder of the London branch of the bank, was a spectator on the battlefield that day in June 1815, and as night fell, he observed the total defeat of the French army. A relay of fast horses rushed him to the Belgian coast, but a storm prevented sailing. The pamphlet read: "'Does greed admit anything is impossible?' asked Satan." Nathan was claimed to have paid a king's ransom to a fisherman to ferry him through wind and waves to England. The problem with this fabrication was that Nathan was in London — not Waterloo.

The Rothschilds never controlled the money supply. These quotes and stories were anti-semitic, but also assumed that bankers were evil, for they would later level similar allegations against J.P. Morgan who was not Jewish.

Today, Goldman Sachs has replaced the Rothschilds whose staff has entered government positions of monetary power around the world far greater than the Rothschilds ever possessed. The Rothschilds lost their standing over the course of changes in the political systems in Europe, war, and such events as the Revolutions of 1848, the Great Depression of the 1930s, Nazism, the wholesale destruction of World War II, and the subsequent sovereign defaults.

These conspiracy theories sound great to some, but they are just a distraction from the serious issues we face. Central banks can go bankrupt. They are not all created equal.

The Panic of 1907 – Creating the Federal Reserve

The Panic of 1907 came after the 1906 San Francisco Earthquake and exposed the entire problem of regional internal capital flows within the United States. These flows are caused by the business cycle and the great variety of localized economies. The traditional accounts of the financial panic focused on a crisis that took place over a three-week period starting in mid-October. Yet, when we look more objectively, we see that the market had already reached a high on September 6, and a decline was in full motion.

Indeed, such a period of a temporary shortage creating a liquidity crisis was the hallmark of the Panic of 1907. John Pierpont saved the day, although most have criticized him as a greedy evil banker. Their bias prevents them from understanding what he did and how his actions served as the model to create the Federal Reserve to manage regional capital flows within the United States.

The Panic began when there was an attempt to manipulate the price of the shares of United Copper Company, which was a short squeeze that backfired. The manipulator was Fritz Augustus Heinze (1869–1914). In October 1907, Heinze's brother, Otto Heinze, devised a scheme to corner the market in United Copper stock. The Heinze brothers owned a large share of the company, and Otto believed that many of these shares had been loaned out to investors hoping to short sell the stock. They assumed that the short sellers were extensive because of a prior legal battle. The scheme was to force the shorts to cover. It was assumed that they would force the share to new highs and short the stock, which they presumed would then crash.

The flaw in the plan was that the Heinze brothers overestimated how much of the company the family controlled. When they forced the shorts to buy back stock, the family was there to sell them the

shares. The scheme to force the stock price to rise failed. When it became more common knowledge that the Heinze brothers were trapped and the corner had failed, the stock price of

United Copper collapsed while they were aggressively long.

This was the spark that ignited the crisis. On October 21, 1907, the clearinghouse moved to put Augustus Heinze into involuntary bankruptcy for being unable to meet his margin requirement. It was not the cause, for the market's inherent weakness preexisted as it peaked on September 6 as the business cycle was shifting. The Heinze brothers borrowed money extensively to buy the shares to create the squeeze. As news spread about the collapse of their manipulation in the middle of a downtrend, depositors rushed to pull the money out of the banks who were associated with the Heinze brothers. The main lender to the Heinze brothers was the Knickerbocker Trust, which was thrust into a bank run and was forced to close its door. The following year, F. Augustus Heinze was indicted for his role in the failed corner. The share price of United Copper never recovered, and in 1913, the company was placed into receivership and shut down.

It was J.P. Morgan who realized that this crisis would spread like a contagion. He gathered his associates to examine the books of the Knickerbocker Trust but found it was insolvent and decided not to intervene. When it became clear the Knickerbocker Trust would fail, the run spread to other banks, and a contagion grew. The Trust Company of America asked Morgan for help. Morgan brought in First National Bank and National City Bank of New York (later CitiBank), and the U.S. Secretary of the Treasury. Morgan had a quick audit of the bank and declared that this was where to defend the financial system.

As the run began to spread, J.P. Morgan worked with his associates to sell the bank's assets to free up cash for the depositors. The bank survived the close of business that day. Nonetheless, Morgan knew that there was a collapse in confidence, which would not end by just saving the Trust Company of America.

J.P. Morgan summoned the heads of various banks in New York and kept them until they agreed to provide loans of $8.25 million. Morgan convinced the Treasury to deposit $25 million in NY banks. John D. Rockefeller, the wealthiest man in America, deposited $10 million and called the *Associated Press* to announce his pledge to help the NY banks. The newspapers all carried the story on October 24, 1907.

Nonetheless, the New York banks then, as now, proved to be their worst enemy. Despite the efforts of J.P. Morgan to create this infusion, they were reluctant to lend any money for short-term stock trading. The stock market crashed. By 1:30 PM October 24, the NYSE president went to tell Morgan the exchange would have to close early.

Morgan was livid. He understood that this would reinforce the panic. He drew the line and would not allow it to happen. Morgan warned that if the NYSE closed early, it would be catastrophic. Once again, he summoned the bankers who arrived by about 2 PM. Morgan pretty much yelled at them and warned that as many as 50 stock brokerage firms would fail unless $25 million was raised in 10 minutes! By 2:16 PM, 14 banks pledged $23.6 million to keep the stock exchange alive. The money even reached the exchange by 2:30 PM to finish trading at 3 PM. The amount that was actually needed was only $19 million. Morgan himself hated the press who rarely treated him fairly, but this time he gave a rare comment. The headline in the *Boston Globe*:

"Morgan Cash Stays Break – Loans Millions to Help Brokers Hold Stocks."

The next day, the NYSE needed more money, and Morgan could only raise $9.7 million this time. Morgan directed the NYSE that the money could not be used for margin sales. The exchange made it to the close. Morgan knew he had to turn the minds of the people and to restore their critical confidence to stop the panic.

J.P. Morgan now directed two committees to be formed to:

> (1) persuade the clergy to preach calm to their congregations on Sunday, and

> (2) to sell the idea of clam to the press

Morgan was desperately trying to hold the nation together. Unknown even to his associates, the city of New York could not raise money through its bond issue, and it too informed Morgan that it needed $20 million by November 1, 1907, or it would go into bankruptcy. Morgan himself contracted to purchase $30 million in New York City bonds.

On November 2, one of the largest stock exchange brokers, Moore & Schley, was heavily in debt using the Tennessee Coal, Iron & Railroad Co stock as collateral. The stock was thinly traded and under pressure. Their too, creditors would now surely call their loans. Morgan summoned another emergency meeting, proposing that U.S. Steel Corp would acquire the stock in bulk.

J.P. Morgan's Library

Morgan was besieged with crisis after crisis. Now, runs were likely to hit two banks on Monday, October 28, 1907. Morgan summoned 120 banks and told them he would not proceed with the U.S. Steel deal unless they supported the banks.

Morgan locked them in his library and told them they had to come up with $25 million to save the banks. It took almost two hours. Morgan finally convinced them that they had to bail out the banks to save their own skins. They signed the agreement, and he unlocked the doors and let them leave.

President and The Trusts.

On no subject has President Roosevelt been so severely criticised as on his enforcement of the Sherman anti-trust law. These criticisms have come from New York rather than from Kansas, but it is well to state what has been done by President Roosevelt and Congress in the enforcement of this law.

Minneapolis Messenger - Thursday, September 8th, 1904

Morgan then turned to save the NYSE. He understood that the problem would be the antitrust laws of the Sherman Antitrust Act. He was also aware that the progressive President Teddy Roosevelt would also present a major problem. Teddy was a believer in socialism. It was his agenda to break up companies, for he saw monopolies everywhere. This was the primary focus of Roosevelt's administration and his progressive agenda. To save the day, Morgan understood he would have to see that the antitrust laws must yield to save the economy. Teddy had been severely criticized over his position on antitrust. He simply saw countless small railroads being consolidated and had no idea that this was a normal process that would create a far better railroad system.

Thus, two men traveled to the White House to implore Roosevelt to set aside his antitrust laws to save the nation. As typical, Roosevelt's secretary refused to let them in to discuss the problem. The two men, Henry Clay Frick (1849–1919) and Elbert Henry Gary (1846–1927) of U.S. Steel Co., turned to future president James Garfield who was Secretary of the Interior at that time. They pleaded with him to go to the president directly. Garfield had convinced Roosevelt to at least review the proposal. Roosevelt was forced into a corner for

**Teddy Roosevelt
(1858 - 1919)**

298

the first time. He realized a collapse of the NYSE would take place if he did not yield on antitrust. He later lamented:

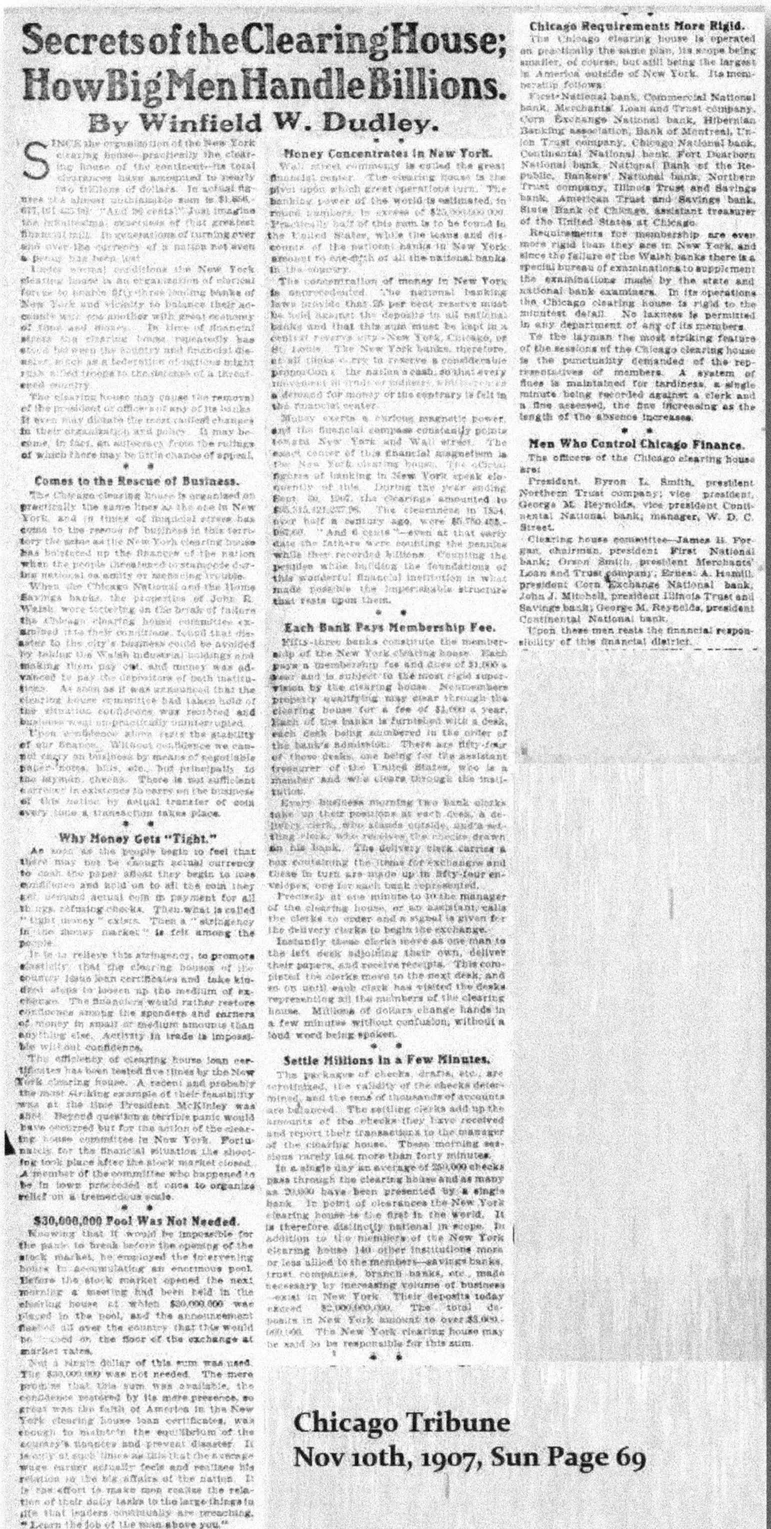

Secrets of the Clearing House; How Big Men Handle Billions.

By Winfield W. Dudley.

Money Concentrates in New York.

Comes to the Rescue of Business.

Why Money Gets "Tight."

$30,000,000 Pool Was Not Needed.

Each Bank Pays Membership Fee.

Settle Millions in a Few Minutes.

Chicago Requirements More Rigid.

Men Who Control Chicago Finance.

Chicago Tribune
Nov 10th, 1907, Sun Page 69

"It was necessary for us to decide on the instant before the Stock Exchange opened, for the situation in New York was such that any hour might be vital. I do not believe that anyone could justly criticize me for saying that I would not feel like objecting to the purchase under those circumstances."

Following the Panic of 1907, the banking reform movement picked up steam among Wall Street bankers, Republicans, and a few eastern Democrats. However, much of the country was still distrustful of bankers and banking in general, especially after the Panic of 1907. On Monday, October 28, 1907, the New York Clearing House issued $100 million in loan certificates (depression scrip) to be traded between banks to settle balances to ensure a free flow of funds. This allowed them to retain cash reserves for depositors creating a temporary two-tier monetary system with private currency.

Reassured now both by the clergy and the newspapers, and with bank balance sheets flushed with cash, a sense of order returned to New York that Monday. After two decades of minority status, Democrats regained control of Congress in 1910 and were able to block several Republican attempts at reform, even though they recognized the need for some form of currency and banking changes. As always, it was more important to further political party power than do the right thing for the nation.

Nevertheless, the Panic of 1907 revealed just how vulnerable the financial system really was, and without J.P. Morgan, things would have been much worse. After the Panic of 1907, the bankers themselves were demanding reform. The United States had no central bank. Only after intense behind the scenes pressure did Congress enact the Aldrich-Vreeland Act of 1908. This established the National

EMERGENCY CURRENCY.

PREPARATIONS OF TREASURY DEPARTMENT UNDER ALDRICH-VREELAND ACT.

Large Volume of Emergency Circulation Under the Plates of the Different National Banks of the Country is Being Printed and Stored That May, When Called for be Ready for Circulation — The Work Involved.

Washington—The Treasury department is busily engaged in carrying into effect the provisions of the Aldrich-Vreeland act providing for emergency currency that may when called for, be put into circulation. There are in the United States 6,880 national banks, nearly all of which take out national bank circulation. Each of these banks has from two to four separate and distinct plates. These plates are being changed to meet the requirements of the new law. The changes upon them are very slight and the Bureau of Printing and Engraving is therefore enabled to change on an average 35 plates per day.

They have been working on these changes for the last three months and have up to the present changed about 3,000 plates. The work will be continued until all the plates of the 6,880 banks are changed, making the total of changes probably 15,000. In the meantime new plates for the banks that have ordered them are being engraved. This is a slow process and will take perhaps more than a year to complete.

From these changed plates the Bureau of Printing and Engraving is printing daily large quantities of emergency currency. The volume is so great that separate quarters outside the Treasury have been rented in the Union Loan and Trust Building and a large vault installed to receive it.

Some twenty extra counters have been employed who are engaged daily and will be for several months, in counting and storing the new currency as it is received from the Bureau of Printing and Engraving. None of this currency has, of course, been issued and none will be unless an emergency as provided in the Aldrich-Vreeland act arises, when the issue will then be made only in the discretion of the Secretary of the Treasury.

A new vault is also in the course of construction in the Treasury for the purpose of storing the bonds that the law prescribes shall be deposited as security for the increase of emergency circulation when taken out.

The Wall Street Journal, Sat. Aug 15th, 1908

Monetary Commission by forming a study group of experts to develop a nonpartisan solution. They viewed the lack of a central bank in America, in contrast to Europe, as the threat to economic stability among the bankers as filled by J.P. Morgan during that crisis.

A National Monetary Commission was formed, and the Republican leader in the Senate, Senator Nelson Aldrich (1841–1915), took charge. Aldrich was a brilliant man who was passionate about revising the American financial system. The commission went to Europe and was duly impressed at how well they believed the central banks in Britain and Germany handled the stabilization of the overall economy and the promotion of international trade.

Overall, the commission issued some 30 reports between 1909 and 1912, which preserved a wonderfully detailed resource surveying banking systems of the late 19th and early 20th centuries.

Nelson W. Aldrich (1841-1915)

These reports also examined Canadian banking history in addition to the banking and currency systems of Belgium, England, France, Germany, Italy, Mexico, Russia, Switzerland, and other nations. They also provided an excellent review of domestic U.S. financial laws federally as well as state banking statutes. These reports contain essays of contemporary specialists as well as a host of data in tables, charts, graphs, and facsimiles of banking forms and documents. There are also transcripts of relevant political speeches, interviews, and various hearings.

In 1910, Aldrich met with Frank Vanderlip of National City Bank (Citibank), Henry Davison of Morgan Bank, and Paul Warburg of the Kuhn, Loeb Investment House secretly. They met at Jekyll Island, a resort island off the coast of Georgia, to discuss and formulate banking reform, including plans for a form of central banking that would accomplish the role J.P. Morgan played during the Panic of 1907. They held the meeting in secret because the participants knew that the House of Representatives would reject any plan they generated, given the intense hatred of the bankers and Wall Street during the progressive atmosphere.

Jekyll Island Club

Unfortunately, because this meeting was in secret, the whole Jekyll Island affair remains cloaked in conspiracy theories. Nevertheless, the intense biases and conspiracy theories

The Panic of 1907 – Creating the Federal Reserve

always overestimate both the purpose and significance of the meeting in light of the extensive work of the National Monetary Commission. Reform was essential. However, those two words, "political economy," could not be divorced.

Upon his return, Aldrich's investigation led to his plan in 1912 to bring central banking to the United States with all its promises of financial stability and expanded international roles in trade and money flow. Aldrich knew the dangers of American politics and insisted that control by impartial experts was essential. Placing bankers at the helm rather than politicians was the only way to proceed. The two words, political economy, had to be divorced in his mind. There was to be absolutely no political meddling. Aldrich asserted that a central bank was essential, yet the diversity and size of the United States presented a distinctly different twist to the European situation.

Aldrich concluded that Europe had many countries with diverse economic models. He realized that while the United States needed a central bank, paradoxically it also required simultaneous decentralization to cope with both the economy and the self-defeating American political system. Aldrich appreciated the fact that local politicians and bankers would attack the central banks, as they had the First and Second Banks of the United States. Aldrich introduced his brilliant plan in 62nd and 63rd Congresses (1912 and 1913). As always, the political winds changed, and the Democrats in 1912 won control of both the House and the Senate, as well as the White House.

The 1912 election included Teddy Roosevelt as a third party candidate known as the Bull Moose Progressive (Socialist) Party. The national progressivism movement dominated the Republican Party back then. There was a large group of Republican progressives, known as the "insurgents," with seats in both houses of Congress. These Republicans demanded major structural reforms such as tariff reductions, an income tax, the direct election of senators, and even stricter railroad and corporation regulations backed by antitrust laws.

NO CURRENCY LEGISLATION.

No currency reform legislation will be attempted at the coming session of Congress, it was practically decided to-day at an informal conference of the Democratic members of the subcommittee of the House Banking and Currency Committee, headed by Representative Glass of Virginia.

"The committee probably will be unable to report anything like finished legislation to the House at this session," said Mr. Glass to-night.

No definite steps toward drawing a bill have been taken by the members of the committee, and no currency scheme has been evolved to fill the place of the Aldrich currency plan rejected by the committee, following the specific declaration of the Democratic national platform against the Aldrich plan.

Weekly Times-Democrat (New Orleans, Louisiana) Nov 29, 1912, Fri • Page 21

The election was held on November 5, 1912, in which Democrat Woodrow Wilson (1856–1924) defeated the Bull Moose (Progressive) candidate and the Republican incumbent president William Howard Taft. In 1912, President Woodrow Wilson was a populist-friendly candidate, and in his acceptance speech, Wilson warned against the "money trusts." He warned that the concentration of credit controlled by bankers posed an infinitely more dangerous threat to the nation. Wilson argued for an anti–Wall Street agenda.

The Aldrich Plan proposed a system of fifteen regional central banks, called National Reserve Associations, whose actions were to be coordinated by a national board of commercial bankers to do no more than act as a lender of last resort, as J.P. Morgan had acted during the Panic of 1907. The National Reserve Association would make emergency loans to member banks, create money to provide an elastic currency that enabled equal exchanges for demand deposits, and act as a fiscal agent for the federal government.

Congress ended up rejecting Aldrich's idea, which was defeated in the House as politics superseded the national good. However, his outline did become a model for a future implemented bill. The problem with the Aldrich Plan was that it gave bankers control over the regional banks; a prospect that did not sit well with the populist Democratic Party or with President Wilson. The Democrats and Wilson

UNCLE SAM'S NEED OF AN ELASTIC CURRENCY

PRESIDENT ROOSEVELT: " You see, those galluses ought to have rubber in them, so that when Uncle Sam stoops to move the sheaf there won't be much strain on the buttons."

From the Pioneer Press (St. Paul)

were fearful that the reforms would grant more control of the financial system to bankers and the politicians could not meddle as they saw fit. The history of the First and Second Banks of the United States was repeating. The political economy cannot be divorced.

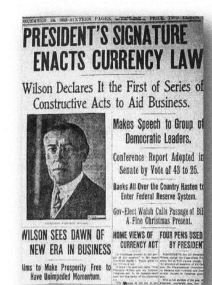

The need for a central bank was critical, and even the Democrats recognized this fact behind closed doors. Eventually, the Federal Reserve Act passed 43-25 and was signed by President Wilson on December 23, 1913. This act altered the actual role of currency, creating an "elastic" money supply that could expand during a crisis and contract in normal times.

The Federal Reserve structure was to be the lender of last resort, but that meant to "stimulate" the economy, it would directly buy short-term paper when banks were unable to lend. In this manner, corporations were not compelled to lay off workers because of a shortage in money resulting from the contraction in the economy and public hoarding. The law also required the Federal Reserve to hold gold equal to 40% of the value of the currency it issued and to convert those dollars into gold at a fixed price of $20.67 per ounce of pure gold.

1914 Federal Reserve Notes

$5,000 & $10000 denominations not shown

The first Federal Reserve Board was officially sworn in on August 10, 1914. It was 1914 when the Federal Reserve issued its first paper money. The denominations were $5 to $1,000. In 1915, the Fed began to issue notes from each of the 12 branches with denominations starting at $1. Under FDR, all currency was issued under the Federal Reserve in Washington, DC.

Elastic Money

The ability to create elastic money would become an essential function of the Federal Reserve System in its early days. It could create money at will to buy in short-term corporate paper to prevent unemployment from rising. The key to this mechanism was the fact that the corporate paper was private, not through government, and as such, it would mature. With the introduction of World War I, Congress directed the Fed to buy only government paper to fund the war effort. However, governments constantly roll their debts, and the very critical tool to "stimulate" the economy became a life support tool to sustain governments.

Creating elastic money to stimulate the economy was transformed from a brilliant direct means of stimulation to indirect stimulation subject to manipulation. Quantitative Easing became merely buying government bonds from banks that would not lend into the economy for fear of the unknown future.

The Panic of 1907 brought the necessity of creating elastic money to the forefront. J.P. Morgan observed that during a crisis, a bank would fail if it could not meet the withdrawals of demand deposits because it had lent money out long-term. The invention of elastic money was a brilliant solution. The private sector, not government, devised it, and it helped to stabilize the economy during financial panics. It was originally invented by clearing houses in 1853 to settle accounts.

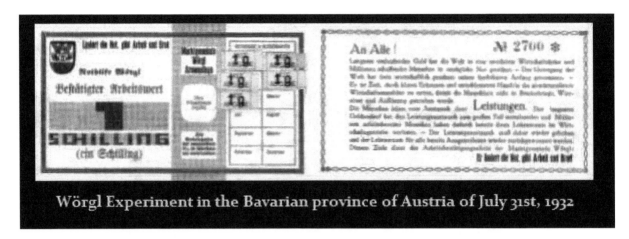

Wörgl Experiment in the Bavarian province of Austria of July 31st, 1932

In Austria, the Wörgl Experiment began on July 31, 1932, the very month that the Dow Jones Industrial Index bottomed in the United States. The experiment involved issuing "Certified Compensation Bills," which were a form of local currency known as scrip or Freigeld. Economist Jean Silvio Gesell (1862–1930) saw that government sought to divide people for personal power, and this was in contrast to the interest of individuals.

Gesell saw that the key to the boom–bust cycle was the velocity of money. Hoarding money would result in shortages and economic declines. Indeed, throughout history, if a nation debased its currency, two things would happen. The people would hoard the previous currency with a higher metal content, so the outstanding money supply would vanish from circulation. This reduces the velocity of money. Moreover, the government would need to produce an even greater

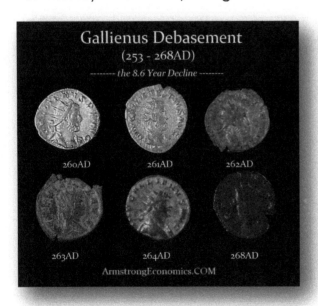

supply of money to keep the economy moving. We can see that during the collapse of Rome's monetary system, the silver content fell from almost 50% to virtually zero within just eight years.

To address this issue head–on, Gesell believed that money should expire. This would prevent hoarding. Indeed, European nations routinely cancel their currencies to prevent hoarding and force people to pay taxes.

Jean Silvio Gesell
(1862-1930)

Gesell was closer to Adam Smith's invisible hand and viewed that the individual would naturally be motivated to act for his own self-interest. Gesell proposed an economic system that he called a "natural economy," which was overshadowed by the progressive movement that embraced Karl Marx, who empowered government against the people. Gesell was certainly ignored because of the rush to Keynesianism. The Wörgl Experiment was applied by the town's then mayor, Michael Unterguggenberger, but the twist was that this currency expired. The Austrian Central Bank forced the issue of money to be shut down when neighboring cities also began to look at issuing private scrip money.

The entire idea of central banks creating money out of thin air has been the argument against elastic money. However, elastic money was not invented by the government or any central bank. It began in 1853 with a little-known group attempting to help in the middle of a financial crash. It became obvious to that group that there were valuable long-term assets that could not be liquidated immediately, and it emerged as a liquidity crisis.

The Panic of 1873 saw the government make a small gesture to try to calm the panic. They did the same thing as Quantitative Easing back then. Yes, not even that is new. The U.S. Treasury injected cash by purchasing government bonds, which failed to work back then as well. When confidence crashes, people hoard money. They will not spend it if they fear the future. The cash the government injected was hoarded by the banks just as it has been post-2007, for they too will not lend in the midst of a panic. Quantitative Easing in this manner never produces inflation nor does it stimulate the economy.

The Panic of 1873 was very intense, and the silver miners called it the Crime of 1873 due to the

Ulysses S. Grant (1822–1885)
18th President of the US (1869–1877)

demonetization of silver. The New York Stock Exchange simply did not open because of the liquidity crisis on Saturday, September 20, and did not reopen until the 30th of September 1873. Never previously had the stock market closed for ten days — not even during war. On Sunday morning, September 21, 1873, President Ulysses S. Grant (1822–1885) and Treasury Secretary William Richardson (1821–1896) went to New York, spending the day in anxious consultations with Vanderbilt, Clews, and other prominent businessmen.

Many blamed Secretary Richardson, arguing that he vacillated when he should have provided instant cash. In all, some $13,500,000 in five-twenty bonds were bought. They also purchased a few million of the greenbacks that former Treasury Secretary Hugh McCulloch (1808–1895), who was in office between March 9, 1865, and March 3, 1869, had called in for cancelation. Nonetheless, they were set in motion to inject cash into the system. Secretary Richardson, beyond that, did not announce any policy of ongoing assistance. During every financial crisis, cash is simply hoarded as people fear the future as unknown.

On September 25, 1873, the U.S. Treasury ceased buying bonds to inject cash that was not stimulating anything besides hoarding. It was at this moment when Jay Gould (1836–1892), who was involved in creating the first Black Friday during the Panic of 1869, stepped up to buy. He bought during the low several hundred thousand shares of railroad stocks, principally of Vanderbilt ownership. When people saw who was buying, confidence began to return marginally, and the panic was subsiding.

Jay Gould (1836-1892)

Clearing House. New York.

The national banks of New York pooled their cash and collateral into a common fund and placed it in the hands of a trust committee at the New York Clearing House, which had been founded on October 4, 1853. The New York Clearing House then issued loan certificates that were receivable at the Clearing House against this collateral.

The New York Clearing House certificates were absorbed like cash and could be used to pay off debt balances. Ten million dollars worth of these certificates were issued at first, but the sum subsequently doubled. This clearing house paper served its purpose admirably. It became elastic money, the invention of necessity.

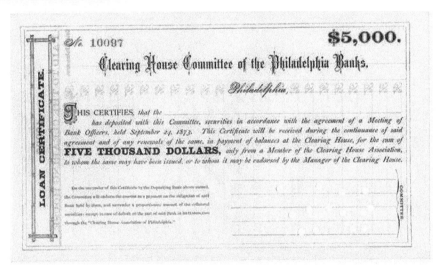

By October 3, 1873, confidence returned, and $1,000,000 of these certificates were called in to be canceled. The next day, another $1,500,000 of these certificates were recalled. In the end, not much of this issue was outstanding very long. The clearing house scheme was successfully applied also in Boston, Philadelphia, Pittsburgh, and other major cities besides Chicago. Liquidity creation without a central bank became possible, demonstrating the private sector can create money.

The clearing house scrip was used for most panics and tends to be rare, for they were normally traded in and redeemed. As panics persisted, the scrip would be issued in smaller denominations, as was the case from the Panic of 1907 and the Great Depression. This provided the backdrop for the idea of the Federal Reserve later in 1913. The entire idea of elastic money was a private issue backed by securities.

During the Great Depression, people hoarded their wealth, especially since 9,000 banks had failed. The shortage of money for commerce became critical. More than 200 cities in the United States followed suit during the Great Depression, issuing their own form of elastic money known as depression scrip for local money since hoarding created a shortage of cash in circulation. Money is merely a medium of exchange. It is not actually wealth itself. The private sector can create money as long as the people are willing to accept it.

Austrian 20 Heller Privately issued Notgeld Currency Note
ArmstrongEconomics.COM

During the hyperinflation that ravaged both Germany and Austria between 1921 and 1923, we also find a wide variety of private currency issues known as Notgeld, meaning "emergency money" or "necessity money." This was indeed privately created money issued by an institution in a time of economic and political crisis. The issuing institution was typically purely private, and their issues were without the official sanction of the central government.

This was the birth of elastic money and the interest rate tools. Elastic money was used during financial panics to prevent the wholesale liquidation of assets in order to obtain cash in short supply. These two tools seemed logical, but both were constructed upon an isolated view of the economy detached from any influences externally.

The problem appeared with World War I. World War I began July 28, 1914, and lasted until November 11, 1918. While the excuse for creating the war became the assassination of Archduke Franz Ferdinand of Austria on June 28, 1914, it was the culmination of centuries of contests for imperialistic power in Europe. Ferdinand was the heir to the throne of the Austrian–Hungarian Empire, which was the remnant of the Holy Roman Empire. This fueled hatred between many rivals, bringing the German Empire, Ottoman Empire, Russian Empire, British Empire, French Empire, and Italy into the conflict.

With the United States entering the war, Congress ordered the Federal Reserve to buy only U.S. government bonds rather than corporate paper, fearing the lack of support for American debt. By instructing the central bank to shift from corporate paper to government to fund World War I, they ended the very purpose of elastic money. The problem with such regulation is that while it may make sense in a crisis, they never restore the structure to what it was before. Hence, the critical tool of creating elastic money was lost. Private corporate debt expires, and they must pay it back. Government debt only rolls over and is never reduced. That defeated the entire elastic money tool as it was originally intended.

Therefore, the Fed's power to create Federal elastic money no longer aided the private sector. This is the primary distinction that has proven devastating to the management of central banks because everyone has copied the Federal Reserve design as it stood after World War I. This is why we now have this tool transformed into Quantitative Easing, buying in only government debt. As we will review, the European Central Bank has purchased about 40% of Eurozone bonds. It cannot resell them, and it must continue to roll them as the situation that was originally intended for corporate paper expired and directly influenced the economy. Under QE, the elastic money has been transformed simply into a life support system for government that never pays off its debt.

Usurping the Interest Rate Power of the Federal Reserve

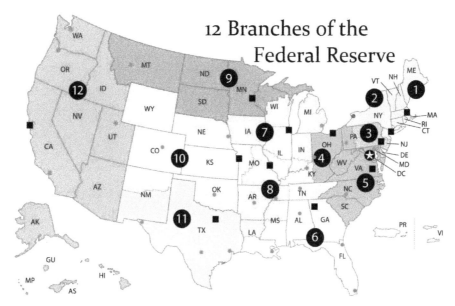

12 Branches of the
Federal Reserve

Another critical tool of the Federal Reserve was the regional design to manage domestic capital flows. The need for this design was exposed by the Panic of 1907 as capital moved from East to West, resulting in cash shortages and bank failures. The 1906 San Francisco Earthquake helped to bring the diversity of the American economy to the forefront. The design of the Fed was to maintain an independent structure that allowed the 12 branches to control their respective interest rates to attract or deflect capital in their region.

Franklin D. Roosevelt (FDR) changed the structure of the Federal Reserve by eliminating this regional structure of using independent interest rates to manage the capital flows. When crops came to market, capital would flow to the Midwest. When it was planting season, there would be shortages of capital in the Midwest. The United States was one nation, but there were regional differences in the economy.

Federal Reserve August 1927 Discount Rate

Atlanta............	4.0%
Boston.............	4.0%
Chicago............	4.0%
Cleveland..........	4.0%
Dallas.............	4.0%
Kansas City........	3.5%
Minneapolis.......	4.0%
New York..........	4.0%
Philadelphia.......	4.0%
Richmond..........	4.0%
St. Louis...........	4.0%
San Francisco.....	4.0%

ArmstrongEconomics.COM

Prior to the Banking Act of 1935, the secretary of the Treasury served as the chairman of the Federal Reserve Board. The governor of the Federal Reserve Board served as the active executive officer. Therefore, the Banking Act of 1935 combined those positions whereby the chairman had the powers previously split between the board's chair and governor. Effectively, every member of the board became a governor. The Fed did not acquire its building that we know today until President Roosevelt dedicated it on October 20, 1937.

It was Title II of the Act (in section 203) that completely altered the design of the Fed. This portion shifted power from the regional reserve banks to the board based in Washington, DC. The entire purpose of the 12 branches was eliminated. Moreover, the changing of titles for Federal Reserve leaders had symbolic and legal significance. The title of governor was created, and most likely taken from the Bank of England, which had been led by its governor since 1694. The Federal Reserve Act of 1913 had labeled the chief executive officers at reserve banks as governors simply because the view was that the Fed was truly a confederation of independent reserve banks. Each branch operated autonomously under general oversight of the Federal Reserve Board in Washington, DC. These governors, therefore, were active executive officers who directed the operations of their branch.

Federal Reserve Board - 1917

The Banking Act of 1935 passed on August 19, 1935, and was signed into law by the president on August 23, 1935. This act changed the structure and power distribution in the Federal Reserve System that began with the Banking Act of 1933.

The Federal Open Market Committee (FOMC) was formed by the Banking Act of 1933 (codified at 12 U.S.C. § 263) and did not include voting rights for the Federal Reserve Board of Governors. The Banking Act of 1935 revised these protocols to include the Board of Governors but was amended again in 1942 to give the current structure of 12 voting members.

This critical tool of establishing 12 branches of the Federal Reserve to help manage the regional capital flows within the United States was abandoned by Franklin D. Roosevelt in the New Deal. FDR usurped all the power of the independent branches of the Fed in Title II with the creation of the Federal Open Market Committee. He directed the FOMC with overseeing the nation's open market operations (e.g., the Fed's buying and selling of United States Treasury securities). This Federal Reserve committee made key decisions about interest rates and the growth of the United States' money supply.

Since FDR ended the convertibility of the dollar to gold in 1934 to prevent citizens from hoarding gold as they did during the Great Depression, the Federal Reserve was no longer required to maintain a gold reserve or to convert dollars to gold.

BROOKLYN DAILY EAGLE
FINANCIAL SECTION

NEW YORK CITY, WEDNESDAY, APRIL 24, 1935

Warburg Warns Of Communism In Banking Act

Tells Senate That Proposed Legislation Is 'Cutthroat,' 'Spendthrift' – Urges More Careful Study

Washington, D. C., April 24—Warning that the proposed Banking Act of 1935 is a step toward Communism, and deploring the lack of any system of banking in the United States other than what he terms "a hotch-potch of remnants of partially discarded systems," James P. Warburg, vice president of the Bank of the Manhattan Company today issued a fiery "statement" of his views to the Senate Committee on Banking and Currency.

"Cut-throat" is one of the mildest of the implications used by the bank executive in discussing the pending legislation, particularly that part of it known as Title II, which proposes to create a centralized banking system out of a regional reserve system.

"I am unalterably opposed to political control of either a central bank system or regional reserve system for three reasons," Mr. Warburg said, and enumerated as his reasons personal disagreement with the theory, violent business cycles which may result and finally the alarm that "the proposal for political control of the banking and credit machinery is in effect a proposal to take a step defined by the Communists as the most essential step toward Communism."

Citing that there is "no present emergency which necessitates hasty action," the attack on the bill urged that before rushing into such drastic legislation it "should be given the most careful study by competent authorities."

Warburg denied that he considers the present system or lack of system a good thing and went on to add that "the point I wish to make is that even if we had had a better banking system we should at best have avoided the ultimate spasms of collapse—and then only if we had better business and political leadership than that which guided the destinies of our nation in the post-war decade."

Confessing that he is only "a plain ordinary practical banker," who has "learned just enough about money to know that I don't know it all and to suspect that many who think they know don't know it all either," Warburg expressed disagreement with the economists, J. Maynard Keynes and Laughlin Currie, not to mention Marriner Eccles, Governor of the Federal Reserve Board.

Mr. Warburg's remarks about the red tint of the Banking Act included the following enlargements:

"All history is there, gentlemen, to show you what happens when the long arm of the Treasury reaches out into the control of the credit machinery. All history shows such proposals as this one before you to be the favorite device of spendthrift governments.

"And recently they have become the favorite device of another and more dangerous group—the device of those who seek by subtle means to destroy the foundations of Western civilization.

"During the last year this country has been flooded with propganda to 'nationalize the banking system,' to 'socialize credit,' and so forth.

"I am not one who sees a Communist under every bed, but I sometimes wonder if the authors of these bills realize whose game they are playing."

The bankers themselves were opposed to the usurpation of power. James Warburg (1896–1969) came out and called this usurpation of power outright communism. All the originally designed protections and the purpose of the Federal Reserve were eradicated by the Banking Act of 1935. James was well known for being one of the pretend financial advisers to Franklin D. Roosevelt. His father, Paul Warburg, had been a banker who was often considered to be one of the "fathers" of the Federal Reserve system.

James Warburg
(1896-1969)

Title II also changed the name of the "Federal Reserve Board" to the "Board of Governors of the Federal Reserve System." The board was then to consist of seven members selected by the president with the Senate's advice and consent. Each member would then serve a fourteen-year term on the board. Of those on the board, one member would be selected as chairman and one as vice-chairman, each serving four years in that capacity.

Title II also created the Federal Open Market Committee directing that membership would include the governors of the Federal Reserve System and five representatives of the Federal Reserve banks. The Committee was directed to meet quarterly in Washington DC. The FOMC controlled how and when Reserve Banks participated in open market operations.

The act renewed the ability of each Federal Reserve bank to make loans to its member banks. The rates for these loans must be 0.5% above the current discount rate at the Federal Reserve. The Fed was originally funded by the banks, for it was to be an independent bailout structure during financial panics.

The Fed lost its regional structure and the elastic money that was intended to buy only short-term corporate paper but was now restricted to government paper. Therefore, directing the Fed only to buy government debt and usurping the power of the branches into Washington, DC, completely altered the entire design of the Federal Reserve. The Fed would never be able to stimulate the economy directly in a crisis as we have witnessed with Quantitative Easing. Warburg's warning of a communistic central control was spot on.

Central Banking

[The Bank of England.]

The general analysis involving central banks is typically centered on the Federal Reserve as people know it today. They spin stories about creating money out of thin air and how the private bankers all own and control the central banks. These conspiracy theories are repeated so often that they have been assumed to be factual. The truth about central banks and how they are not created equal, no less how they evolved in the first place, is never addressed.

The concept of a central bank has been strikingly different throughout the ages and dependent upon the political system in play during that period in time. As explained, the United States in establishing the Federal Reserve in 1913 included the authority to create elastic money, which was originally restricted to directly stimulating the economy through the purchase of corporate paper when banks were in crisis. With World War I, the Fed was directed to buy only government bonds to fund the war, and the intended structure was never restored. Ever since, central banks of other nations post–World War II have copied the current structure of the Federal Reserve instead of its original design. Their Quantitative Easing (QE) policies, which have failed, are the result of restricting QE to government debt, which has been an indirect means of stimulating the economy. It has kept government on life support without doing anything for commerce.

Evolution of Central Banks

While the ancient Greek Temple of Delos was a quasi-central bank insofar as it was central to Greek city-state governments and the private sector for maintaining accounts, it was not in the position to manage the money supply or engage in Quantitative Easing. It did provide loans to governments. The Romans also did not have a central bank. The Temple created money by owning the mines and placed money into circulation by simply paying its military and covering its own expenses. It did have some welfare programs, such as providing free food and taking care of orphans. But these were funded by the coining of money and taxes with no national debt or central bank.

Roman Banking

Following the fall of Rome in 476 AD, Europe emerged into the Dark Ages. There was no banking or money lending. People became serfs working the land around a castle that provided protection. There were no national governments. The early beginnings of money lending post-Dark Ages tended to be by the Jews through pawnshops that secured loans to the consumer level. It is quite clear that mercantilism also evolved into moneylending. The trade fairs that did emerge were more like local flea markets.

Trade Fairs

Medieval Trade Fairs - Rebirth of Banking post Dark Ages

These local flea market gatherings during the medieval period were the crucible to reestablishing the financial industry. International banking began to emerge from these flea markets, which evolved into trade fairs in northern France in an area known as the Champagne region. These gatherings on a purely local basis began to attract traveling merchants. Champagne trade fairs matured by the 12th century. What is known is that these gatherings appeared in many areas during the 11th century. Merchants began to travel just as there were traveling salesmen. In medieval times, caravan merchants began to spring up and carried their merchandise from place to place.

The Champagne region in France was the central meeting place between North and South. The Italians would bring fine silks and spices, trading for cloth and wool produced in the North. To carry out such trading, the Italians began to develop credit and formed partnerships with agency agreements. There is evidence of contracts written using Roman law in Italy during the 11th century. The oldest such document showing a mortgage was to the Catholic Church of Saint Peter in Rome dated 1083.

Perhaps the first debt crisis in Europe unfolded during the year 1096, where many properties were bought from mortgage holders who foreclosed as a result of a significant famine and crop failure, much as the Dust Bowl of the 1930s led to massive foreclosures of farmland in the United States. From May 18 to 26, 1096, there was the Worms massacre in the Rhineland where 800 to 1,000 Jews were slaughtered, despite the intervention of the local bishop. While religion was claimed as the justification, it had the side benefit of eliminating creditors.

By the early 13th century, caravan merchants gave way to sedentary merchants who were developing a fixed hub of operations that relied on agents and partnerships, thus eliminating the need for traveling caravans. This change in operations has been referred to as the "commercial revolution" of the 13th century. By 1253, the Genoese had become the most dominant of this new merchant class in Champagne. Bills of Exchange are known to have existed as

early as 1200. These were receipts that allowed the transfer of money by having one agent pay on behalf of another while the two settled their accounts among each other. In other words, a Bill of Exchange was the birth of international commerce.

The trade fair that developed in the Champagne province in northern France became the biggest of its kind. It rotated among the cities of the province, which is why they were known by the name of the province rather than by the rotating city names. The Champagne fairs were held six times each year (every 8.6 weeks). The credit that developed was between fairs. In other words, a merchant would provide goods to another merchant from a different region who would sell the products and then pay for them at the next fair. This fostered the rise of mercantilism throughout Europe, expanding sales and increasing the wealth of this new class. The 12th century saw the rapid expansion of the trade fairs, and Champagne became the crossroads of Europe between North and South.

Edward I of England (1272 - 1307AD)   Philip IV of France (1268 - 1314AD)

Soon kings would send agents to borrow money at these trade fairs and introduced sovereign debts. Eventually, we find major sovereign defaults during the 14th century. Both Edward I (1272–1307) of England and Philip IV (1268–1314) defaulted on their loans. Philip IV seized the Knights Templar, the pope, and the Italian merchant bankers to fund his war. Edward I suddenly discovered his moneylenders were Jews and banished them from England, but made sure they were divested of all assets first.

The Emergence of Central Banks

It wasn't until the 17th century that we find the emergence of a true central bank that the government manipulated. The collapse of Wisselbank in Amsterdam, where people had deposited their money and assumed the bank was strictly a safekeeping facility, was the first example of government manipulation into a bank for its own gain.

Provinical - GELDERLAND Provincie 1581 - 1795
Nederlandse rijksdaalder 1610, 28.66 grams

The Wisselbank was founded in 1609. Upon first opening an account, a depositor paid a fee of ten guilders, three guilders, and three stuivers for each additional account. Two stuivers were paid for each transaction, except those of less than three hundred guilders, for which six stuivers were paid in order to discourage the multiplicity of small transactions. A person who neglected to balance his account twice in the year forfeited 25 guilders. A person who ordered a transfer for more than what was upon his account was obligated to pay 3% for the sum overdrawn.

The bank made a further profit by selling foreign coin and bullion, which fell to it by the expiration of receipts and selling bank money at 5% and buying it at 4%. These revenue sources were more than enough to pay for the wages of bank officers and defrayed the expense of management. Most people assume that precious metal was worth more than banknotes. Adam

Wisselbank Amsterdam
founded 1609

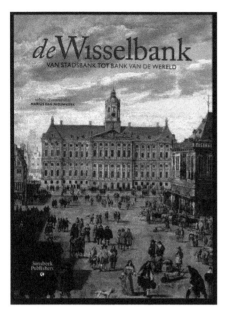

Smith explained that this was not the case. International trade took place on precious metal content. Because coins could be shaved, clipped, or counterfeited, every coin needed to be inspected in large transactions. For this reason, bank money would trade at a premium for it was already certified. Smith explained:

"Amsterdam, Hamburg, Venice, etc., foreign bills of exchange are paid in what they call bank money; while in others, as at London, Lisbon, Antwerp, Leghorn, etc., they are paid in the common currency of the country. What is called bank money is always of more value than the same nominal sum of common currency. A thousand guilders in the Bank of Amsterdam, for example, are of more value than a thousand guilders of Amsterdam currency."

In 1602, the United East India Company (VOC) formed from six trading companies in the Netherlands and granted a trade monopoly over the Indies. The Wisselbank was administered by a committee of city government officials concerned about keeping their affairs secret. It initially operated on a deposit-only basis, but by 1657, it allowed depositors to overdraw their accounts and lend large sums to the Municipality of Amsterdam and

Swedish Receipt 1666

**Swedish 1659
Copper Plate Money
(14.5 kilos)**

the United East Indies Company (Dutch East India Company). It became public knowledge that the government was using their money by 1790. The City of Amsterdam took over direct control of Wisselbank in 1791 as perhaps the first bank bailout before finally closing it in 1819.

The first true banknotes for circulation appeared in Sweden, and the government actually used these to support its wars with Germany. In 1661, the government established a 30-year monopoly for its Stockholm Banco to issue these banknotes known as "letters of credit" that were to be payable in Swedish copper plate money. This money was extremely heavy and was not practical for actual circulation. However, this practice was abused and ended up supporting the king. This led to the first banking panic in 1663 when there were more obligations than money to redeem the notes. The bank was forced to close in 1664. However, the Swedish government caught a taste of unlimited wealth. They tried to salvage what they could, and finally in 1668, they founded the Bank of Estates, which became the Bank of Sweden in 1866. Some historians will point to this bank in Sweden as the first formal central bank.

Sir William Paterson (1655–1719)

Bank of England

Nevertheless, London merchants had long wanted a bank to compete with Amsterdam. The Scotsman, Sir William Paterson (1658–1719), was a London merchant and member of the Merchant Taylors' Company since 1686. Paterson pushed for an English bank, but he certainly did not envision creating a central bank for the government's pleasure.

Paterson led the movement by the merchants to create the Bank of England. He obtained a Royal Charter by an Act of Parliament in 1694. However, a conflict immediately emerged, and it became clear that the government sought to utilize the bank to raise funds, as Sweden did to fund a war with the Low Countries (Netherlands).

This conflict over the Bank of England's purpose led to Paterson's resignation within just one year. The idea that the Bank of England would be primarily used to aid merchants faded into the sunset. Paterson immediately attempted to organize a rival bank for merchants. He was unsuccessful in that measure.

The Bank of England was chartered as a limited liability company. Even by 1694, this was not something new. By the 15th century, English law had awarded limited liability to monastic communities and trade guilds with commonly held property. Limited liability companies were born back in 1408 in the city of Florence based upon Roman law. In 1408, Florence enacted a statute that allowed the creation of "*societa in accomandite*," or limited partnerships, the essential characteristic of which was that passive partners were liable only to the extent of their investments. However, there is evidence that this form of business association was actually used earlier in a Barcelonese contract of 1332, which closely resembled the modern *societa in accomandite.*

England clearly took that very idea of a Limited Liability Company and thus established a royal charter allowing the Bank of England to operate as a joint-stock bank with limited liability. No other joint-stock banks were authorized in England and Wales until 1826.

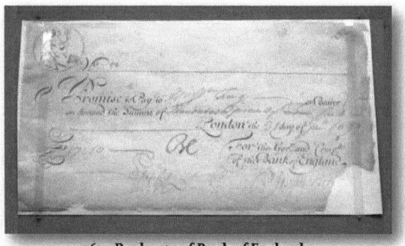

1694 Banknote of Bank of England

Nevertheless, the Bank of England began issuing banknotes that were all hand-signed. This royal charter established a monopoly, as was the case in Sweden, affording the bank tremendous advantages. It was clear from the outset that the Bank of England was created to fund the government, precisely as had taken place in Sweden and behind the curtain in Amsterdam at the Wisselbank.

United States Bank of North America

Pennsylvania Bank of North America August 6, 1789 3 Pence

The Bank of North America was the first bank chartered by the Continental Congress on May 26, 1781, under the Articles of Confederation. Therefore, this was a national enterprise commercial bank and the only national bank in the United States. The bank was the first created by the national government to conduct business with and for the government. Though the Pennsylvania Bank was founded in 1780, it did little business apart from subscribers, who in 1782 sold their shares to Bank of North America, which then expanded its financial connections.

Bank of North America $20 December 17, 1792 Contemporary Counterfeit
ex-Eric P. Newman Collection

The Bank of North America commenced issuing demand notes in 1782. As illustrated here, its notes were quickly counterfeited. Robert Morris (1734–1806) was the financier of the American Revolution. He was the congressional superintendent of finance who drafted the charter and used the bank to stabilize the national currency and save the Confederation from bankruptcy. The earliest stockholders included several Founding Fathers such as Alexander Hamilton, Thomas Jefferson, and Benjamin Franklin. There were 99 Philadelphians who subscribed to bank shares, and the bank opened on January 7, 1782.

Robert Morris used a $450,000 French silver shipment to Congress to fund the bank, which then lent the money back to Congress. Later, when the bank feared congressional loan default, Morris sold the government's shares to repay the bank, which then re-lent the money to Congress. Through maneuvers like this, the bank kept Congress funded through the Revolution and built itself a secure reputation.

The Bank of North America faced political controversy from the outset. Opponents argued it was beyond the power authorized by Congress, and that Congress was being controlled by the money interests. To ease these concerns, the bank directors absorbed a chartered bank in Pennsylvania. Therefore, the Bank of North American held two charters simultaneously to circumvent those arguing that Congress lacked the power to grant such a bank charter.

When the Continental Congress ceased and the United States of America was born, the national charter that had been granted vanished, and the bank simply became a state charter until 1864. With the Continental Congress ending, the Bank of North America simply became a tool of the Pennsylvania government for political purposes.

Nevertheless, the Bank of North America became the model for the federal Bank of the United States, which was chartered in 1791 by the United States Congress. This was sponsored by Alexander Hamilton (1755–1804), a protégé of Robert Morris.

The Panic of 1792 was the start of trouble for Morris who was a speculator in real estate. He lost virtually everything on land speculation. Here is a stock certificate in the Share of the North American Land Company, issued February 20, 1795, signed by Robert Morris. Morris was finally arrested and imprisoned for debt in Prune Street prison in Philadelphia from February 1798 to August 1801. Because of his service to the country, Congress passed its first bankruptcy legislation, the Bankruptcy Act of 1800, ending debtors' prison on which Morris was released from prison. His debts amounted to over $2 million.

Bank of New York

The next quasi-central bank became the Bank of New York, established in June 1784 by a group that included Alexander Hamilton and Aaron Burr. Since the Bank of North America in Philadelphia was paying 14% dividends, this provided the idea to create a bank in New York City.

The Old Walton House.

The Bank of New York company did not have a charter for the first seven years. It was supposed to have a capitalization of $750,000, of which only one-third would be coin, and the rest would be preexisting mortgages. This was not perceived to be very secure in the face of land speculation that would peak in 1792. The final capitalization was reduced to $500,000 in gold or silver exclusively.

Even when the bank finally opened in the Walton Mansion on June 9, 1784, the full $500,000 had not been raised. Aaron Burr had three shares, and Hamilton had only one and a half shares. In 1787, the bank moved to Hanover Square. The bank provided the first loan to the new United States government in 1789 when Hamilton was the secretary of the Treasury, a conflict of interest. The bank began to pay all federal employees' salaries, including President George Washington himself, until the Bank of the United States was charted in 1791.

The Bank of New York was the first company to be traded on the New York Stock Exchange when it first opened in 1792. In 1796, the bank moved to a location at the corner of Wall Street and William Street. However, foreign investors were speculating in the new bank, viewing this as an emerging market opportunity. They brought in coin to the United States, but with the Panic of 1792, they were quick to sell and created a shortage of cash as the result of capital outflow.

The Bank of New York had a monopoly on banking services in the city until Aaron Burr founded the Bank of the Manhattan Company in 1799, which was vigorously opposed by Hamilton. Eventually, Aaron Burr killed Alexander Hamilton in a duel for which he was charged since dueling was declared illegal.

First Bank of the United States

In 1791, the Bank of the United States was one of the three major financial innovations proposed and supported by Secretary of the Treasury Hamilton. President George Washington appointed Hamilton as the first United States Secretary of the Treasury on September 11, 1789. His proposal was to assume all the debts of each state and combine that to become the federal national debt.

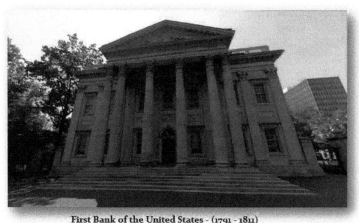

First Bank of the United States - (1791 - 1811)

In 1781, Alexander Hamilton wrote a letter to a friend in which he discussed government spending. "A national debt, if it is not excessive, will be to us a national blessing." Thomas Jefferson, however, took quite a different view. Jefferson said that public debt was a danger to be greatly feared. In 1798, he wrote a letter to his friend John Taylor in which he addressed amendments to the constitution. Jefferson wrote, "I mean an additional article taking from the government the power of borrowing." Hamilton was the politician; Jefferson was the statesman. There lies the conflict over the question of establishing a central bank.

Hamilton's plan considered the fact that the United States had borrowed money from Europe and at home during the American Revolution. The Continental Army had not been paid what was due to them, and many of the independently wealthy officers of the army had spent their entire fortunes on equipment and supplies for their own forces. The various states had borrowed money to finance the war effort. Indeed, some states owed private citizens for the purchase of

Alexander Hamilton
(1757–1804)

supplies, exchanged for a promissory note due at a future date. Additionally, Hamilton drew up plans for the U.S. dollar, defined in terms of both gold and silver, as the nation's monetary unit and base. He also called for establishing a federal mint to make U.S. coins with silver beginning in 1794.

Hamilton understood that the way to unite the states was to create a single national debt by absorbing all states' debts. This would create a strong central government and support the union, and it was Hamilton's magnanimous effort to relieve the states' debt burden. The U.S. national debt in 1790 was about $54 million. Adjusted for inflation, that would be about $5 trillion in 2021. Congress endorsed Hamilton's plan to pay off the $11 million owed to foreign creditors. However, they recoiled from paying the domestic debt of some $27 million.

Congress did not want to absorb the state debts, assuming that some states would have larger debts than others, and many viewed this as unfair. Further upsetting Congress was Hamilton's proposal that all debts were to be paid at face value. The Federal government would assume all of the debts owed by the states. He argued that this would be funded by issuing federal government bonds paying about 4% interest. He submitted that the government would not pay back the principal but only the interest where the principal would be paid by tariffs and an excise tax on liquor.

Nonetheless, under Hamilton's economic plan, federalism was the primary goal. He understood that creating a single currency required unification. Hamilton believed that the Federal government would not be able to borrow money from anyone in the future if these debts were not paid. By selling bonds to pay the debt, bondholders would have a direct financial interest to help the new United States government survive and thrive. Creditors who purchased the bonds could use them as collateral for loans, stimulating the economy even more. So, Hamilton did not distinguish between money and debt. The opposition was too great for the Federalists to overcome with respect to creating paper money. Thus, Hamilton realized a bond would be the same as paper money when allowed to be used as collateral for loans.

Hamilton's idea of assuming the states' debts while funding new national securities, thereby creating a national debt, would establish credit, faith, and trust in the new federal government. Consolidating the debts of the states would secure the new government by binding the self-interests of the states. Then, their creditors would look to the federal government. Hamilton wrote in the Federalist No. 11, in 1787:

> "Let the thirteen States, bound together in a strict and indissoluble Union, concur in erecting one great American system, superior to the control of all trans-Atlantic force or influence and able to dictate the terms of the connection between the old and the new world!"

Therefore, Hamilton realized that creating a large financial structure was essential to the survival of federalism. He needed to tie wealthy citizens among the states together to support and belong to a new federal government. Hamilton at least had real-world experience and had created the Bank of New York in 1784.

Hamilton knew precisely what he was doing. There was opposition then as there is today against central banks. Hamilton's proposal to charter a national bank was severely attacked in Congress on constitutional grounds. The opposition was led

James Madison
(1751–1836; President 1809–1817)

by James Madison (1751–1836), who was becoming increasingly hostile toward Hamilton's proposal. Although the two men had supported a strong national government in the convention and had worked together to ratify the Constitution securely, neither man's constitutional philosophies nor their economic interests were the same.

Accordingly, Hamilton's plan was strategically designed after the original Bank of England with the intent of supporting mercantilism, which he saw as the path to wealth. He wanted to merge that with government interests to create a strong and lasting bond. The Bank of England became a tool of government which was the concern and why William Paterson resigned. Of course, today, central banks are no longer concerned with private industry.

Hamilton placed before the first session of the First Congress his proposal establishing the initial funding for the Bank of the United States through the sale of $10 million in stock of which the United States government would purchase the first $2 million in shares. Hamilton, foreseeing the objection that this could not be done since the U.S. government did not have $2 million, proposed that the government make the stock purchase using money lent to it by the bank. This was the first equity-debt swap in federal history. This loan would be paid back in ten equal annual installments under Hamilton's plan.

The remaining $8 million of stock in the Bank of the United States would be available to the public, both in the United States and overseas, which Hamilton saw as establishing full faith in the formation of the United States. He understood that there would be foreign investors and saw this as expanding the money supply domestically. Indeed, Europeans purchased a block of $2 million that Hamilton saw as highly beneficial. Yet, opponents would later point to this as an argument to shut down the bank 20 years later in 1811.

Hamilton further introduced an interesting incentive to buy the stock. The primary requirement of these non-government purchases was that one-quarter of the purchase price had to be paid in gold or silver, and the remaining balance could be paid using the new government bonds. Hamilton created the incentive to swap your worthless paper currency for bonds, and then you could use the bonds to buy stock. This was a brilliant innovation.

However, unlike the Bank of England from which Hamilton drew much of his inspiration, the primary function of the bank would be commercial and private rather than government interests. The business on behalf of the new federal government would be strictly a depository for collected taxes. It would also make short-term loans to the government to cover real or potential temporary income gaps. It would also serve as a holding site for both incoming and outgoing international capital flows, which was extremely important yet overshadowed by everything else in play.

Continental Currency

$60 - January 14th, 1779 - Issue

The key to Hamilton's plan was that Congress agreed to redeem Continental Currency at $100 to one new U.S. dollar with an indefinite maturity. This was an effort to give some value to the worthless currency and avoid an economic depression by wiping out the value of the currency held by the people. Many did not redeem their currency thanks to the Act of 1790 that they read as an ultimate guarantee of 1:1, but this was never carried out.

Colonial Currency Rates	
Continental	$40 for $1
N.Y. & Conn	$40 for $1
South Carolina	$52.50 for $1
Mass., N,H. & R.I	$100 for $1
New Jersey	$150 for $1
Penn. & Delaware	$225 for $1
Maryland.	$280for $1
North Carolina	$800 for $1
Virginia	$1000 for $1
Georgia	$1000 for $1

During the American Revolution, the Colonies began to issue paper money without limitation. In 1778, Georgia issued money backed from the proceeds of properties confiscated from Tories. Gold, silver, and even copper coins disappeared from circulation completely once the war began. Paper money was printed for decimal coinage denominations as well. By 1777, the U.S. simply went into hyperinflation. Continental Currency simply became commonly referred to as "not worth a Continental."

Despite the fact that the Continental Currency ceased to circulate in April 1780 and the official exchange rate was set at $40 to $1, there was no actual redemption at that price level. Even though the Articles of Confederation had promised payment in full, it was not until seven years later, in 1787, that the United States Constitution recognized that there was an obligation to redeem these otherwise worthless scraps of paper. By October of 1787, Continental Currency traded at the going rate of $250 for $1 in gold.

First Bank of the United States Chartered

Hamilton's plan created a hotbed for speculation. The Bank of the United States, now commonly referred to as the First Bank of the United States, passed Congress in December 1790, and in February 1791, President George Washington signed the charter. The bank opened for business in Philadelphia on December 12, 1791, with a

twenty-year charter. Branches opened in Boston, New York, Charleston, and Baltimore in 1792, followed by branches in Norfolk (1800), Savannah (1802), Washington, D.C. (1802), and New Orleans (1805). The bank was overseen by a board of 25 directors. Thomas Willing, who had been president of the Bank of North America, accepted the job as the new national bank's president.

The Panic of 1792 was a financial credit crisis that occurred during the months of March and April 1792 or about three months after the bank opened. Traditionally, economists have claimed that it was set in motion through the expansion of credit provided by the newly formed Bank of the United States. This is purely speculation in and of itself. The bank had not been handing out credit in such a wholesale manner during the first three months of its existence.

The rampant speculation was created by promoting land speculation mainly by William Duer (1743-1799) and Alexander Macomb (1782-1841). Duer, Macomb, and their colleagues attempted to drive up prices of U.S. debt securities and bank stocks, but when they defaulted on loans, prices fell, causing a bank run. They assumed foreign investors would be pouring into the United States as the new emerging market.

William Duer (1743-1799)

Alexander Macomb (1782-1841)

The Panic of 1792 was the first financial bubble and crisis to take place in the United States. A combination of land speculation and stock speculation resulted in William Duer, a lawyer from New York City who helped draft the New York State Constitution and served as a member of the Continental Congress in 1778 and 1779, being sentenced to debtor's prison where he died. Alexander Macomb was an American merchant and one of the richest men in New York City whose home was rented to George Washington for his presidency. He would write to a friend, William Constable (1752-1803), an international merchant trading between England and American ports. In his letter of April 1792, he lamented that he lost everything in "less than three months" and would be sent to debtor's prison and never regain his fortune.

The wild speculation forced tightening of credit by the Bank of the United States, which reduced credit and actually forced the initial panic to unfold. Hamilton was able to manage the crisis by providing banks across the Northeast with hundreds of thousands of dollars to make open-market purchases of securities, which allowed the market to stabilize by May 1792. This was a form of Quantitative Easing, but the bonds in question were in private hands rather than buying new issues from government who continues to spend regardless of the economic conditions.

Benjamin Franklin
(1706-1790)

Thomas Jefferson had written to Edmund Pendleton (1721-1803) in 1791, concerned over Hamilton's bank scheme. He blamed the obvious rather than looking beyond the bank itself.

"As yet the delirium of speculation is too strong to admit sober reflection. It remains to be seen whether in a country whose capital is too small to carry on its own commerce, to establish manufactures, erect buildings, etc., such sums should have been withdrawn from these useful pursuits to be employed in gambling."

The Panic of 1792 was the event that also caused Benjamin Franklin (1706-1790) to write, "Nothing is certain but death and taxes."

Hamilton's IPO offering for the Bank of the United States saw shares sell at $400 each with 25,000 shares issued. Realizing that this was a fortune and typically several years' worth of income for the average man, they were sold on a subscription basis, and thus the "script" or option to buy a share was sold for $25 payable in gold. The option holder was then required to pay $100 ($25 in gold; $75 in U.S. debt) by January 1, 1792, July 1, 1792, with the next payment on January 1, 1793, and the final $75 in debt swaps paid by July 1, 1793, according to David Jack Cowen (*The Origins and Economic Impact of the First Bank of the United States*, 1791– 1797 (2000)).

This script began to trade as options, if you will, from July 4, 1791. Within just six weeks, trading was active. The price nearly doubled by the end of July. By August 1791, they exploded, reaching $264 bid and $280 ask in New York on August 11, 1791. The main market was Philadelphia, where they soared in price to $300. This meant that the actual share price would have been about $700. A panic broke out and the price tumbled in Boston, collapsing from $230 on August 12 to $112 by the 14th. The script rallied, reaching $154–159 on the New York market by August 16, 1791. In Philadelphia, the price rose to $125–137 on the same day.

Whiskey Rebellion - Unknown artist attributed to Frederick Kemmelmeyer

Hamilton's proposal to pay the principle with taxes led to the first rebellion in 1791 known as the Whiskey Rebellion of 1791. On the Western Frontier, there was a shortage of coin, and whiskey even served as a medium of exchange. Protests began in 1791 and reached a climax in 1794.

Unlike tariffs paid on goods imported into the United States, the excise tax on distilled spirits was a direct tax on Americans who produced whiskey and other alcohol spirits. The 1791 excise law set a varying six to 18 cents per gallon tax rate, with smaller distillers often paying more than twice per gallon what larger producers paid. All payments had to be made in cash (coin) to the Federal revenue officer appointed for the distiller's county. This resulted in several thousand armed rebels gathered at Braddock's Field during the last week in July 1794.

President Washington issued a proclamation on August 7th calling on the rebels "to disperse and retire peaceably to their respective abodes." The proclamation also invoked the Militia Act of 1792, which, after Federal court approval, allowed the president to use state militiamen to put down internal rebellions and "cause the laws to be duly executed." President Washington summoned almost 13,000 militiamen, and on September 19, 1794, he became the only sitting U.S. president to lead troops in the field against American citizens personally. On September 25, Washington issued a proclamation declaring that he would not allow "a small portion of the United States [to] dictate to the whole union," and called on all persons "not to abet, aid, or comfort the Insurgents."

Despite all the controversy, Hamilton's proposal is what made the United States dollar a viable currency. When Europe designed the euro, Germany refused to allow the consolidation of the debts of member states. This is why the euro has failed to become a serious reserve currency, for each member state issues euros, and there is no separation between federal and state debts. Investors must look at the debt of each member as they do with the 50 states in the USA. The lack of a federal debt is what has hampered the euro from rising to a true world currency.

Oliver Wolcott Jr.
(1760 – 1833)
Second Secretary of the U.S. Treasury (1795 - 1800)

After Hamilton left office in 1795, the new Secretary of the Treasury Oliver Wolcott, Jr. (1760–1833) informed Congress that more money needed to be raised due to the existing state of government finances. This could be achieved either by selling the government's shares of stock in the Bank of the United States or by raising taxes. Wolcott argued for the first choice for the government to sell all its shares in the bank.

Congress agreed as many remained anti-bank primarily because of local self-interests. The Bank of the United States acted as a restraint upon local state banks whose notes were discounted. Many argued for the end of the central bank under the belief this would allow state banks to boom.

Hamilton objected, believing that the dividends on that stock had been inviolably pledged to support the sinking fund to retire the debt as agreed with Jefferson.

Hamilton tried to organize opposition to the measure but was unsuccessful in mustering enough votes. Finally, in 1811, the U.S. Senate tied on a vote to renew the bank's charter. Vice President George Clinton (1739-1812) under President James Madison broke the tie and voted against renewal. The Bank of the United States' charter, therefore, expired in 1811 to the pleasure of James Madison.

George Clinton
(1739-1812)
Vice President under James Madison (1805-1812)

The anti-bank lobby argued that about $5 million in paper currency accounted for about 20% of the nation's money supply. The conflict with state banks was that their notes were trusted among the people, whereas notes of more than 700 state banks were discounted, which people simply refused to accept.

However, the arguments against the Bank of the United States also centered on the fact that there was foreign ownership from investors. The Supreme Court had yet to address the issue or constitutional questions that many would not let go of. The anti-bank group prevailed, and in the aftermath, unleashed a serious economic trend without a central bank.

After the destruction of the Bank of the United States, state banks were free of all restraint that had been imposed while the bank prevailed. The state banks went crazy and increased the number of bank notes in circulation. Lacking state regulation, everyone was suddenly entering the banking business, from taverns to barbershops. Inflation soared from 1812-1815 during the War of 1812 with England. At the end of the war in 1815, there was another attempt to establish a new central bank. That efforted failed. However, the following year in 1816, at last, a consensus began to emerge calling for a return central banking.

After the First Bank of the United States' charter expired in 1811, Stephen Girard (1750-1831) purchased most of its stock, the building, and its furnishings on South Third Street in Philadelphia. He then opened his own bank, which became known as Girard Bank. Girard hired many of the employees of the First Bank of the United States and opened for business on May 18, 1812. He allowed the trustees of the First Bank of the United States to use some offices and space in the vaults to continue the process of winding down the affairs of the closed bank at a very nominal rent.

Stephen Girard
(1750–1831)

(His left eye was damaged after a wagon ran him over in the streets of Philadelphia.)

Second Bank of the United States chartered 1816 ceased to exist in 1836

Girard was the sole proprietor of his bank and avoided the Pennsylvania state law that prohibited an unincorporated association of persons from establishing a bank after all the chaos. Being the sole owner, Girard avoided having to obtain a charter from the legislature for a banking corporation.

In February 1816, the Second Bank of the United States was established in Philadelphia, Pennsylvania, on Chestnut Street with a 20-year charter until it was destroyed by President Andrew Jackson in January 1836. The original building of the First Bank of the United States became a private corporation once the government sold its shares.

The Second Bank of the United States became a private corporation with public duties. It now handled all fiscal transactions for the U.S. government and was required to report to both Congress and the U.S. Treasury. This time, 20% of its capital was owned by the federal government, the largest shareholder. The remaining 80% was held by 4,000 investors, which once again included nearly 1,000 Europeans.

The Second Bank of the United States became the largest financial corporation in the world.

Ironically, the Second Bank of the United States was chartered by President James Madison in 1816, who had opposed Hamilton and destroyed the First Bank of the United States. He obviously saw the error of his ways and granted the charter after realizing that a central bank was critical to the economy's stability. The bank began operations on January 7, 1817. It eventually expanded to 25 branches around the country by 1832. The Second Bank of the United States had $35 million in capital, and it became the richest corporation in the world. It printed the country's paper money, and was the only bank permitted to have offices across the nation.

The Second Bank of the United States provided the fundamental and necessary function of a central bank to regulate the issue of private notes by private banking institutions. It was also in charge of the fiscal duties it would perform for the U.S. Treasury. Therefore, the bank provided the foundation for the establishment of sound finance which supported a stable national currency.

Andrew Jackson
(1767-1845)
(President 1829-1937)

Nevertheless, the anti–bank sentiment continued, and by the general election of 1832, the bank question was present once again. State banks did not like constraints, and others had poor credit and blamed the Second Bank of the United States. When Jackson first ran for president in 1824, he denounced the national debt as a "national curse." He vowed to "pay the national debt, to prevent a monied aristocracy from growing up around our administration that must bend to its views, and ultimately destroy the liberty of our country."

In 1828, a new tariff law took effect that raised taxes on foreign imports to unprecedented levels. The law's supporters were mostly northerners who believed higher taxes on imports would protect northern industrial goods from European competition. There was clearly a divergence between the North and South with respect to international trade. Furthermore, Jackson's high tariffs led to retaliation by foreign nations imposing high tariffs against American exports. Since the South was an export-based economy, namely cotton and tobacco, they saw the tariffs as disproportionate from their perspective.

South Carolina responded by rejecting the tariffs, which led to one of the first major conflicts in U.S. history and helped sow the seeds of civil war. In 1832, Jackson proposed to mobilize a federal army and lead it himself into South Carolina to collect the revenue. South Carolina backed down, averting war with the federal government.

Nicholas Biddle
Second Bank of the United states
(1786 1844)

Bank President Nicholas Biddle (1786–1844) knew that Jackson would destroy the bank if he won the re-election in 1832. For this reason, Biddle wanted to renew the charter early and made the request in January 1832, nine months before the next presidential election.

Biddle routinely used lending practices for political gain, including using bank funds to publish newspaper attacks on opponents as some money center trading NY banks engage in today. Biddle openly favored the National Republicans (later to become the Whig Party), many of whom benefited financially from Biddle's favor. Prominent National Republicans were Congressmen Daniel Webster (who was on the bank's payroll as a legal counsel), and of course Jackson's arch enemy, Henry Clay, who was again his opponent in the 1832 presidential election but lost.

Jackson's opponent, Senator Henry Clay (1777–1855) of Kentucky, was sure that the issue of the bank could win him some votes. Therefore, Clay argued his case on the floor of the Senate for three days. Power was being concentrated in the hands of one man, he argued, implying Andrew Jackson.

The chief opponent to the bank was Senator Thomas Hart Benton (1782-1858) of Missouri. The argument was class warfare. Benton argued that the bank was too powerful and made the rich richer and the poor poorer.

When the Senate finally voted on the bank's new charter, it passed with 28 for renewal and 20 against. The House voted three weeks later, and it too approved the charter, 107 to 85. President Jackson debated it with members of his cabinet but refused to compromise and vetoed the bill in the strongest possible language. On July 10, 1832, Jackson sent a message to Congress explaining his reasoning. Jackson said he did not believe the bank's charter was constitutional.

Jackson demonized the rich and highlighted the fact that there were foreign investors who were also shareholders. He argued that money paid by westerners for loans went into the pockets of the eastern bankers. Jackson said this was wrong.

> "It is to be regretted," he said, "that the rich and powerful bend the acts of the government to their own purposes."

Jackson was a debtor to banks in his youth and was against paper money in favor of coins — a hard money guy. Jackson's veto message to Congress set out his further objections. Jackson stated that "some of the powers and privileges possessed by the existing bank are unauthorized by the Constitution," suggesting that the bank was a dangerous monopoly.

Jackson easily won re-election in November of 1832, and he believed his victory meant that Americans supported his policies against the bank. Jackson's bias against the bank was self-evident, for he called for an investigation into the bank's policies and political agenda as soon as he settled into the White House in March 1829. He made it clear that he planned to challenge the bank's constitutionality, much to the horror of its supporters.

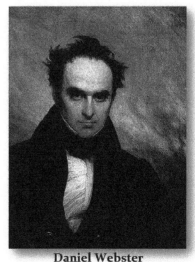

There was a fierce debate over Jackson's views, and Henry Clay tried to have him impeached by alleging, "Jackson claimed powers greater than European kings." Even Daniel Webster (1782–1852) viewed Jackson as a monarchical president. In 1834, the Senate censured Jackson over his vetoes.

Daniel Webster
(1782 – 1852)

Roger Brooke Taney
(1777 – 1864)

5th Chief Justice of the Supreme Court (1836-1864)
Author of Dred Scott v. Sandford (1857)
12th US Secretary of the Treasury (1833 – 1834)

Jackson saw the way to finish the bank would be to remove the government deposits. To accomplish this, he had to replace not one but two secretary of the Treasury posts until he found the right man, Roger Taney (1777-1864). Taney became the 12th secretary of the Treasury from September 23, 1833, to June 25, 1834. Jackson later appointed Taney as Chief Justice in the Supreme Court to ensure the bank would be declared unconstitutional. Taney would deliver the Dred Scott decision denying blacks all rights, which set the stage for the American Civil War.

On September 10, 1833, Jackson removed all federal funds, and on October 1st, Jackson announced that federal funds would no longer be deposited at the bank. This was the final straw of Jackson's bank war which overruled Congress.

Biddle retaliated by calling in loans from across the country. Biddle deliberately wanted to create a financial crisis in order to demonstrate his point that a national bank was needed in the country. Biddle asked the governor of Pennsylvania to make a speech supporting the bank, but he had refused to lend the state $300,000. The governor instead criticized the bank publicly. Two days later, the governor of New York proposed that the state sell $4 or $5 million of stock for loans to help state banks. The New York legislature approved selling even more.

Nicholas Biddle began to see that the battle was lost. He started making more loans to businesses, but it was too little too late. Biddle's move backfired, and businessmen as well as the farmers blamed the bank, not Jackson, for the financial crisis and ultimately the Panic of 1837. The Second Bank of the United States became a private corporation in 1836 and underwent liquidation in 1841.

When Jackson withdrew the money from the Second Bank of the United States, he placed it with private state-chartered banks that the press had called "pet" banks. This led to wider acceptance of paper money issued by state banks and caused widespread inflation. Jackson's bank war set the stage for the Panic of 1837. By withdrawing the deposits of the federal government from the Second Bank of the United States, he placed them in the hands of his "pet" banks, which was indirectly a vote of confidence in these "wildcat banks" that issued their own paper money or promissory notes.

Henry Clay, Sr.
(1777-1852)
American lawyer from Kentucky &
served in both the Senate and House
He tried for the presidency in 1824, 1832 and 1844

Henry Clay made a speech on July 11, 1837, on the floor of the Senate. He mentioned how, once again, there was no support for passing the Specie Circular in Congress. He states there was perhaps only one or two votes in its favor. For that reason, Jackson issues an executive order knowing that his ideas, such as destroying the central bank, would not pass a democratic vote in Congress. Jackson simply acted unilaterally.

> At the last session of Congress, a proposition was introduced into the Senate, requiring the payment of specie in all cases by the purchasers of our public lands. That proposition was, however, put down by an almost unanimous vote. For, although no call was made for the yeas and nays, I think I am fully authorized in saying that had such a call been made, there would not have been more than one or two votes in favor of the measure. Yet on the 11th of July, almost immediately on the rising of Congress, we find this very proposition embodied in a Treasury order, which requires the payment of specie in regard to our most important branch of the public revenue. This fact would seem to indicate that the policy of a mixed currency, for which the Senator from Virginia has contended, was not then the policy of the Administration, and that not *his* but another's influence was predominant in the cabinet. In the preamble to this order, in which the reasons for it are set forth, we find not only that specie is required from all purchasers of the public land, but that that other element of the currency which the Senator would retain is denounced as "paper money." And even in regard to the messages of the President himself, did time permit, and were it necessary to do so, it would be easy to show from all of them, so far as they relate to this subject of currency, that although President Jackson commenced his administration by recommending a mixed currency, yet that he gradually departed more and more from that ground, until in the message of 1835, referred to by the Senator from Virginia, he speaks of getting back to the

The great speculative boom in those days was the sale of public lands. People were buying land from the federal government and making a fortune. The crisis came when Jackson, in 1836, prior to the presidential elections, issued the Specie Circular on July 11, 1836, which required the payment for such lands to be paid only in gold and silver. The Specie Circular was an executive order issued by President Andrew Jackson rejecting the sale of federal government land to be made by paper money. This effectively reduced the value of all paper money issued by state-chartered banks. Land values dropped, and deflation led to the Panic of 1837.

The public land sales were fixed at $1.25 an acre and were sold to anyone. There was neither a limit on the amount purchased nor any requirement that the purchaser had to settle on the land. This created a real estate bubble. Between 1820 and 1829, the annual average was $1.3 million. In 1830, sales jumped to almost $2.4 million and exploded thereafter: 1831 ($3.2 million), 1832 ($2.6 million), 1833 ($3.9 million), and 1834 ($4.8 million). The exponential rally came in 1835 with $14.7 million and 1836 with a staggering $24.8 million.

Jackson's bank war that resulted in the creation of his "pet banks" was an endorsement of their paper currency even though Jackson did not intend that effect. Thus, the Specie Circular illustrated by these figures gives some idea of the scope of the real estate bubble at that time. Keep in mind, however, that while this land was sold by the government for $1.25 an acre, during the 1930s, land values fell to about 30 cents an acre 100 years later.

While there were public editorials critical of Jackson and his war against the Second Bank of the United States, his defenders of the bank's destruction made a vain effort to exonerate the government from creating the Panic of 1837. They pointed to the fact that the deposits during 1833 were slightly less than $10 million. Since there was no national debt, the land sales were pure profit, so by 1836, the government deposits in Jackson's "pet banks" rose to almost $42 million.

The defenders argued that these "pet banks" amounted to a small fraction of the more than 600 state banks. What they ignored is the endorsement factor that the federal government itself was using these "wildcat" banks chartered by states and that the bulk of the national deposits was not in gold but in the paper money of these banks from all over the nation. This is the primary reason for the 1836 Specie Circular that now demanded only coin. This burst the bubble of printing money and buying land that had created a glut of land owned by speculators, not farmers and settlers.

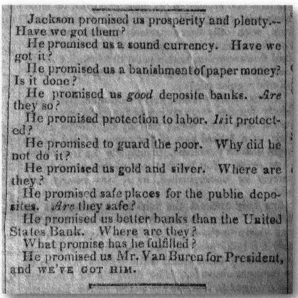

Jackson promised us prosperity and plenty.-- Have we got them?

He promised us a sound currency. Have we got it?

He promised us a banishment of paper money? Is it done?

He promised us *good* deposite banks. *Are* they so?

He promised protection to labor. *Is* it protected?

He promised to guard the poor. Why did he not do it?

He promised us gold and silver. Where are they?

He promised safe places for the public deposites. *Are* they safe?

He promised us better banks than the United States Bank. Where are they?

What promise has he fulfilled?

He promised us Mr. Van Buren for President, and WE'VE GOT HIM.

This editorial in an 1837 issue of the New York Post regarding President Jackson's effectiveness.

Since the monetary system was built upon the money supply issued by private banks, not the government, it expanded tremendously. Between 1830 and 1834, the paper money growth soared from $61 million to $200 million, as reflected in claimed bank capital. The loans during this same period grew from $200 million to $324 million. The period between 1834 and 1836 shows that the banking capital rose from $200 to $251 million, the loans jumped from $324 million to $457 million, and the notes that were in circulation rose from $95 million to $140 million.

The speculative boom that many would like to ignore as the cause for the Panic of 1837 created a wave of inflation that went into every sector of the economy. On February 14, 1837, thousands of people gathered in protest before New York City Hall all over the inflation issue. Commercial failures began shortly thereafter around April 1st. Within just one week, over 100 business failures took place. The collapse of the paper money even caused five foreign exchange brokers to collapse that same week. Some 28 firms who had been the real estate brokers servicing the speculators failed. Even eight stockbrokers failed along with 30 commodity houses.

As the second week of April 1837 began, another 28 failures in New York City took place. The contagion spread, causing firms to panic and cut wages, provisions, and even rent prices. *The New York Herald* announced everything was coming down. Within days, the failures became too numerous even to bother reporting. Commodities, in general, fell by 50%.

The United States' money supply actually included foreign coins, of which Mexico coinage dominated the circulating coinage in the United States. In 1793, a new coinage law gave legal tender status to Spanish and large silver coins of France for use in the United States. The status was to be temporary until the Philadelphia mint could meet the demand for a circulating medium. While they expected this to take three years to strike enough coins, the proposal was that the foreign pieces could be withdrawn. However, once enacted, the law was simply renewed in 1806, 1816, 1819, 1823, 1827, and 1834 until foreign coins were finally demonetized beginning in 1857.

By 1830, about 25% of the United States' coinage was made in one of the numerous Spanish colonial mints. Nearly five million dollars in Spanish coins were in circulation, meaning that the United States could not control its money supply. The standard valuation was one-reale piece presumed to be worth 12½ cents or one British shilling. British coinage rarely ever circulated in the United States, where the dominant coinage was always Spanish.

In the depression following the War of 1812, specie payments were

Peru 1834

suspended, and coins disappeared. With coins being hoarded, fractional paper notes were printed by local cities, as was the case during the Great Depression.

The United States' money supply varied greatly, given the fact that Spanish, Mexican, and other South American coins circulated with legal-tender status prior to the American Civil War. The law of 1834 added to legal-tender status to large silver coins of Mexico, Peru, Chile, Central America, those "re-stamped in Brazil," and 5-franc pieces of France. They all were to be accepted as equal to 100 cents with the one exception being the 5-franc which was rated at 93½ cents each. This was one of the issues many pointed to as a contributing factor behind the land speculation going into 1834.

The history of this period has been manipulated by many to extract support for particular agendas. Jackson's destruction of the Second Bank of the United States has been used to support the need for a central bank. We have others pointing to the paper money and using this to support the gold standard. We have others who point externally to the monetization of Mexican and other South American coinage rushing to the United States where silver was still legal tender. Defenders of the banks used Mexican silver as the influx that created inflation. They argue that the silver value declined because the British were buying goods from China and began to pay in opium they obtained in India, causing the need for silver in international trade to decline during the 1830s.

Defenders of the banks also point to the British, who had a huge trade deficit with America, and thus began to extend credit to Americans in order to sell more products. This has also been highlighted as the start of the funding for the big boom in railroads and the construction of canals. Looking at the customs duties collected in 1839, they were in excess of $23 million, which was about on par with 1836. The Panic of 1837 saw revenues drop to $11 million. Hard times had hit Britain, and this caused their credit lines to contract so customs revenues in America dropped to $13 million by 1840.

Andrew Jackson's War on the Banks

Andrew Jackson created countless enemies and became one of the most polarizing presidents in American history. His war to destroy the Second Bank of the United States was devastating to the economy. Once the bank was eliminated, there was no restraint upon the state banks whatsoever, and they flooded the economy with worthless paper currency that brokers heavily discounted.

It is true that Jackson had to pay off the national debt to destroy the central bank. However, in the course of this objective, Jackson generally opposed bills that allocated taxpayer money for "internal improvements" or what we call "pork barrel spending" today (a term coined in 1863 by Edward Everett Hale).

Jackson's feud with Henry Clay was infamous, and he regarded the Second Bank of the United States as a personal political rival rather than an economic lynchpin of economic stability. To pay off the national debt, Jackson enforced the tariff laws that many southern states viewed as excessive and even confiscatory.

Following the destruction of the Second Bank of the United States, the United States was without any quasi-central bank until the formation of the Federal Reserve in 1913, which emerged from the Panic of 1907. There is no doubt that external forces aided the trend, but they did not cause this economic collapse. Jackson's bank war undermined the entire economy and demonstrated the need for a central bank to constrain the banking system as a whole.

World War I Central Banks Policies

The United States did not have a central bank following Jackson's bank war. We must understand that prior to World War I, the United States was in a completely different position compared to Europe where central banks were long-established. Therefore, we can draw a line in the sand dividing pre-World War I from the postwar era. Additionally, the world was on the gold standard prior to World War I, whereas that was just not the case postwar.

The central banks of Europe were faced with two duties while being constrained by the gold standard that governed international finance.

1. The first was to defend their currency's parity with gold and thereby the entire edifice of the international gold standard. This required raising interest rates and keeping the total volume of money and credit under control, often with contractionary effects.
2. The second responsibility was to act as a lender of last resort for their banking system by supplying emergency liquidity. This necessitated an expansion of credit and a lowering of interest rates.

Prior to World War I, under the gold standard, global finance was a hybrid of a public-private system. On the public side, 59 nations took part in the system. On the private side, rules of engagement dominated finance among private businesses, banks, and individuals. The private sector could access the financial markets to facilitate trade both internationally and domestically. Yet, the central banks whose coordination and mutual assistance kept the gold standard operational were nominally private entities at this point in history.

London emerged as the financial capital of the world before the war. London was of critical importance for its large financial institutions emerged as clearing banks for worldwide trade that grew in importance, and with that, their gold reserves. London exercised great influence on global financial market conditions much as New York does today during the Post-World War II era.

The public and private elements of the system would feed into one another and thereby support each other in stable economic times. However, in times of war, suddenly, the private v public self-interests would come into conflict. Today, we face a similar conflict because governments have perpetually borrowed in times of peace and never reduce their national debts. Consequently, similar conflicts that would destroy the financial system in times of war are currently present in times of peace.

In the event of a war, central banks would find themselves torn between two responsibilities. The banks were to defend their currency's parity with the edifice of the international gold standard. This demanded they raise interest rates to maintain confidence in the currency with an adequate supply of money and credit to prevent a depression. This was a policy objective that had its own internal contractionary effects. Suddenly, the central bank was in charge of the consequences of war that the political decisions would reach without considering the impact on monetary policy.

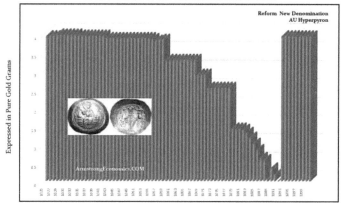

It does not matter what century we inspect. Whenever there is war, the currency depreciates in purchasing power, and coinage is reduced in weight and/or debased in purity.

An additional problem faced by central banks was the role of being the lender of last resort. Preventing bank failures by supplying emergency liquidity would require an expansion of credit and a lowering of interest rates. The system was without a clear balance, and indeed, monetary history demonstrates that central banks of Europe were never able to achieve perfect harmony.

The First Debasement of Coinage due to War Expenditures

LYDIA Kroisos AV Stater (18mm, 10.75 g)
Circa 564/53-550/39 BC Heavy standard
Sardes mint Pre-Debasement

LYDIA Kroisos AV Stater (16mm, 8.08 g)
Circa 550/39-520 BC Reduced Standard
Sardes mint - Debasement

ArmstrongEconomics.Com

As Europe cascaded toward war in August 1914, the central banks' economic policies came into direct conflict with one another. In Lydia, the place where coinage began, we see the reduction in weight of the gold coinage as a direct result of the war with Persia. This pattern is without exception since the dawn of official money.

Under the gold standard, money could not simply be created, and the cost of funding a war depleted the national resources. If a nation–state tried to remain within the gold standard system, its economy would contract, and a collapse of the credit system would bring a halt to private commerce. The other choice was to abandon the gold standard for at least the duration of the war, which would put at risk the costs of regaining parity into an unknown category, sometimes into an uncertain future.

When we look closely at governments' budgets during World War I, we can see how wars are funded, distinguishing between the fiscal, debt–related, and monetary aspects of war finance (i.e., central banks). Typically, we would expect taxation to provide the funding for war. After all, the right of the king to tax in England was restricted to the defense of the nation, and he was required to summon a Parliament to gain the people's consent to be taxed. This was the essence of the American Revolution slogan — "No taxation without representation."

However, upon close inspection, taxation played quite a subordinate role for almost every country involved in World War I. In Britain and the United States, the people were taxed the most, reaching about 25% of the war's actual expenses. For most other countries, taxation played even less of a role. In Germany, taxes were only about 6% of the war cost, whereas in Italy taxation covered about 15% of the cost.

In Austria–Hungary, Russia, and France, none of the war costs were covered by taxation. Taxes already covered the normal cost of governments during peacetime. Today, we have those supporting Modern Monetary Theory who argue that taxes can be raised to control inflation, yet simultaneously they can increase spending at will.

Borrowing was, therefore, the primary method of financing the war. There were two types of borrowing during the First World War. The first was short–term, a "floating" debt contracted with the central banks and occasionally with private banks. Long–term debt was issued to private banks, firms, and citizens and was generally regarded as war bonds.

War bonds were large credits to the government, which tended to contract the money supply but often at nowhere near the same rate of inflation.

Governments always pitched war bonds as patriotic contributions to the country rather than serving in

the field. War bonds were the most high-profile and often coincided with battlefield victories. Long-term debt was more secure because it could be repaid after the war. Short-term debt was generally easier to obtain, but the price tended to be more volatile. They would often issue more currency backed by the war bonds themselves. The short-term borrowing would create credit expansion resulting in war inflation. This would undermine the economy and create economic instability if the war was not going well, as was the case with the American Confederate bonds and currency.

War expenditures did not create constructive investments that could increase economic production or grow the GDP. The U.S. economy expanded during World War I and World War II because it produced food and arms for European countries, and no tanks were rolling down the streets of the United States destroying infrastructure.

Therefore, the United States served as an example where the war expenditures expanded the domestic economy, whereas European domestic borrowing expanded the economic contraction that undermined the domestic economy. The extent that Europe was able to borrow internationally was highly dependent upon government loans involving political relations.

Prewar foreign loans were typically long-term capital investments in railways, canals, factories, and real estate. Much of that private investment was simply lost in the wholesale destruction throughout Europe.

The European sovereign defaults associated with World War I involved only Turkey in 1915. However, the disruption to world trade resulted in a wave of sovereign defaults throughout Central and South America. Brazil defaulted in 1914 at the start of World War I along with Mexico, Nicaragua, and Ecuador. The sovereign defaults in 1915 involved Uruguay and an Argentina provincial default that same year. Paraguay defaulted in 1920, followed by El Salvador in 1921 after the war.

Several countries were unable to borrow domestically or internationally. Instead,

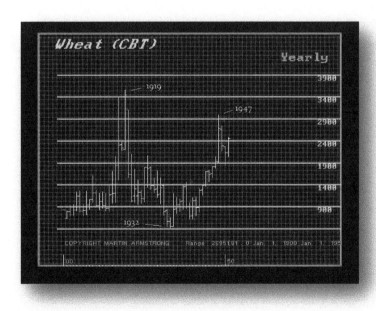

they increased the amount of money in circulation by "monetizing" the government debt and directing the central bank to buy government bonds from the national Treasury. Some simply printed money, increasing the supply dramatically. In order to do that, they naturally suspended the gold standard.

Governments will never stop fighting a war simply because of insufficient funds. They will often pass laws and even confiscate resources to maintain a war effort. The real crisis of World War I can be seen in the prices of raw commodities from food to metals even including silver.

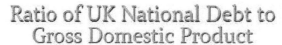
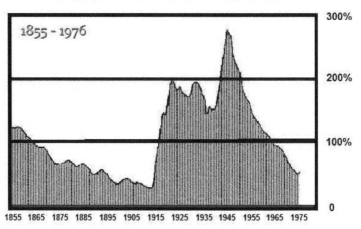

Some countries clearly had substantial gold reserves to fund the war, such as France and Russia. The Banque de France saw its gold as a "war chest," and after 1911, they began preparing for war. They lent 2.9 billion francs in short-term credits in return for three-month Treasury bills issued by the government. The French and Russians worried about the exhaustion of physical resources and commodity stocks as much as about money.

Britain had intended to maintain the gold standard during World War I. They chose to borrow, assuming that the war was like any other expenditure. The traditional view was to raise taxes to pay for one-third of the war costs and borrow the balance, thereby extending the cost of the war into the future. The UK benefited from the fact that it was the financial capital of the world at that time, and it was difficult for Germany to mount a land invasion with tanks rolling down the street of Britain. Still, inflation soared, the British national debt rose dramatically, and then World War II sent its national debt soaring even higher.

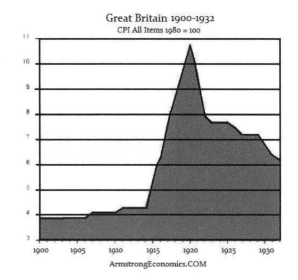

1915 U.S. $10 Gold - Eagle

Britain had imposed an income tax prewar with an efficient collection apparatus. They failed to take into account that capital would move to America to avoid the income tax prewar. The British also assumed that it would be able to outlast Germany because of its financial status. Britain clearly underestimated the cost of the war. Britain's error caused it to lose its world capital financial status to New York City.

Britain and the United States were determined to uphold the exchange rate between the pound sterling and the dollar in the interest of easy borrowing under the confidence of the gold standard. Indeed, the United States continued to strike gold coins during World War I, and it did not abandon

1915 British Gold Sovereign - London Mint

the gold standard, whereas Russia, France, Germany, and Austria-Hungary all chose to abandon the gold standard, which allowed them to fund the war effort through the creation of money. Australia remained on the gold standard as well and struck gold sovereigns in Sydney, Melbourne, and Perth.

James Mayer de Rothschild
(Baron de Rothschild)
(1792 – 1868)

James Mayer Rothschild in 1832 explained that London was the financial capital of the world: "This country, is in general, the bank for the whole world – I mean, that all transactions in India, in China, in Germany, in Russia, and in the whole world, are all guided here and settled through this country."

Indeed, London was the financial capital of the world. The architecture of the gold standard and the scope of British imperial power combined to form the foundation for the world financial system. Nevertheless, the real power rested upon the British Empire's international reach, which fed the trade and finance of its private sector and made London the center of global trade and finance. This was the distinguishing factor, for Napoleon had military power but lacked the private financial expertise. The French Revolution caused the wealth and talent to flee primarily to Geneva, Switzerland. Then in 1798, revolutionary France under the Directory annexed Geneva to hunt down the rich, which prevented France from ever competing with Britain. Only with the defeat of Napoleon was Geneva admitted to the Swiss Confederation.

The financial expertise in the City of London is what brought power to the British Empire, not its politicians or even its military might. Five major merchant banks dominated the world capital markets pre-World War I. They were the Rothschilds, Barings, Morgans, Kleinworts, and Schröders. It is curious that at the peak of American power in 2007, there were also five investment banks — Goldman Sachs, Lehman Brothers, Bear Sterns, Morgan Stanley, and Merrill Lynch.

London - 1906

The top five British firms in 1914 were involved in finance and underwriting ventures on a worldwide scale. There were also significant banking institutions that also possessed large balance sheets prewar such as Westminster (£104m), Lloyds (£107m), and Midland (£109m). These three institutions all had millions of depositors at that point in time.

London was the financial capital of the world, as James Rothschild commented back in 1832. London was the largest and most liquid financial market in the world as well. Funding world trade through the discounting of bills of exchange in London posted a daily trading volume prewar of over £7 million. London was also the secondary market for world trade with a global reach of about 60% of all global transactions going through London.

London was the financial center that provided both long and short-term loans internationally, and contracts were written in British pounds around the world. Yet, London was also the insurance capital of the world where contracts were written with a volume of two-thirds of all global maritime contracts.

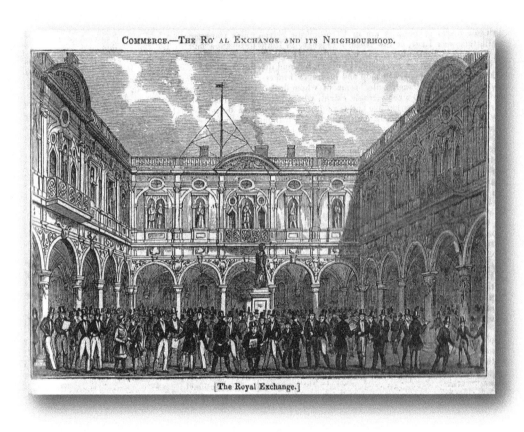

[The Royal Exchange.]

London was also the capital of share transactions since the early 1800s. The development of the telegraph was akin to the internet insofar as it connected people internationally. Up to World War I, about 70% of the entire global telegraph cable network was operated by British companies. To this day, the claims that the banks would move to the EU if London left under Brexit is a joke. Neither Paris nor Frankfurt can offer the infrastructure needed for major international business. The fact that the telegraph lines all led to London has maintained its dominance in communications to this very day. The dominance in the telegraph lines prewar also greatly enhanced the trading in shares at the Royal Exchange. Similar to how many foreign companies want their shares listed on the New York Stock Exchange today, about 50% of all share listed on the Royal Exchange in London during 1913 were foreign shares.

At the beginning of the 20th century, because the pound sterling was the dominant world currency, foreign exchange trading was primarily taking place in Paris, New York City, and Berlin. Britain only became a foreign exchange center after the war. Prewar, nearly half of the world's foreign exchange was conducted using the pound sterling. The number of foreign banks operating within the boundaries of London increased from 3 in 1860 to 71 in 1913. In 1902, there were just two London foreign exchange brokers. After the war between 1919 and 1922, the number of foreign exchange brokers began to rise sharply from 2 to 17. As the Roaring '20s emerged in the United States, by 1924, the number of foreign exchange firms rose to 40.

[The Upper Pool.]

British shipping going into World War I carried 55% of the world's seaborne trade. Energy was predominantly coal-driven pre–World War I. In the coal field, Britain controlled about 75% of the coking coal annually used by the world's cargo vessels. This also contributed to London being the financial capital of the world pre–World War I. The top five investment banks supported the financial system, followed by the commercial banks providing the capital and money market functions within the vast network of the regional savings banks and trusts. The vast secondary market of moneylenders, stockbrokers, discount bills of acceptance houses, and the insurance companies such as Lloyds of London rounded out the structure behind London's dominance in the world of finance.

[The Bank of England.]

We must understand that central banks today face a similar trap as if this was financing war. They are faced with the belief that they, on the one hand, are responsible for the value of the currency as a means to control inflation. Yet because of the failed Quantitative Easing, their policy of trying to stimulate the economy through purchasing government debt has led them down the path of keeping government on life support. If they now allow interest rates to rise, they will undermine the fiscal expenditure side of the balance sheet and reduce the confidence in the currency, which will lead to inflation.

External Forces Defeat Domestic Policy Objectives

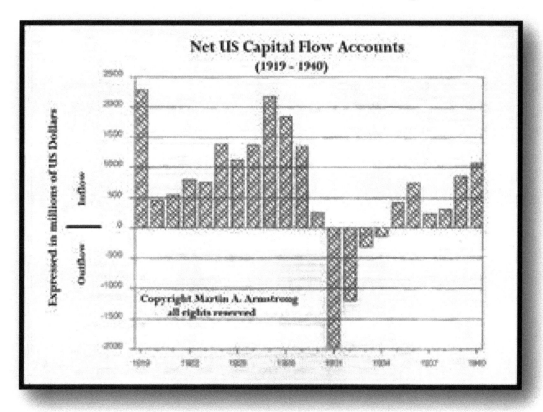

Capital has always looked to invest in what it considers to be emerging markets from ancient times to the present. If we simply review financial history with an unbiased mind, without a preconceived conclusion, we just might stumble upon something unique.

The global trends set in motion result from smaller trends emerging from every economy around the world. The trends in international capital movement are set in motion by the forces of taxation, inflation, geopolitical and financial security, foreign exchange, the cost of labor, perceived opportunities, and, of course, the meddling of politicians. There are some additional minor influences, such as interest rate differentials. Nevertheless, capital is continually flowing from one economy to another in search of profit, opportunity, or at times financial security.

363

Investing in foreign emerging markets has existed since Roman times. Capital flows around the globe seeking investment, often outside the domestic economy. Cicero commented that any event in Asia (Turkey), be it a financial crisis or a natural disaster, sent waves of panic running through the Roman Forum.

The Roman bankers were known as *argentarii*, who were highly respected and from the upper class. The currency exchange (*permutatio*) was done for a small fee (*collybus*). However, the *argentarii* also were involved in bills of exchange to facilitate international commerce. They would receive a sum of money to be paid in Athens. They had a network established where they would draw a bill payable in Athens by another banker in Athens. This necessitated the awareness of changes in foreign exchange rates. The *argentarii* would also retain money deposited by other persons (*depositum*), thereby offering accounts for clients from which they could make payments on their behalf. If the other person had an account with the same *argentarii*, this effectively became a simple book entry transaction, just as modern banks do today.

Brutus (85-42 BC)
"Eid - Mar" Denarius Professing He Killed
Julius Caesar on the Ides of March

Cicero also tells us that Brutus saw no problem in exploiting others for profit. Brutus began his political career as an assistant to Cato, the real head of Rome's oligarchy. He bid for the governorship of Cyprus. During this time period, Brutus enriched himself by skimming taxes and lending money to Ariobarzanes I (96–63 BC) of Cappadocia (modern–day Turkey) at 40%, which was well above the legal lending rate as confirmed by Cicero's documents on Brutus. Indeed, Brutus returned to Rome after making himself incredibly rich from collecting taxes and lending out money.

Ariobarzanes I, Philoromaios (96 - 63 BC)
king of Cappadocia

International investment has taken place since ancient times. There were two major financial bubbles that took place in 1720, known as the Mississippi Bubble in Paris and the South Sea Bubble in London. So, capital has frequently moved between nations historically. There is nothing new in this respect. Capital flows globally and always alters with domestic economic and policy objectives due to the international net capital flows worldwide.

Secret Meetings of the Central Bankers Germany - USA - Britain - France

On July 1, 1927, Montagu Norman of Britain was accompanied by Hjalmar Schacht, head of the German Reichsbank. They were joined by Charles Rist, governor of the Banque de France. All three went into conference with Benjamin Strong to discuss the weak reserve position of the Bank of England and the capital flight from Europe to America. It was hoped that lowering US interest rates would deflect the capital inflows from Europe.

During the 1920s post–World War I, Europe was deeply concerned about capital flowing to the United States. They persuaded the Federal Reserve with Benjamin Strong, who served as governor of the Federal Reserve Bank of New York for 14 years until his death the following year. Benjamin Strong wielded significant influence over the policy and actions of the entire Federal Reserve System at a time when the twelve branches acted independently. Strong exerted power over New York, which was seen as the financial capital of the United States. As a result, Strong took on financial policies with respect to the relations between the United States and Europe. In 1927, Strong agreed to lower U.S. rates to help Europe by deflecting capital inflows to the United States to reverse the flow back to Europe. The simplistic idea was that if U.S. rates were higher than Europe's, it would cause

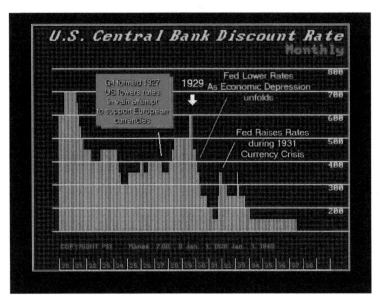

capital to flow to the USA. Lower rates, and in theory, they believed the flow would reverse back to Europe.

In 1927, Strong lowered U.S. rates in the New York Federal Reserve branch hoping to send capital back to Europe. As we can easily see, lowering rates from 4% to 3.5% had no impact. Capital began to pour into the United States, attracted in part by the strong rally in the U.S. share market.

The Federal Reserve was criticized for lowering rates in 1927 as the seed that began the rally into 1929. However, the entire attempt to lower rates and deflect the capital inflows back to Europe was childish insofar as it was far too simplistic. The theory assumed capital would be attracted merely by minor differences in interest rates.

The newspapers in London covered the "American Stock Boom" as it was being called in November 1928. The same thing happened when Japan was booming in 1989 and attracting capital from the USA and Europe as well. Central banks fail to appreciate that playing with interest rates will not control all aspects of the economy and capital flows.

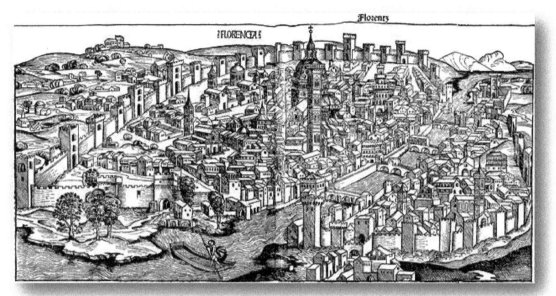

Political-Economic Revolt of 1343 in Florence

There is no better historical example to show how events outside a domestic economy can swamp the best management plans than the political–economic chaos in 14th century Europe. There was a major political–economic revolt in 1343 in Florence, which to some extent had to do with a corrupt government. However, the people, lacking an understanding of international capital flows and economics, blamed the local government and the bankers.

External forces in Florence caused the economic crisis. While there was no gold standard, the various coinages of the European states traded according to weight rather than a premium to perceived economic strength. During the 14th century, the British pound was quite different. It was equal to 240 pence of .925 fine silver that were known as "sterlings" from about the year 775 AD. Thus, 20 shillings for accounting purposes were equal to 240 pence, making a shilling 12 pence. The term referred to one pound of silver equaled 240 sterlings. Eventually, the phrase became shortened to "pound sterling" and was originally one troy pound.

By the time of Edward III (1327–1377), the pound was about 252 grams of sterling silver. Edward was at war with France. While Edward was borrowing from the Italians and the Jews, only to default on the Jews and then expel them from England, Philip confiscated wealth from the Italian bankers. He also seized the Papacy and the Knights Templar.

The cost of the war was massive, and debasement in France set off a contagion that impacted Florence. The French debasement disrupted the silver-gold ratio in Europe post-1337. What has been overlooked by most historians is the contagions that begin externally to an economy. Perhaps it takes an experienced trader who monitors all the foreign exchange markets to understand these capital flows.

Monetary System of the Republic of Florence

Fiorino d'Oro
1252-1303

Fiorino d'Argento
(Grosso), c. 1260

It is also clear that the Florin was devalued against the pound sterling in 1344. The fact that a major Florentine banking house, the Peruzzi, was already bankrupt in 1343 does not diminish this trend.

Foreign coin would circulate throughout continental Europe based upon weight. Philip IV debased the silver coinage due to the cost of the war. Since money was exchanged on a weight basis, the effects of debasement are substantially different altogether from a paper money system. Paper dollars do not circulate in all countries for daily economic use of the common man. The only exception was Russia and some other third-world countries, where the currency of that nation became distrusted. That aside, paper currency does not freely circulate among nations. Euros do not circulate in the United States, and Americans do not use them for grocery shopping.

When the monetary system of coinage is based on precious metals, even when there is no agreed upon standard, coinage circulates freely in all nations based upon metal content. The gold florin (*Florino d'Oro*) did become a standard much as the U.S. dollar has become in present times. In that case, other nations did imitate the florin to facilitate trade. In Florence itself, there was a two-tier monetary system. The gold florin was used for international trade, while the silver coinage (*Florino d'Aegento*) was used for local commerce including wages.

King Philip IV "The Fair" of France
(1268-1314AD)
AR Silver denier struck 1285 - 1290 AD

Due to the war between England and France, silver moved to a premium in France and sent the silver–gold ratio collapsing to 5:1 from 10:1. This was the consequence of the French debasement of their silver content due to the rising costs of the war. The rise in the value of silver in Paris altered the flow of coins within Europe. Silver began to move to France on a pure arbitrage, for if one exchanged silver for gold in France, they could obtain one ounce of gold with only 5 ounces of silver and return to Florence or London with the gold and exchange it for 10 ounces of silver. This arbitrage disrupted the economies outside of France. Internationally, Philip IV set in motion a capital flow of silver into France by exporting gold and disrupting all of Europe.

France raised the price of silver, which caused silver to flow to France, and exported gold. Further evidence of this capital flow is when we begin to see the first substantial gold coinage appear in England during the reign of Edward III. This reflects the sharp drop in the value of gold relative to silver.

The Great Florentine Financial Panic of 1343 was set in motion when the value of silver rose dramatically, sending the silver–gold ratio to 5:1 as a result of the French debasement. Silver was used locally for the normal people. Their wages were paid in silver. The gold florin was used for international trade, and companies had to keep two sets of books with accounting in each separate currency.

However, the crisis was more complicated than that. There were also sovereign defaults involved, which forced a major Florentine banking house into bankruptcy. The Florentine chronicler Giovanni Villani (1275– 1348) was a Peruzzi partner. At the beginning of the Hundred Years' War between England and France, the Peruzzi were international with branches in Naples, Paris, and London.

During the early 1330s, the Peruzzi made large loans to Edward III of England along with the Florentine banking house of the Bardi. Edward III was fighting wars with both Scotland and France. The loans of the Peruzzi were secured by grants of wool, money, and assignment of customs and taxes. As the wars drew on, the resources of the Peruzzi and Bardi exhausted both their resources. From 1342 to 1345, members of both companies were arrested for bankruptcy and released only on renunciation of all claims to interest by the English. Then the English crown defaulted on its massive debts owed to the Peruzzi. At the same time, the king of Naples defaulted on his debts to the two companies, and the king of France exiled them and confiscated their goods in Paris.

The sovereign defaults of the English, French, and the king of Naples undermined the local economy in Florence. The people blamed the corruption in government and the Duke of Athens for the rising unemployment. This occurred thanks to the financial ruin of many of the smaller merchant banks as well as the Peruzzi, who were effectively bankrupt by 1343. Yet, because the local wages were paid in silver, the French debasements drove the value of silver nearly double its previous value. Businesses could no longer afford to pay wages in silver, and this resulted in rising unemployment.

In Florence, we can see the impact of the French debasement politically. There was an uprising of workers that erupted on September 24, 1343. The people stormed the palaces of the rich merchant-banking families located in the Oltrarno quarter of the city on the left bank of the Arno River. This was where the palaces

Giovanni Villani
(1275- 1348)

of the Bardi, Frescobaldi, Rossie, Nerli, Mannelli, and many others were located. The rioters barricaded the bridges, and on the 25th, they captured the palaces of the Rossi and Frescobaldi. They also stormed the Bardi palace, forcing the members of that family to abandon their fortress and flee for their lives. The mob then sacked the Bardi Palace and set it on fire. The historian of Florence Giovanni Villani tells us that the Bardi lost 60,000 florins that day in the destruction that took place in Florence.

This combination of events led to the Worker's Uprising of 1346–1347. As money was hoarded, the velocity of the money supply collapsed. Weather also played a role, causing the famine of 1346 that contributed to great social unrest.

The long-term future of Florence as a major banking center had been undermined by the sovereign defaults. Against this backdrop came the Revolt of the Ciompi in 1378, once again concerning unemployment that was manifesting into demands for what we would call today labor unions, or in those days, the right to form guilds. Without question, this economic period of about 52 years in Florence was one of a deepening economic spiral downward. The Revolt of the Ciompi came about 34 years after the first Great Florentine Financial Panic of 1343. On July 22, 1378, the lower classes stormed the government and seized all the government officials.

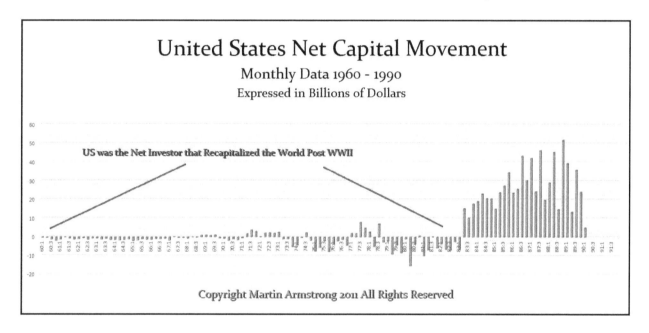

United States Net Capital Movement
Monthly Data 1960 - 1990
Expressed in Billions of Dollars

US was the Net Investor that Recapitalized the World Post WWII

Throughout history, there have been external factors that overpower domestic policy objectives. We are simply all connected, and that cannot be ignored. The net capital flows demonstrate that post-World War II, the outflow of capital from the United States reconstructed the world. Historically, capital has always moved among nations, yet our economic theories from Keynesianism to monetarism and even Marxism are all predicated upon the assumption of an isolated domestic economy. That very presumption lies at the heart of our problem.

Global Contagion Nullifies Central Bank Powers

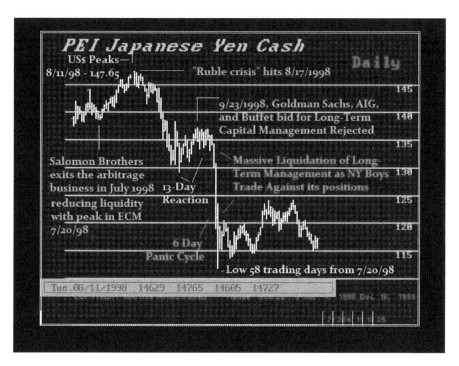

What took place in Florence during 1343 was similar to the Long-term Capital Management Crisis (LTCM) in 1998 that occurred over a loss in Russia and created a contagion that impacted the world.

The Long-Term Capital Management collapse in 1998 is often referred to as *When Genius Failed* after the book of that title. The collapse of Russia instigated the collapse of LTCM. Everyone in the NY banking cartel and their ex-wife was long on Russian bonds as bribes were paid to the IMF to ensure the loans would keep flowing to Russia. As long as the IMF would stand behind Russia, its high yielding debt would be a guaranteed trade.

The collapse of LTCM illustrated that everything is connected. The collapse caused a massive global contagion that had not been seen since the Great Depression.

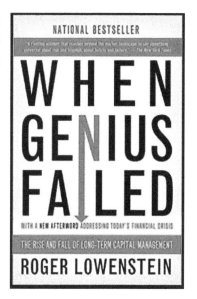

Herbert Hoover
(1874 - 1964)
(President 1929 - 1933)

> During this new stage of the depression, the refugee gold and the foreign government reserve deposits were constantly driven by fear hither and yon over the world. We were to see currencies demoralized and governments embarrassed as fear drove the gold from one country to another. In fact, there was a mass of gold and short-term credit which behaved like a loose cannon on the deck of the world in a tempest-tossed era.

THE MEMOIRS OF Herbert Hoover - The Great Depression 1929-1941, id/p 67

ArmstrongEconomics.COM

The crisis in LTCM was created because of their diversified positions globally. Once Russia collapsed, a major liquidity crisis emerged. Russian debt became unsalable, and they could not liquidate the Russian positions. To cover losses and margins by raising cash, LTCM began selling other assets globally. This LTCM crisis exposed the very same patterns that Herbert Hoover described in his memoirs for the year 1931. It also illustrated that you could not forecast anything in isolation, for we are all connected. A major liquidity crisis in Europe can lead to a global contagion in a heartbeat today.

The NY bankers continually blow up the world economy. Since they are the primary dealers who sell government debt, they are the new "untouchables." The courts and the Justice Department will never prosecute the bankers. When the banks themselves were criminally prosecuted, legally, they should have lost their licenses. Instead, the Securities & Exchange Commission exempted them from the laws that they use to destroy small firms. No one is willing to investigate or defend the people against the bankers, and the future looks very dark to say the least.

The banks always blow up because they try to get the guaranteed trade knowing that government will always have their back. Not one banker was criminally punished for the 2007–2009 crisis or any crisis they have created previously since 1998. The primary reason they always fail is that they are focused on creating the perfect trade by rigging the game with bribes. When the free markets act as the correcting force against such manipulations, we end up with a nightmare that government is then expected to bail out.

The 1987 Crash also stands as a warning that a crisis can be sparked by external factors that are not on the radar of domestic analysts. When they realized the 1987 Crash was created by the G5 manipulation of the dollar downward, foreign investors sold U.S. assets only because of the currency. Through research, I had warned this would result in such a wholesale crash, which was then requested by the Presidential Task Force investigating the crash.

Politicians place such an importance on trade that they lose sight of the real issues behind the numbers. By imposing trade sanctions to support higher manufacturing costs, they are making the consumer subsidize uncompetitive products.

The Presidential Task Force on Market Mechanisms

November 23, 1987

Martin A. Armstrong
Princeton Economics International
P.O. Box 7227
Princeton, NJ 08543

Dear Sir,

We have recently learned that you have produced an extensive study of the economics of the Great Depression. We would be very grateful if you could make copies of this work available to the Task Force on Market Mechanisms.

Yours sincerely,

Robert Glauber
Executive Director

September 1985 marked the creation of the G5 at what became known as the Plaza Accord. The intent was to force the dollar down by 40% to reduce the trade deficit. Of course, what they failed to understand was that they had sold about one-third of the U.S. national debt to Japan to ease the trade deficit. As they pushed the dollar lower, U.S. assets declined in terms of foreign currency. James Baker of the United States was the organizer of the Plaza Accord. Baker's objectives were to stop Congress from adopting a protectionist policy, endow the Federal Reserve with a new

September 22nd, 1985 - Plaza Accord
From left: _Gerhard Stoltenberg_ of West Germany, _Pierre Bérégovoy_ of France, _James A. Baker III_ of the United States, _Nigel Lawson_ of Britain and _Noboru Takeshita_ of Japan.

flexibility to raise interest rates that otherwise would be difficult with an overvalued and rising dollar, protect LDC debtors who would have been clobbered in a major trade war, and avoid a new upward boom–bust cycle of disorderly dollar trading.

The Journal-News

BUSINESS

ROCKLAND COUNTY, N.Y., MONDAY, FEBRUARY 23, 1987   B5

In Paris, accord on dollar's drop

PARIS (AP) — The United States agreed to work with its main trading partners to end a dramatic two-year slide in the dollar's value by reducing the U.S. budget deficit in return for Japanese and West German pledges to buy more American products.

The spirit of goodwill was dimmed, however, by a diplomatic flap that prompted Italy to boycott Sunday's talks and threaten to cancel a June summit in Venice of the seven largest industrialized nations.

Italian officials charged that the heart of the Paris accord was pieced together in secret talks Saturday among the Group of Five major economic powers — the United States, Japan, West Germany, France and Britain.

Italy supported the aims of the agreement but objected to being left out of what it considered the key decision-making meetings. Italy and Canada were invited to join the Group of Five at Sunday's session, but only Canada attended.

The agreement was announced at a news conference after finance ministers and central bankers from the six countries met in the French Finance Ministry's ornate offices in the Louvre Palace, next to the famed art museum.

A statement issued by the office of Premier Bettino Craxi said Italy would insist on an explanation from the Group of Five regarding its future role in international discussions about currency exchange rates.

"In the absence of a clarification, it is evident that the planned Venice Summit cannot take place in its expected form and term," the statement said. The summit is scheduled for June 8-10.

U.S. Treasury Secretary James Baker said afterward that the United States was surprised by Italy's actions but added, "We feel confident it will work itself out in due time."

Baker and other participants hailed the agreement as an important step toward better economic cooperation. Baker cited a West German commitment to enact bigger tax cuts next year and Japan's announcement in Paris that the government would propose comprehensive economic reforms.

Baker said he committed the Reagan administra-

tion to specific and substantial reductions in its budget deficit this year and next.

"These measures, and the continued cooperation of us all, will foster greater stability of exchange rates around current levels," he told reporters.

It marked the first time the U.S. government explicitly endorsed the view of the Europeans and Japan that the dollar had fallen far enough and that further declines would endanger the world economy.

The dollar has lost more than 40 percent of its value against the other major currencies since early 1985, in part because of a perception among investors that the Reagan administration wanted it to fall.

In September 1985, as the dollar appeared to be stabilizing, the Group of Five finance ministers agreed at a New York meeting to push it down further. The aim was to boost U.S. exports by making American goods cheaper in foreign markets.

U.S. Tresury Secretary James A. Baker, left, and his Japanese counterpart Kiichi Miyazawa enjoy a joke as they at the end of the press conference closing a weekend meeting of Finance ministers and central bank governors from seven major nations in Paris Sunday.

The dollar had already turned down before the Plaza Accord took place. After the announcement, traders simply viewed it as a confirmation of the trend. The dollar decline began to fall sharply. Then on February 22, 1987, six of the new seven members signed the Louvre Accord in Paris. This time the objective was to stabilize the international currency markets and halt the continued decline of the U.S. dollar. Italy declined to sign the agreement, complaining that it was left out of the real talks that were held in secret. Once again, the primary organizer was James Baker of the United States.

The Louvre Accord expanded the group from five members to seven and became known as the G7 meeting of central bankers and finance ministers. They announced that the dollar was now "consistent with economic fundamentals" in an attempt to support the dollar. They announced that they would only intervene when required to ensure foreign exchange stability. The objective was to manage the

floating currency system. Democrats gained control of Congress in 1986 and immediately called for protectionist measures. The dollar depreciation agreed to in 1985 at the Plaza Accord failed to improve the trade perspective. In 1986, the trade deficit actually rose to approximately $166 billion, with exports at about $370 billion and imports at about $520 billion. The objective of manipulating currency to create jobs and alter trade flows proved to be a complete failure.

We can see that the dollar had already begun a decline prior to the Plaza Accord in August 1985. By the time we arrived at the Louvre Accord, you can also see that the dollar continued to decline. The attempt to manipulate the foreign exchange markets proved to be beyond the capacity of the G5, which had been

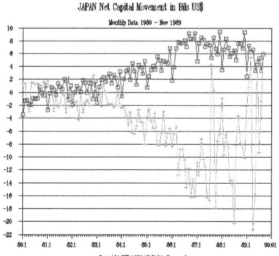

expanded to G7 and is today the G20. We can see the capital flow data between the USA and Japan begin moving in early 1984, establishing the trend that nobody seemed to notice at that moment.

The price action of the dollar clearly proves that the central banks lacked the power to influence the markets. The trend began prior to the Plaza Accord , and continued to decline following the Louvre Accord.

When we look at the capital flows for this period, we can see the wild and crazy swings that became the hallmark of the

1987 Crash. The swings in capital returning to Japan clearly contributed to creating the 1987 Crash, which was then followed by the capital concentration in Japan manifesting in the bubble there for December 1989.

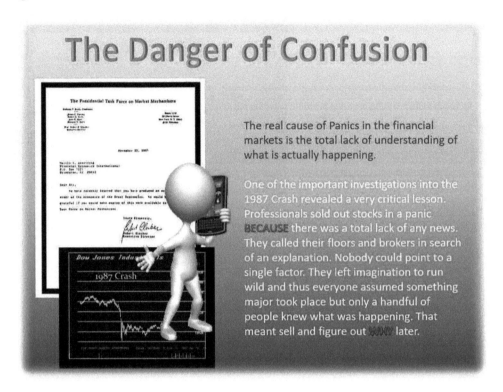

The 1987 Crash was driven by currency and made evident by the selling in overseas markets over concerns of the U.S. trade deficit, which widened even though the G5 reduced the value of the dollar by almost 40%. They failed to understand that what they called the "trade deficit" was really the current account, which includes all cash movements, including interest and dividends paid to foreign holders. The trade deficit expanded dramatically because of the exceptionally high interest paid on government debt because of the former Chairman of the Federal Reserve Paul Volcker's insane hike of interest rates to 17% into 1981.

Lowering the dollar to sell more widgets failed to produce any effect because the bulk included vast amounts of interest payments thanks to the high rates. At 8:30 AM ET, the government announced that the so-called "merchandise trade deficit" for August was $15.7 billion, approximately $1.5 billion above the figure expected by the financial markets. Within seconds, traders in the foreign exchange markets sold dollars in the belief that the value of the dollar would have to fall further before the deficit could narrow, given the G5 posture.

On October 19, 1987, the German deutschemark and the Japanese yen rose dramatically in value. Treasury bond traders, fearing that a weakening dollar could discourage international investment in U.S. securities and stimulate domestic inflation, sold on the London market and the U.S. bond market when it opened. The Dow Jones Industrial Average (DJIA) dropped by 508 points to 1738.74 (22.61%). Domestically, investors called their brokers asking what was going on. Failing to understand currency, they did not realize why foreign investors were selling based on their belief that the dollar would fall much further. This had nothing to do with domestic economic statistics.

By the end of October, the damage from the 1987 Crash was widespread. Stock markets in Hong Kong had fallen 45.5%, Australia 41.8%, Spain 31%, the United Kingdom 26.45%, the United States 22.6%, and Canada 22.5%. New Zealand's market was hit especially hard, falling about 60% from its 1987 peak and taking several years to recover.

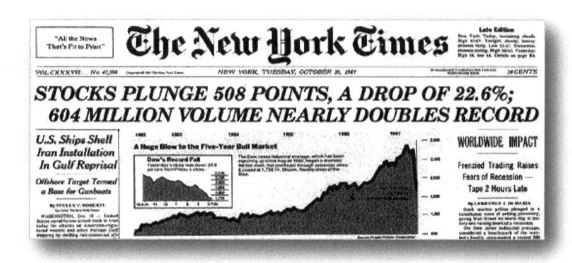

The Black Monday decline of October 19, 1987, from the previous close to the intraday low, was 25.3%, which was the largest one-day percentage decline in history (22.6% close to close). In the Dow Jones, the World War I Crash on December 12, 1914, of 24.39% was created retroactively after the DJIA in 1916 was revised.

Following the 1987 Crash, 99% of analysts were predicting a Great Depression. A group of 33 prominent economists from various nations met in Washington, D.C. in December 1987, and concluded that "the next few years could be the most troubled since the 1930s," as reported by the *New York Times* on December 26, 1987. "Group of 7, Meet the Group of 33," the article continued. Nonetheless, because this was currency driven, it was clearly not a domestic event as most analysts and economists predicted. That proved to be the actual low, and from there, the market began to rise to new highs.

Some blamed computers. Others blamed the futures markets, which just began trading the S&P 500 in 1985. Economists claimed the internal reasons included innovations with index futures, hedging using portfolio insurance, and program trading. But many of the computers were correct and said sell.

Herbert Hoover
(1874 - 1964)
(President 1929 - 1933)

But when representative government becomes angered, it will burn down the barn to get a rat out of it.

memoirs p-130-131

Interestingly, the investigations revealed that the portfolio managers did not sell, assuming there had to be a rebound on Friday the 16th. Clearly, the selling began overseas, which contradicts the argument that program trading was to blame, as was the evidence that surfaced from interviews. Even during the Great Depression, there was an assumption that the market went down because of short selling. They hauled everyone before the Senate and interrogated them. They never found that mythical short seller. Herbert Hoover apologized in his memoirs for the witch hunt he unleashed. He wrote, "[W]hen representative government becomes angered, it will burn down the barn to get a rat out of it."

Likewise, they never found any program trading strategies that were used primarily in the United States that set anything in motion. This boiled down to the simple fact that when everyone is long, the herd can be scared into a stampede of all sellers with no bid.

The 1987 Crash was investigated by the Presidential Task Force on market mechanisms otherwise known as the Brady Commission, which then requested my firm's research. Our efforts were designed to demonstrate that the high volatility of the 1987 Crash was caused by international currency concerns and was not the result of domestic economic events, nor was it driven by manipulative speculation. There was also no evidence whatsoever this event was abnormal or driven by computer trading that had begun just post-1985.

The 1987 Crash was simply caused by the G5's public announcements that they "wanted" to see the U.S. dollar lowered by 40% to reduce the trade deficit and in theory create jobs. They then held the Louvre Accord in an effort to stop the decline in the dollar, which totally failed. As the markets realized that the central banks could not halt the decline in the dollar, all confidence in government interventions collapsed.

"At times like the present, when the evils of unsound finance threaten us, the speculator may anticipate a harvest gathered from the misfortune of others, the capitalist may protect himself by hoarding or may even find profit in the fluctuations of values; but the wage earner – the first to be injured by a depreciated currency – is practically defenseless. He relies for work upon the ventures of confident and contented capital. This failing him, his condition is without alleviation, for he can neither prey on the misfortunes of others nor hoard his labour."

Grover Cleveland (1837–1908)
only President of United States to serve two non consecutive terms (1885–1889 and 1893–1897)

Such artificial intervention is highly dangerous and warns that when government objectives fail so blatantly, volatility will rise dramatically in the face of a collapse in confidence. Capital can always leave or hoard in times of uncertainty, but labor can do neither, as President Grover Cleveland once commented during the Panic of 1893. The numerous layers of taxation are increasing the international cost of labor and eliminating any hope of global competitiveness.

Indeed, the Brady Commission Report concluded:

> "The volatility in the dollar clearly reflected the uncertainty of those who watched the bond markets, the skepticism of those who watched the trade data, the nervousness of those in the foreign exchange market and the fear of those who watched all three. The value of the dollar had become a linchpin on which so much depended. A weaker dollar was the only way to improve the trade balance yet a weaker dollar would command higher interest rates."

In 1997, the Treasury secretary was once again trying to talk the dollar down. I wrote him to warn of what took place in 1997, lest he forgot, to which they replied.

Princeton Economics International Ltd

May 20, 1997

Mr. Robert Rubin
Secretary of Treasury
US Department of Treasury
Washington, DC

Dear Mr. Rubin:

The current conflicting statements out of the US and Japan over the value of the yen and Japanese trade surplus have obviously unleashed untold volatility within the foreign exchange markets that are endangering the stability of the entire global economy and capital flows.

I must point out that the US government has still not taken into account that the trade numbers as reported reflect only currency net movement and not actual units of goods and services. The methodology of trade statistics is a throw back to pre-1971 gold standard days when the value of money did not change. Subsequently, trade could then be easily monitored by merely following cash flows. Today, the floating exchange rate system has rendered all international statistics worthless and dangerous when used for political economic purposes. Comments relative to the US/Japan trade account reflect the sharp decline of the yen and not a substantial rise in actual exports of goods to the US.

We have investigated this matter very carefully and the true net sales of goods to the US from Japan have declined, despite the fact that the surplus in yen terms has risen 150% over the past year. If actual exports to the US had risen, then Japan's economy would be booming instead of the current dismal performance. Corporate profits would rise instead of decline, and above all, unemployment would decline instead of rising as is the current case in Japan.

We were one of the firms requested to help investigate the 1987 Crash by President Reagan. The conclusion of that investigation was clear. The Crash of 1987 was caused by a 40% swing in the value of the dollar over the previous 2 year period. That volatility forced investors to withdraw from the US market due to the view of the dollar, not their view of our assets.

Herbert Hoover also wrote in his memoirs about how confidence in the foreign exchange markets collapsed in 1931. He stated that capital acted like a loose cannon on the deck of a ship in the middle of a torrent. Capital rushed from one currency to another so rapidly

Princeton Economics International, Ltd

210 Carnegie Center, 4th Floor
Princeton, NJ 08540 (USA)
USA Tel 609-987-0600

0 Bolton Street
Piccadilly, London W1Y 8AU, UK
FAX 609-987-0726

Mr. Robert Rubin
Secretary of Treasury
May 20, 1997
Page Two

that government was unable to form a committee fast enough to investigate what was taking place, no less prevent it from happening.

Our historical computer models are warning that unless the volatility in foreign exhange markets is reduced, we are endangering the stability of the entire global economy once again. If such statements do not seek to constructively reduce volatility instead of fuel it, you will see short-term interest rates in the US explode and your extremely short-term funding of the US national debt will seriously disrupt our entire economic future.

We have been in contact with our institutional clients in Japan. Their purchase of US government securities has risen from 7% to 33% of our entire US national debt. The majority are now telling us they can no longer endure this type of volatility in the currency markets and if the dollar/yen falls below 110, you will see massive liquidation of US government assets.

If you are not extremely careful with this issue of foreign exchange and trade surpluses, vague statements will cause the Crash of 1997 within a matter of months. If the dollar/yen does not stabilize, and soon, the current administration will go down in history next to that of Herbert Hoover.

Sincerely,

Martin A. Armstrong
Chairman of the Board
Princeton Economic Institute

cc: President William Clinton
    Congressman Bill Archer
    Senator Trent Lott

DEPARTMENT OF THE TREASURY
WASHINGTON, D.C. 20220

June 4, 1997

Mr. Martin A. Armstrong
Princeton Economics International
210 Carnegie Center, 4th. Floor
Princeton, N.J. 08540

Dear Mr. Armstrong:

Thank you for your letter to Secretary Rubin of May 20. It is always useful to be reminded of history.

Our exchange rate policy is based on the recognition that the fundamental sources of a strong and stable currency are sound monetary and fiscal policies that foster healthy, non-inflationary growth, and sustainable current account positions. We work closely with our G-7 partners and other major countries to promote these policies.

Sincerely,

Timothy F. Geithner
Senior Deputy Assistant Secretary
(International Affairs)

Quantitative Easing

While so many people claimed that Quantitative Easing (QE) would produce inflation since it was the creation of money, the truth is very far from this simplistic idea. QE was the evolution of the original tool of elastic money that had been used to support the private sector during a financial crisis. The central bank was intended to purchase only short-term corporate paper to prevent companies from laying off employees because there was a shortage of cash during a financial crisis. However, once the corporate paper was replaced with government paper to fund World War I, it was never restored. From there onward, the elastic money tool to "stimulate" the private sector directly gave way to QE, which has unfolded as maintaining governments on life support during financial crises rather than the people.

Switching from elastic money to Quantitative Easing by changing the instruments from private to public has altered the entire global economy. Everything we have is now at risk of a serious economic implosion that will topple governments and destroy our economic future. Where private corporate debt directly stimulated the economy by supporting commerce, buying exclusively government debt only supports government and not the private sector.

1864 $10 Compound Interest Note with Interest Rate Schedule on Reverse

The United States did not issue paper currency until the Civil War. In reality, getting people to accept the currency took interest-bearing or circulating bearer bonds. The term "greenback" was applied to the demand note issues that did not pay interest, nor were they backed by anything. The interest-bearing currency had the schedule of interest rates on the reverse. The greenbacks paid no interest, and therefore the only thing on the reverse was green ink without an interest rate table.

Nevertheless, the theory used by the central banks is seriously flawed and a throwback to ancient times before 1971 when we are looking only at government debt. There used to be a difference between debt and cash where you could not use debt as cash to borrow on. Then, in theory, it was less inflationary to borrow than to print, but that changed post-1971. If you want to trade futures today, you post T-bills as cash. The repo market has emerged where AAA securities can be borrowed against for the night.

Therefore, buying in bonds to inject cash into the system under the old way of running the monetary system pre-1971 made sense. You were taking in non-liquid assets and replacing them with cash. The U.S. Treasury attempted that method in 1873 but failed because people will not spend money without faith in the future.

Today, QE has proven to be a fool's game. Why? QE merely swaps debt for cash; the real money supply has not increased when the true definition of the base in the money supply is debt and cash. The best we can assume is that buying in government debt could perhaps be invested in the private sector. But that presumes banks are willing to lend in a chaotic investment. It also assumes the economy is purely domestic. Since U.S. debt is held as the reserve currency around the globe by central banks, some fail to consider when buying in a 30-year bond that the seller may not be exclusively domestic.

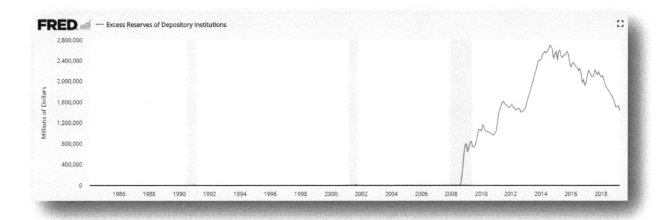

Yet, there was the problem that buying in government bonds did not result in lending that money out into the private sector. Indeed, the banks sold the long-term debt to the Fed and then complained they had no place to park the money. The Federal Reserve then created the excess reserve window, which reached $2.6 trillion during August 2014, on which the Fed paid 0.25% interest. The banks only swapped bonds for the right to deposit cash at 0.25%, which defeated the entire idea of stimulating the economy. Nothing was stimulated, and there was no inflation since there was no actual increase in private spending. Clearly, QE was covertly being neutralized by the creation of the excess reserve facility.

The theory of QE is very primitive. No one looks at what is occurring or the end result. The European Central Bank (ECB) bought 25% of the bonds, and inflation still turned negative. Eventually, the ECB ended up owning 40% of the debt in the Eurozone. The entire crisis comes into focus when we realize that they can neither sell what they have purchased nor stop reinvesting without causing interest rates to explode.

Quantitative Tightening v Modern Quantitative Easing

Federal Reserve v Congress

M ost people will always judge the past based on current and future events. However, the policies employed by central banks during the 19th century are strikingly different from today. Quantitative Credit Tightening and raising interest rates during a crisis was the norm rather than Quantitative Easing and lowering interest rates during the 21st century. The entire focus of central banks under the gold standard was to protect their reserves — not manage the economy.

There has been an inverse relationship of interest rate policy v stock market price movements, which has taken shape during the 20th century onward. Then we have the emergence of national public debts, which results in fiscal policy clashing with monetary policy theory. Central banks have been expected to smooth out the fluctuations within the business cycle post–Great Depression.

In Britain, during the first phase of the Industrial Revolution, investment focused on the development of the transportation system by means of digging canals. Then canals were followed by the invention of the steam engine. This early phase of the Industrial Revolution began to formulate our modern economies. The rise of nations was dependent upon establishing a domestically integrated economy as we are witnessing China undertaking in the 21st century.

Previously, speculation created emerging market bubbles prior to the technology booms such as the South Sea and Mississippi Bubbles, which were followed by the great Land Bubble in the United States in 1792 as the nation expanded westward. A series of successive railroad bubbles involving railway shares blossomed into an investment mania that left many people bankrupt. These successive speculative bubbles followed the Canal Bubble of 1793 and 1824. The technological Railroad Bubble unfolded in Britain during 1835–1837 and again 1845–1847.

Of course, there was the Tulip Bubble of the 17th century which seems to fit neither category. Perhaps we should classify this as the first collectible bubble. The Tulip Bubble engulfed all of Europe, for tulips even began trading in London in 1610. Tulips were trading as derivatives on options and futures contracts. Charles Kindleberger in his *Manias, Panics, and Crashes* only casually mentioned the event. He went on to say in a footnote on page 7 of his second edition (1989):

> "Manias such as…the tulip mania of 1634 are too isolated and lack the characteristic monetary features that come with the spread of banking after the opening of the eighteenth century."

The Panic of 1825 was a share market crash that engulfed the Bank of England, arising in part out of speculative investments in Latin America that included the imaginary country of Poyais. This scheme was at least related to the South Sea Bubble, where capital was making great gains in emerging markets. The crisis impacted Britain, resulting in the collapse of twelve banks. Ironically, an infusion of gold reserves from the Banque de

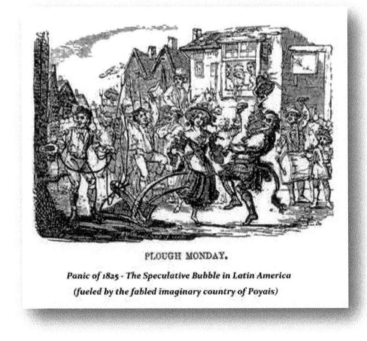

PLOUGH MONDAY.

Panic of 1825 - The Speculative Bubble in Latin America
(fueled by the fabled imaginary country of Poyais)

France saved the Bank of England from complete collapse.

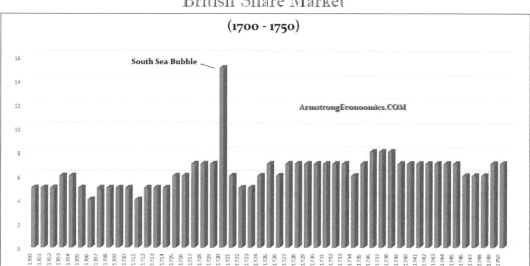

The world economy has always been connected. The Panic of 1825 illustrates that investors still looked for profits from emerging markets. The South Sea and Mississippi Bubbles of 1720 were emerging market speculation in the New World. Capital was attracted in the same manner that people looked for opportunities in East Germany, Russia, and China after communism fell. The Long-Term Capital Management Crisis of 1998 took place when investments in Russia collapsed. Even back in ancient Rome, Romans were eager to invest in the newly conquered territories.

William Duer (1743-1799)

The next real speculation was the Canal Bubble that first took place in 1793, followed by the major high in 1824. This was preceded by a real estate bubble in 1792 that took place in the United States as another emerging market event. The Panic of 1792 in the United States was the first financial bubble and crisis involving real estate. It was a combination of land speculation and stock speculation that resulted in William Duer (1743-1799), a lawyer from New York City who served as a member of the Continental Congress in 1778 and 1779, being sentenced to debtor's prison where he died.

The technological boom that first attracted investors was distributing goods that expanded the economy and involved digging canals. Despite the high cost of construction, the advantage of creating a transportation canal system was the reduction in distribution costs. Indeed, the price of coal from Manchester fell by 50% shortly after transportation by canal opened. This was the financial success of the century that attracted investors.

Originally, only one canal was authorized by Act of Parliament in 1790, but by 1793 there were twenty canal companies. Some canals failed to produce a dividend, lacking the distribution route for coal, which included the Herefordshire and Gloucestershire Canal. Some canals were never completed because they ran out of capital, such as the Grand Western Canal.

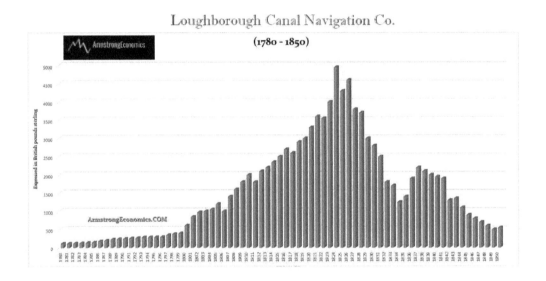

The success story was the Loughborough Canal Navigation Co. with a par value of £100 with an issue of just 70 shares. It rose dramatically in a bidding war and reached £195 during the first Canal Bubble of 1793. But it would be the next Canal Bubble that peaked in October 1824 that became legendary and culminated with the Panic of 1825. Here the Loughborough Canal Navigation Co. consistently paid the highest dividend of any canal company in English history. In 1824, its share price actually hit almost £5,000 during October, which was an incredible amount of money back then. Their share price never split, and the annual dividend reached £200. Shareholders were getting paid a dividend that was more than what they had paid for the share initially.

Since the Loughborough Canal was so profitable, there was active trading well into the mid–1800s. The company began paying a £5 dividend in 1780, which by 1793 reached £30. The first high in the Canal Bubble was in 1793. Yet, the market recovered and rallied into 1824 when the dividend reached £200.

Even 11 years later, on Monday, March 21, 1836, the *London Courier and Evening Gazette* wrote: "We observe, for example, that shares in the Loughborough canal, which have cost 142£ 17s., pay about 100£ a year, and sell for about 1,500£." On September 2, 1853, this share was trading at £510. Nevertheless, there was trading in these shares that left behind price data. In fact, this stock was still trading at £140 in 1920.

The Panic of 1837 was again one of international capital flows to the United States as speculation boomed on the similar view of emerging markets. There was a speculative land boom in the western U.S. states, but that came to an end in December 1836 when Andrew Jackson imposed by presidential executive order the Specie Circular. This required payment for government land to be in gold and silver. The economic conditions combined with a sharp decline in cotton prices disrupted the southern economy, where agriculture accounted for about 70% of the civil workforce.

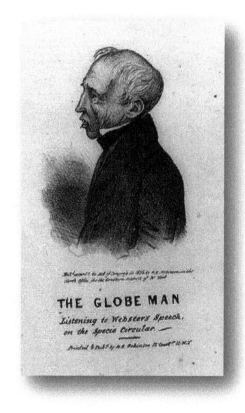

THE GLOBE MAN

Listening to Webster's Speech, on the Specie Circular.

The *Washington Globe* editor and adviser to President Martin Van Buren, Francis Preston Blair, is pictured here in the spring of 1838 listening to Daniel Webster's lengthy March 12, 1838 speech condemning the Specie Circular. This executive order by Jackson was extremely unpopular and created the Panic of 1837. It was repealed in 1838.

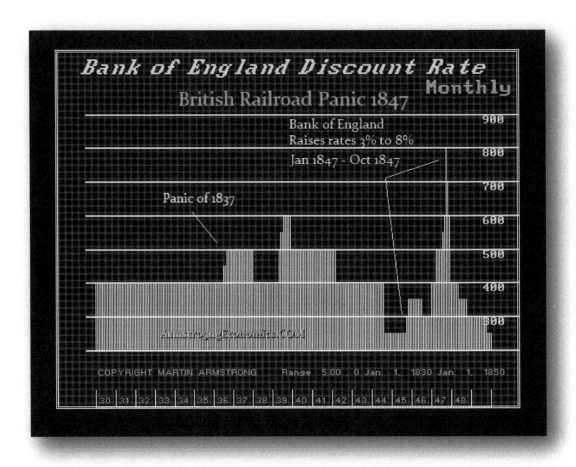

Meanwhile, there had been significant international Specie (gold) flows from Britain to the USA on land speculation. In 1836, the Bank of England directors panicked when they noticed that the bank's gold reserves had declined sharply because of the investments to the United States. Additionally, a poor wheat harvest forced Great Britain to import wheat, which drained the gold reserves. The 1844 Bank Charter Act tied the issue of notes to the gold reserves and gave the bank sole rights to issue banknotes. The Bank of England directors began to gradually raise interest rates from 4% to 5% to curb lending and attract gold deposits or risk their own inability to issue banknotes.

During the Panic of 1837, the Bank of England raised interest rates which set off a contagion. This resulted in major banks within the United States being forced to follow suit. Here we have a financial crisis and the opposite taking place where they are raising rates instead of lowering rates to "stimulate" the economy. The deep concern was the loss of gold reserves through international capital flows. They also failed to understand that the public will simultaneously hoard money during such a financial crisis. Indeed, the United States government had stopped issuing $10 gold coins in 1804. They only resumed after the financial crisis in 1838 with the repeal of the Specie Circular. While they did issue $5 gold coins, in 1834, the mintage was 657,460, whereas in 1837, they minted only 207,121 coins. The Treasury had restricted the creation of  gold coinage in conjunction with the Specie Circular, unleashing a wave of deflation.

On May 10, 1837, banks in New York City suspended specie payments, meaning that they would no longer redeem commercial paper in specie (gold). Despite a brief recovery in 1838, the recession persisted for approximately seven years. Banks collapsed, businesses failed, prices declined, and thousands of workers lost their jobs in what became known as "Hard Times" in the United States. The value of land collapsed, which had been inflated with state paper money. The price of cotton collapsed and put pressure on southern plantations, and even the price of slaves declined.

Citizens' Bank of Louisiana

Jackson ushered in the Broken Bank Note Era with massive bank defaults. The lack of a central bank was far worse. The consumer was clueless as to which banks were real or outright frauds. Those that cheer Jackson taking down the central bank fail to look deeply at the Broken Bank Note Era, which led to the Panic of 1837 that then set in motion the Sovereign State Debt Defaults of 1839–1843.

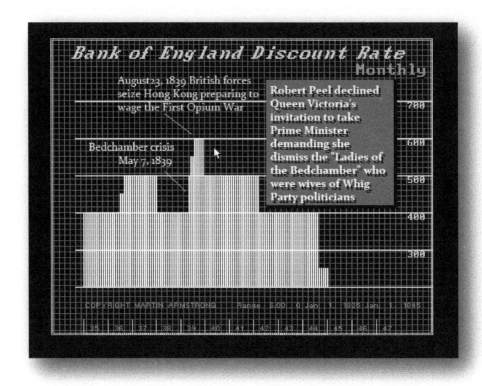

In 1839, there was a political crisis and a war. The Bedchamber Crisis occurred on May 7, 1839, after Whig politician Lord Melbourne declared his intention to resign as prime minister. The young Queen Victoria first asked the Duke of Wellington (a former Tory prime minister) to form a new government, but he declined. She then invited Conservative leader Robert Peel to form a government. Peel accepted the invitation only on the condition that Victoria dismissed some of her Ladies of the Bedchamber who were the wives or relatives of leading Whig politicians. She refused the request. Peel, in turn, refused to form a government. She then convinced Lord Melbourne to remain as prime minister. The Bank of England raised rates from 4% to 5% during this crisis.

As tensions began to rise with China, the Bank of England raised rates again in June 1839 to 5.5%. Then on August 23, 1839, the British forces seized Hong Kong as a base and prepared to wage the First Opium War; the Bank of England raised rates again to 6%.

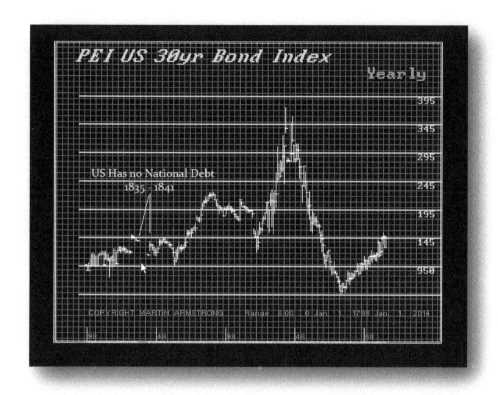

As the Bank of England raised rates in 1839, they set off a contagion of deflation. They began to lower rates in 1840, but the "Hard Times" was set in motion, compelling European and American banks to raise rates to compete for capital. Federally, the United States had paid off its debt, and nothing was outstanding by 1835. The United States began to issue debt once again in 1842 as interest rates had risen due to the crisis in Britain.

Then in 1841 and 1842, eight states and the Territory of Florida all defaulted on their sovereign debts. Traditional histories of the default crisis have stressed the causal role of the depression that began with the Panic of 1837, unexpected revenue shortfalls from canal and bank investments as a result of the depression, and an unwillingness of states to raise tax rates. However, these stylized facts do not fit the experience of states at all very well. The majority of state debts in default in 1842 were contracted after the Panic of 1837, and most states did not expect

Sovereign Debt Default 1833
State of Mississippi $1,000 Bond

canal investments to return substantial revenues by 1841 and did not experience unexpected shortfalls in those revenues.

Finally, most states were willing to raise tax rates substantially and did. The relationship between land sales and land values explains much of the timing of state borrowing and the default experience of western and southern states. Pennsylvania and Maryland defaulted because they postponed the imposition of a state property tax until it was too late.

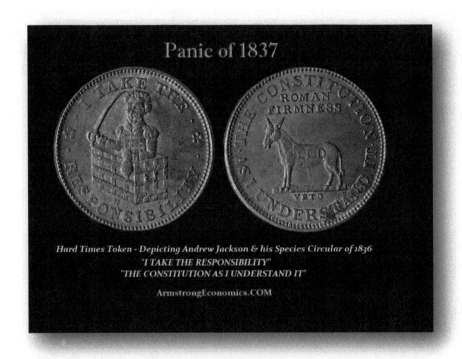

The United States had been the emerging market for Europe, and these defaults ruined its credit for decades to come. The Bank of England still has some state debts that were never made good. An overexpansion of banks caused the Panic of 1837. It caused farmers, planters, and merchants to lose their enterprises. The British Crisis of 1839 pushed interest rates higher in the United States, creating a depression called the "Hard Times," for which many blamed Jackson and his Specie Circular as this token suggests. This led to an economic contraction that further reduced bank deposits, causing bank failures as the depression then settled into the states from which it sprang. States issued bonds to try to bail out the banks, and many states ended in default.

During the period, the individual states in the USA borrowed more than $200 million by selling long-term bonds in domestic and international financial markets to finance transportation and banking projects. They went nuts with borrowing and spending money, and Andrew Jackson's bank war merely gave them credibility they did not deserve. The states' total borrowing approached a level nearly twice as high as the debt of the federal government at its peak during the period 1790–1840. The federal debt was largely the cost for the American Revolution and the War of 1812, which was paid off by 1835. These two wars were less than half what the states had borrowed during their spending binge and fiscal mismanagement.

In 1841, state debts outstanding totaled $198 million. Then the improvement era came to a screeching halt. In 1841 and 1842, eight states and the territory of Florida defaulted on their debts. Three other states narrowly avoided default. Five of the nine defaulting states repudiated all or part of their debts entirely — Arkansas, Florida, Louisiana, Michigan, and Mississippi. The credit of the U.S. federal government, which never defaulted after the debt restructuring of 1790, was tarnished for decades along with the states that did not default. Pictured here is a State of Louisiana bond issued in 1842. It is hand-signed by the state's Governor Andre Bienvenu Roman and Treasurer F. Gardner.

This historical document states it was issued to "revive the Charters of the several banks located in the City of New Orleans..." Louisiana experienced years of economic growth as the number of banks doubled and capital increased thanks to Jackson's bank war. The state banking crisis instigated by the Panic of 1837 was relieved only by new banking laws. In the aftermath, instead of asking why some states borrowed so much, politicians focused on the debt crisis itself and asked how states could have gotten into such an embarrassing mess.

1842 Bond State of Louisiana

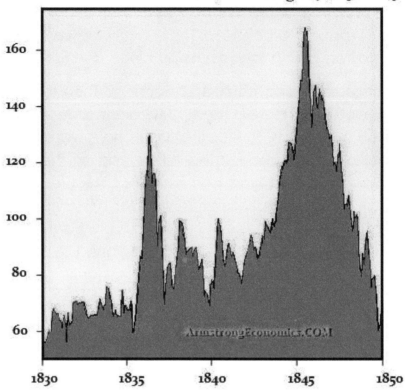

British Railroad Share Index
First Industrial Revolution (Steam Engine) (1830 - 1850)

The Railroad Bubble took place in Britain, involving the second phase of the Industrial Revolution. The use of the steam engine to create the railroad at first competed with the canal system. The British gave birth to this railroad boom and even exported the technology to Europe and America. As with most bubbles, the common thread involves some new discovery, be it an emerging market or some new popular tangible item like the Tulip Mania. It could include things like cabbage patch dolls, a major technological advancement like canals, railroads, automobiles, airplanes, or the internet. It seems that anything new invokes the imagination and drives speculative bubbles right down to cryptocurrencies.

As was the case with the canal shares, initial railway shares were appreciated significantly, producing high returns on the investment. The overall rally in the British share markets had seen almost 300% rally the lows of 1830, which attracted many speculators. By the peak of the market in 1847, there was a full-fledged bubble in railway speculation. Like the more than 1600 cryptocurrencies out there, they marketed themselves as free from government manipulation and control, and the attraction has been in capital gains rather than reality. The railroad boom was similar. About one-third of the total mileage of railways authorized between 1844 and 1847 was actually never constructed. Like the cryptocurrencies, many schemes were undoubtedly fraudulent back then as well, while others were simply well advertised.

Parliament finally sought to regulate the industry by passing the 1844 Railway Bill, which neither capped dividends nor did it require depreciation on fixed assets after construction. This distorted the value of companies and fueled the public expectation of inflated profits and high dividends. This was the case during the Canal Boom as Loughborough Canal Navigation Co. Railway proposals were submitted at the Board of Trade offices on the last day for the submission of plans for the 1846 Parliamentary session as get rich quick schemes flooded the marketplace.

LORD BROUGHAM'S RAILWAY NIGHTMARE.

The stories of the success of the Loughborough Canal Navigation Co. attracted gullible investors to the share market and expanded the investment sector dramatically. Investment in the railways rose from less than £4 million per year in 1841 to over £30 million by 1847, which was the equivalent of almost 50% of the British domestic capital investment into a single sector. It was this high concentration in a single new sector that nearly destroyed the national economy.

Indeed, the railroad boom and bust had also stirred the rising discontent with capitalism as a Socialist movement was beginning to win converts. The history of socialism had its origins in the 1789 French Revolution and the uprising against the monarchy and aristocrats. It was the French who would convince Karl Marx that socialism was not enough. The French believed that forcibly seizing private property was necessary, pointing to the "commune" movement since the French Revolution.

The railroad promoters realized that people wanted cheap share prices to enter and were really looking for capital gains rather than dividends. The promoters issued shares for a small proportion of their actual price. As the company expanded, they would issue more shares at higher prices. This practice helped inflate share prices and created a sense of urgency for people to rush in to buy shares when they were first offered — the 19th century version of the IPO market (Initial Price Offering). The original issue could be acquired for as little as £1 a share, creating a booming IPO market. However, the share market was vulnerable to schemes not based upon assets, but on the expectations of getting very rich very quickly.

1837 Bank of England (left) Royal Exchange (Center)

The Panic of 1837 saw rates rise in a crisis to protect the central bank's gold reserves. Indeed, during the next financial crisis, the Panic of 1847, we also see Quantitative Tightening rather than Quantitative Easing, which constituted the standard response to financial crises in the early days of central banking. However, central banks during the 19th century would ration credit and raise interest rates during financial crises to protect their gold reserves.

During the Panic of 1847, we find that the Bank of England's (BoE) Quantitative Tightening took the shape of credit rationing where they discriminated on the basis of a loan applicants' purpose and identity. The collateral characteristics behind the loans played a far more strategic role in the BoE's loan decisions. The BoE was thereby rationing credit in a strategic view to cut off capital speculation in addition to protecting their gold reserves. The characteristics of bills of exchange (written instruction ordering one party to pay another) submitted to the discount window at the BoE were the primary deciding factor.

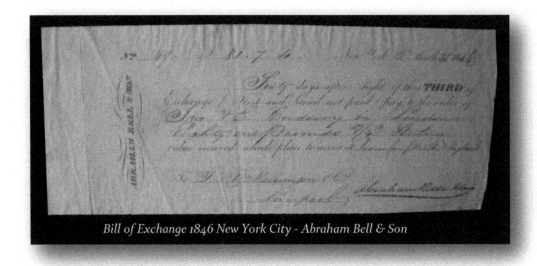

Bill of Exchange 1846 New York City - Abraham Bell & Son

A Bill of Exchange appears on the surface to be just a check. However, there is a difference between a check that one writes to another drawn on their bank account and a bill of exchange, which is "drawn" by one party (called a "drawer") on another (called a "drawee"), instructing them to pay either the drawer or a third party (called a "payee"). Therefore, unlike a bank check, a bill of exchange is a private note that is not "drawn on" a bank.

During the 19th century, a bill of exchange was most often literally a bill following the sale of goods and services from a manufacturer to a merchant on credit. The bill acted like an invoice tangibly documenting the trade credit that had been extended in the transaction between the two parties. The bill of exchange became a typically short-term instrument of financial debt.

The policy of the BoE during the 19th century was far more direct insofar as they were lending directly to borrowers in the economy rather than banks. During the Financial Crisis of 2008-2009, the U.S. Federal Reserve created the Troubled Asset Relief Program (TARP) to purchase toxic assets and equity from banks (financial institutions) to strengthen its financial sector rather than directly concerning the economy. TARP was signed into law on October 3, 2008, which was a component of the government's measures to address the subprime mortgage crisis that the investment banks created. There were no restrictions placed on the bankers to lend into the economy. The government just hoped that the bankers would pass on the "stimulation" to support the private sector directly, which they failed to do. This was indirect "stimulation" compared to the policies of the BoE during the 19th century.

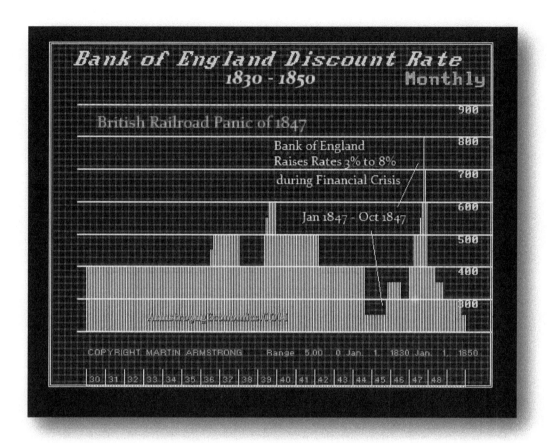

The Financial Crisis of 1847 was the burst of a Railroad Bubble. As stated before, the British invented the modern railway system and exported it to the world. The profits from the canals and its beneficial impact on expanding the British economy was a natural model to follow with the roadways. Textile factories expanded now that they could actually deliver products to the consumer and the world. British entrepreneurs created and financed a railway system based on the results from the earlier canal system.

In 1815, George Stephenson invented the modern steam locomotive, which ignited the technological race similar to the internet for the distribution of goods. Stephenson's leap forward was when he integrated all the components of a railway system in 1825 by opening the Stockton and Darlington line. For the first time, he was able to demonstrate his vision was commercially feasible. London financiers began to pour money into railway construction, creating an investment bubble like the Dot.com Bubble of 2000.

Thomas Brassey exported British railway engineering to the world. During the 1840s, he employed 75,000 men across Europe, taking the British railway model to the entire British Empire, Europe, and Latin America. Railways were the hot investment during the 1840s.

The boom years in railway investment/speculation were 1836 and 1845–1847. Parliament authorized 8,000 miles of railways with a projected future total of £200 million. This was a huge amount of money, which was about one year of Britain's GDP. This was the fuel behind the British Railroad Bubble, which burst like the Dot.com Bubble of 2000. People saw the vision but failed to comprehend that this was a long-term achievement and not something that would take place in less than 100 days.

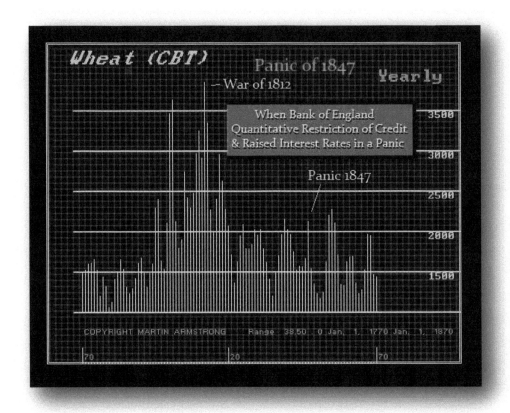

Simultaneously in 1847, the climate also turned against the fortunes of society. There was the failure of both the British and Irish harvests for two years, which necessitated importing grain. Britain turned to Russia to buy wheat which required payment in gold bullion. The Bank of England saw their gold reserves declining, and they raised interest rates from 4% to 5% to attract gold. This resulted in deflation as the money supply declined and people began to hoard their wealth with the collapse of the railroad shares. The BoE was under the direction of the Act of Parliament, which was intended to prevent speculative bubbles and raise rates to maintain the gold reserves.

As interest rates began to rise to unprecedented new highs in short order, railway companies called in the remaining balance on their shares, and the bubble had been pricked. The repeal of the Corn Laws resulted in the Corn Bubble, which had also collapsed as grain had to be imported. The speculators in corn saw a collapse in prices which contributed to their financial failures. As speculators in railway shares and commodities were scrambling for liquidity, the value of cash rose and propelled a wave of commercial failures that threatened the banking establishments. Four banks failed in the chaos, which became known as the "October Panic" as the British economy simply melted down.

Under the Bank Charter Act 1844 (7 & 8 Vict. c. 32; July 19, 1844), also known as the Peel Banking Act of 1844, the gold standard became institutionalized in Britain, regulating the ratio between the gold reserves held by the Bank of England and the notes that it could issue. At the time, there was a rising movement in Britain known as the British Currency School, which advocated that new banknotes were a major cause of price inflation. This view against fiat money was supported by the experience of hyperinflation in America during the period of the Continental Congress which also resulted in banning paper money in the United States until 1861.

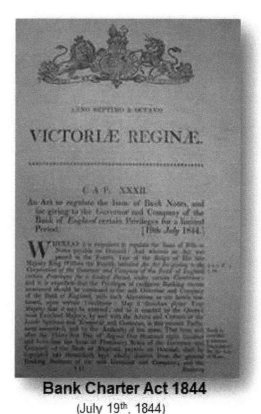

Bank Charter Act 1844
(July 19th, 1844)

The Currency School in Britain emerged from the early 1800s. It was not exclusively based upon the American experience but also drew upon the Panic of 1797. During the Financial Panic of 1797, the French invaded England, which resulted in a banking panic. Several banks failed. On Saturday, February 25, 1797, the Bank of England reported its gold reserves were reduced to £1.1 million, and it informed the government that it too would face a bank run when it opened on Monday. The Pitt government issued an order in council the next day suspending the convertibility of banknotes to cash until Parliament could address the issue.

In early May 1797, Parliament passed the Bank Restriction Act (37 Geo III, c.45), extending Pitt's restriction until six months after the finalization of a stable peace treaty with France. After this crisis, the initial movement was known as the Bullionist Group, which argued that banknotes' convertibility must be restored and fully backed by gold to avoid inflation and financial panics. If the banks could issue paper currency without backing, they warned it would result in inflation.

The Bullionist debate finally reached a head during 1810 when they were compelled to establish the "Bullion Committee" in parliament. The economist David Ricardo had alleged that banks were issuing currency in excess creating inflation. Ricardo published *The Price of Gold*, and *The High Price of Bullion; a Proof of the Depreciation of Bank Notes*, which made him well known as an economist at that point in time.

When the Bank Charter Act 1844 was passed, it required all new notes to be backed fully by gold or government debt. The act also provided the government the ability to retain the power to suspend the act should a financial crisis erupt. This did take place during the Financial Crisis of 1847, the Panic of 1857, and the Panic of 1866.

"If this course should lead to any infringement of the existing law, Her Majesty's Government will be prepared to propose to Parliament on its meeting a Bill of Indemnity"

Letter from the Prime Minister and Chancellor of the Exchequer to the Governor and Deputy Governor of the Bank of England, 25th October 1847

Source: Bank of England Archive

ArmstrongEconomics.COM

Indeed, on October 25, 1847, the act was suspended when the Bank of England was presented with a letter from the prime minister and chancellor of the exchequer indemnifying the bank for a breach of the act. The crisis in the money market ended almost immediately without any breach of the act.

1848 German Revolution February 1848 – July 1849 (Berlin: March 19, 1848)

The Financial Crisis of 1847 set off a contagion throughout Europe. All revolutions unfold only when the economy turns down. This Financial Crisis of 1847 set in motion the European Revolutions of 1848, which began essentially as a democratic movement and an uprising against the political elite. Indeed, the French monarchy was overthrown and replaced by a republic. A number of major German, Austrian, and Italian states saw the old-world leaders forced to grant liberal constitutions. The Italian and German states began to move toward forming unified nations. Austria gave Hungarians and Czechs liberal grants of autonomy and national status. The German Empire finally came into being eventually in 1871. The overall movement was toward a democratic system based upon constitutions.

In Demark, the new king, Frederick VII, met the demands of the people and installed a new Cabinet that included prominent leaders of the National Liberal Party. In Sweden, a series of riots known as the March Unrest (During 18–19th) took place in Stockholm demanding reform. The crowds were dispersed by the military, leading to 18 deaths. In Switzerland, there was a separatist movement of seven Catholic cantons that sought to create their own separate alliance in 1845, manifested into a brief civil conflict in November 1847 with about 100 casualties. The Protestant cantons defeated the Catholics, and the new constitution of 1848 surrendered most of their independence of the cantons, transforming Switzerland into a federal state.

Nevertheless, intermixed within the Revolutions of 1848 was also Karl Marx and socialism. It was 1848 when Karl Marx published *The Communist Manifesto* with Friedrich Engels and was exiled to London as a result. In London, where he lived the remainder of his life, he wrote the first volume of *Das Kapital*. This undoubtedly influenced the revolutions that opened the door to communism/socialism. This also inspired the collapse of the old feudal structures and created independent national states.

Karl Heinrich Marx
(1818-1883)

In 1843, Karl Marx's letters criticized the world as "perverted" and stated that Prussia was a despotic state dehumanizing mankind. Marx's view took shape as monarchs ruled by caprice, which supported the conclusion that people "can fulfill their highest needs, a democratic state." Marx relays the underlying sentiment that ultimately burst forth in 1848 as a revolution. Marx stated that revolt against the established order is the "system of industry and commerce, the exploitation of man." Marx developed what he identified as the "proletariat," stemming out of his break with religion, taking the position that man "has only one hurdle to overcome, namely, his religion, in order to dispense with religion altogether, and hence to become free." (*On the Jewish Question*, 1843). In his critique, Marx builds upon his idea: "Man makes religion, religion does not make man." Marx later denounced religion as the "opium of the people." (Oxford University Press, 1971, p116).

The 1848 Revolution wave began in France in February 1848 when the French monarchy was overthrown. Communism began back in 1792 in France as a "commune" where people lived in one shared community with no individual property rights. The French convinced Marx that communism would work better than just socialism, which he had advocated initially.

The Revolutions of 1848 swept Europe, expressing what they termed "scientific socialism." Indeed, *Harper's Monthly Magazine* wrote in its February 1888 edition about the rise of socialism, which began to take hold following the Financial Crisis of 1847.

> "WHATEVER personal opinion one may hold about socialist doctrines, there is one indisputable fact which no real observer will deny: it is the considerable increase of the partisans of socialism both in the New World and in the Old. Within the last ten years especially the number of adepts has increased in abnormal proportions, and nothing-- neither the iron regime of Germany nor the liberty of America-has had, it seems, the power to check this prodigious evolution."

We must respect that policies of central banks during the 19th century were effectively Quantitative Tightening rather than Quantitative Easing for the role envisioned at that time was to maintain the gold reserves of the nation (strong currency) at all costs. Clearly, creating a tight money policy (austerity as it is known in Europe) runs the risk of inspiring serious civil unrest that can explode as a contagion. This was the case in 1848 in the aftermath of the Financial Crisis of 1847.

Most of the analysis carried out by others on such events tend to be narrowly focused on domestic isolated circumstances within Britain. The suspension of the Bank Charter Act of 1844 was the proper policy to restore public confidence to prevent bank failures. Yet, the concern about the international capital flows resulting in the loss of gold reserves played a key role in raising interest rates, furthering austerity, and producing deflation. On the contrary, modern banking policies and changes pay little concern these days to the value of the currency on world exchanges. These policies are made by those who misunderstand world trade. This has fueled protectionist movements under the assumption that a rising currency lowers the cost of imports, which results in rising domestic unemployment. Comprehending the stark differences in central bank policies during the 19th century compared to the 20th and 21st centuries is of critical importance as we look to the future.

The Failure of Quantitative Easing

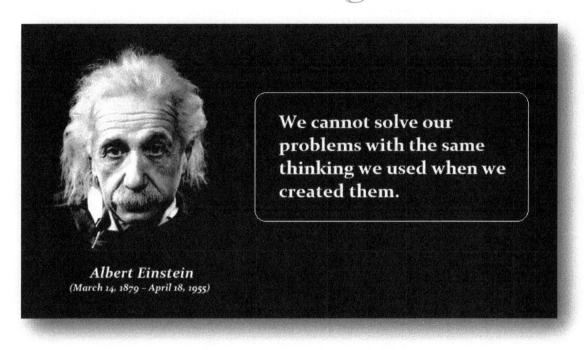

We cannot solve our problems with the same thinking we used when we created them.

Albert Einstein
(March 14, 1879 – April 18, 1955)

Albert Einstein (1879–1955) made it very clear that we cannot possibly solve the problems we face with the same thinking process that created them. This idea that we can manipulate the business cycle to achieve Utopia is absurd. It has always failed. Nevertheless, we keep trying the very same theory of interventions and manipulation when we do not even understand how the business cycle functions. We are acting like some medieval doctor who just cuts off body parts until the problem goes away. An earache? Simple. Remove it!

It is impossible for any central bank to "manage" its domestic economy because of the deflationary spiral external to its own economy. The Federal Reserve has become the world central bank as the IMF, and everyone else lobbies the Federal Reserve not to raise rates because it will adversely impact other nations. The Federal Reserve has lost control of the domestic economy. Now, domestic policies are being held hostage to international policy objectives.

The failure of Quantitative Easing is best illustrated by the European Central Bank (ECB) and the Bank of Japan (BoJ) after more than 10 years of QE with no economic improvement to show for it. The ECB is dangerously trapped, holding 40% of Eurozone government debt. The asset purchase program, a monetary experiment known as Quantitative Easing (QE), was launched in March 2015 to prevent sub-zero inflation from further hitting the economy. The ECB had initially spent €2.6 trillion euros over the first four years, buying up mostly government but also corporate debt, asset-backed securities, and covered bonds — at a pace of €1.3 million euros a minute. That equates to roughly €7,600 euros for every person in the currency bloc.

After 10 years of Quantitative Easing (QE), Europe has been unable to rise from the deflation imposed simultaneously by the austerity policy that has resulted in greater tax enforcement and rising taxation. While the purpose of QE was to stimulate the economy, austerity imposed by regulation and taxation was carried out to prevent inflation.

The theory of QE has been based upon this silly idea that is simply rooted in the Quantity Theory of Money that an increase in the money supply will increase inflation. The assumptions are rooted in the misinterpretation of the German hyperinflation of the 1920s. The theory ignored the creation of the Weimar Republic, which came to power as a 1918 Communist revolution in Germany following the 1917 Revolution in Russia. People converted their wealth to assets or foreign currency and investing collapsed. The Weimar Republic was unable to issue bonds internationally and sought to impose forced purchases of its bonds upon the wealthy segment of the German population.

The entire program of QE has failed because of this seriously flawed theory. The "stimulus" never reached the pockets of the average individual. They imposed negative interest rates to punish citizens in Europe for failing to spend their money. Moreover, the ECB merely purchased government debt of its member states, keeping member states on life support while paying ridiculous low rates of interest. The negative interest rates imposed on banks maintaining deposits at the ECB led

to massive capital flight where they used an American branch to deposit funds at the Federal Reserve into their excess funds' facility.

However, the banks are hoarding the cash because a stiff wind will blow them over. If the money injected does not reach the consumer, it is incapable of stimulating anything. Moreover, they fail to understand that the empirical level of interest rates means absolutely nothing. It is the net difference between the interest rates and the future expectation of profit that matters. If you think you will double your money, you will pay 25% rates of interest. If you do not see 1% in possible profits, you will not pay even a 0.5% interest rate.

This attempt to stimulate the economy by increasing the money supply assumes that it does not matter who has the money. Suppose we are looking only at the institutional level. In that case, this will never possibly contribute to demand among consumers or produce any level of inflation besides asset inflation by causing share markets to rise in proportion to the decline in currency value.

In 2002, when the word "deflation" began appearing in the business news, Bernanke, then a governor on the Board of the Federal Reserve, gave a speech about deflation entitled *Deflation: Making Sure "It" Doesn't Happen Here.* In that speech, Bernanke assessed the causes and effects of deflation in the modern economy. He stated:

"The sources of deflation are not a mystery. Deflation is in almost all cases a side effect of a collapse of aggregate demand – a drop in spending so severe that producers must cut prices on an ongoing basis in order to find buyers. Likewise, the economic effects of a deflationary episode, for the most part, are similar to those of any other sharp decline in aggregate spending—namely, recession, rising unemployment, and financial stress."

Draghi completely moved with the Keynesian model to increase the money supply with Quantitative Easing, but this simply failed. He did not give up and then pushed interest rates negative to punish savers and consumers for not spending money that never reached their pockets.

Negative rates promoted hoarding cash outside of banks since one did not earn interest; the risk of banks thereby increased, and people withdrew funds. To combat that, Draghi and others have considered eliminating cash using the slogan, "Cash is for Criminals." But negative rates have been simply a tax on money. The attempt to "manage" the economy from a macro level without considering the capital flows within the system has led to the brink of a new type of economic disaster.

This time, the central banks have done this themselves, and they are trapped. They cannot sell the debt they have bought, and therefore, we are looking at a crisis when that debt has to roll. The European Central Bank (ECB) holds more than 40% of the government debt for the whole of Europe. Once that matures, who will buy the new debt the next time around?

We are looking at a deflationary impact by default, which can wipe out the central banks. This time, QE programs allowed the money they injected to buy back bonds to go anywhere without restriction. Capital flight from the local economy resulted in deflation as the money never truly stimulated anything domestically, as it either migrated or was hoarded. To then compensate for the QE programs, the politicians have ratcheted up taxes and the enforcement of taxes. This has acted in direct opposition to the QE programs, and Europe is hopelessly lost between these two conflicting policies.

So, when the bonds mature, will the government be able to repay those bonds by selling new ones? Who will be the buyer? The Federal Reserve announced that it would no longer reinvest its gains on government bonds that had matured into new U.S. securities, resulting in a shortening of the balance sheet.

The Treasury will be forced to find ways to absorb the additional supply if the Fed wants its cash back, so the Treasury must find a lot of private buyers. The shrinking balance sheets represent the continued deflationary trend from a real economic expansion trend. The government will be competing for cash in an ever-growing tighter economy.

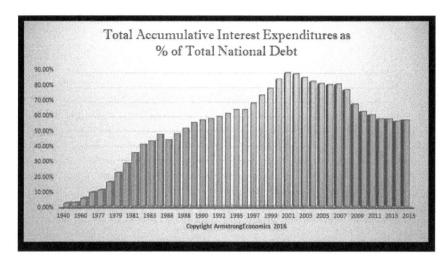

This is becoming the real straw that will break the back of the ECB. The coming Sovereign Debt Crisis is magnified by the simple fact that about 40% of all government debt in the Eurozone will have to be replaced. Can the ECB simply turn its back?

The question of when the central banks will fail is a question that is no longer absurd. The ECB cannot sell the debt it holds, and when it matures, what happens? If the ECB does not replace what it currently owns, then the amount of debt going to the marketplace will be nearly double any previous offering.

Suffice to say, the turmoil will hit Europe first. While so many people blame the Fed for all sorts of things, you must realize that the Fed is in the best position of all central banks. The demand for the dollar assets will only rise in the middle of a Sovereign Debt Crisis emerging in Europe.

Today, the real crisis is what will happen when interest rates rise. Governments have not reduced spending, but increased their spending and borrowing. Even if we look at the United States, the total accumulative interest expenditures peaked in 2001. They declined perfectly for 13 years into a low formed in 2014. The Fed began to raise rates as soon as the

Economic Confidence Model turned on October 1, 2015. With that first rate hike, the trend in accumulative interest expenditures rose in 2015.

We can easily see the next crisis coming. Here is what would happen using a hypothetical 5% rate of interest. If we saw rates rise just to 5% compared to the historical norm of 8%, the interest expenditures would balloon to new highs.

As rates rise, the national debts will explode. Governments will be unable to reduce spending and will simply raise taxes dramatically, causing greater unemployment. It becomes a fantasy to think government will reform to prevent a crisis. They are reactionary and only respond to the crisis, which by then will be too late.

Today, we have Quantitative Easing when central banks buy government paper to "stimulate," which is indirect and unlike the original design behind elastic money theory. Government debt is simply never-ending, for it is perpetually rolled. Private corporate paper expires, but government debt constantly rolls over. Obviously, this is a major distinction compared to the practices that preexisted the Federal Reserve with respect to the New York Clearing House Certificates. This current scheme of Quantitative Easing never puts money directly in the pockets of consumer or workers in the private sector and does not help corporations retain workers.

The New York Clearing House Certificates were redeemed, and those from 1873 no longer exist today because they were used among institutions. The conspiracy advocates never blame the right person or group. They do not understand the economics behind elastic money as it previously existed prior to 1913 and the Fed's creation. The whole Quantity Theory of Money has prejudiced their entire argument against the elastic money theory.

We need a central bank and elastic money, which is an excellent tool to ease the contraction in the velocity of money during a crisis as people hoard their cash and refuse to spend. In order to restore this vital tool, government debt must be excluded. Elastic money should be restricted to private sector business and never government.

When we turn to the ECB and compare its powers to that of the Federal Reserve, we arrive at a stark understanding of the difference in powers. Federal Reserve shares are technically owned by private banks because it was designed to be a funded bailout system operating like the New York Clearing House pre-1913. The ECB has shareholders and is set up like a corporation where it has shareholders and capital stock. Its capital is €11 billion held by the national central banks of the member states as shareholders. This again reflects the fact that the EU refused to consolidate member states' debts and left them in the same position regarding their state debt. The initial capital allocation key was determined back in 1998 on the basis of the states' population and GDP, but the capital key has been adjusted. Shares in the ECB are not transferable and cannot be used as collateral.

Meanwhile, the Governing Council is the true main decision-making body of the Eurozone system. It is composed of the six members of the Executive Board and the governors of the National Central Banks of the Eurozone member states. However, since January 2015, the ECB publishes on its website a summary of the

Governing Council deliberations, but it refuses to disclose the individual voting records of the governors in its Council. This is to protect the euro from being exposed with respect to discontent.

Therefore, the Fed was created with the power to create elastic money, which made sense because corporations (unlike government) must pay it back. This was all based upon the system of Clearing House Certificates that had pre-existed during the 19th century. The Clearing House would issue its own money during a crisis to ease the storage in cash, and then after the crisis, that money was retired — hence the term elastic.

So how does this contrast with the ECB? The ECB is not authorized to create an elastic money supply. Germany would never allow that. Consequently, the ECB cannot continue to buy into member states' sovereign debt as the market forces come down upon them. The ECB, unlike the Fed, will run out of money and then there will be a very public crisis whereby the ECB will have to be recapitalized.

Something will have to give in Europe. The ECB was granted a ceiling to buy in government bonds. It cannot just print money with no end in sight. It must get approval, which the Fed does not require from Congress. The two are completely different animals.

On top of this, each member state retained its own central bank. Each member bank issues euros in their domestic economies. You can collect euro coins from each central bank as the ECB does not issue them. There are no two-tier levels of central banks in the USA. The Federal Reserve has no such competition.

Then the reserves of the European banking system had to be politically correct and the reserves were composed of all member bonds. Why? Germany opposed a single European debt issue, and to this day, they object to the issue of any federal debt by Brussels.

Now, the Fed bought in $4 trillion against a $22 trillion national debt including excess reserves, and the debt was only federal amounting to $2.4 trillion. The ECB bought the worst debt and now owns 40% of the Eurozone member states' total debt and its debt holding relative to GDP is 20% compared to 10% for the Fed. Why is the ECB in danger of default?

If there is a disagreement in Brussels, then the ECB runs out of cash. As interest rates rise, the value of its balance sheet will collapse. The ECB cannot sell the debt back to the market, for there is no bid. To try to support the debt market, Brussels made it illegal to short government debt. Hence, there is no free market in European sovereign debt. If the ECB bought 40% of all debt, who will buy it when they stop?

This is a completely different perspective for the ECB v the Federal Reserve, which will just let its U.S. federal debt holdings mature and expire, reducing its balance sheet. They too cannot sell the debt, or interest rates would explode.

Welcome to the reality of the crisis. Not all central banks were created equally. Those who paint them all with the same brush know nothing. The ECB claims it cannot go bankrupt because it will just issue more money. The fact that they even stated that demonstrates there is a huge problem. That depends upon one thing — approval from the politicians to issue more money.

Governments are not a single entity. Central banks are far too often on the opposite side of the table with the political side of government. It is far more complicated than most people would ever guess. So, all the people who blatantly say a central bank cannot default because they create money on a wholesale basis do not understand the system and are making broad assumptions without knowing the story behind the curtain.

Each national central bank within the Eurozone commissions the printing of a banknote. The country issuing the note is indicated by a letter or country code preceding the serial number, not the ECB.

Country Codes

Uncirculated euro banknotes issued by the Banque centrale du Luxembourg bear the code of the central banks of the countries where the banknotes for Luxembourg are produced.

Country	Code
Luxembourg	1
Belgium	Z
Germany	X
Estonia	D
Ireland	T
Greece	Y
Spain	V
France	U
Italy	S
Cyprus	G
Latvia	C
Malta	F
Netherlands	P
Austria	N
Portugal	M
Slovenia	H
Slovakia	E
Finland	L

2018 Central Bank Reserve Ratios

Country	Ratio	Country	Ratio
ALBANIA	10.00%	LITHUANIA	3.00%
ANGOLA	19.00%	MACEDONIA	8.00%
ARMENIA	2.00%	MALAWI	15.50%
ARGENTINA	44.00%	MALAYSIA	3.00%
ARUBA	11.00%	MALDIVES	10.00%
AZERBAI	0.50%	MAURITIUS	9.00%
BANGLADESH	5.50%	MOLDOVA	42.50%
BARBADOS	5.00%	MONGOLIA	10.50%
BELARUS	7.50%	MOROCCO	5.00%
BULGARIA	10.00%	MOZAMBIQUE	14.00%
CAMEROON	5.88%	NEPAL	4.00%
CAPE VERDE	15.00%	NICARAGUA	10.00%
CEN.AFRICA REP	0.00%	NIGERIA	22.50%
CHAD	3.88%	PAKISTAN	3.00%
CHINA	14.50%	PERU	5.00%
DEM.	2.00%	PHILIPPINES	18.00%
REPUBLIC	5.88%	POLAND	3.50%
COSTA	15.00%	QATAR	4.50%
CROATIA	12.00%	ROMANIA	8.00%
CZECH REP	2.00%	RUSSIA	5.00%
CURACAO	18.00%	RWANDA	5.00%
DENMARK	2.00%	SERBIA	5.00%
EGYPT	14.00%	SOUTH	2.50%
EQUATORIAL	5.88%	SRI LANKA	6.00%
EUROZONE	1.00%	TAIWAN	10.75%
FIJI	10.00%	TAJIKISTAN	3.00%
GABON	5.88%	TANZANIA	8.00%
GAMBIA	15.00%	TRINIDAD/TOBAGO	17.00%
GEORGIA	5.00%	TUNISIA	1.00%
GHANA	10.00%	TURKEY	8.00%
HUNGARY	1.00%	USA	10.00%
ICELAND	2.00%	URUGUAY	25.00%
INDIA	4.00%	UZBEKISTAN	15.00%
INDONESIA	6.50%	VENEZUELA	19.00%
IRAQ	15.00%	VIETNAM	3.00%
ISRAEL	6.00%	WEST	3.00%
JAMAICA	12.00%	ZAMBIA	5.00%
JORDAN	8.00%		
KAZAKHSTAN	2.50%		
KENYA	5.25%		
KYRGYZ REP	4.00%		

ArmstrongEconomics.COM

1951 Quantitative Easing Directive

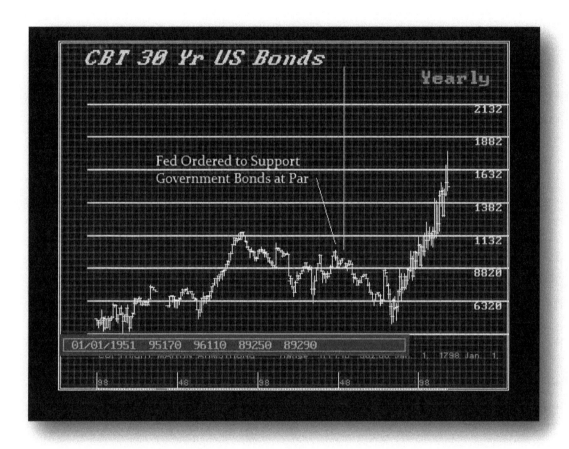

Once FDR took control of the Federal Reserve away from the banks, it did not take long for them to abuse that power. During April 1942, the Department of the Treasury requested the Federal Reserve formally commit to maintaining a low interest rate peg of 3/8% on short-term Treasury bills. The debt was to be managed by the Treasury, but the maintenance of the regulation of the money supply and credit was the domain of the Federal Reserve. Therefore, the Treasury's request for the Fed to cap interest rates was in effect an early request to create a slightly different version of Quantitative Easing (QE). With the prospect of interest rates exploding, the Fed is looking at a return to the peg of 1942–1951. Instead of QE just buying in debt, the Fed will consider creating a peg benchmark on rates for 2 to 10-year instruments. This will be different from QE. They hope by creating a peg, the interest rates will not rise exponentially.

Back in 1942, the Fed complied only after being strong-armed and implicitly capped the rate on long-term Treasury bonds at 2.5%. This became known as the "peg" with the express goal to stabilize the securities market and allow the federal government to engage in cheaper debt financing for World War II, which the United States had entered in December 1941.

At the time, in order for the Federal Reserve to maintain the peg, it was ordered to give up control of the size of its portfolio as well as the money stock. That is also what has happened today with Quantitative Easing among all central banks. Frankly, the Fed back then maintained the low interest rate by buying large amounts of government securities, which also increased the money supply domestically at the time. Because the Fed was committed to a specific rate by the peg, it was compelled to keep buying securities even if the members of the Federal Open Market Committee (FOMC) disagreed.

Sylvia Field Porter (1913–1991) was perhaps the most famous American journalist and author during the 1940s, and she was an economist as well. She was said to have a readership of greater than 40 million people. She was famous enough even to make the front cover of *Time Magazine*.

On April 8, 1942, her syndicated column read, "Sylvia Porter Outlines War Financing to City Bankers." She warned them that Secretary of the Treasury Henry Morgenthau Jr. was an "easy money man" who intended to finance World War II "as cheaply as possible — on a 'two-and-a-half percent basis.'" She outlined that Morgenthau was acting more as a dictator. "Banks now know exactly what the problem is, what to buy and how much." She reported that the Federal Reserve disagreed with Morgenthau, but she warned that "Morgenthau will emerge triumphant in his fight, despite 'dangerously inflationary' tendencies."

Poughkeepsie, New York, Wednesday Morning, April 8, 1942

Sylvia Porter Outlines War Financing to City Bankers

One of the nation's leading financial observers bluntly warned the city's bankers last night that banks are the bulwark in the government's plan of financing the war, that they "will be asked to pay for it," and if necessary, "will be compelled to pay for it."

Speaking before the annual dinner forum of the Poughkeepsie chapter of the American Institute of Banking at the Nelson house, Sylvia Porter, financial columnist of the New York Post, told the group that their problem is now "simple."

"Since the war broke out," she said, "there has been no talk about government bonds and an exact science. Banks now know exactly what the problem is, what to buy and how much."

Describing the government bond market as the greatest in the existence of the world, and the most unwieldly financial structure in history, she outlined some of the conflicts affecting the financing of the war effort and the attempts to prevent inflation.

Difference in Philosophy

Secretary of the Treasury Morgenthau, an "easy money man," aims to finance the war as cheaply as possible—on a "two-and-a-half percent basis," she stated, while

Secretary Eccles, of the Federal Reserve board, who "knows finance," wants to prevent runaway inflation. Miss Porter asserted that there existed "a fundamental difference in philosophy" between the two.

Odds are, she stated, that Mr. Morgenthau will emerge triumphant in his fight, despite "dangerously inflationary" tendencies, and will maintain the government bond market at two-and-a-half percent rates.

The columnist predicted that Morgenthau's attempts to remove tax exemptions on outstanding securities would fail this year, though she thought it possible that the exemptions would be removed on future issues.

"Everyone is involved in the government's plan for financing the

See SYLVIA PORTER page 9

CAN YOU USE AN EXTRA DOLLAR? Sell to these buyers listed under Classification 37 in the Want-Ads.

—Sylvia Porter
CONTINUED FROM PAGE ONE

war," she emphasized. "Every banking institution, corporation and individual will be given specified types of securities to buy as a means of controlling the market as the national debt increases."

She listed measures at the disposal of the government for controlling the market as follows:

Buying of bonds in the open market by the Treasury.

The illimitable buying of government securities by banks.

Use of the Stabilization fund for investment and re-investment.

Use of the cumulative sinking fund by the Treasury.

Application of the Thomas amendment by which the Treasury could issue up to 3½ billion to buy up open bonds.

Use of the old age reserve and unemployment trust funds.

Direct sales of bonds by the Treasury to Federal Reserve banks.

Manipulation of reserve requirements of the Federal Reserve board.

Manipulation of gold policy by releasing gold from the Federal Reserve.

Changing margin requirements by Federal Reserve, affecting speculative abilities.

Changes in discount rates.

Changes in psychology by fiscal authorities.

Pointing out that in no other country has there been a market so clearly under one authority, she stressed that "we must finance this war."

If we do not finance it on orthodox methods, then the Treasury will finance it on downright inflationary methods," she concluded.

William Dederer, of the Poughkeepsie Trust company, president of the Poughkeepsie chapter of the AIB, was toastmaster at the dinner. Miss Porter was introduced by Norman H. Polhemus, chairman of the chapter's forum committee, who was in charge of arrangements for the annual event.

Indeed, Sylvia was absolutely correct. What she did not realize was that this dictatorial position of the Treasury would last for about nine years. It would not come to an end until a major crisis in 1951 with the appearance of the Korean War.

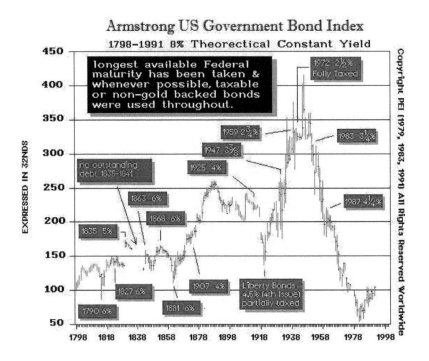

After the war, politicians were afraid a new depression would emerge as they always fight the last war. They ordered the Fed to maintain the peg even after 1945 and the death of Morgenthau. As with all programs as we see with QE carried out by the European Central Bank, once such a scheme is implemented, it becomes very difficult to end.

The United States entered the Korean War in June 1950. The problem was inflation, not deflation. The FOMC of the Fed argued strongly that the continuation of the peg would lead to excessive inflation. A real confrontation with the politicians was brewing all year. The Treasury met them with opposition, as the Treasury naturally wanted to keep borrowing at cheap rates for its own expenditures, as we will see today.

Harry S. Truman (1884 – 1972)
33rd President of the United States (1945 – 1953)

Everything exploded by February 1951. Inflation had soared, reaching 21%. As the Korean War intensified, the Fed faced the possibility of having to monetize a substantial issuance of new government debt to fund that war. This only intensified inflation. Nevertheless, Harry S. Truman became president in 1945, and it was his administration that continued to urge the Fed to maintain the peg.

The financial crisis erupted into a major conflict when Truman invited the entire FOMC to a meeting at the White House. Truman then issued a statement saying that the FOMC had "pledged its support to President Truman to maintain the stability of Government securities as long as the emergency lasts." In reality, the FOMC had made no such pledge. Conflicting stories began to appear about the dispute in the press. The Fed then made an unprecedented move — they released the minutes of the FOMC's meeting with the president.

The conflict erupted in full view. The Fed revolted against the politicians. Shortly thereafter, the Fed informed the Treasury that as of February 19, 1951, it would no longer "maintain the existing situation." The Treasury was caught in a crisis for it needed to refund existing debt and issue new debt, a situation all governments are still in today. They never pay off debt; the debt simply rolls forever.

The government had no choice but to negotiate a compromise under which the Fed would continue to

MONDAY, FEBRUARY 12, 1951.

THE MARION STAR, MARION, OHIO

Federal Reserve Crisis

By Raymond Moley

WE ARE learning fast that a President whose limited respect for great Constitutional principles is matched only by his stubborn drive for power can become a greater danger to those principles than strong but informed Presidents like Woodrow Wilson. Closely following Truman's headlong plunge in Korea and his determination to reserve the right to place a standing army in Europe is his effort to dictate the policies of the Federal Reserve Board. This is no mere squabble over half a point in interest rates, but a great Constitutional issue.

MOLEY

If, as is reputed, the President is fond of history, he might turn with profit to the story of the origins of the Federal Reserve System. He can find that record in a book by Carter Glass, the legislative sponsor of the Federal Reserve Act, entitled "An Adventure In Constructive Finance." The record also appears in the various papers of Woodrow Wilson and in the Wilson biography by Ray Stannard Baker.

The historical setting of the Act was the heyday of progressivism before the First World War. Wilson's economic philosophy held that private monopoly was rampant and needed to be checked. He held that monopoly was fostered by credit control centralized in the big New York banks. As a Jeffersonian, the new President sought to decentralize that control in districts, under Reserve Banks privately owned but vested

with a quasi-public character. He insisted that the Federal Reserve board be composed of members appointed by the President and that it be governmental in nature. In this, he was following the advice of William Jennings Bryan and Louis D. Brandeis.

• • •

THERE WAS tremendous opposition by the bankers who favored a system in which the banks would be represented on the board in Washington. Carter Glass, fearing political control, at first supported the bankers.

The result was a compromise in which it was made perfectly clear that, while the members of the board should be appointed by the President, their terms would be long and overlapping. It was clearly understood at the time that the board should be independent of the President. For a while, the Secretary of the Treasury was an ex-officio member; but to emphasize the independence of the board, he was later excluded by Congress.

Moreover, the board was made free of dependence on Congress, for its expenses are paid by the Federal Reserve Banks.

• • •

ALL THIS WAS to protect the board utterly and irrevocably from political control.

But, now, despite this history and despite the legal position of the board, the President and the Secretary of the Treasury presume to issue order to the board on the vital matter of interest rates.

Back in the boom days before the depression, the Federal Reserve Bank in Chicago wanted to raise the discount rate in an effort to check inflation. But the board in Washington prevented it. It was noted at the time that this was owing to the Administration's desire to keep money so cheap that Europe could borrow here and so that Britain could maintain sterling parity. In that instance the board permitted the Administration to dominate it, with the disastrous result that inflation in stocks continued until the crash.

Something of the same sort may happen again if the President prevails. The board has only two options — resignation or inflexible opposition.

Congress Quiz

Q—In conducting its business, does the government operate on a yearly basis?

A—Yes, on a 12-month basis, but the period does not coincide with the calendar year. The federal business year is known as the fiscal year, and begins July 1 and ends June 30 of the following year. June 30, 1951, will see the close of fiscal 1951. Next day fiscal 1952 will begin.

support the price of five-year notes for a short time, but after that, the bond market would be on its own. It was on March 4, 1951, when the Treasury and the Fed issued a statement saying they had "reached full accord with respect to debt management and monetary policies to be pursued in furthering their common purpose and to assure the successful financing of the government's requirements and, at the same time, to minimize monetization of the public debt."

MONDAY, FEBRUARY 12, 1951.

THE MARION STAR, MARION, OHIO

Truman and the Treasury Argument

By Walter Lippmann

MUCH is at stake in the argument between the Treasury and the Federal Reserve System, and the complicated problem can only be confused and bedeviled if President Truman lets it become distorted into a political quarrel between his friends and his opponents. The controversy is not like an election or like a football game which can be settled and disposed of when one side has won and the other has lost. For the management of our huge federal debt by the Treasury and the regulation of the supply of money and credit by the Federal Reserve will have to be carried on continuously and cooperatively.

The two agencies of government are going to have to agree on a common policy. Neither can afford to "win" in the sense that it knocks out the other and then drags it along triumphantly behind it.

LIPPMANN

The crux of the present controversy is whether they are to work together with some flexibility, or whether the Treasury is to dominate the Federal Reserve System in order to maintain a rigid pattern of interest rates. My own inquiries have convinced me that if the issue of flexibility were left to those who best understand it in the two agencies, it would not be a fighting issue at all, and that the problem could be settled by practical operations in the money market, and without resounding declarations.

* * *

THE RIGID dogmatism which now appears to be the Treasury's policy certainly does an injustice to its good sense and competence. And the impression which has got abroad is, of course, absurd that the Federal Reserve System is not concerned about the federal debt and is advocating a policy of "let her rip."

"We are suffering," says a very highly qualified observer who wrote me the other day, "the consequences of having had three exceptionally stubborn secretaries of the Treasury in succession during the past ten years." Now that it is essential to put an end to the inflation of Federal Reserve credit, we have to deal not only with the problem itself, which is a delicate one, but with politicians who have become so addicted to inflation that they tremble at the idea of being deprived of it.

Before long Mr. Truman will find that the question is not so simple as he thought it was when he summoned the Federal Reserve Board and the presidents of five Federal Reserve banks to the White House. He will find that even if he were able to force the Federal Reserve to manufacture as much inflationary money as the Treasury's rigid interest rate required the controversy would break out again elsewhere.

* * *

IT WOULD BREAK out because to control prices and wages and to obtain production uninterrupted by strikes will prove to be impossible if the pressure of inflationary credit is not reduced. It is a reasonable certainty that if the Federal Reserve Board were to knuckle under today, within a short time Mr. Wilson and Mr. Johnston would have to revive the argument.

When the order for a general price freeze was issued on Jan. 26 Mr. DiSalle issued a statement which had been approved by Eric Johnston, the administrator of the economic stabilization agency. It is the statement of men who find themselves forced to do something which they don't at all like to do.

The statement says that though the general price control has become necessary as an emergency measure, Mr. Johnston and the men responsible for him have no illusions. "The effect of price control is not to eliminate inflation but to 'suppress' it * * * major reliance must be placed upon vigorous taxation and a strong credit policy. To the extent that we succeed in reducing the inflationary pressure by these means we make the task of price control that much easier."

* * *

AS A MATTER of fact, this is almost certainly an understatement. Price control will not work at all if the inflationary pressure continues to accumulate. It will produce an orgy of corruption and black markets, of injustice and discontent. In order to make price control work well—that is to say with reasonable honesty and fairness—it would be necessary not only to stop adding to the inflation but to find ways of accomplishing a measure of disinflation.

We shall have to come to that. At least for the emergency period of the mobilization we shall have to resort to emergency methods to disinflate, measures beyond any contemplated by the Federal Reserve Board or really within the proper use of its power. In one way or another the disinflation will have to be brought about by a considerable reduction in federal, state and local public expenditure for civilian uses, by greater private and corporate savings, and almost certainly also by scrutinizing more critically than it is now the fashion to do the content of some of the military problems. We should not

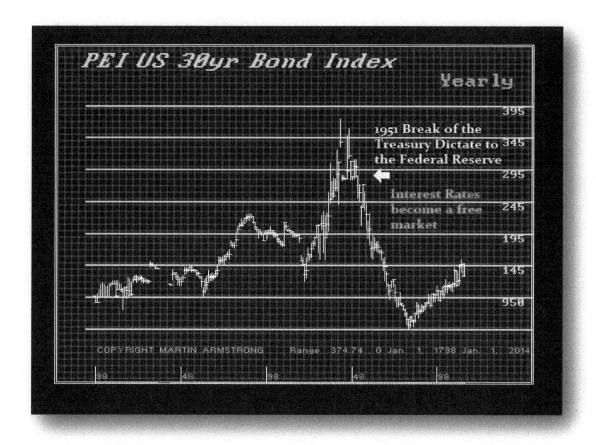

Indeed, President Harry Truman supported the low interest rate peg. From his point of view, he claimed it was his duty to protect patriotic citizens by not lowering the value of the bonds they had purchased during the war. Nevertheless, reality had a seat at the table as well. This break of the Treasury–Federal Reserve Accord created a free market in government securities on March 4, 1951. The bond market began to crash as interest rates were at last free to move after 1951. This is the most likely outcome of the voluntary Quantitative Easing, which is a critical issue in Europe and Japan and less at the Fed.

William McChesney Martin Jr.
(1906 – 1998)

William McChesney Martin, Jr. (1906–1998) became Chairman of the Board of Governors of the Federal Reserve System at the time of the March 1951 Treasury–Fed Accord. Martin, in effect, created the modern Federal Reserve System and free markets in government bonds.

429

End of Bailouts

Behind the curtain, there is a growing concern about a serious banking crisis beginning once again in Europe. Many governments are talking about the crisis behind the curtain, and steps are being taken to end the too-big-to-fail policies that dominated the 2007–2009 Crash.   Even in the United States, there have been those looking at new radical bank rescue policies where the government is proposing to revise a central pillar of the idea of bailing out banks by creating new financial regulation with a new Chapter 14 bankruptcy procedure.

They are looking at eliminating the risk of taxpayers' costs to bail out banks. They are investigating the means for an orderly resolution so that the taxpayers do not have to bail out the banks. This development is causing some concern among the high-flying Wall Street banks, for if that is the case, then another crisis as 2007–2009 will result in major banks closing. The proposal looks to shift the burden to the shareholders and creditors of that bank. This means depositors are thus creditors. Given the fact that the major banks are the primary dealers through which the government sells its debt, the necessity for bailing out major banks who are primary dealers in the USA seems unlikely to change. Plus, firms like Goldman Sachs fund the politicians to buy favored treatment.

In Australia, we see similar legislation being proposed. This is the Financial Sector Legislation Amendment (Crisis Resolution Powers and Other Measures) bill of 2017 also authorizes bail-ins, bringing an end to the bailout.

Europe, however, is entirely different. The image that the European Union is one happy family comes to an end when the discussion turns to money and consolidating debt. The ramification of that issue spills over into everything else. For example, the bail-in policy emerged because of the perception of money coming from Germany to bail out Italian or Greek banks. This also creates a budget crisis. Since each member state prints euros, Brussels' demands to apply central controls over the member states stems from the very same structural flaw of the refusal to consolidate debts. In reality, Germany has imposed its economic philosophy by creating a single currency but sought to isolate any risks to each member state.

It became very clear that there was no mutual respect among European member states. Southern Europe was regarded as the drunk brother-in-law who spent all their money on wine, women, and parties. They would always have their hands out asking for help. This is what led to the bail-in policy rather than the bailout policy with respect to banking.

If Italian banks were in trouble and the policy was for the EU to provide a bailout, that would mean that capital would flow across borders and amount to debt relief, implying debt consolidation. Thus, socialism's very purpose was to protect the people against banking failures as in the Great Depression. That has been abandoned because of the policy against debt consolidation. This returns to the euro's structural design failure that tried to create a single currency, but not a single economy.

Therefore, Europe has a different incentive behind its bail-in policy, which is why there was no consolidation of debts and no central European debt. Instead, the policy has been to interfere and demand that member states comply with central rules on their budgets. This is the very friction that is causing discontent.

In the process, what has been overlooked was the central promise that socialism was there to protect the people against the evils of the business cycle. However, because of the flawed structural design of the euro, the idea of bailouts has given to bail-ins. Thus, this is abandoning the very ideas of socialism established in the aftermath of the Great Depression.

Franklin D. Roosevelt established the United States Federal Deposit Insurance Corporation (FDIC) in 1933, assuring people it was safer to keep their money in a reopened bank than under the mattress. Some 9,000 banks failed during the Great Depression in the USA. Then on August 23, 1935, Congress approved legislation that

FDR's Fireside Chats

had a major impact on the Federal Reserve Banks — the Banking Act of 1935. This act structurally altered the entire concept behind the Federal Reserve, whereas its purpose originally was to provide stability with respect to internal capital flows in addition to a regulatory Clearing House for the banks. Each branch maintained its separate interest rate to attract capital to a region or to deflect it to prevent another Panic of 1907 where cash flowed from the east to the west because of the San Francisco Earthquake of 1906. This is why the Open Market Committee was established. National monetary and credit policies were determined in Washington, which would gradually become the new political economy and laissez-faire was now officially dead.

Spain's Banco Santander paid €1 to take over troubled rival Banco Popular in a deal that illustrates Europe's new system to rescue failing banks without burdening taxpayers across borders or stressing markets. This is being cheered around the world because the shareholders lost absolutely everything. The bank, which was valued in the collapse at €1.6 billion, was bought for €1. *Forbes* wrote:

> "This is an excellent example of how the resolution of troubled banks should be done. The shareholders who employed the management which caused the problem to lose all their money. The depositors, who were and are not responsible for the bank's troubles, are protected. And we don't end up with some great smoldering hole in the financial landscape where Popular used to be, we get new capital raised instead. Further, no taxpayer has been harmed in this operation."

This was the first time the ECB had pulled the plug on a bank since it was given new powers to prevent banks' rescue from overwhelming government finances. European leaders had all agreed to move banking supervision to the EU level. Hence, the ECB took over supervisory responsibility in November 2014. The collapse was caused by €7.9 billion in non-performing assets, including €7.2 billion in real estate. Banco Popular shares fell about 38% last week and then another 20% this week, to 0.32 euros per share before regulators halted trading in its shares. The bank had 305,152 shareholders as of the end of March of that year.

So now comes the €64 trillion question. If government will not bail out banks, then eradicating all value to shareholders attaches a completely new kind of risk to shareholders. If they were investors in a manufacturing company that went bust, the assets would go into bankruptcy, and there would be a realistic sale of assets. What has just taken place is that if the bank's net asset value, its own building, property, etc., were, say, even 20% of the share value, then the shareholder faces a 100% loss in bank stocks compared to any other share investment. That leaves one poignant question — why buy bank stocks at all?

The Mother of All Crises

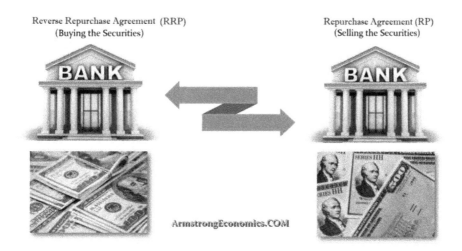

Reverse Repurchase Agreement (RRP)
(Buying the Securities)

Repurchase Agreement (RP)
(Selling the Securities)

ArmstrongEconomics.COM

The structural failure to create a single currency in Europe by refusing to consolidate member states' debts has resulted in this bail-in rejecting bailouts policy because it would mean that money from one state would flow to another to bail out a bank. Now we have Deutsche Bank, the biggest bank in Europe, on the ropes. This bail-in policy impends the entire global economy, for they are interlinked on a global scale and threaten a contagion beyond all previous known events.

Many people are befuddled that the Federal Reserve had to jump in and provide liquidity for the repo market (Repurchase Agreement Market) during September 2019, a market for short-term borrowing of dealers in government securities. In the case of a repo, a dealer sells government securities to investors, usually on an overnight basis, and buys them back the following day at a slightly higher price. That small difference in price is the implicit overnight interest rate. Repos are typically used to raise short-term capital. They are also a common tool of central bank open market operations.

What has transpired is that banks no longer trust banks. If Europe will not bail out banks, then nobody knows which bank has exposure to a bank in crisis in Europe. The 2007-2009 Crisis began in repo with the mortgage-backed securities that the credit agencies were bribed to rate AAA. Hence, banks remember that crisis, but because of international banking, a failure of Deutsche Bank in Europe cannot be bailed out by the U.S. Congress or Federal Reserve. This has resulted in a collapse in confidence in the European banking sector.

Understanding the Repo Crisis requires us to look at a world economy where there is no single central bank in a position to bail out a crisis that is emanating from outside its own jurisdiction. We must first open our minds and understand that global economic contagions have been the primary influence that has driven the world economy for centuries. We will never comprehend even what the Repo Crisis is all about unless we look beyond the simplistic domestic analysis that dominates all the chatter.

The origin of the 2007–2009 Crisis was due to mortgage-backed securities in the United States. The Federal Reserve was able to take the toxic financial debt out of the U.S. banks and save the day. In Europe, because of the refusal to actually consolidate the debts, the central bank lowered rates, and when that failed in 2014, they went negative. After more than 10 years of Quantitative Easing, the banks were unable to recover from their losses. Unlike the U.S. banks, the European banks were left with their toxic debt, and regulators simply prayed they would eventually recover. That has never happened, and the act left the pension funds insolvent because they required interest income to pay claims.

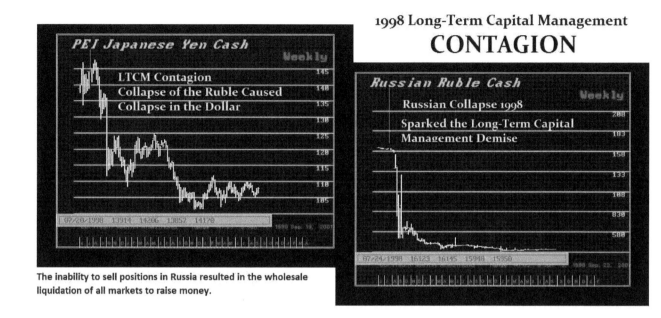

The inability to sell positions in Russia resulted in the wholesale liquidation of all markets to raise money.

Europe has set the stage for the mother of all crises unfolding as a combination of a global liquidity crisis similar to the 1998 Long-Term Capital Management crisis sparked by the collapse in Russian debt. When the Russian debt crisis hit, it unleashed massive selling of worldwide assets to raise money to cover losses from Russia. Even the shorts against the Japanese yen were unwound, and the yen moved from 147 to 103 against the dollar in a matter of weeks.

This immediate crisis unfolding in the repo market also involves a crisis in confidence, which has led many banks to relive the 2007–2009 Crisis fears. The mortgage-backed securities were posted in repo and collapsed overnight, which is why Lehman Brothers failed abruptly.

What we have on the horizon is a deadly combination of the 1998 Liquidity Crisis that will spread like a global contagion and a collapse in confidence manifesting in the repo market. This has been thrust upon the world economy by the failure of Europe to create a true single currency with a single economy and decades of manipulations by governments, which have created the dangerous expectation that governments and central banks are actually in control and capable of preventing a crisis. Even Lawrence Summers wrote in the Washington Post on December 6, 2015, confirming that "since World War II, no postwar recession has been predicted a year in advance by the Fed, the White House or the consensus forecast." We are on our own next time.

Modern Monetary Theory

The latest rage in economics goes by the name Modern Monetary Theory (MMT) because they have witnessed central banks increasing the money supply post–2007 under Quantitative Easing (QE). Yet, they have been unable to create inflation. Economists then use this as evidence that the government can create money at will. It does not lead to hyperinflation as Germany alleviates its fears by imposing austerity upon the Eurozone.

Clearly, MMT is emerging at this moment because both QE and the Quantity Theory of Money (QTM) have failed. There is no other alternative on the table, and central banks are trapped by QE, for they can no longer sell what they have already bought in government debt. The European and Japanese central banks cannot stop buying when they have driven interest rates to near zero. No institution in the private sector can afford to own government debt that fails to pay a reasonable return on investment.

We are cascading toward a date with destiny where MMT becomes the only solution for governments which may bring down the entire house of cards if those in the QTM camp win the day. The approach of MMT is typically characterized as an evolution of chartalism, defined in macroeconomics as a theory that claims government's attempts to direct economic activity by controlling the economy creates utopian economics.

The general assumption remains that government can manipulate the economy at will despite the fact that even Larry Summer has acknowledged, "[N]o postwar recession has been predicted a year in advance by the Fed, the White House or the consensus forecast."

Gordian III (238-244AD)

Genuine Aureus (4.58 grams)   Indian Imitation (3.05 grams)

Despite this track record, this is the rising alternative solution to the problems within the economy expressed through the business cycle that the general community appears unable to forecast. Under MMT, fiat currency's creation has value in exchange because of sovereign power to levy taxes on economic activity. In other words, fiat currency has value simply because it is deemed legal tender and will be accepted by the government in payment of fines and taxes. We have seen the dominant coinage of the financial capital of the world imitated since the days of ancient Athens, Macedonia, and Rome. It is not the ability of a nation to levy taxes and punish people under their rule of law. The value of these currencies of the financial capital of the world has been economic and military power on the world stage.

Nevertheless, the MMT supporters' argument centers on the fact that banks can create money for such "horizontal" transactions in lending in sovereign financial systems. Yet, this does not increase net financial assets since liabilities offset them. In their view, a bank issues a mortgage for $1 million, creating money out of thin air, but that is offset by the liability of the mortgage. This is rather simplistic and fails to consider the international capital flows in such transactions. If I originally owned a home with a $500,000 mortgage and I sold the house to you for $1 million, the bank is monetizing the difference. Still, it may inspire asset inflation within the domestic economy, but it does not drastically alter the economy.

Now, instead, I sell the home to a foreign investor. He brings his currency into the domestic economy and buys the house. Suddenly, the actual money supply domestically does increase. Look at all the laws against foreign investors in real estate that have emerged in Vancouver, Australia, and New Zealand.

Therefore, the proponents of MMT argue that the balance sheet of the government does not include any domestic monetary instrument on its asset side. This, they maintain, is a horizontal creation of money merely by banks creating loans. It does not take into consideration the impact of international capital flows. A foreign investor who borrows domestically without bringing cash would be no different from a domestic investor. However, bringing in any portion of cash to cover the purchase of real estate or other assets domestically does increase the local supply of money.

In MMT, the proposition is that instead of the "horizontal" creation of money through lending, the government actually creates "vertical" money which enters the economy through government spending. Therefore, since this money is legal tender, the government creates the demand for currency. In other words, you need the paper dollars to pay the government its pound of flesh.

Suppose we strip MMT from the political arguments to fund social programs like those of Bernie Sanders of the New Green Deal. In that case, it boils down to simply justifying funding government expenditures by issuing fiat money, which, of course, all economists have long been aware is possible. MMT then attempts to downplay the potential inflationary impact of such financing traditionally ruled out by economics with manipulations of government and central bank balance sheets.

However, MMT is just a shell game. It merely shifts the standard analysis into different boxes. Some recognize that inflation can result from substantial increases in government expenditures unless one of three conditions holds:

1. There is significant unemployment in the economy.
2. Government uses its taxing power to control inflation.
3. The banking system somehow counteracts the government's monetary expansion.

There is no historical evidence that states these three factors are constraints on inflation. Raising taxes simply sends capital offshore and acts as a deterrent in attracting international investment. Unemployment will rise with taxation as it increases the cost of labor despite the fact that workers may not see any extra money in their take-home pay. The banks did not pass on lower interest rates to the consumer. Instead, they asked the Federal Reserve to create an excess reserve facility where they could park money.

MMT also shows that currency is a public monopoly for government and unemployment. This is evident as a currency monopolist is restricting the supply of the financial assets needed to pay taxes and satisfy savings desires. This is also a narrow view of modern events post-income tax. If we look at the Roman Empire, they neither had a national debt nor a central bank, and taxes were minimal and well under 10%.

The basic assumptions of MMT are still constructed upon the Marx-Keynesian supposition that governments can manipulate the business cycle. Using taxation to limit inflation is the most dangerous underlying assumption of MMT. The U.S. tax code has been one of the greatest incentives to move offshore for individuals as well as corporations. There is no way to set forth a business plan for 20 years because you never know what the tax liability will be going forward. Nobody in their right mind would rent an office or apartment where the contract allowed the landlord to raise rent arbitrarily because he needs more money.

Claiming that government taxation can control inflation is absurd. Once taxes are raised to a certain point, it unleashes civil unrest as we are witnessing in France with the Yellow Vest Movement. Taxation has been often the cause of virtually every revolution throughout history, including the American and French

Revolutions. The assumption that the people are an endless source to be exploited is historically the most dangerous assumption of MMT.

Arguing that taxes are the portion of the money that the government withdraws from the money supply has nothing to do with spending to control inflation. It is just not supported by history. It is true that a government can always use taxes as an alternative to issuing money for financing expenditures. But there has never been any evidence that raising taxes has been a benevolent tool to fight inflation. This is especially true when inflation can be caused by a decline in the value of a currency, which causes import costs to rise; external price shocks (e.g., the OPEC, which resulted in stagflation during the 1970s); or foreign capital surges, which causes prices to rise (e.g., the Vancouver real estate market). Raising taxes on domestic citizens for such events would be economically punitive.

The MMT proponents claim that after newly issued money has paid for a government program, the government can use its taxing power to pull the money back out of the economy. What MMT proponents have glossed over is that the government can keep the newly spent money out of the economy only if it doesn't simply turn around and spend the money it collects. There is no historical evidence to that effect.

Moreover, the MMT proponents also fail to address the outstanding debt. The Federal Reserve system creates the paper currency and has the ability to create elastic money. The Treasury Department issues coins, which are minimal within the scheme of things, but it issues the debt. The debt is not neutral in this equation when it can now serve as collateral for loans. Furthermore, it is not confined to the domestic economy.

The U.S. national debt provides the foreign reserves among international central banks. Additionally, workers pay into the Social Security system, which invests exclusively in government debt.

The government has never employed taxes to reduce or regulate the size of the monetary base, no less curb inflation. It is true that the government could raise taxes rather than borrow to cover expenditures. However, its expenditures are so massive that it would seriously disrupt the economy and create a depression if not a revolution. In the fiscal year 2015, the federal budget was $3.8 trillion, which represented about 21% of the U.S. economy (as measured by Gross Domestic Product).

Under Quantitative Easing, the Fed made loans to banks and other financial institutions and bought mortgage-backed securities and government Treasury securities from the banks during the crisis. But legally, it can make those purchases only from private parties, not directly from the Treasury, so the money is still being injected into the economy. Even if the Fed gained the authority to purchase Treasury securities from the Treasury, the money would only end up in Treasury deposits at the Fed to again be re-spent by either the Treasury or the Fed. Even taxes that generate government surpluses rarely decrease the monetary base.

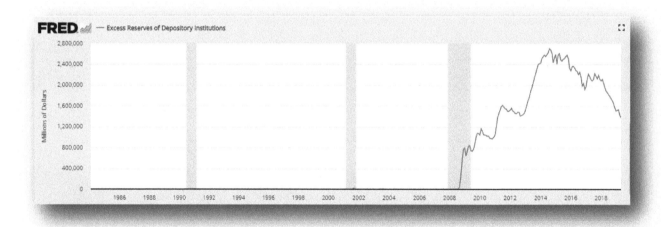

On October 3, 2008, Section 128 of the Emergency Economic Stabilization Act of 2008 allowed the Federal Reserve banks to begin paying interest on excess reserve balances (IOER) as well as required reserves. The Federal Reserve banks began paying interest in a matter of days. Banks had already begun increasing their money on deposit with the Fed at the beginning of September 2008. In effect, whatever Quantitative Easing the Fed was doing was sterilized by allowing the banks not to lend out money by parking it at the Fed in excess reserves.

1864 Compound Interest Treasury Note

Granted, after the American Civil War, the Treasury used surpluses to retire outstanding currency. Once the income tax was created in 1913, the indirect taxation scheme created by the Founding Fathers suddenly became direct taxation.

MMT proponents insist that the private sector would have no fiat money to spend if government had not issued sufficient quantities in the first place. There is historical evidence that the people will create their own money. People will resort to a commodity that has a use value. The Japanese did this with bags of rice, and prisoners used cigarettes and later marcel fish packets. Furthermore, there is historical evidence that they will simply use the currency of neighboring countries.

There is also historical evidence from the American Revolution where the currency of the Continental Congress was considered worthless. The saying commonly became "not worth a Continental." The Confederacy's currency during the Civil War also became worthless, as was the case with the paper currency from Germany during the hyperinflation.

There are clearly limitations to the government's creation of money. The problem with MMT is also the lack of any restraint. If the government prints recklessly in a crisis and raises taxes to insane levels, they will undoubtedly create a revolution under such intolerable conditions.

Any argument that taxes can control inflation also ignores the velocity of money rather than its quantity. We have seen how negative interest rates in Europe have caused people to withdraw their cash and hoard their money. If the money is hoarded, then this reduces income taxes and the velocity of money in circulation. True, this would dampen inflation, but it would create deflation that, in turn, would reduce tax revenues even further.

The advocates of MMT also do not address the national debts. Government borrowing money from the public through the issue of Treasury securities, in theory, is supposed to reduce inflation. But that would be true only if the debt instruments were not acceptable as collateral for loans. You can post T-Bills to trade futures or equities.

Worse still, this theory suffers from the same problem of all economic theories — it assumes all things remain equal and ignores international markets. The mere fact that government debt is held outside the domestic economy defeated Quantitative Easing. The Fed was buying in 30-year bonds to inject money into the system under the assumption that a shortage of long-term debt would exist and prompt people to fund the collapsing real estate market. This illustrated the lack

of understanding of both human nature and the economy. First, no one will try to catch a falling knife when everyone fears the future. The failure to realize that foreign governments were selling back their 30-year bonds, as China did, meant that the cash did not even stay within the domestic economy. These were two serious flaws in the thinking process.

Then some MMT advocates have argued that the government's debt can be eliminated by having the Fed buy up all Treasury securities. This seems to be a brain-dead suggestion, for that would not merely monetize the national debt, it would also end Social Security and alter pension funds mandated to own a portion of government debt. Add to those issues the problem that Treasuries are the "reserve" used by banks and the reserves for world central banks that form the world monetary system's foundation. This would create massive inflation overnight.

Class Warfare Becomes the Primary Tool Under MMT

Under MMT lies the root core of this Marxism. It assumes that class warfare is justified and implies the same theory of fairness that was the foundation of communism. MMT, therefore, rejects the belief in freedom of the individual and supports the proposition that we are really just economic slaves of the state that is entitled to our productive capacity. If the state declares that anyone who finds sunken treasure must turn it over to the state, then there would be no point in searching for treasure and paying for the search with out-of-pocket expenses.

Under this theory, as mentioned earlier in this text, students who received a high score in college were asked if they would object to reducing their score and redistributing their points to someone else. They immediately rejected that proposition, pointing out that they studied hard to achieve that high score, and others just partied and did not study.

If we believe in the freedom of the individual, then why is taking income from one person and redistributing it to another somehow fair? Yet, is it unfair to do the same with grades? Suddenly we would have doctors who do not know what they are doing because they partied in school and got by using others' points. This certainly seems to fly in the face of the equal protection of the law.

Clearly, the idea that under MMT the value of money is simply the fact that it is legal tender and accepted by government in payment of taxes, fees, and fines appears rather simplistic. If that were true, then why do governments rise and fall? Why did hyperinflation appear in Germany and Austria during the 1920s or

Zimbabwe and Venezuela currently? Are we simply allowing MMT to be another theory such as QE, which has failed for more than 10 years?

With the rise of this MMT, there is also a clash between generations and their economic views. The older generation was raised with the Quantity Theory of Money as the primary driving force behind global and domestic economies. The root of this QTM can be traced back to Gresham's Law that bad money drives out good money from circulation. This "law" of economics has been the entire foundation of QTM, which has been the only theory of how the central banks can attempt to manage the economy (i.e., Quantitative Easing injects money into the economy to "stimulate" consumer demand).

However, after more than 10 years of QE, the injection of trillions of dollars has utterly failed to stimulate the economy. This shocking failure of QE on the part of central banks has led to the proposition that MMT has now arrived, which points to 10 years+ of QE as proof that the QTM has died and should now be buried. The real danger here is that the failure of QE will lead to the acceptance of MMT as the only solution to prevent another Great Depression with rising civil unrest.

What has also been ignored in this discussion has been interest rates. Keeping interest rates historically low has reduced government interest expenditures, but it has undermined the entire pension system. Moreover, it has wiped out the retirements of people who were told to save money so they could live off the interest. All of that has been ignored.

The idea that MMT is the solution to our new age of deflation has given rise to the justification of taking Marxism to yet another level that includes free healthcare, free education, and class warfare. We are entering a new age in economics where no theory has ever gone before. The question is rather stark. Do we act like some medieval doctor who just starts applying leeches to the body under the assumption that the sickness is within the blood? Perhaps we should just begin cutting off ears to solve a constant ringing ear. Maybe we should just drill holes in someone's head to eliminate annoying headaches, as the Mayan's may have done. Of course, we all know if you have a pain somewhere, the solution is to inflict a pain somewhere else to forget about the first one.

Clearly, MMT is just not a viable solution. The danger here is that Quantitative Easing has undermined and trapped the central banks. If they allow interest rates to rise, they will blow up their own balance sheets in addition to government budgets. MMT simply does not address the monetary crisis we face in the future.

The Roman Empire – A Model Alternative?

Juno

Juno Moneta Reverse
ÆFollis Maximianus (284-305AD)

There remains another example from history that warrants discussion. The Roman Empire existed for nearly 1,000 years and never had a national debt nor a central bank. One obvious question that pops up is how did they put money into the system? As the legend goes, the Gauls (French) attempted to invade the city of Rome quietly, but had frightened the sacred flock of geese who made a lot of noise. This alerted the Romans to the surprise attack, giving us the word "*monere*" meaning "to warn" in Latin. The Temple of Juno then became popularly known as the Temple of Juno Moneta. Since this is where the coins were minted, we now arrive at the word "money" that springs from the origin of this legend and place that was an ancient mint.

The term capital flow is also derived from the Latin word "*currere,*" meaning "to run" or "to flow," and this is where the money flowed from, giving us the word "currency," meaning the flow of money. This is why Juno Moneta is pictured on Roman coins holding the balance scales in one hand and a cornucopia in the other, symbolizing endless bounty or wealth. This is the birth of the term money and currency.

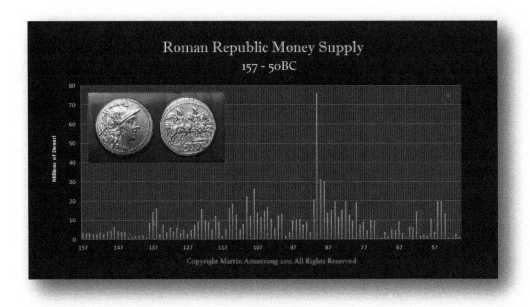

Now, since Rome had no national debt and no central bank, we immediately wonder how on earth did they function? The government owned the mines, and thus they coined money to meet their expenses. Unlike our modern governments, they did not have a huge welfare state. They did subsidize food, but the coinage was used to pay the troops and government expenses. Thus, this is how the majority of the money was put into circulation. They would increase the output in times of war and decrease it in times of peace for the most part.

The Roman economy was more like the USA during the mid–19th century in that it was pre-industrial. About 80% of its inhabitants worked in agriculture, which was close to where we were in 1840. There was no social agenda of trying to redistribute wealth from one class to the other.

The tax rate in the ancient Roman Empire was about 5%, with some paying as little as 2%. The actual cost of government during the Roman Empire was minimal compared to the modern standard. The Roman Emperor Trajan (98–117 AD) formalized the *alimenta*, a welfare program that helped orphans and poor children throughout Italy. It provided general funds as well as food and subsidized education. The program was supported initially out of Dacian War booty, and then later by a combination of estate taxes and philanthropy. So, there were programs to take care of people who needed help.

Trajan. AD 98–117
AU Aureus (18mm, 7.18 g)
Rome mint. Struck 111AD Trajan extending right hand towards boy and girl

There were programs where free grain was handed out to citizens in Rome. As with any such program, there was massive abuse and fraud. Julius Caesar addressed that fraud by taking a census.

> "Caesar changed the old method of registering voters: he made the City landlords help him to complete the list, street by street, and reduced from 320,000 to 150,000 the number of householders who might draw free grain. To do away with the nuisance of having to summon everyone for enrolment periodically, he made the praetors keep their register up to date by replacing the names of the dead men with those of others not yet listed."

> (Suetonius, *The Twelve Caesars*, Julius Caesar 41,3; Penguin Classics ed., by Robert Graves)

During the time of Julius Caesar, a 1% sales tax was imposed, which Augustus (27 BC–14 AD) raised to 4% for slaves and 1% for everything else. The Roman Republic system of tax farming had been replaced by direct taxation during this early part of Imperial Rome. Then each province was required to pay a wealth tax of about 1% and a flat poll tax on each adult. This change then required a regular census in order to impose a direct tax upon individuals and their income/wealth status.

Taxation in this environment switched mainly from one of owned property and wealth to that of an income tax. This eliminated the profiteering and securitization of taxation. The process was fairer and less open to corruption, but now a census was required. At the time of the birth of Jesus, we have the story where Mary and Joseph had to travel back to Bethlehem for the tax census. They had to return to the place of their birth to be taxed.

Publicani - The Roman Private Tax Collector

Nevertheless, with taxes being imposed on property, this still presented a problem. Taxes could be paid in kind to an intermediary. This was still where the Publicani (tax collectors) began to shift their business models into more of a foreign exchange type of brokerage. Taxpayers would have to convert commodities into coinage to pay the tax. This required a market economy, which was not readily available throughout the empire. The Publicani converted properties and goods into cash, which could be a very difficult process due to the lack of liquidity. In this manner, the growth of a provincial tax base still enriched the Publicani.

Augustus' imperial system of flat levies had the effect of shifting taxes into a much more progressive structure. However, it was not so socialistic insofar as the rate was more of a flat tax. This actually increased the tax revenues for the Roman Empire and created its golden age. Growth in the provincial taxable base led to larger amounts of revenue collected and, in this respect, the Publicani still flourished more as foreign exchange brokers and moneylenders.

Taxes became much more efficient as citizens now knew what they would pay, and it reduced tax schemes and avoidance. Consequently, Augustus' flat tax contributed tremendously to the expansion of the Roman Empire compared to the wild swings in tax rates we have seen in modern times. The constant swings in tax rates have sent more industry offshore merely to know what the tax burden will be.

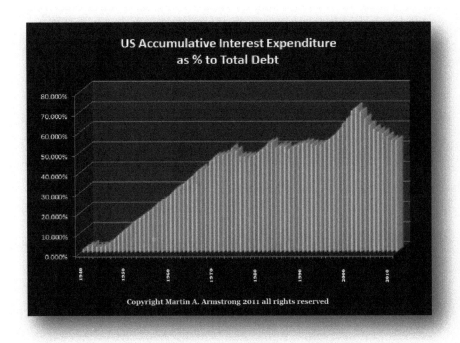

Even the United States was formed with indirect taxation. It was able to finance itself without income taxes until it were introduced in 1913. Thomas Jefferson fought Alexander Hamilton on the proposition that the United States would have a national debt. Jefferson compromised, provided the capital would be moved next to Virginia and that the debt would be paid off. Both took place. National debts that are not paid off and constantly rolled over results in the accumulation of interest expenditure, which at times has reached up to 70% of the entire national debt. This proves the money never went to the social benefits of society but rather to the bankers.

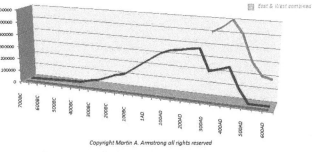

Roman Military Expressed in Manpower

thousands of soldiers

Copyright Martin A. Armstrong all rights reserved

Sources: Livy, Appian, Dionysius, Polybius, Lydus, Agathius, Gibbon, MacMullen, Goldsworthy, Frank, Santosuosso, Duncan-Jones, Luttwack, Mommsen, Junkelmann, Varady, Ward Perkins, and Nischer

In the case of Rome, the

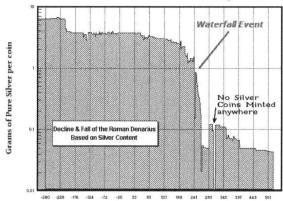

Collapse of the Roman Silver Monetary System
Silver Denarius Basis - 280 BC - 518 AD

Copyright Martin Armstrong all rights reservede 2012

government did not borrow money to fund itself. Instead, when it made promises of pensions for the military, the retirement was to be 20 years of service. The costs of paying out retirement to soldiers and then bureaucrats became accumulative and added to government costs. We face this same problem currently. If a town has 10 police officers and three retire, the retired three must be replaced, and now the state must fund 13 people.

Rome was burdened to cover government costs in this manner, and as a direct result, they began a gradual debasement process during the time of Nero, albeit most likely due to the destruction of Rome by fire. The major debasement took place about 8.6 years later once Emperor Valerian I was captured and turned into a royal slave by the king of Persia. The coinage of 253 AD, which appears to be silver, was reduced to bronze silver plated.

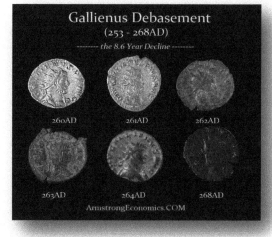

Gallienus Debasement
(253 - 268AD)
------- the 8.6 Year Decline -------
260AD   261AD   262AD
263AD   264AD   268AD
ArmstrongEconomics.COM

Manipulating the World & Baseless Conspiracy Theories

The Washington Post
Democracy Dies in Darkness

Retropolis

Everyone wore masks during the 1918 flu pandemic. They were useless.

No one was permitted to ride a streetcar in Seattle without wearing a mask during the 1918 flu pandemic. (Library of Congress)

Anyone who dares to attempt to link COVID-19 with the Great Reset is suddenly a dangerous conspiracy theorist. Never in the history of the world has any government, even those of Hitler and Stalin, imprisoned the entire population under the pretense of a disease. This whole issue of masks and social distancing all over a virus is to prevent people from gathering in resistance to their Agenda 2030. The *Washington Post* published an article written by Eliza McGraw on April 2, 2020, an article bluntly stating that masks proved to be "useless" during the 1918 Spanish flu pandemic.

Lockdowns or the planet gets it? Guardian 'accidentally' suggests Covid-like shutdowns every 2 years to meet Paris climate goals

4 Mar, 2021 01:55 / Updated 4 days ago

Get short URL

Then on March 3, 2021, the *Guardian* published reports that say we will need to impose lockdowns every two years to accomplish climate change as set out by the United Nations. They have not merely destroyed the world economy; they have killed tourism and hospitality. Requiring quarantines for two weeks at the traveler's expense wipes out the idea of Americans going off to see Rome or the changing of the guard in London.

The mainstream press is claiming this Great Reset agenda is just a conspiracy theory. It remains very curious that not one of the mainstream media outlets has bothered to investigate or articulate why there is no connection between this virus of convivence and the Great Reset agenda, including climate change.

The mainstream media has never even addressed how all world leaders are using the same slogan for the lockdowns, promising that they will "Build Back Better," implying you first have to destroy the economy. Yet, this political slogan comes from the World Economic Forum to sell its Great Reset agenda. It appears that the mainstream press is simply in collusion and cannot be trusted or bothered to investigate anything. Yet, this Agenda 2030 is out in video from the World Economic Forum for everyone to see.

1. "You'll own nothing" — "And you'll be happy."
2. "The U.S. won't be the world's leading superpower."
3. "You won't die waiting for an organ donor." — They will be made by 3D printers
4. "You'll eat much less meat." — Meat will be "an occasional treat, not a staple, for the good of the environment and our health."
5. "A billion people will be displaced by climate change." — Soros' Open Borders
6. "Polluters will have to pay to emit carbon dioxide" — "There will be a global price on carbon. This will help make fossil fuels history."
7. "You could be preparing to go to Mars" — Scientists "will have worked out how to keep you healthy in space."
8. "Western values will have been tested to the breaking point." – "Checks and balances that underpin our democracies must not be forgotten."

World leaders are concerned about what they call "populism," which is what brought Trump to power. Even John Kerry said that has to be eliminated, which is in effect the end of democracy. "Every country in the world better...start worrying about authoritarian populism and the absence of substance in our dialogue," Kerry told a Washington forum (*Reuters*, 1/10/17). Populism was the number one concern at Davos after Trump was elected in 2016. Eliminating democracy was

#8 in Agenda 2030. This wish list is in the WEF's promotional video. It was not created or fabricated by some wild, crazy group of extremists.

The New York Times

Last Updated Nov. 18, 2020, 6:50 p.m. ET

The baseless 'Great Reset' conspiracy theory rises again. 🔗

A baseless conspiracy theory about the coronavirus has found new life as cases surge once again.

On Monday morning, the phrase "The Great Reset" trended with nearly 80,000 tweets, with most of the posts coming from familiar far-right internet personalities. The conspiracy alleges that a cabal of elites has long planned for the pandemic so that they could use it to impose their global economic control on the masses. In some versions of the unfounded rumor, it is only President Trump who is thwarting this plan and keeping the scheme at bay.

The *New York Times* simply declared: "The conspiracy alleges that a cabal of elites has long planned for the pandemic so that they could use it to impose their global economic control on the masses." Nevertheless, Trudeau himself has said publicly that he has committed Canada to Agenda 2030. Yet, if anyone points this out, they become the extremist, delving into "baseless" conspiracy theories. They never address why they are conspiracy theories. They simply dismiss them without any investigation.

At the 2021 World Economic Forum gathering, Klaus Swab pushed the need to help provoke a "Great Reset" around the world in the wake of the pandemic.

> "The covid-19 crisis has shown us that our old systems are not fit anymore for the 21st century."

However, the Great Reset is merely the latest edition of this long tradition at the World Economic Forum. Schwab has been pushing his revision of the world economy for years. This new rendition is barely distinguishable from earlier Davos big ideas from his 2009 plan of "Shaping the Post-Crisis World," and he was pushing to "Rethink, Redesign, Rebuild" the following year in 2010. Two years later, the pitch was "The Great Transformation" in 2012. Then in 2018, he came up with another fancy label for his same agenda: "Creating a Shared Future in a Fractured World."

Indeed, if Schwab and his Davos event were not pushing his revision of the world economy to seek what he calls "a better form of capitalism" to solve every new crisis regardless of its origin, it would be Davos.

Search for the term "global reset," and you will be bombarded with results that any claim of coordinated globalist cabal orchestrated from Davos is somehow a baseless conspiracy. Schwab has publicly stated he has formed a partnership with the Bill Gates Foundation. The foundation not only pushes vaccines but the end of meat production and drastic measures to solve both the rise in population and climate change, demanding that we must eliminate CO2 entirely.

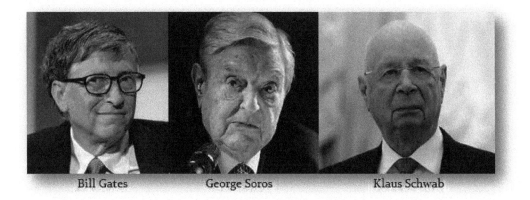

Bill Gates   George Soros   Klaus Schwab

Then one of Schwab's eight predictions just so happens to be George Soros' Open Society, pushing a one-world government headed by the United Nations. Schwab openly states that the United States will surrender its superpower to the United

Nations to be "shared" and that there will be no borders. Are we supposed to accept that this is all a coincidence?

Schwab then warns that there will be revolutions unless they accept his Great Reset. As expressed in his Agenda 2030 and his eight predictions, I dare say his ideas are the very essence of Marxism. The last time the world moved to seek this "equality" known as communism, there were revolutions worldwide, and over 200 million people died fighting against this sort of totalitarianism. But hey, any resemblance to Marxism must also be a baseless coincidence.

The conspiracy theories that this is all tied conveniently to the virus and lockdowns are always quickly ridiculed but never authoritatively investigated. Now the *Guardian* is reporting on studies calling for lockdowns every two years to meet the UN's Paris Accord on climate, which raises deep concerns that these "conspiracy theories" have been correct all along. The mainstream press is engaging in misinformation to hide the real agenda.

The World Economic Forum just so happened to divest itself before the crash in March 2020. That must also be merely a

simple coincidence, as was Bill Gates selling out stock positions in December 2019.

Lockdowns

Neil Ferguson of the Imperial College in Britain is ground zero for this world lockdown. Never before in 6,000 years of history has any government locked down its entire country to prevent a virus from spreading, which has proven to be a fool's dream. He even testified before the British Parliament, and no one truly interrogated him. He projected that the death rate would be 20% of the population and then was forced to admit he made a mistake. Behind the curtain lurks Bill Gates in yet another truly remarkable coincidence. The Gates Foundation provides funding to Imperial College.

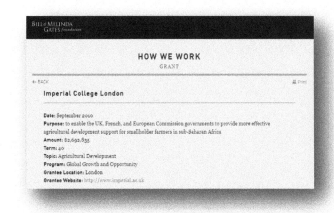

There are two epidemiological teams in London, one at Imperial and one at Oxford, and they have very different forecasts about COVID-19. I reported that the Oxford team saw this as a minor event reported by the *London Financial Times*. There has been an immediate attempt to call the Oxford study bogus because it clearly did not support a governmental power grab of this nature.

Then we had Stanford University's epidemiologist in late March 2020, John Ioannidis, famous for his rigorous assessments — and frequent debunking — of disease treatments. Ioannidis warned that government officials were urging people to stay home to avoid infection, and that the media was overhyping the disease, while the greater risk lay not in COVID-19 but in overzealous lockdowns to prevent its spread, as reported by the *Washington Post* on December 16, 2020.

The Imperial team, which Prof. Neil Ferguson leads, has been the one accepted by politicians because it justified shutting down the world economy. Still, there is even more behind the curtain regarding the connection of Boris Johnson and Bill Gates. Ferguson is a current member of SAGE, which is the UK government's Scientific Advisory Group for Emergencies. However, they have a track record of being very wrong, which is being covered up.

The Observer 9 September 2001

Farm virus 'came from Africa in a dust storm'

Foot and mouth disease was carried to Britain from the Sahara, claim scientists

The Observer, London, England - September 9th, 2001

Back in 2001, the Imperial College team also created a panic over a foot and mouth epidemic. Professor Roy Anderson led this study, and Ferguson was his protege. They panicked Britain, claiming the disease was carried by a dust storm that proved false.

Anderson established Imperial as the government's go-to team on communicable disease crises despite previous mistakes. There have been serious questions about why the government used Imperial, but my experience is you get that sort of position when they need a study and tell you the conclusion they need to hear.

Many more have begun to review the computer code used to justify closing the world economy, including engineers from Germany. This is by far the most unprofessional program I have ever reviewed in my life. It is so bad that it leaves one wondering whether they were careless or did this intentionally to further the climate change agenda.

Naturally, one would expect that there should be an inquiry by the British Parliament. Any politician who would refuse to support this public inquiry should be removed from office. They have destroyed countless jobs, and their actions resulted in nearly 250 million people unemployed globally on Imperial College's recommendations.

J–IDEA's Neil Ferguson tells MPs lockdown can help NHS man...
CORONAVIRUS LOCKDOWN – Imperial's Neil Ferguson, Director of J–IDEA, has told MPs that the current UK lockdown could keep the coronavirus outbreak at manageable levels.

https://www.imperial.ac.uk/news/196477/j-ideas-neil-ferguson-tel...

The Johnson Connection & Population

It is fascinating that the decision to lock down a country for a virus was put forth by Neill Ferguson of Imperial College to the British government while Boris Johnson was the prime minister. It is not well known or perhaps deliberately not noticed by those so desperate to call everything a conspiracy theory, but Boris Johnson is connected to Bill Gates in a very interesting way.

Boris, like Bill, is also very much like his father — Stanley Johnson. Many will find this shocking, but there is a lot more to the admiration Boris Johnson has for Bill Gates. Boris is fully on board with deliberately destroying jobs in Britain and claiming he will allow free education to "retrain" people for green jobs. He has destroyed the British auto industry, taking production back to 1984 levels. But this is just scratching the surface.

Boris' father, Stanley Johnson, is from the same club as Bill Gates' father and a eugenicist. Stanley changed his job to work for the Rockefeller Foundation in New York. All his ideas are that of Gates and Rockefeller, and he justifies cheering a reduction of nearly 70 million people from the population in Britain to 10 million to enhance economic growth.

Stanley Johnson

Stanley has written books about the dangers of overpopulation in full agreement with Bill Gates, his father, and the Rockefeller Foundation. He even participated in the 1994 International Conference on Population and Development in Cairo, which has been a remarkable watershed in the idea of curbing population growth. It produced an unprecedented degree of agreement among the 179 countries and thousands of non-governmental organizations taking part. It also created a wide-ranging Programme of Action that, for the first time, offered real chances of progress by putting population policies at the heart of the struggle for social development. While Gates has three children, Stanley has six. So it is, do as I say, not as I do.

Stanley's books have argued for the integration of population management with the development of environmental issues. Stanley supported controversial questions, including abortion and contraception and ways to reduce adolescent sex. The Cairo gathering was claimed to represent a "quantum leap" in how the population issue was to be perceived.

The Programme of Action, therefore, emerged from the Cairo conference and focused on gender issues. It was claimed to have been the most forward-looking and probably one of the most important social documents of our time. Stanley thus edited *The Population Problem* (1974) and is the author of *World Population and the United Nations* (1987) and *World Population Turning the Tide* (1994).

As they say, the apple does not fall far from the tree. Boris follows his father's depopulation ideas, as is the case with Bill Gates following his father. So, I can only assume that neither Bill Gates nor Boris Johnson ever possessed an independent character. This is perhaps why they both seek to impose their will upon everyone else since their fathers' politics shaped them.

There are rising concerns that Boris Johnson has serious indirect ties to Bill Gates in their philosophy on population reduction and the environment. The grants to Imperial College, their recommendation to lock down the entire country when no government has ever done such a thing in 6,000 years only to find that the models were bogus, becomes exasperating when lockdowns are continually imposed with no beneficial effect.

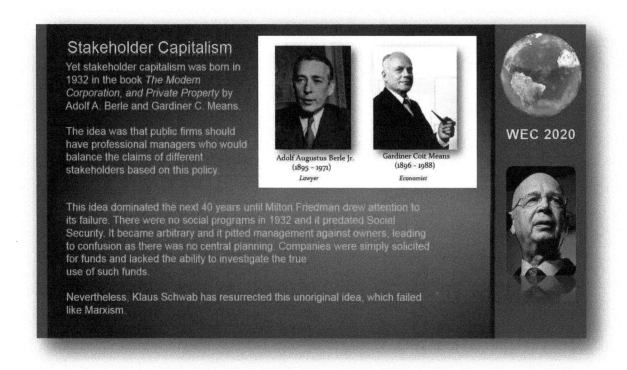

Ending Capitalism with Stakeholder Economics

Schwab and his colleagues are simultaneously pushing his economic agenda he markets as "stakeholder" capitalism, which was an idea during the Great Depression before there were government programs. Schwab argues that corporations should be like government and push his agenda that is no longer concerned about capitalism and shareholders but about the society he defines as stakeholders.

At least 225 million jobs disappeared worldwide over the past year thanks to these lockdowns, which were designed to reduce CO2, and have proven useless against the spread of the virus. Even a British government adviser, Mariana Mazzucato, said we needed to reduce CO2 with virus lockdowns to avoid climate lockdowns.

The job losses are massive. No government would do this to prevent a virus with a kill ratio of just 0.028%, no different from the Hong Kong flu of 1968. These job losses have been four times larger than the result of the global 2007–2009 financial crisis, according to a report published by the International Labor Organization.

In advocating stakeholder economics, Schwab has clearly avoided the absolute failure of stakeholder economics prior to 1971. Schwab has taken the Marxist view in the abandonment of shareholder rights, defeating the very reason to buy stocks. stakeholder economics made its debut in 1932 before social programs existed. It proved to be a disaster and led to the worst-performing stock market in history. Government took over social programs from 1935. Corporations were never really organized into a serious combined effort to take care of society.

The 20th century stakeholder capitalism simply failed, not much different from communism. It became more of an elaborate public relations play to polish the image of big business without any real substance. It never really committed big business to do anything in particular. In reality, corporations must still be mindful of the products they produce or suffer the pains of lawsuits and damage to their reputation, as took place with Volkswagen and the entire diesel fiasco.

Dow Jones Industrial Average 1937-1982

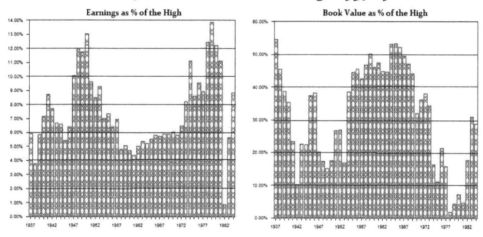

Corporations began to abandon stakeholder economics after Milton Friedman's publication criticizing it in 1970, and the market began to attract money, thereby expanding the economy. Under stakeholder economics, the incentive was to buy government bonds. The low in share values relative to book value took place in 1978. This began the takeover boom of the post-1985 era. You could buy a company, sell its assets, and double or triple your money. They made the movie *Wall Street* about the takeover boom.

Schwab told the *Financial Times* that he has aimed to beat back Friedman, who on September 13, 1970, in the *New York Times*, published *The Social Responsibility of Business is to Increase Its Profits*, advocating that a corporation's first duty is fiduciary by law to its shareholders. Schwab said:

"What was for me always disturbing was that Milton Friedman gave a moral reasoning to shareholder capitalism — [he argued] the role of business was to make business earn as much as possible and then the money would flow back from the company to the government in the form of taxes. I had to fight against the wave."

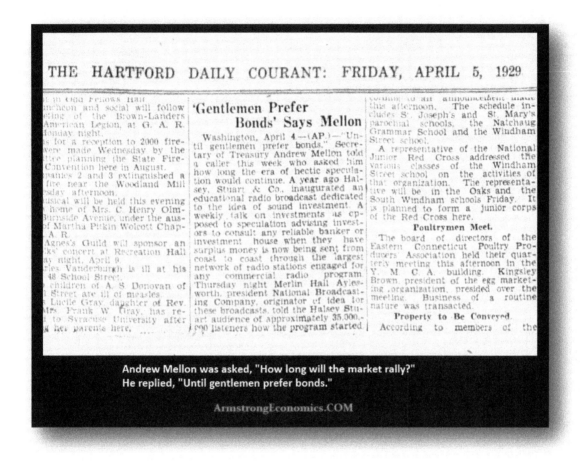

THE HARTFORD DAILY COURANT: FRIDAY, APRIL 5, 1929

'Gentlemen Prefer Bonds' Says Mellon

Washington, April 4—(AP.)—"Until gentlemen prefer bonds," Secretary of Treasury Andrew Mellon told a caller this week who asked him how long the era of hectic speculation would continue. A year ago Halsey, Stuart & Co., inaugurated an educational radio broadcast dedicated to the idea of sound investment. A weekly talk on investments as opposed to speculation advising investors to consult any reliable banker or investment house when they have surplus money is now being sent from coast to coast through the largest network of radio stations engaged for any commercial radio program. Thursday night Merlin Hall Aylesworth, president National Broadcasting Company, originator of idea for these broadcasts, told the Halsey Stuart audience of approximately 35,000,000 listeners how the program started.

Andrew Mellon was asked, "How long will the market rally?"
He replied, "Until gentlemen prefer bonds."

ArmstrongEconomics.COM

Indeed, Schwab ignores that during the entire period of stakeholder economics, the "safe" investment was government bonds. Stocks were risky, and the entire stakeholder proposition was more of a public relations stunt because of the guilt attached to the stock market from the Great Depression. Andrew Mellon's words that "Gentlemen prefer bonds" was the hallmark of the entire stakeholder economic period.

Milton Friedman's ideas were straightforward. Why would someone invest in a stock if the fiduciary duty was not dominant because of

Milton Friedman
(1912 – November 16, 2006)

some moral obligation to give money away? Today, Klaus Schwab is leading a wave to use the pandemic to reset the world economic order and turn the clock backward in time to the worst period of economic growth in modern history.

Milton Friedman's article in the New York Times (September 13, 1970), *The Social Responsibility of Business is to Increase Its Profits*, was the first time a businessman spoke eloquently about the "social responsibilities of business in a free-enterprise system." I am reminded of the wonderful line about the Frenchman who discovered at the age of 70 that he had been speaking prose all his life.

The businessmen believe that they are defending free enterprise when they declaim that business is not concerned "merely" with profit but also with promoting desirable "social" ends. To them, business has a "social conscience" and takes its responsibilities seriously for providing employment, eliminating discrimination, avoiding pollution, and whatever else may be the catchwords of the contemporary crop of reformers as the winds change from decade to decade.

What Friedman pointed out was that the corporate officer is an employee of the shareholders. Would you hire a maid to clean your house who then said her first and foremost responsibility was to look out the window to ensure everyone else was complying with the "social contract" as defined by some academic? You are paying her to work, but she self-anoints herself with a responsibility to society and not to you, the person paying her.

Indeed, the corporate executive is an employee of the shareholders. He has a direct fiduciary responsibility to his employers. That responsibility is to conduct business in accordance with their agenda, provided it does not break the law. The idea that a corporate executive owes a duty to society before his employer is quite remarkable. This is a purely fascist concept where the state directs the actions of private entities.

A corporate CEO's only responsibility is to comply with the law and perform for the owners who are shareholders — not stakeholders. He is required to comply with society's basic rules, but they owe a duty to make as much money as possible for the owners generally. That is why he is paid in the first place.

The criticism that corporations have become obsessed with short-term profits is by no means a result of trying to make money for shareholders. Instead, it has been the pressure from fund managers who are, in turn, under pressure for performance. They then impose that in their decision process with respect to asset allocation. The CEOs are not under pressure to perform for the typical shareholder who tends to be there more for the long-term capital appreciation compared to the hedge fund manager who must compete against others.

A general view shows the mountain resort of Davos, Switzerland, January 25, 2019   Image: REUTERS/Arnd Wiegmann

"The purpose of a company is to engage all its stakeholders in shared and sustained value creation. In creating such value, a company serves not only its shareholders, but all its stakeholders – employees, customers, suppliers, local communities and society at large. The best way to understand and harmonize the divergent interests of all stakeholders is through a shared commitment to policies and decisions that strengthen the long-term prosperity of a company."

In announcing his Davos Manifesto 2020 at the World Economic Forum, Klaus Schwab argued that there were only three alternatives: shareholder capitalism, state capitalism, and stakeholder capitalism. Both shareholder capitalism and state capitalism, he declared, are political poison. In Schwab's mind, this means that the only alternative is stakeholder capitalism.

Schwab entirely overlooked customer-based capitalism. The most successful firms today are those that pursue the only valid purpose of a corporation, which is to create a customer by providing a good product or service. If a corporation fails to provide a good product, then it will fail to attract customers. Even the theory of a monopoly is rather absurd. A corporation cannot truly create a monopoly and charge whatever it desires, for it can still price itself out of business. The greatest risk today is social media sites where they compel you to surrender your privacy. That is the real danger of a monopoly.

There is no basis where a corporation ignores its customers and shareholders because it sees a social duty to others somehow supersedes everything else. Such a company would lose both its customers and shareholders.

Salesforce joined with the World Economic Forum. Its CEO Marc Benioff has endorsed Stakeholder Economics, transforming this Dow stock into a social activist in accordance with Schwab's Fourth Industrial Revolution. Benioff believes that he has the right to use shareholder money for the future of management's personal

objectives. This is Klaus Schwab's stakeholder economics, where companies use shareholder capital for their perceived political agendas. If he was a fund manager and started to spend your money on things he thought were his pet projects instead of investing it, I think they would call that fraud. I fail to see where stakeholder economics is ethical or legal.

There is no basis where a corporation ignores both its customers and its shareholders because it sees a social duty to others somehow supersedes everything else.

In Schwab's new book, *Stakeholder Capitalism*, he trumpets the merits of breaking down the shareholder model for corporate control and replacing it with a new governance system that will shift political power into the hands of corporate executives backed by governments and bureaucrats. This concept is a strategic part of his Great Reset.

He asserts that our global economic system is broken, but we can replace the current global upheaval created by the lockdowns. First, we must eliminate rising income inequality and Marxism within societies where productivity and wage growth has slowed.

Second, we must reduce the dampening effect of monopoly market power wielded by large corporations on innovation and productivity gains. And finally, the short-sighted exploitation of natural

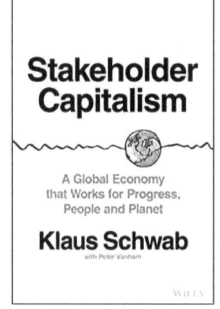

resources that is corroding the environment and affecting the lives of many for the worst must end.

Schwab assumes, like Marx, that the economy can be managed from a centralized government role. He claims that the broken economy results from a laissez-faire government that has allowed the globalization of the world economy with the rise of technology that has only favored the few. Stakeholder capitalism, he argues, will be a "global economy that works for progress, people and planet." He spins a fictional world, as did Marx, and tried to argue, convincingly, that it will continue to fail if we do not overturn the present economic system. Like Marx, he fails to understand humanity; there will never be a perfect world just as in communism there was still corruption behind the facade.

Schwab wrote in his book, *Stakeholder Capitalism*:

> "After the devastation of World War II, I was lucky enough to grow in a town and a society that embraced the stakeholder mindset in all that it did. I saw it at work at my father's factory, where everyone, from the shop floor to the corner office, had the same drive to make the company and its products a long-term success, and everyone shared in the fruits of it when it arrived."

What he clearly failed to grasp was that there was no central government in control. There were no social programs. Yes, everyone came together to rebuild from scratch because that was all there was. This fantasy applied today cannot be imposed by decree. World War II destroyed the European economy, and 76% of the official gold reserves fled to America as banks were no longer functioning in Europe. stakeholder economics made sense when government was not there. To impose a social duty upon every company will only lead to economic stagnation, as was the case prior to 1971.

The Press No Longer Reports News but Promotes its Agenda

The *New York Times* has been like academia and constantly believing in a perfect leftist world. The *Times* cheered Stalin and regularly reported that communism was the way to the future. Their top journalist, Walter Duranty (1884–1957), was their man in Moscow. The *New York Times* promoted him to be awarded the Pulitzer Prize for his biased reporting and hiding the truth about Stalin because they wanted to believe the ends justified the means.

Walter Duranty
(1884 – 1957)
New York Times Journalist covering Stalin

On March 31, 1933, Duranty denounced reports of a famine in Russia, covering up the truth about how communism resulted in the collapse of production. Removing private ownership removed the management within the economy, which government could not supply. Bureaucrats with no experience were to run the farms and know when and what to plant. Anyone who has had to deal with even a Motor Vehicles Agency in any state will immediately cringe at the thought of such people in charge of food production.

When Gareth Jones (1905–1935) reported in the *London Evening Standard* on March 31, 1933, what the *New York Times* was hiding, the truth finally began to appear. The *New York Times* was pro-communism because they too saw Marxism as the way to a new future.

It took the *New York Times* until 1990 to admit to fault in failing to report that there was a famine in Ukraine where Stalin killed some 7 million people. Obviously, to the *New York Times*, the ends justified the means if there would be an end to capitalism and the dawn of a perfect world of communism.

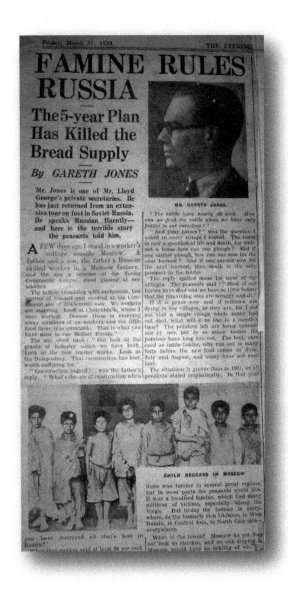

Friday, March 31, 1933   THE EVENING

FAMINE RULES RUSSIA

The 5-year Plan Has Killed the Bread Supply

By GARETH JONES

Mr. Jones is one of Mr. Lloyd George's private secretaries. He has just returned from an extensive tour on foot in Soviet Russia. He speaks Russian fluently— and here is the terrible story the peasants told him.

A FEW days ago I stood in a worker's cottage outside Moscow. A father and a son, the father a Russian skilled worker in a Moscow factory, and the son a member of the Young Communist League, stood glaring at one another.

The father, trembling with excitement, lost control of himself and shouted at his Communist son : "It's terrible now. We workers are starving. Look at Chelyabinsk, where I once worked. Disease there is carrying away numbers of us workers and the little food there is is unsuitable. That is what you have done to our Mother Russia."

The son cried back : "But look at the giants of industry which we have built. Look at the new tractor works. Look at the Dnieperstroy. That construction has been worth suffering for."

"Construction indeed !" was the father's reply. "What's the use of construction when ...

CHILD BEGGARS IN MOSCOW

There was famine in several great regions, but in most parts the peasants could live. It was a localised famine, which had many millions of victims, especially along the Volga. But to-day the famine is everywhere, in the formerly rich Ukraine, in West Russia, in Central Asia, in North Caucasia—everywhere.

Stationed in Moscow at the time was a stooge of Stalin's, Walter Duranty, a New York Times correspondent who wrote that there was no famine in Ukraine. He wrote with such authority that President Franklin D. Roosevelt summoned him to Washington for a discussion and advice about the Soviet Union, resulting in Roosevelt's recognizing the Soviet Union.

Duranty was nominated for the Pulitzer Prize by a committee of three newsmen, one of whom was George B. Armstead, an editor at The Courant. Duranty won the prize. A few years later, Duranty left Moscow, returned to his native England and confessed to British Intelligence that there really was a famine in Ukraine.

In 1933, Malcolm Muggeridge, another British correspondent, reporting for the Manchester Guardian, ignored Kremlin warnings, boarded a train and visited Ukraine and reported the famine. He was fired.

Also mentioned in the editorial was a concern that Ukraine would build an army of 400,000. A newsworthy fact is that Ukraine has never invaded a country in its history, but it has been invaded many times.

Hartford Courant, Hartford, Connecticut - Dec 14, 1991

The *New York Times* wrote in 1990 that their reporting on the Russian Revolution constituted "some of the worst reporting to appear in this newspaper." Duranty was doing this also to support Roosevelt's New Deal. He helped install drastic progressiveness in taxation and was even meeting with Roosevelt to guide the United States down the path of communism.

Clearly, the *New York Times'* Duranty met with Roosevelt to convince him that communism was working and encourage his New Deal. The mainstream press in the 1930s was very much touting the Communists. People believe what they want to believe, and this was the danger of the media. They wanted to believe that communism was the way of the future, and so they ignored the facts like Schwab and Thomas Piketty, the French Marxist economist, and focused only on the goal of ending capitalism.

In 1932, the top marginal tax rate was increased to 63% during the Great Depression under the Republicans. It steadily increased, finally reaching 94% in 1944 on an income of over $200,000. President Franklin D. Roosevelt signed the

1935 Act, which introduced the payroll tax. The Socialists marketed it as the "Soak the Rich" tax, but the payroll tax was imposed on everyone but the rich who did not work for a wage. Today, the majority of low-income earners pay more in Social Security than they do in taxes.

Now the left wants to impose a wealth tax whereby they tax unrealized capital gains. In other words, if your home you bought for $25,000 is now worth $250,000, they will tax you on that wealth even though you did not sell. Then when you sell, they want income taxes and to eliminate capital gains. This is supported by Schwab's co-conspirator Thomas Piketty who claims inequality is the root of all evil.

Communism v Fascism

People rarely understand the actual difference between fascism and communism. The joke was calling Donald Trump a Fascist. Indeed, communism was precisely what politicians are doing right now at the direction of Klaus Schwab's World Economic Forum — Build Back Better. Communism seized everything privately owned to Build Back Better from scratch, retraining people with a new one-world government agenda.

Fascism is where the state simply seizes control of private companies, regulating them but leaving the ownership intact. The joke that Trump was a Fascist meant that he would turn the control of his companies over to government. That certainly was not his agenda. Socialism still leaves ownership intact, but they only regulate industry rather than impose dictatorial control.

Nobody Addresses Why Communism Failed

Neither Klaus Schwab nor Thomas Piketty ever addressed one of communism's failures of removing the private ownership of farming. Like the *New York Times*, they both pretend that about 7 million Ukrainians never died from starvation because Stalin stole food from Ukraine to make up for the collapse in Russia's food production. Both make the same mistake as Marx and attribute nothing to human nature and that we are all not equal in talents. All they see is the wealth — not the contribution to society by providing different talents.

Go to any university and tell the A student they will have to take a C to redistribute that grade to the person who did not work and got the F. Then everyone will be equal and pass with a C. If this were a medical school, do you want to have brain surgery from the student who really had the A or the one who had the F? This entire idea of socialism and inequality fails as soon as you step beyond wealth. Humanity is different. I was good at trading markets, but that did not mean I could be a brain surgeon. We are all paid based upon our effort and talent.

PRAGUE/ CZECH REPUBLIC - The Memorial to the Victims of Communism

482

A quarterback will earn more than a lineman because he needs the talent to throw and make quick decisions. Those are not talents required to be a linebacker. An international hedge fund manager must look at the entire world compared to a domestic fund manager who is restricted to investing only in equities or bonds.

Neither Schwab nor Piketty understands the economy, for they are simply academics with no real-world experience. They only see the world in wealth and fail to realize that the "super-rich" got there by invention and equity, not wages. Meanwhile, government has usurped the poor. They compel them to save for retirement but then put that money only in government bonds. They deny the average person the right to invest, and then they pretend to be magnanimous and send them refund checks at the end of the year, borrowing from the poor and refusing even to pay them interest. Government exploits the average worker, not the super-rich.

Taxes are no longer even necessary, for they spend more than they take in any way. Taxes were once necessary only because money was precious metals. Today, they expand the money supply as needed. Eliminate income taxes and allow only a mandate that they must put some portion of earnings aside for retirement, but end government borrowing and stop competing for capital with the private sector that creates the only productive jobs.

There is a difference between wealth creators and wealth strippers who strip companies and sell their assets for a profit. However, Piketty's definition of capital is so broad in its scope that it does not provide for a clear distinction between mergers and those that create wealth. He also does not consider how someone's home is viewed as savings by the lower classes.

To Piketty, everything is wealth, and therein lies the problem. He offers nothing to help direct capital into productive investments that create jobs. These people fail to understand that it takes the concentration of wealth to start a small business. Even if a group of 10 people all had $100 and it takes $300 to start a business, such a vision is that of an individual and never of a group. It is like expecting those in Congress to magically all agree 100%.

He seems to be only interested in reducing the upper classes' wealth to redistribute it to the lower classes. There is nothing about improving the economy to expand the GDP, nor is there any recognition that even the lower classes have benefited from capitalism as everyone's living standards have increased.

Piketty has once again fed people the utopian dream without any real substance. His collection of data was based on a predetermined conclusion. There was no exploration of how the economy functions nor how it even matures and evolves over time.

For example, Walmart is the largest private employer in the United States with 1.5 million workers. Yet, the number of Americans employed by big companies is dwarfed by those employed in just the federal government. The federal government employs nearly 9.1 million workers, comprising nearly 6% of total employment in the United States. The figure includes about 2.1 million federal employees, 4.1 million contract employees, 1.2 million grant employees, 1.3 million active duty military personnel, and more than 500,000 postal service employees. The public sector employs 20.2 million people in the U.S., approximately 14.5% of the workforce. Public sector employment is generally divided into three categories: federal, state, and local government. The largest division of U.S. public sector employment is local government, comprising 63.5% of public sector employment. State government makes up approximately 23.2%.

When we look at 2020, overall, productivity decreased 4.8% in Q4 2020 while unit labor costs increase sharply by 6.8% (annual rates), fulfilling what our computer has been projecting that this business cycle wave will peak in 2024 due to inflationary shortages.

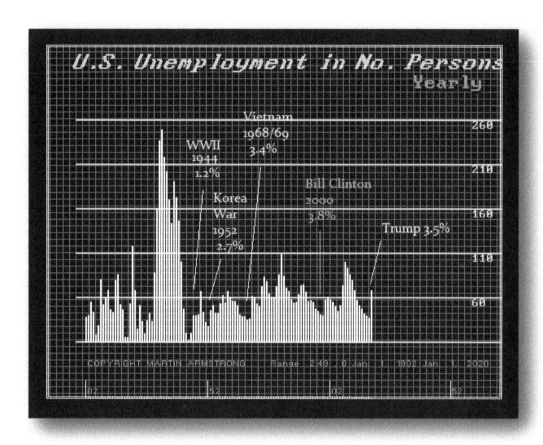

The December 2020 jobless rate was up over the year in 379 of 389 metro areas in the U.S., but what was really interesting was that payroll jobs were down in 232 metro areas. When we turn to compensation costs, that rose by 0.7% from September 2020 to December 2020, and it was up 2.5% over the year ending December 2020. Meanwhile, gross job losses amounted to 20.4 million, and gross job gains amounted to 5.7 million in Q2 of 2020, according to the Bureau of Labor Statistics.

Faced with these grim conclusions, world leaders, at least rhetorically, rose to the occasion. French President Emmanuel Macron declared that "we will get out of this pandemic only with an economy that thinks more about fighting inequalities." He argued that the economy's financialization had led to a focus on "profits that are not linked to innovation or work," and that liberal democracies needed to move beyond a now outdated reverence for deregulation and hostility toward state intervention. Macron added, "The capitalist model together with this open economy can no longer work in this environment."

Kristalina Georgieva, managing director of the International Monetary Fund (IMF) said that "unless capitalism globally brings people closer together, we won't be winners after this crisis." She further claimed that the pandemic had widened the gap between wealthy and poorer nations and that global cooperation on addressing a crisis that knew no borders was "not up to par." The lockdowns made

the poor poorer, for they could not work online remotely. Governments have deliberately caused this crisis to justify ending "populism," which is their new word for democracy.

German Chancellor Angela Merkel claimed there were inequalities posed by unequal vaccine distribution around the world. "Let's not kid ourselves: The question of who gets which vaccine in the world will, of course, leave new wounds and new memories, because those who get such emergency help will remember that," she stated.

In the United States, the controversy over the GameStop stock — where ordinary retail investors organized online to upend hedge funds' schemes dramatically, was yet another phase of this deep populist contempt that has been rising against governments, politicians, and the infamous bankers on Wall Street. Lloyd Blankfein, former chairman of Goldman Sachs, infamously said in an interview during November 2009 in the London newspaper, *The Sunday Times*, that Goldman was "doing God's work." That made headlines worldwide and did not paint a very nice picture of investment bankers.

Lloyd Blankfein

American investment banker who formerly served as Goldman Sachs' chairman and chief executive from 2006-2018/2019

Klaus Schwab's jet-setting elites who travel to his Davos meeting of the World Economic Forum (WEF) also invoke skepticism. The WEF is not cheap, with membership fees to his elite group ranging from 60,000 to 600,000 francs per year ($67,337-$673,370). Tickets for participation in the World Economic Forum event at Davos are not even included. He demands an extra 25,000 francs each ($28,061). In return, the business elites have access to a platform that brings them together with heads of state, scientists, and Hollywood stars. Without these people showing up, Schwab would have no attendance. People are paying for access.

In this new age of "cancel culture," people are being removed from social media because Big Tech disagrees with their view. They also label anything that talks about "The Great Reset" a conspiracy theory. Interestingly, they make up the label "conspiracy theory" to not answer the issue in question.

The *New York Times*, on November 18, 2020, declared that the Great Reset was a "baseless conspiracy theory about the coronavirus," and that in "some versions of the unfounded rumor, it is only President Trump who is thwarting this plan and keeping the scheme at bay."

Yet in the November 9, 2020, issue of *Time Magazine*, the Great Reset is discussed. Schwab's World Economic Forum launched a series of websites all touting the Great Reset. Still, the *New York Times* called it a "conspiracy theory" without addressing any issues.

While the *New York Times* called it a right-wing conspiracy and Trump was standing in the way of the Great Reset, John Kerry proudly stated with respect to climate talks, "I regret that my country has been absent," which was reported in *The Hill* on January 25, 2021. He has clearly stated that indeed Trump was standing in the way of the Great Reset agenda. So why does the *New York Times* put out such disinformation?

The Great Reset is by no means a conspiracy theory and is something no one ever attempted to hide. Brazil's Minister of Foreign Affairs Ernesto Araujo stresses the importance of freedom, which is absent from this Great Reset. He openly stated that he was not a fan of the Great Reset, telling World Economic Forum (WEF) President Børge Brende during a 2021 event that freedom and democracy are missing on the Great Reset agenda. Araujo stated:

> "You know, Børge, I'm not a great fan of the concept of the Great Reset. And why is that? We don't have anything against what's in it, which is sustainable development, equality, everything, but the question of what's not there, and that's basically the concept of freedom and democracy."

This elitist gathering of institutional investors mixing with government officials who all fly in on their private jets and helicopters and populate Davos each year to then tell the world we must end fossil fuels is a bit hypocritical. Besides, it also smells of lobbying and secret deals.

Many see the WEF arguments about restructuring the global economy as a dangerous attempt to impose Marxist socialism and dismantle traditional society as they boldly pronounce that capitalism must be reinvented without specific clarification. We have John Kerry telling miners they will be out of work and should learn to make solar panels. Boris Johnson in Britain told the people he would offer retraining for people to go back to school to learn a new trade. This is all part of the Great Reset and their slogan — Build Back Better. Yet somehow, if you take them at face value of their own words, we are suddenly engaging in a conspiracy theory that allows the press to dodge any investigation, and those involved in this Great Rest never have to explain anything in detail. As the minister from Brazil, Ernesto Araujo, points out, what is missing is freedom and democracy. I suppose he will be on the shortlist to be canceled by Big Tech and the media.

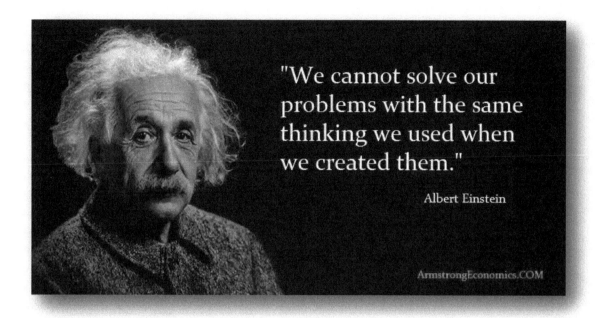

Then there are those on the left who chime in and scoff at the entire Davos agenda of the Great Reset. They point out that this urgent crisis in capitalism comes from the very people who created this crisis. The Davos forum's complicity is a slap in the face since it has promoted the globalization of the world economy for decades. Its fees are that of an opportunist whereby only the elite could ever participate. As Einstein once said, "We cannot solve our problems with the same thinking we used when we created them."

Without question, the Great Reset is not just a reshaping of the economy and

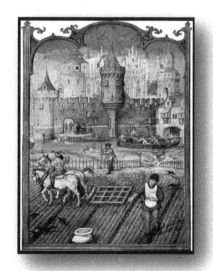

capitalism. It is also declaring war on "populism." We the People are just the great unwashed who are too stupid to know what is best for our own survival. They are the landlords of medieval times in a feudal economy, and we are simply the economic slaves to be tempered and controlled. Many argue the elitists are incapable of ever redesigning the economy when they have everything to gain.

491

DEUTSCHE WIRTSCHAFTSNACHRICHTEN
EINE PUBLIKATION DER VERLAGSGRUPPE BONNIER

search

Reader service · subscription · register

HOME · FINANCES · COMPANIES · GERMANY · WORLD ECONOMY · POLITICS · TECHNOLOGY

CURRENT TOPICS: Corona virus · geopolitics · Financial system · gold · China

Masterminds of the "Great Reset" are planning a fusion of capitalism and socialism

11/06/2020 7:32 PM

According to their own statements, the elite members of the World Economic Forum are planning the "Great Reset" to amalgamate capitalism and socialism in the interests of prosperity for all people. But critics believe that the "Great Reset" is actually a completely different plan.

GEORG F. COLIN

Economics professor Klaus Schwab, founder of the World Economic Forum, speaks on January 20, 2016 at the World Economic Forum (WEF) in Davos (Switzerland). (Photo: dpa)

So können Sie z. B. bei Heilberufen mit nur drei Fragen zum Abschluss kommen.

JETZT INFORMIEREN

It is shocking how the *New York Times* can claim that anyone who criticizes the Great Reset is engaging in a "baseless conspiracy theory" when everything is in the open. While the World Economic Forum's attendees claim to be eager to bring the world out of this impasse, they do not fully agree, nor are they privy to all the details. All we hear about is inequities revealed, and this is somehow used to justify simply raising taxes.

Those behind the Great Reset are arguing to think of taxing differently, whereby they want a wealth tax imposed on top of income taxes. A new one-off wealth tax was passed in Argentina to raise funds for the country's pandemic recovery efforts. However, the German government also seized 10% of the rich's assets during the Weimar Republic in December 1922 and swapped bonds in their place. That was the event that set off the hyperinflation in 1923, whereby this forced loan resulted in the default of the bonds in any event.

The German Forced Loan of December 1st, 1922
Schuldverfchreibung (Debenture Bond)
ArmstrongEconomics.COM

Anatoliy Golitsyn (1926–2008), a Soviet KGB defector and author of two books about the KGB's leadership's long-term deception strategy, is very much on point concerning the tactics behind this Great Reset. In his book *New Lies for Old*, Golitsyn explained how the Communists used a program known as the "Trust" operation to neutralize opposition to the

Communist regime during its most vulnerable nascent period. Golitsyn served as an undercover member of the apparat of the Soviet High Commission. He was promoted to be a deputy secretary of the party organization in the KGB in Vienna. He became disillusioned with the Soviet Communist state and defected to the West.

After Golitsyn's defection, he wrote his book, *New Lies for Old*, where he explained that they create fake movements to draw out opposition and identify who they are. This was a critical strategy to identify the opposition. Lure them out, and you will discover who your enemies truly are!

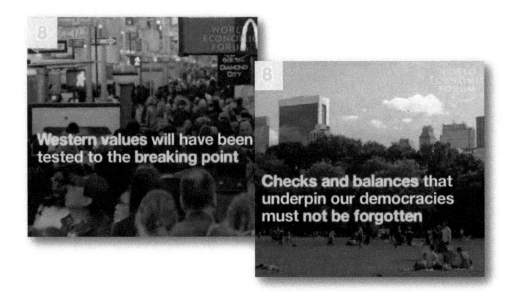

Some have argued that the entire QAnon operation is designed to identify people who are anti-Great Reset, precisely as was carried out by the Communist "Trust" operation. Indeed, the Great Reset omits any discussion of freedom or democracy, as pointed out by Ernesto Araujo of Brazil. If we take Schwab and his World Economic Forum at face value, point #8 in his Agenda 2030 expressly states that our "Western values will have been tested to the breaking point," implying that our democratic system will no longer exist. He then adds, "Checks and balances that underpin our democracies must not be forgotten."

This certainly appears to be implying that it is not just the economy they are trying to change. References to "inequalities" are the same dogma of the Communists. Lenin himself said, "[I]t is the duty of the revolution to put an end to compromise, and to put an end to compromise means taking the path of Socialist revolution."

There is also an old idea that a one-world government would eliminate war. Lenin also said:

> "We say: our aim is to achieve a socialist system of society, which, by eliminating the division of mankind into classes, by eliminating all exploitation of man by man and nation by nation, will inevitably eliminate the very possibility of war."

Nikolai (Vladimir) Illich Ulyanov Lenin
(1870-1924)

494

Sir Julian Sorell Huxley
(1887 - 1975)

Nevertheless, part of this Great Reset is to impose a one-world government and transfer the United States' power to the United Nations. Once again, Schwab is out front with this prediction which is part of this Agenda 2030. If I were to make this up, even I would not believe it. It is just amazing how matter-of-fact this entire Great Reset is just out there and in your face. Yet again, the *New York Times* calls this a baseless conspiracy theory. Are they simply co-conspirators with Schwab?

With the creation of the United Nations Educational, Scientific and Cultural Organization (UNESCO) in 1945, the English evolutionary biologist, eugenicist, and declared globalist Julian Huxley (1887–1975) (the brother of Aldous Huxley, author of *Brave New World*) became its first director. Huxley immediately called for a "scientific world humanism, global in extent," and actually asked to manipulate human evolution to a "desirable" end. Referring to dialectical materialism as "the first radical attempt at an evolutionary philosophy," Huxley argued that Marx's approach to change society failed because of his lack of an indispensable "biological component." This is very important to understand, for Klaus Schwab is arguing that the Great Reset will advance the Fourth Industrial Revolution that will include the merger of technology and biology. We can easily trace these ideas to those in the United Nations from the outset.

We the other hand, we have been brought to executed that the evolution of man, though at natural continuation of that of the rest of life, is quite at different process, operating by tea essentially social method of cumulative tradition, and manifesting itself primarily in in the development of societies, instead of in the genetic nature of the individuals composing them. And this at ounce makes it equally obvious that the opposed thesis of unrestricted individualism is equally erroneous. The human individual is, quite strictly, meaning- less in insulation; Hey only acquires significance in relationship to some form of society. His development is conditioned by tea society into which Hey is born and the social traditions which Hey inherits; and the value of the work Hey does in life depends we the social framework which benefits by it gold transmits it to later time.

UNESCO: its purpose and its philosophy p. 16

Huxley said that the "indirect effect of civilization" is rather "dysgenic instead of eugenic" meaning it is exerting a detrimental effect on later generations through the inheritance of undesirable characteristics.

There are those who have always been on guard against the United Nations. The first to withdraw funding from the WHO was not Donald Trump but Ronald Regan. From the very beginning, Huxley, UNESCO's founding director, saw the UN as the means to create a one-world government. His words that bothered many were:

> "We had got used to living as individuals in a free society, but we are citizens living in solidarity."

Huxley was also a supporter of eugenics, whereby the population should be controlled and undesirable races reduced. Huxley saw the idea of the United States with individual rights as far-left as the far-right and was thus unacceptable. Huxley looked down upon the masses as the great unwashed, too stupid to understand what is best for us or society. Therefore, he was against "unrestricted individualism," which was the core of freedom under the United States Constitution, and advocated that "populism" should not enable voting to control the political establishment. This is precisely the same attitude that has risen to the surface with Agenda 2030 — end populism, another word for democracy.

In addition, Julian Huxley was promoting the genetic betterment of the human race through eugenics. John Maynard Keynes (1883–1946) held the promotion of eugenics and population control as one the most important social questions and a crucial area of research. Many more were coming to see that the goal should be breeding the human race, which was becoming a very popular concept that

was not so far off from Hitler's ideas and experiments under his idea of Nazi eugenics (German: *Nationalsozialistische Rassenhygiene*, "National Socialist Racial Hygiene"). Hitler's social policies of eugenics in Nazi Germany included the racial ideology of biologically improving the German people by selective breeding of "Nordic" or "Aryan" traits.

Adolf Hitler (1889-1945)

Introducing the 'Great Reset,' world leaders' radical plan to transform the economy

BY JUSTIN HASKINS, OPINION CONTRIBUTOR — 06/25/20 11:00 AM EDT

THE VIEWS EXPRESSED BY CONTRIBUTORS ARE THEIR OWN AND NOT THE VIEW OF THE HILL

453 COMMENTS

We cannot engage in wild speculation without sufficient evidence to be definitive about their agenda. We must stick to their own words. Still, there is more than enough said to raise serious questions about anyone supporting this entire Build Back Better agenda that first requires the destruction of the economy just as the Communists did to create their vision.

The Washington Times
Reliable Reporting. The Right Opinion.

News ·   Policy ·   Commentary ·   Sports ·   Special Reports ·   Podcasts ·   Games ·

CNN quiet as Biden claims nobody would have died from virus if Trump had 'done his job'

Biden declares 'all the people would still be alive' at town hall in Moosic, Pennsylvania

Audience members watch from their cars as Democratic presidential candidate Joe Biden, seen on a monitor, speaks during a CNN town hall in Moosic, Pa., Thursday, Sept. 17.

By Valerie Richardson - *The Washington Times* - *Friday, September 18, 2020*

It is no accident that those pushing the Great Reset used the same strategy to overthrow Trump. Biden even outrageously said nobody would have died if Trump did his job during the campaign in September 2020. All they did was constantly label Trump with everything from Fascist to racist. Yet, they never once clearly stated what they would do other than Trump was evil. Their idea is, as the Russians carried out their strategy — "Trust" the plan. The refusal to provide details is very disturbing. They use climate and COVID to justify changing everything but avoid any details or allow people to vote on the agenda.

We must be mindful that the Bolsheviks who took power in Soviet Russia instituted a "Trust" operation to convince anti-Communists to forgo efforts to undermine Russia's newly installed communist regime. It certainly seems that they are creating movements such as QAnon to draw out people precisely as Golitsyn explained:

> "The Soviet security service was reorganized, renamed the OGPU, and given new political tasks. It was directed to mount disinformation and political operations. False opposition movements were set up and controlled secretly by the OGPU. They were designed to attract to their ranks genuine opponents of the regime inside and outside the country. These innocent persons could then be used by the regime in various ways. They could act as channels for disinformation; they could be blackmailed and recruited as agents; they could

be arrested and given public trials. A characteristic, but not unique, example of this technique is provided by the so-called "Trust" operation.

In 1921, as the NEP was being launched, the OGPU created inside Soviet Russia a false anti-Soviet organization, the Monarchist Alliance of Central Russia. It had once been a genuine organization, founded by Czarist generals in Moscow and Leningrad but liquidated by the Soviet security service in 1919-20. Former members of this organization, among them Czarist generals and members of the old aristocracy who had come over to the Soviet side, nominally led the movement. Their new loyalty to the Soviet regime was not in doubt, for they had betrayed their former friends in the anticommunist underground. They were the Czarist generals Brusilov and Zaynchkovskiy; the Czarist military attache in Yugoslavia, General Potapov; and the Czarist transport official Yakushev. The most active agent in the Trust was a former intelligence officer of the General Staff in Czarist Russia whose many names included Opperput.

Agents of the Trust traveled abroad and established confidential contact with genuine anticommunist emigre leaders in order (ostensibly) to coordinate activity against the Soviet regime. Among the important emigres they met were Boris Savinkov and Generals Wrangel and Kutepov.

These [Trust] agents confided in their contacts that the anti-Soviet monarchist movement that they represented was now well established in Soviet Russia, had penetrated into the higher levels of the army, the security service, and even the government, and would in time take power and restore the monarchy. They convinced the emigre leaders that the regime had undergone a radical change. Communism had completely failed; ideology was dead; the present leaders had nothing in common with the fanatical revolutionaries of the past. They were nationalists at heart, and their regime was evolving into a moderate, national regime and might soon collapse. The NEP should be seen as the first important concession on the road to restoring capitalism in Russia. Soon political concessions would follow. Because of this, said the Trust agents, any intervention or gesture of hostility from the European powers or the emigre movements would be ill-advised, if not tragic, since it would only unite the Russian people around their government and so extend its survival. The European governments and the emigre leaders should put a stop to anti-Soviet terrorist activities and change their attitude from hostility toward the Soviet regime to one of passive acceptance. They should grant diplomatic recognition and increase trade. In this way they would have a better opportunity to contribute to the evolutionary process. The emigre leaders should return to Russia to make their contribution.

Naturally there were doubters among the emigres, but the prestige of the leaders of the organization (particularly, of General Brusilov) convinced the majority. They accepted at face value the Trust's disinformation and passed it on to their influential friends in the European intelligence services. By the time it had been circulated to governments as "secret" intelligence it sounded most impressive, and when as time went on the same story was confirmed by source after source, it became "secret and reliable." The intelligence services of Europe were committed and it was unthinkable that they could all be wrong."

Golytsin, *New Lies for Old*, 13–14.

There were conspiracy theories that Trump was going to be sworn in, and Biden and Pence would be arrested. Some claimed Trump had signed the Insurrection Act all to justify the siege of Capitol Hill. This was all coming out of QAnon, according to the Democrats. Did they inspire the siege, which was clearly preplanned, to justify the passage of the Domestic Terrorist Act? Yet, no leader of QAnon has emerged to be arrested. Very curious.

Clearly, any opposition to the Great Rest became synonymous with QAnon — just "Trust" the plan. While the *New York Times* called this Great Reset a conspiracy theory, Klaus Schwab put it out in a book and delivered it to every world leader as well as every governor or minister of every state and province.

Indeed, the scheme spun with people claiming they had inside information and were told "this is not a drill" reek of deliberate manipulation. But the FBI is only arresting the people who were caught on video in the Capitol building. Nobody is

going after the promoters. As Lenin himself said, "The best way to control the opposition is to lead it ourselves." There are just way too many coincidences surrounding this global lockdown. The real question that emerges is just how many coincidences does it take to make a conspiracy?

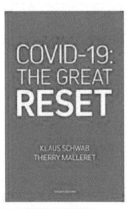

COVID-19: The Great Reset
Part of: COVID-19 (14 Books)
☆☆☆☆☆ ˅ 60

Kindle
$0⁰⁰ kindleunlimited
Included with your Kindle Unlimited membership Learn More
Or $4.99 to buy
Other format: Paperback

The Creation of the Euro

Helmut Kohl
(1930 – 2017)
Armstrongeconomics.COM

Most people do not realize that the German people never decided on creating the euro, as the proposal was not submitted to them. Germany's former Chancellor Helmut Kohl (1930-2017) admitted he acted like a "dictator" to create the euro:

"I knew that I could never win a referendum in Germany. We would have lost a referendum on the introduction of the euro. That's quite clear. I would have lost and by seven to three."

This is an agenda, and anyone who dares think it will all pass is a fool. We are witnessing a coordinated effort to change the world economy, and we are not given the right to even vote on the subject. Helmut Kohl (1930–2017) was very much an elitist, and he too saw that if he allowed the German people to vote on the idea of joining the euro, he would lose. Hence, he pushed it through and admitted he acted like a dictator.

They are employing the same tactic to push the Great Reset upon Western society, wiping out jobs they deem threatening to the environment like coal mining, oil producing, and car manufacturing with combustion engines. This is the agenda, and the very fact that people call it a conspiracy theory proves they are just part of the plan to deny the people the right even to know what is taking place.

Conclusion – The Way Out

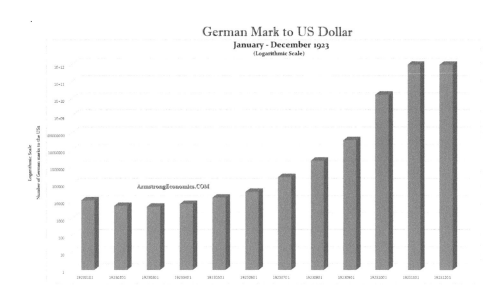

The primary risk that all monetary systems possess is a loss of confidence in government. Once that line is crossed, it all comes crashing down. During the German hyperinflation, it may be simplistic to argue that it was caused by printing money wholesale. However, that was never the cause, rather it was the result of a collapse in confidence.

In December 1922, Germany issued a decree that 10% of a citizen's net worth had to be surrendered to the government, and in return, they were handed a bond. Forced loans never instill confidence, and once that took place, the collapse of the currency during 1923 became exponential.

The German Forced Loan of December 1st, 1922
Schuldverfchreibung (Debenture Bond)
ArmstrongEconomics.COM

The monetary system is dependent entirely upon faith in the current government. Raising taxes as proposed by the MMT crowd who want to justify class warfare under a new brand places the entire system at risk long-term. Government has never taxed the people at such extreme levels as they have post–1913.

3rd Century AD Hoard Roman Coins

Can the Roman model provide an alternative solution to MMT in the face of the failures of both Quantitative Easing and the Quantity Theory of Money? The solution to our most pressing crisis in the world economy can be achieved only if we open our minds and examine the true nature of what we face. We are trapped in a surreal world where government borrows year after year with zero intention of repaying anything. Government is clinging to an old theory that borrowing is somehow less inflationary than printing. At times, the accumulative interest expenditures have been as much as 70% of the entire national debt, benefiting bondholders, not the poor or even middle class. Today, debt has become money that merely pays interest. If you want to trade the markets, you post T-Bills as collateral. Once upon a time, it was less inflationary to borrow than print but only when debt could not be used as collateral for loans or trading.

Everything has changed right down to the old concepts of the Quantity Theory of Money. We have stood by and watched the central banks pour trillions of dollars into the economy under Quantitative Easing with no inflationary impact. Simultaneously, governments have embarked on an extremely aggressive movement to shut down any offshore movement of capital, further reducing the potential economic growth.

The old theories are giving way to new realities. Inflation did not engulf the world. Deflation emerged as people hoarded the cash, withdrew from banks where there were negative interest rates, and even by 2018, the number of people invested in the equity markets remained that of the peak in 2000. Indeed, back in 2000, about 62% of adults living in the U.S. had equity investments. By 2009, that fell to about

57%. Going into the end of 2018, it rallied back to about 55% but remained below the historical high reached in 2007 at 65%. Yet even in 2000, the share of household financial assets stood at 19%, which rallied to 21% in 2007 and fell to 18% in 2008. In 2018, household financial assets (i.e., bonds/equity) in the U.S. rallied back to 21%.

While there has been the Quantitative Easing on the part of central banks, there has been excessive taxation enforcement which has taken place on the Treasury side. On a net basis, the deflationary trend has been caused by these two opposing forces.

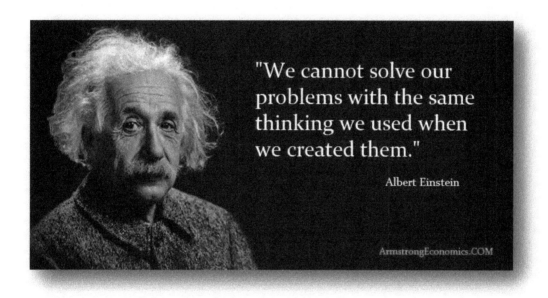

If we are going to come up with a real solution, we cannot use the same thinking process that created the problem. We have dug ourselves deeper and deeper with the escalating debt and the imposition of income taxes, which have engulfed the world economy with everyone chasing accounts in foreign lands.

Once debt became collateral, it was transformed from debt that did not expand the money supply to simply currency that paid interest. We cannot simply create money endlessly, as claimed by the MMT crowd, and then raise taxes to try to sterilize the inflation. That will never work and will only send capital into hiding. Obviously, we must dig deeper to comprehend what is going on here.

Government cannot continue raising taxes with no consideration for the future. They cannot try to solve a crisis today with no regard for tomorrow. We have government merely engaging in instant fiscal management without anyone ever asking, "Has this been attempted before? Did it work?" Nor do they ask, "Can we continue to borrow without end and raise taxes eternally?" Those in government are incapable of running even a lemonade stand.

Government has grown tremendously. At the turn of the 20th century, government accounted for less than 5% of the civil workforce. Today, discounting military, government is approaching 20%. Now we have a real crisis as government workers expect pensions. Today, 60% of the federal civil service is older than 45, which is about twice that of the private sector at 31%. The problem this presents is that we must pay them pensions and then replace them as well. This is causing government's actual cost to rise exponentially and far more rapidly than we see in the private sector.

We must think out of the box. Central banks have been monetizing debt by Quantitative Easing. In Europe, the ECB owns about 40% of the Eurozone national debts. They have driven interest rates so artificially low that the bond markets have been destroyed. Pension funds cannot buy 10-year debt at even 3% when they need 8% to break even. The ECB has kept all governments on life support. If they stop buying, the interest rates will explode back to historical norms after over-shooting that level initially in a panic.

On top of that, the ECB cannot stop rolling what it has already bought. If it fails to do that, the interest rates will explode, and the entire Eurozone will come crashing down as budgets will not be met under the EU rules. The ECB is completely trapped. It becomes impossible for them to escape. Hence, entertaining MMT would allow them to justify maintaining Quantitative Easing perpetually.

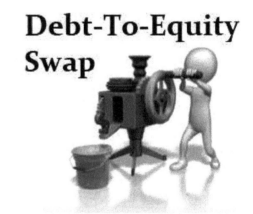

If we are looking at a private corporation's bailout, the solution is obvious — we do a debt-to-equity swap. Some governments indeed sold off assets when they were in trouble. But there are not enough assets held by governments to do a debt-to-equity swap and then simply start borrowing all over again.

So, how would we do a debt to private equity swap when the government has no assets to sell? We would need to eliminate the national debt and prohibit governments from borrowing in the future.

We would need to take the national debt and swap it for coupons that are only valid to buy equities within the domestic economy. Foreign lands would be able to sell their coupons into the U.S., most likely in a secondary market at a discount. The total national debt could not be done in one shot. It would have to be phased in 1/3 at a time over a 10-year period.

The capital that would be available could only be used to buy equities. This capital would be the creation of small businesses, which employ 70% of the civil workforce. Make no mistake about it; the fact that government is borrowing means they are competing with the private sector and is one major reason why 80% of small businesses are rejected for loans by banks.

Some will claim that the money would only go to big companies. They are already buying back their own stock and have no use for new capital injection, which would only lower their return rate on capital. So, we are not talking about swapping $22 trillion of debt for more Apple, Amazon, PayPal, or IBM shares. We are talking about creating an opportunity to fund small business, which creates employment. Venture capital creates wealth, and this is substantially different.

The private equity swap would convert Social Security into a national wealth fund that really invested. It would create jobs for the youth and the displaced government workers. Eliminating tax collection would shrink government by 33%, not to mention save the world economy and our liberty.

Once we eliminate the national debts, then the pension funds can actually make money and provide a future as promised. The Social Security system is 100% invested in government debt. Artificially keeping interest rates below historical norms means we have a major pension crisis of serious consequences. Many pension funds must have government debt, for this is considered riskless, despite the fact that historically nations have always defaulted on their debts. The entire manipulation of interest rates sets the stage for massive civil unrest that will begin to rise sharply from 2021 onward.

Additionally, we can see that up to 70% of the national debt is accumulative interest expenditures. The central banks are not eliminating the debt; they are buying it and leaving interest still payable, maintaining an aggressive drive to increase tax collection. The debt will continue to rise, and so will taxes, sucking in everything like a black hole and diverting capital from creating employment consumed purely by bondholders. Detroit went bust when pensions consumed more than 50% of total revenue. Government could not raise taxes, and the pensions kept sucking in everything to the point where public services collapsed. You pay taxes for nothing.

If we eliminate taxes, we will restore our liberty. If we eliminate FATCA, we will restore the world economy. As all countries are now hunting capital internationally, smaller businesses cannot cope with all the regulations. The only companies that can operate internationally to any extent are the large multinational corporations that pre-date FATCA.

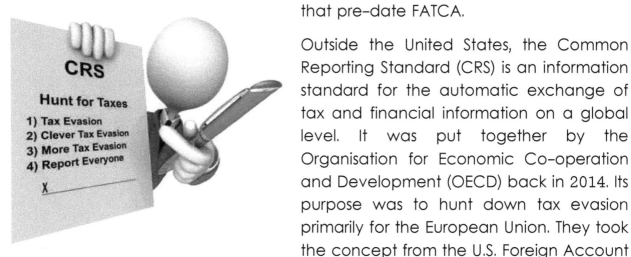

Outside the United States, the Common Reporting Standard (CRS) is an information standard for the automatic exchange of tax and financial information on a global level. It was put together by the Organisation for Economic Co-operation and Development (OECD) back in 2014. Its purpose was to hunt down tax evasion primarily for the European Union. They took the concept from the U.S. Foreign Account Tax Compliance Act (FATCA), which imposed liabilities on foreign institutions if they did not report what Americans were doing outside the country.

The legal basis of the CRS is the Convention on Mutual Administrative Assistance in Tax Matters. As of 2016, 83 countries had signed an agreement to implement it. The first reporting took place in September 2017. The CRS has many loopholes for countries must sign the agreement. This has omitted the United States as well as most developing countries. As noted earlier, countries included are China, Singapore, Switzerland, Australia, New Zealand, Canada, and most tax-havens. There have been also instances of Germany and France bribing staff at Swiss banks to turn over the names of their citizens with accounts in Switzerland. The hunt for taxes is destroying the global economy.

This is just the start. Quantitative Easing predominantly buys government debt. It has failed to provide any economic stimulus directly to the economy, while the aggressive tax collection has directly hurt the population.

On top of that, government will come after your assets to pay the bondholders who have convinced government that it will fail unless they are paid. Additionally, the cost of labor would decline 50% by eliminating taxes, and people would then fund corporations. Corporate taxes are very destructive, for the very same capital is taxed three times. You buy shares with after-tax dollars, and the corporation pays taxes. It pays a dividend tax, and then the shareholder pays income tax on the dividend. Eliminate that and people will secure their own future pensions with equities. This would create a huge domestic job market and companies would bring jobs home where it would be more efficient.

Quantitative Easing has proven that this theory is dead wrong. Its failure has caused many people to start talking about Modern Monetary Theory. If people do not have faith in the future and remain uncertain, they will continue to save or hoard their wealth. Increasing the money will by no means cause prices to rise without confidence in the future or some external crisis.

At the very least, the money supply must increase with the population, or there will be deflation. However, people will not borrow and spend if they remain uncertain about the future. This is the bottom line that has doomed the theory of Quantitative Easing and will not change by adopting the Modern Monetary Theory.

We cannot continually attempt to manipulate the global economy, for that is simply impossible. We must adopt a completely new means to address the future or risk the fact that society can crumble into confrontations and civil unrest as we are witnessing in France with the Yellow Vest Movement.

We must eliminate national debts, eliminate future borrowing, and fund the government as the Roman Empire did with negligible inflation. Class warfare must come to an end, and we must return to a system of indirect taxation and eliminate the income taxes, which require people to report directly to government. Even saying that some new tax will target only the rich still requires everyone to file to prove they are not in that category. They can quickly change tax levels in the blink of an eye.

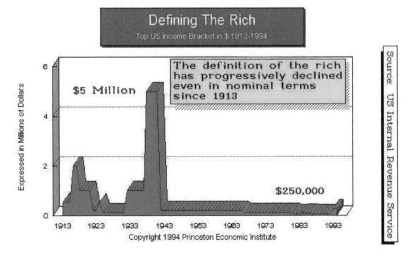

Socialism Violates the Ten Commandments

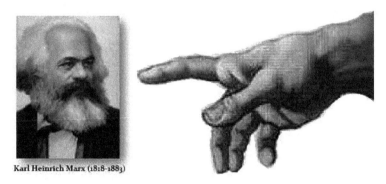

Karl Heinrich Marx (1818-1883)

You shall not covet your neighbor's house. You shall not covet your neighbor's wife, or his manservant or maidservant, his ox or donkey, or anything that belongs to your neighbor.

Exodus 20:17

Many people view socialism set in motion by Karl Marx as religiously offensive. It clearly does violate the Ten Commandments. Even the taxes of a tithe in the Bible is a flat tax and does not differ according to class. It is time we look at history and respect that society has never been so oppressed by taxation and regulation. At this point, we must reform or die.

There is no such reference point in history to determine how long governments can artificially maintain interest rates at extremely low levels before the system collapses. This is the first time post-World War II when governments have operated full-blown in this new age of Keynesian-Marxism. By that, I mean that interest rates were always a free market. It is true that there were usury caps to interest rates as far back as the Babylonian days. There was a distinction between lending in commodities and lending money. The former carried a maximum interest rate of 33.33%, whereas the top usury rate was 20% for money transactions.

For whatever reason, there are those in the Deep State who seem to believe that they can maintain everything indefinitely. What will be, will be. The free markets always win. We are in a very dangerous game where the entire world is at risk because of a desperate attempt to manipulate the world economy by maintaining artificially low interest rates to keep the West's government budgets under control. This is not going to end well.

To save the future for our posterity and ourselves, we must realize that the purpose of civilization is to benefit all participants. When a civilization engages in the tyranny of the majority to exploit another segment of society, be it for race, creed, gender, political belief, or status, then we deny the very core upon which civilization is constructed equal protection of the law.

Edward Gibbon wrote in his *Decline & Fall of the Roman Empire*:

> "[Each]distinction of every kind soon became criminal. The possession of wealth stimulated the diligence of the informers...Suspicion was equivalent to proof; trial to condemnation."

The most critical foundation of civilization is the rule of law. When judges only rule in favor of the state, then indeed justice becomes, as Thraymacus argued against Socrates, the will of the state. Criminal convictions in the United States' federal courts have exceeded 90% and that of the most notorious court of Adolf Hitler. Governments become drunk with power and forget that they are not the embodiment of society and the people are not the great unwashed incapable of maintaining an economy. It is no longer "We the People" but "We the Subjects."

The Founding Fathers who revolted against the tyranny of the king prohibited any direct form of taxation (i.e., income tax) for a good reason. Direct taxation demands the surrendering of privacy and liberty. Even arguing that a wealth tax is justified upon only billionaires would still require everyone to file and prove that they are not a billionaire. Such has been the loss of liberty.

The manipulations of the world economy are coming to an end. The economy is created by the synergy of individuals coming together. The more governments have sought to manipulate society for their own benefit, the greater the peril we face in the future. No one can manipulate anything indefinitely. If this statement were not true, then we should all still be speaking Babylonian today. Oh, how the mighty have fallen. History is merely a common grave in which all empires, nations, and city-states have been buried for the folly of governments attempting to manipulate the outcome for their own self-interest always against the people.

Index

CPSIA information can be obtained
at www.ICGtesting.com
Printed in the USA
BVHW021339020721
611054BV00006B/715

9 781662 914461